Specialist Computing's

Computer Jargon

Dictionary and Thesaurus

By
Eddie Martin

To Howard + Anne
Best Wishes
Eddie

5th January 2004

First published in 2004 by

Specialist Computing Limited

PO Box 128
Tonbridge
Kent
TN12 7WD
United Kingdom

www.specialist-uk.com
Email: sales@specialist-uk.com
Fax: +44 (0) 1892 723717

ISBN 0-9546186-0-2

A catalogue record for this book is available from the British Library.

Printed and bound in the UK by Biddles Limited, King's Lynn.

Preface

This book was written as a valuable help to the uninitiated but can be used by anyone interested in computer terminology. It constitutes Words and Phrases regularly used in regard to computers, associated equipment and software, which have found their way into our everyday language.

The book not only provides Dictionary definitions of computer jargon but also includes a Thesaurus with each jargon definition linking Words and Phrases of similar meaning.

Each Word or Phrase is in alphabetical sequence and is shown in **'bold type'** with its description in 'normal type'. The Thesaurus entries are in alphabetic order in *'italic type'* and follow each description if applicable. The linked Thesaurus items are separated by semi colons.

If a Word or Phrase has more than one meaning, each definition is described and is preceded by a number. e.g. (1), (2).

There are only a few Words or Phrases that refer to company names or products as the aim of the book is purely jargon related. This ensures that the book can be kept to a reasonable size.

Some Words and Phrases used in computer terms and which have the same meaning as in the English language are not included.

A number of acronyms appear as Words and their full titles are always described in the descriptions whilst there are also entries in the Dictionary for the full titles.

Synonyms also appear and are linked to each other with the Thesaurus.

Any abbreviations used are described in full in the descriptions.

Happy hunting.

16 Bit

A term describing the architecture of a computer in which data is stored in 16 bit registers, or transferred from one part of a computer to another in a 16 bit wide data bus.

See Also: *286; 32 Bit; 386; 64 Bit; 8 Bit; Address; Address Bus; Advanced Technology; Analogue Computer; AT; Binary; Binary Digit; Bit; Bits Per Second; BPS; Bus; Channel; Data Bus; Digital; Eight Bit; Extended Technology; Gbps; Least Significant Bit; Local Bus; LSB; Mbps; Most Significant Bit; MSB; Register; Sixteen Bit; Sixty Four Bit; System Bus; Thirty Two Bit; Transmission Channel; XT;*

1st Generation

A term referring to computers built using electronic valves.

See Also: *2nd Generation; 3rd Generation; 4th Generation; Advanced Technology; Analogue Computer; AT; Computer; Desktop; Digital Computer; EDS; Electronic Data System; Environment; Equipment; Extended Technology; Hardware; IBM (tm) Compatible; Kit; Laptop; Machine; Mainframe; Micro; Microcomputer; Midrange System; Minicomputer; Multi Platform; Notebook; Number Cruncher; Palmtop Computer; PC; Personal Computer; Portable; Standalone; System; Tower Computer; Turnkey; XT;*

286

A processor in a computer which preceded the 386 processor. It has clock speeds that vary from 10 to 20 MHz and a 16 bit data transfer bus.

See Also: *16 Bit; 386; 486; Advanced Technology; ALU; Application Specific Integrated Circuits; Arithmetic and Logic Unit; ASICS; AT; Central Processing Unit; Chip; Chipset; Clock Speed; Computer Power; Co-processor; CPU; Extended Technology; IC; Integrated Circuit; Maths Co-processor; Megahertz; MHz; Microprocessor; Parallel Processor; Power; Processor; Reduced Instruction Set Computing; RISC; Silicon Chip; Sixteen Bit; XT;*

2nd Generation

A term referring to computers, which were built using transistors and also the programming languages used on them.

See Also: *1st Generation; 3rd Generation; 4th Generation; Advanced Technology; Analogue Computer; AT; Computer; Desktop; Digital Computer; EDS; Electronic Data System; Environment; Equipment; Extended Technology; Hardware; IBM (tm) Compatible; Kit; Laptop; Machine; Mainframe; Micro; Microcomputer; Midrange System; Minicomputer; Multi Platform; Notebook; Number Cruncher; Palmtop*

Computer; PC; Personal Computer; Portable; Standalone; System; Tower Computer; Turnkey; XT;

3.5 Inch

(1) A floppy disk which is 3.5 inches in diameter with a storage capacity of up to 1.44 Mb. (2) The disk drive to take a 3.5 inch disk.

See Also: *5.25 Inch; Archive; ATAPI; Attachment Packet Interface; Backing Store; Backup; Bits Per Inch; Block; Boot Disk; BPI; Cluster; Computer Power; Configuration; Crash; Cylinder; Defragment; Density; Device; Directory; Disk; Disk Drive; Disk Map; Disk Pack; Disk Size; Disk Storage; Diskette; Double Density; Drive; EIDE; Enhanced Intelligent Drive Electronics; Equipment; FDD; Five and a quarter; Fixed Disk Drive; Floppy Disk; Floppy Disk Drive; Format; Fragmentation; Grandfather, Father, Son; Hard Disk Drive; Hardware; HDD; Head Crash; Heads; High Density; IDE; Indexed Sequential Access Method; Integrated Drive Electronics; ISAM; Keyed Sequential Access Method; Kit; KSAM; Machine Crash; Magnetic Disk; Mass Storage; Medium; Pack; Peripheral; Power; Read/Write Head; Recording; Recording Device; Recording Medium; Root Directory; Save; Sector; Seek Time; Storage; Store; Sub Directory; Three and a Half; Track; Volume; Winchester Disk; Wipe; Write; Write Protect;*

32 Bit

A term describing the architecture of a computer in which data is stored in 32 bit registers, or transferred from one part of a computer to another in a 32 bit wide data bus.

See Also: *16 Bit; 486; 64 Bit; 8 Bit; Address; Address Bus; Analogue Computer; Binary; Binary Digit; Bit; Bits Per Second; BPS; Bus; Channel; Computer Power; Data Bus; Digital; Eight Bit; Gbps; Least Significant Bit; Local Bus; LSB; Mbps; Most Significant Bit; MSB; PCI; Peripheral Component Interconnect; Power; Register; Sixteen Bit; Sixty Four Bit; System Bus; Thirty Two Bit; Transmission Channel;*

386

A processor in a computer which superseded the 286 and preceded the 486 processors. The clock speeds vary from 16 to 40 MHz and it has a 16 bit data transfer bus.

See Also: *16 Bit; 286; 486; Advanced Technology; ALU; Application Specific Integrated Circuits; Arithmetic and Logic Unit; ASICS; AT; Central Processing Unit; Chip; Chipset; Clock Speed; Computer Power; Co-processor; CPU; Extended Technology; IC; Integrated Circuit; Maths Co-processor; Megahertz; MHz; Microprocessor; Parallel Processor;*

Power; Processor; Reduced Instruction Set Computing; RISC; Silicon Chip; Sixteen Bit; XT;

3GL

A third generation high-level computer programming language, which can be used on different processors, e.g. COBOL, BASIC. The language is converted to machine code by a compiler or an interpreter.

See Also: *3rd Generation; 4GL; ADA; ALGOL; APL; BASIC; C or C++; CLIPPER; COBOL; CODASYL; Code; Code Generator; Compiler; Compiling; Conference On DAta SYstems Languages; CORAL; FORTH; FORTRAN; Fourth Generation Language; High Level Language; Instruction Set; Interpreter; LISP; LOGO; NATURAL; PASCAL; PERL; PICK; PILOT; PL/1; Practical Extraction and Reporting Language; Program; PROLOG; RPG; Software; Software System; Source Code; Syntax; System; System Software; Third Generation Language; Visual Basic;*

3rd Generation

A term referring to computers which were built using integrated circuits and also the programming languages used on them.

See Also: *1st Generation; 2nd Generation; 3GL; 4th Generation; Advanced Technology; Analogue Computer; AT; Computer; Desktop; Digital Computer; EDS; Electronic Data System; Environment; Equipment; Extended Technology; Hardware; IBM (tm) Compatible; Kit; Laptop; Machine; Mainframe; Micro; Microcomputer; Midrange System; Minicomputer; Multi Platform; Notebook; Number Cruncher; Palmtop Computer; PC; Personal Computer; Portable; Standalone; System; Third Generation Language; Tower Computer; Turnkey; XT;*

486

A processor in a computer which superseded the 386 processor. It has clock speeds from 25 MHz upward and a 32 bit data transfer bus.

See Also: *286; 32 Bit; 386; Advanced Technology; ALU; Application Specific Integrated Circuits; Arithmetic and Logic Unit; ASICS; AT; Central Processing Unit; Chip; Chipset; Clock Speed; Computer Power; Co-processor; CPU; Extended Technology; IC; Integrated Circuit; Maths Co-processor; Megahertz; MHz; Microprocessor; Parallel Processor; Power; Processor; Reduced Instruction Set Computing; RISC; Silicon Chip; Thirty Two Bit; XT;*

4GL
A fourth generation high level computer programming language.
See Also: *3GL; 4th Generation; ADA; ALGOL; APL; BASIC; C or C++; CLIPPER; COBOL; CODASYL; Code; Code Generator; Compiler; Compiling; Conference On DAta SYstems Languages; CORAL; FORTH; FORTRAN; Fourth Generation Language; High Level Language; Instruction Set; Interpreter; LISP; LOGO; NATURAL; PASCAL; PERL; PICK; PILOT; PL/1; Practical Extraction and Reporting Language; Program; PROLOG; RPG; Software; Software System; Source Code; Syntax; System; System Software; Third Generation Language; Visual Basic;*

4th Generation
A term referring to computers which were built using solid state electronic circuits and also the programming languages used on them.
See Also: *1st Generation; 2nd Generation; 3rd Generation; 4GL; Advanced Technology; Analogue Computer; AT; Computer; Desktop; Digital Computer; EDS; Electronic Data System; Environment; Equipment; Extended Technology; Fourth Generation Language; Hardware; IBM (tm) Compatible; Kit; Laptop; Machine; Mainframe; Micro; Microcomputer; Midrange System; Minicomputer; Multi Platform; Notebook; Number Cruncher; Palmtop Computer; PC; Personal Computer; Portable; Standalone; System; Tower Computer; Turnkey; XT;*

5.25 Inch
(1) A floppy disk, which is 5.25 inches in diameter with storage capacities that vary from 360k to 1.2Mb. (2) The disk drive to take a 5.25 inch disk.
See Also: *3.5 Inch; Archive; ATAPI; Attachment Packet Interface; Backing Store; Backup; Bits Per Inch; Block; Boot Disk; BPI; Cluster; Computer Power; Configuration; Crash; Cylinder; Defragment; Density; Device; Directory; Disk; Disk Drive; Disk Map; Disk Pack; Disk Size; Disk Storage; Diskette; Double Density; Drive; EIDE; Enhanced Intelligent Drive Electronics; Equipment; FDD; Five and a quarter; Fixed Disk Drive; Floppy Disk; Floppy Disk Drive; Format; Fragmentation; Grandfather, Father, Son; Hard Disk Drive; Hardware; HDD; Head Crash; Heads; High Density; IDE; Indexed Sequential Access Method; Integrated Drive Electronics; ISAM; Keyed Sequential Access Method; Kit; KSAM; Machine Crash; Magnetic Disk; Mass Storage; Medium; Pack; Peripheral; Power; Read/Write Head; Recording; Recording Device; Recording Medium; Root Directory; Save; Sector; Seek Time; Storage; Store; Sub Directory; Three and a Half; Track; Volume; Winchester Disk; Wipe; Write; Write Protect;*

64 Bit
A term describing the architecture of a computer in which data is stored in 64 bit registers, or transferred from one part of a computer to another in a 64 bit wide data bus.
See Also: *16 Bit; 32 Bit; 8 Bit; Address; Address Bus; Analogue Computer; Binary; Binary Digit; Bit; Bits Per Second; BPS; Bus; Channel; Data Bus; Digital; Eight Bit; Gbps; Least Significant Bit; Local Bus; LSB; Mbps; Most Significant Bit; MSB; Register; Sixteen Bit; Sixty Four Bit; System Bus; Thirty Two Bit; Transmission Channel;*

8 Bit
A term describing the architecture of a computer in which data is stored in 8 bit registers, or transferred from one part of a computer to another in an 8 bit wide data bus.
See Also: *16 Bit; 32 Bit; 64 Bit; Address; Address Bus; American Standard Code for Information Interchange; Analogue Computer; ASCII; Binary; Binary Digit; Bit; Bits Per Second; BPS; Bus; Byte; Channel; Data; Data Bus; Data Type; Digital; Eight Bit; Gbps; Least Significant Bit; Local Bus; LSB; Mbps; Most Significant Bit; MSB; Register; Sixteen Bit; Sixty Four Bit; System Bus; Thirty Two Bit; Transmission Channel;*

A/P
Analyst Programmer. A person who designs and programs a computer system.
See Also: *Analyst; Analyst Programmer; B/A; Business Analyst; Code; Contractor; Data Base Analyst; Data Processing Manager; DBA; Design; Development; DPM; Full Project Life Cycle; Language; Logical Design; Loop; Physical Design; Program; Program Specification; Programmer; Programming Language; Project Life Cycle; S/A; S/P; Software; Software Development Cycle; Software House; Specification; Structured Design; Structured Program; System Analyst; Systems Programmer; Technical Author;*

Abort
(1) To manually stop the running of a program before it has finished. (2) An unexpected termination of a computer program.
See Also: *Application; Batch Processing; Bug; Code; Crash; Debug; Debugger; Died; Downtime; Esc; Escape; Hangs; Head Crash; Hung; Interrupt; Job; Machine Crash; Mean Time Between Failure; MTBF; Off Line; Program; Program Crash; Recovery; Restore; Roll Back; System Hangs; Timeout; Virus;*

Absolute Address
(1) A location in a computers memory where data is stored. (2) The reference number of that location.
See Also: *Address; Block; Bubble Memory; Buffer; Cache Memory; Conventional Memory; Core; Core Dump; Disk Cache; Flash Memory; Magnetic Core; Memory; Operand; RAM Disk; Register; Relative Address; Store; Upper Memory; Virtual Memory; VM; Volatile Memory; Working Storage; Workspace;*

Accelerated Graphics Port
AGP or Advanced Graphics Port. A slot on the PC motherboard in which a graphic card is housed.
See Also: *Advanced Graphics Port; AGP; AGP Slot; Digital Video Interface; DVI; Expansion Slot; Fax Card; Graphics; Graphics Card; Motherboard; PCB; PCI; PCMCIA; Peripheral Component Interconnect; Personal Computer Memory Card International Association; Port; Printed Circuit Board; Slot; Sound Card; Video Card;*

Acceptable User Policy
(AUP). Rules provided by an Internet Service Provider detailing the use of their services.
See Also: *American National Standard Institute; Anonymous FTP; ANSI; AUP; CCITT; CCTA; CERN; Conseil Europeen pour la Recherche Nucleaire; Consultative Committee International Telegraph and Telephone; File Transfer Protocol; FTP; Host; International Standards Organisation; Internet; Internet Protocol; Internet Service Provider; IP; ISO; ISP; MP3; Net; Netiquette; Newbie; Point Of Presence; Point to Point Protocol; POP; PPP; Protocol; Provider; Service Provider; Simple Mail Transfer Protocol; Site; SMTP; TCP/IP; The Net; The Web; Transmission Control Protocol/Internet Protocol; WAP; Wap Internet Service Provider; Website; Wireless Application Protocol; WISP; World Wide Web; WWW;*

Access
(1) The reading or writing of information to a peripheral device. (2) Being connected to a file, system or network.
See Also: *Access Time; Bluetooth (tm); Channel; Client Server; Dead Lock; Deadly Embrace; Device; Dial In; Dial Up; Direct Access; Direct Memory Access; DMA; Drive; File; File Server; File Sharing; Gateway; Handshake; I/O; Information Superhighway; Input/Output; Interface; Log In/Off; Modem; Modulator Demodulator; Network; Online; Parallel Interface; Password; Peripheral; PING; Point Of Presence; Point to Point Protocol; POP; Port; PPP; Protocol; Proxy Server; R/W; Random*

Access; Read; Read/Write; Recording Device; RS232; RS423; Seek Time; Sequential Access; Serial Access; Serial Interface; Server; System; T-1; T-3; Transmission Channel; Universal Serial Bus; USB; WAP; Wi-Fi; Wireless Application Protocol; Wireless Fidelity; Write; Write Protect; XMODEM; YMODEM; ZMODEM;

Access Time
The time it takes to extract or record information on a storage device. Normally quoted in milliseconds.
See Also: *Access; Baud Rate; Bits Per Second; BPS; Characters Per Second; CPS; Device; Direct Access; Gbps; Kbps; Mbps; Microsecond; Million Instructions Per Second; Millisecond; MIPS; Ms; Nanosecond; Ns; Pico Second; Random Access; Recording; Recording Device; Seek Time; Sequential Access; Serial Access;*

ACK
Abbr. of Acknowledgement. An acknowledgement code sent from a device that has just received data to the device that sent the data indicating an error free transmission.
See Also: *AMR; Asynchronous; Automatic Message Routing; Communications; Data Communications; Data Transmission; Datacoms; Duplex Transmission; Full Duplex; Half Duplex; Handshake; HD; Multiplex; Multiplexer; Parallel Transmission; Parity Bit; PING; Serial Transmission; Simplex Transmission; Synchronous; Telecommunication; Telecoms; Transmit;*

Acoustic Coupler
A device used with a telephone handset in sending and receiving data along a telephone line from one computer to another.
See Also: *ADN; Advanced Digital Network; Asymmetrical Modem; Asynchronous; Bits Per Second; BPS; CCITT; CCTA; Communications; Consultative Committee International Telegraph and Telephone; Data Communications; Data Transmission; Datacoms; Device; Dial In; Dial Up; Download; Duplex Transmission; Equipment; FDDI; Fibre Distributed Data Interface; Fibre Optics; Full Duplex; Gbps; Half Duplex; Handshake; Hardware; HD; Interface; Kbps; Kit; Mbps; Modem; Modulator Demodulator; Multiplex; Multiplexer; Online; Optical Fibre; Parallel Transmission; Peripheral; Protocol; RS232; RS423; Serial Interface; Serial Transmission; Simplex Transmission; Synchronous; Telecommunication; Telecoms; Teleprocessing System; TPS; Transfer Rate; Transmit; V90; XMODEM;*

ADA
A high level computer programming language used mainly in real time applications.
See Also: *3GL; 4GL; ALGOL; APL; BASIC; C or C++; CLIPPER; COBOL; Code; Code Generator; Compiler; Compiling; CORAL; FORTH; FORTRAN; Fourth Generation Language; High Level Language; Instruction Set; JAVA; JAVASCRIPT; Language; LISP; LOGO; Module; NATURAL; PASCAL; PERL; PICK; PILOT; PL/1; Practical Extraction and Reporting Language; Program; Programming Language; PROLOG; RPG; Software; Source Code; Structured Program; Syntax; Third Generation Language; Visual Basic;*

Address
(1) A location in the computers memory, identifiable by a number. (2) The unique identifier of an e-mail, website or a web page address.
See Also: *16 Bit; 32 Bit; 64 Bit; 8 Bit; Absolute Address; Anchor; Anonymous FTP; Binary Digit; Bit; Block; Bookmark; Bubble Memory; Buddy List; Buffer; Cache Memory; Conventional Memory; Core; Core Dump; Disk Cache; DNS; Domain Name; Domain Name Server; Domain Name System; Dot; Dump; Eight Bit; Electronic Mail; E-mail; E-mail Address; Flash Memory; Hit; Home Page; Hyperlink; Hypertext; Internet Protocol Address; IP Address; Link; Magnetic Core; Mailing List; Memory; Operand; Packet; Packet Switching; Register; Relative Address; Site; Sixteen Bit; Sixty Four Bit; Stack; Store; Thirty Two Bit; Universal/Uniform Resource Locator; Upper Memory; URL; Volatile Memory; Webring; Website; Working Storage; Workspace;*

Address Bus
A communication path used to carry data from one point in a computer to another. i.e. by 8, 16 or 32 bit.
See Also: *16 Bit; 32 Bit; 64 Bit; 8 Bit; Binary Digit; Bit; Bits Per Second; BPS; Bus; Channel; Data Bus; Digital; Eight Bit; Gbps; Kbps; Local Bus; Mbps; Sixteen Bit; Sixty Four Bit; System Bus; Thirty Two Bit; Transmission Channel;*

ADN
Advanced Digital Network. Refers to a 56kbps leased line.
See Also: *Acoustic Coupler; ADSL; Advanced Digital Network; AMR; Asymmetric Digital Subscriber Line; Asymmetrical Modem; Asynchronous; Asynchronous Transfer Mode; ATM; Automatic Message Routing; Bandwidth; Baud Rate; Binary Digit; Bit; Bits Per Second; BPS; Broadband; CCITT; CCTA; Characters Per Second; Communications; Consultative Committee International Telegraph and*

Telephone; CPS; Data Communications; Data Parity; Data Transmission; Datacoms; Dial In; Dial Up; Digital; Direct Connection; Duplex Transmission; FDDI; Fibre Distributed Data Interface; Fibre Optics; Firewire; Full Duplex; Gbps; Half Duplex; HD; Information Superhighway; Integrated Services Digital Network; ISDN; Kbps; Leased Line; Mbps; Multiplex; Multiplexer; Narrowband; Node; Open Systems Interconnect; Optical Fibre; OSI; Parallel Transmission; Parity Bit; Serial Interface; Serial Transmission; Simplex Transmission; Synchronous; T-1; T-3; Telecommunication; Telecoms; Teleprocessing System; TPS; Transfer Rate; Transmit; V90;

ADSL
Asymmetric Digital Subscriber Line. A digital connection to the Internet using an ordinary telephone line instead of a modem which allows for fast data transfers.
See Also: *ADN; Advanced Digital Network; Asymmetric Digital Subscriber Line; Asynchronous; Asynchronous Transfer Mode; ATM; Bandwidth; Baud Rate; Binary Digit; Bit; Bits Per Second; BPS; Broadband; CCITT; CCTA; Characters Per Second; Communications; Consultative Committee International Telegraph and Telephone; CPS; Data Communications; Data Parity; Data Transmission; Datacoms; Dial In; Dial Up; Digital; Direct Connection; Duplex Transmission; FDDI; Fibre Distributed Data Interface; Fibre Optics; Full Duplex; Gbps; Half Duplex; HD; Information Superhighway; Integrated Services Digital Network; ISDN; Kbps; Leased Line; Mbps; Multiplex; Multiplexer; Narrowband; Open Systems Interconnect; Optical Fibre; OSI; Parallel Transmission; Parity Bit; Serial Interface; Serial Transmission; Simplex Transmission; Synchronous; T-1; T-3; Telecommunication; Telecoms; Teleprocessing System; TPS; Transfer Rate; Transmit; V90;*

Advanced Digital Network
(ADN). Refers to a 56kbps leased line.
See Also: *Acoustic Coupler; ADN; ADSL; AMR; Asymmetric Digital Subscriber Line; Asymmetrical Modem; Asynchronous; Asynchronous Transfer Mode; ATM; Automatic Message Routing; Bandwidth; Baud Rate; Binary Digit; Bit; Bits Per Second; BPS; Broadband; CCITT; CCTA; Characters Per Second; Communications; Consultative Committee International Telegraph and Telephone; CPS; Data Communications; Data Parity; Data Transmission; Datacoms; Dial In; Dial Up; Digital; Direct Connection; Duplex Transmission; FDDI; Fibre Distributed Data Interface; Fibre Optics; Firewire; Full Duplex; Gbps; Half Duplex; HD; Information Superhighway; Integrated Services Digital Network; ISDN; Kbps; Leased Line; Mbps; Multiplex; Multiplexer;*

Narrowband; Node; Open Systems Interconnect; Optical Fibre; OSI; Parallel Transmission; Parity Bit; Serial Interface; Serial Transmission; Simplex Transmission; Synchronous; T-1; T-3; Telecommunication; Telecoms; Teleprocessing System; TPS; Transfer Rate; Transmit; V90;

Advanced Graphics Port
(AGP or Accelerated Graphics Port). A slot on the PC motherboard in which a graphic card is housed.
See Also: *Accelerated Graphics Port; AGP; AGP Slot; Digital Video Interface; DVI; Expansion Slot; Fax Card; Graphics; Graphics Card; Motherboard; PCB; PCI; PCMCIA; Peripheral Component Interconnect; Personal Computer Memory Card International Association; Port; Printed Circuit Board; Slot; Sound Card; Video Card;*

Advanced Technology
(AT). The basis in which some personal computers were designed which used a 286 chip.
See Also: *16 Bit; 1st Generation; 286; 2nd Generation; 386; 3rd Generation; 486; 4th Generation; Analogue Computer; AT; Chip; Chipset; Computer; Cross Platform; Desktop; Digital Computer; EDS; Electronic Data System; Environment; Equipment; Extended Technology; Hardware; IBM (tm) Compatible; Installation; Kit; Laptop; Machine; Micro; Microcomputer; Multi Platform; Notebook; OEM; Original Equipment Manufacturer; Palmtop Computer; PC; Personal Computer; Platform; Portable; Reduced Instruction Set Computing; RISC; Silicon Chip; Sixteen Bit; Standalone; Tower Computer; Turnkey; XT;*

AGP
Advanced Graphics Port or Accelerated Graphics Port. A slot on the PC motherboard in which a graphic card is housed.
See Also: *Accelerated Graphics Port; Advanced Graphics Port; AGP Slot; Digital Video Interface; DVI; Expansion Slot; Fax Card; Graphics; Graphics Card; Motherboard; PCB; PCI; PCMCIA; Peripheral Component Interconnect; Personal Computer Memory Card International Association; Port; Printed Circuit Board; Slot; Sound Card; Video Card;*

AGP Slot
An internal slot in the computer, which provides a faster path for data when used with an internal graphic's card.
See Also: *Accelerated Graphics Port; Advanced Graphics Port; AGP; Expansion Slot; Fax Card; Graphics; Graphics Card; Motherboard; PCB; PCI; PCMCIA; Peripheral Component Interconnect; Personal*

Computer Memory Card International Association; Port; Printed Circuit Board; Slot; Sound Card; Video Card;

AI
Artificial Intelligence. A computer science, which attempts to computerise human learning and reasoning.
See Also: *Analogue; Application; Artificial Intelligence; EDS; Electronic Data System; Expert System; FL; Fuzzy Logic; Information Technology; IT; Leading Edge; Package; Software Package; Software System; State of the Art; Virtual Reality; VR;*

ALGOL
ALGorithmic Oriented Language. A high level computer programming language mainly used for mathematical and scientific applications.
See Also: *3GL; 4GL; ADA; APL; BASIC; C or C++; CLIPPER; COBOL; Code; Code Generator; Compiler; Compiling; CORAL; FORTH; FORTRAN; Fourth Generation Language; High Level Language; Instruction Set; JAVA; JAVASCRIPT; Language; LISP; LOGO; Module; NATURAL; PASCAL; PERL; PICK; PILOT; PL/1; Practical Extraction and Reporting Language; Program; Programming Language; PROLOG; RPG; Software; Source Code; Structured Program; Syntax; Third Generation Language; Visual Basic;*

ALU
Arithmetic and Logic Unit. The part of a central processing unit, which performs arithmetic and logical operations.
See Also: *286; 386; 486; AND gate; Application Specific Integrated Circuits; Arithmetic and Logic Unit; ASICS; Boolean Algebra; Central Processing Unit; Chip; Chipset; Clock Speed; Co-processor; CPU; FL; Flip Flop; Fuzzy Logic; IC; Integrated Circuit; I-OR gate; Large Scale Integration; Logic Gate; LSI; Maths Co-processor; Microprocessor; Motherboard; NAND gate; NEQ gate; NOR gate; NOT gate; Operator; OR gate; Parallel Processor; Processor; Silicon Chip; Transistor; Very Large Scale Integration; VLSI; X-OR gate;*

American National Standard Institute
(ANSI). An organisation which determine standards within the computer industry. Pronounced "ansee".
See Also: *Acceptable User Policy; ANSI; AUP; BCS; CCITT; CCTA; CERN; CODASYL; Conference On DAta SYstems Languages; Conseil Europeen pour la Recherche Nucleaire; Consultative Committee International Telegraph and Telephone; EBCDIC; Extended Binary*

Coded Decimal Interchange Code; IEE; International Standards Organisation; ISO; NCC;

American Standard Code for Information Interchange
(ASCII). A standard 8-bit format in which data is stored as a character that makes it compatible across different hardware and software systems. ASCII is pronounced "askey".
See Also: *8 Bit; ASCII; ASCII Files; Binary Digit; Bit; Bit Pattern; Byte; Character; Data; Data Type; EBCDIC; Eight Bit; Extended Binary Coded Decimal Interchange Code; Format; Hex; Hexadecimal; Information; Least Significant Bit; LSB; Most Significant Bit; MSB; Octal;*

AMR
Automatic Message Routing. A procedure in which an electronic device automatically routs messages depending on information contained in them.
See Also: *ACK; ADN; Advanced Digital Network; Analogue Digital Converter; AND gate; Asynchronous Transfer Mode; ATM; Automatic Message Routing; Black Box; Boolean Algebra; Client Server; Communications; Data Communications; Data Parity; Data Transmission; Datacoms; Dial In; Dial Up; Direct Connection; Distributed System/Network; Duplex Transmission; EFT; EFTPOS; Electronic Fund Transfer; Electronic Fund Transfer Point of Sales; Ethernet; FDDI; Fibre Distributed Data Interface; Fibre Optics; FL; Flip Flop; Full Duplex; Fuzzy Logic; Gateway; Half Duplex; HD; Integrated Services Digital Network; Intranet; I-OR gate; ISDN; LAN; Leased Line; Local Area Network; Logic Gate; Modem; Modulator Demodulator; Multiplex; Multiplexer; NAND gate; NEQ gate; Network; Node; NOR gate; NOT gate; Optical Fibre; OR gate; Parallel Transmission; Parity Bit; Protocol; Ring Network; Serial Transmission; Server; Simplex Transmission; Star Cluster; Star Network; Telecommunication; Telecoms; Teleprocessing System; Token Ring; TPS; V90; Very Large Scale Integration; VLSI; WAN; Wide Area Network; X-OR gate;*

Analogue
(1) A peripheral device which processes data analogous as opposed to digitally. e.g. speedometer. (2) Information which changes continuously and sent direct from an analogue device. e.g. speedometer reading.
See Also: *AI; Analogue Computer; Analogue Digital Converter; Application Specific Integrated Circuits; Artificial Intelligence; ASICS; Device; Digital Analog Converter; Hand Held Device; IC; Integrated*

Circuit; Interface; Light Pen; MIDI; Musical Instrument Digital Interface; Peripheral; Remote Device; Voice Activated;

Analogue Computer
A computer which operates with input direct from devices that receives continuous readings of speed, quantities etc. i.e. not from digital input.
See Also: *16 Bit; 1st Generation; 2nd Generation; 32 Bit; 3rd Generation; 4th Generation; 64 Bit; 8 Bit; Advanced Technology; Analogue; Analogue Digital Converter; AT; Computer; Cross Platform; Desktop; Digital Computer; Distributed System/Network; EDS; Eight Bit; Electronic Data System; Environment; Equipment; Extended Technology; Hand Held Device; Hardware; IBM (tm) Compatible; Information Technology; Installation; IT; Kit; Laptop; Light Pen; Machine; Mainframe; Micro; Microcomputer; MIDI; Midrange System; Minicomputer; Multi Platform; Musical Instrument Digital Interface; Notebook; Number Cruncher; OEM; Original Equipment Manufacturer; Palmtop Computer; PC; Personal Computer; Platform; Portable; Sixteen Bit; Sixty Four Bit; Standalone; Thirty Two Bit; Tower Computer; Turnkey; Voice Activated; XT;*

Analogue Digital Converter
A device that converts continuous analogue signals to digital signals which then enable a computer to process the data. e.g. converting temperature to digital format.
See Also: *AMR; Analogue; Analogue Computer; Automatic Message Routing; Device; Digital; Digital Analog Converter; Equipment; Flatbed Scanner; Front End Processor; Hand Held Device; Hardware; Interface; Kit; Light Pen; MIDI; Musical Instrument Digital Interface; Optical Scanner; Peripheral; Scanner; Voice Activated;*

Analogue Monitor
A visual display unit or terminal which supports an unlimited number of colours.
See Also: *Anti Glare Screen; Cathode Ray Tube; CGA; Colour Graphics Adaptor; CRT; Device; Digital Monitor; Display; EGA; Enhanced Graphic Adaptor; Environment; Equipment; Extended Video Array; Graphics Card; Hardware; High Resolution; Installation; Intelligent Terminal; Interlaced; Kit; LCD; Liquid Crystal Display; Low Resolution; Monitor; Monochrome; Paint Screen; Peripheral; Plasma Screen; Prompt; Resolution; Screen; Screen Burn; Split Screen; Super Twist LCD; Super VGA; Super Video Graphics Array; SVGA; Terminal; TFT; Thin-Film Transistor; Touch Screen; Twip; VDT; VDU; VGA; Video Card; Video Display Terminal; Video Graphics Array; Video Random*

Access Memory; Visual Display Terminal; Visual Display Unit; VRAM; XGA;

Analyst

A person who analyses and designs a computer system.

See Also: *A/P; Analyst Programmer; B/A; Business Analyst; Contractor; Data Base Analyst; Data Flow Diagram; Data Model; Data Processing Manager; DBA; Design; Development; DFD; DPM; Flowchart; Full Project Life Cycle; Hand Holding; Logical Design; O & M; Object Oriented Analysis; Object Oriented Design; Object Oriented Programming; OOA; OOD; OOP; Organisation & Methods; Physical Design; Programmer; Project Life Cycle; S/A; S/P; Software Development Cycle; Software House; Specification; Structured Design; System Analysis; System Analyst; Systems Programmer; Technical Author; Walkthrough;*

Analyst Programmer

(A/P). A person who designs and programs a computer system.

See Also: *A/P; Analyst; B/A; Business Analyst; Code; Contractor; Data Base Analyst; Data Processing Manager; DBA; Design; Development; DPM; Full Project Life Cycle; Language; Logical Design; Loop; Physical Design; Program; Program Specification; Programmer; Programming Language; Project Life Cycle; S/A; S/P; Software; Software Development Cycle; Software House; Specification; Structured Design; Structured Program; System Analyst; Systems Programmer; Technical Author;*

Anchor

The starting point or destination of a hyperlink.

See Also: *Address; BBS; Browser; Bulletin Board System; Cookie; Cybercafe; Cyberspace; DNS; Domain Name; Domain Name System; E-mail Address; Extensible Hypertext Markup Language; eXtensible Markup Language; Hit; Home Page; HTML; Hyperlink; Hypertext; Hypertext Mark-Up Language; Information Superhighway; Internet; Internet Protocol; Internet Protocol Address; IP; IP Address; Link; Net; Page; Portal; Search Engine; Site; Spider; The Net; The Web; Thumbnail; Universal/Uniform Resource Locator; URL; Webring; Website; World Wide Web; WWW; XHTML; XML;*

AND gate
A logic gate on a chip which operates with binary digits where an output logic value 1 only occurs if all inputs have a logic value 1. e.g. Inp=1 and Inp=1 then Out=1, Inp=1 and Inp=0 then Out=0.
See Also: *ALU; AMR; Arithmetic and Logic Unit; Automatic Message Routing; Binary; Binary Digit; Bit; Boolean Algebra; Chip; Chipset; Expert System; FL; Flip Flop; Fuzzy Logic; I-OR gate; Large Scale Integration; Logic Gate; LSI; NAND gate; NEQ gate; NOR gate; NOT gate; OR gate; Silicon Chip; Transistor; Very Large Scale Integration; VLSI; X-OR gate;*

Anonymous FTP
The way in which users gain access to a remote server using the File Transfer Protocol without having an account on that server. The e-mail address is used as a password and 'anonymous' is assigned as the user name.
See Also: *Acceptable User Policy; Address; AUP; Client Server; Client Server Protocol; Cookie; Dial In; Dial Up; E-mail Address; Ethernet; File Transfer Protocol; FTP; FTP Site; FTPmail; Interface; LAN; Local Area Network; Mirror Site; Network; Network Information Centre; NIC; Protocol; Remote Device; Ring Network; Server; Star Cluster; Star Network; TCP/IP; Token Ring; Transmission Control Protocol/Internet Protocol; WAN; Wide Area Network; XMODEM; YMODEM; ZMODEM;*

ANSI
American National Standard Institute. An organisation which determine standards within the computer industry. Pronounced "ansee".
See Also: *Acceptable User Policy; American National Standard Institute; AUP; BCS; CCITT; CCTA; CERN; CODASYL; Conference On DAta SYstems Languages; Conseil Europeen pour la Recherche Nucleaire; Consultative Committee International Telegraph and Telephone; EBCDIC; Extended Binary Coded Decimal Interchange Code; IEE; International Standards Organisation; ISO; NCC;*

Anti Glare Screen
(1) A visual display unit screen whose surface does not reflect light. (2) A device which covers a screen to stop the reflection of light while allowing the screen to be viewed.
See Also: *Analogue Monitor; Cathode Ray Tube; CGA; Colour Graphics Adaptor; CRT; Device; Digital Monitor; Display; EGA; Enhanced Graphic Adaptor; Equipment; Extended Video Array; Graphics Card; Hardware; High Resolution; Installation; Intelligent Terminal; Interlaced; Kit; LCD; Liquid Crystal Display; Low Resolution; Monitor;*

Monochrome; Paint Screen; Peripheral; Plasma Screen; Prompt; Resolution; Screen; Screen Burn; Split Screen; Super Twist LCD; Super VGA; Super Video Graphics Array; SVGA; Terminal; TFT; Thin-Film Transistor; Touch Screen; Twip; VDT; VDU; VGA; Video Card; Video Display Terminal; Video Graphics Array; Video Random Access Memory; Visual Display Terminal; Visual Display Unit; VRAM; XGA;

API

Application Program Interface. An interface which allows services provided by the operating system to be used by programs.

See Also: *Applet; Application; Application Program Interface; Code; Cookie; Device Driver; Disk Operating System; DLL; DOS; Driver; Dynamic Link Library; Graphical User Interface; GUI; Interface; Interrupt; Interrupt Request; IRQ; Linux; MCA; Micro Channel Architecture; Network Operating System; NOS; Operating System; OS; OS/2; Overlay; Program; Software; Software Driver; Structured Program; System Software;*

APL

A Programming Language. A high level computer programming language.

See Also: *3GL; 4GL; ADA; ALGOL; BASIC; C or C++; CLIPPER; COBOL; Code; Code Generator; Compiler; Compiling; CORAL; FORTH; FORTRAN; Fourth Generation Language; High Level Language; Instruction Set; JAVA; JAVASCRIPT; Language; LISP; LOGO; Module; NATURAL; Page Description Language; PASCAL; PDL; PERL; PICK; PILOT; PL/1; Practical Extraction and Reporting Language; Program; Programming Language; PROLOG; RPG; Software; Source Code; Structured Program; Syntax; Third Generation Language; Visual Basic;*

Applet

A program downloaded over a network and run on the user's computer to create animation or sound, for example.

See Also: *API; Application; Application Program Interface; Browser; Call; Chain; Cookie; Cyberspace; Daemon; DLL; Dynamic Link Library; Extensible Hypertext Markup Language; eXtensible Markup Language; Function; HTML; Hypertext Mark-Up Language; Instruction Set; Internet; Invoke; Loop; Macro; Memory Resident; Mix; Module; Nesting; Net; Program; Script; The Net; XHTML; XML;*

Application
A collection of programs designed to carry out a specific task. e.g. word processing, accounting.
See Also: *Abort; AI; API; Applet; Application Program Interface; Artificial Intelligence; Batch File; Batch Processing; BBS; Bespoke; Bulletin Board System; CAD; CADCAM; CADMAT; CAE; CAI; CAM; CASE; Case Tool; CBT; Computer Aided Design; Computer Aided Design and Manufacturing; Computer Aided Design Manufacture and Test; Computer Aided Engineering; Computer Aided Instruction; Computer Aided Manufacturing; Computer Aided Software Engineering; Computer Based Training; Configuration; Desk Top Publishing; DTP; EDS; Electronic Data System; Expert System; Freeware; Geographical Information System; GIS; Information System; Integrated Systems; IS; Mail Merge; Meta-Search Engine; Multi Platform; Office Information System; OIS; Package; Program; Releases; Search Engine; Shareware; Software; Software House; Software Package; Software System; Spider; Spreadsheet; System; Turnkey; Vertical Market; Word Processor; WP;*

Application Program Interface
(API). An interface which allows services provided by the operating system to be used by programs.
See Also: *API; Applet; Application; Code; Cookie; Device Driver; Disk Operating System; DLL; DOS; Driver; Dynamic Link Library; Graphical User Interface; GUI; Interface; Interrupt; Interrupt Request; IRQ; Linux; MCA; Micro Channel Architecture; Network Operating System; NOS; Operating System; OS; OS/2; Overlay; Program; Software; Software Driver; Structured Program; System Software;*

Application Specific Integrated Circuits
(ASICS). Chips designed for specific tasks. e.g. controlling a washing machine.
See Also: *286; 386; 486; ALU; Analogue; Arithmetic and Logic Unit; ASICS; Central Processing Unit; Chip; Chipset; Clock Speed; Co-processor; CPU; Graphics Card; IC; Integrated Circuit; Large Scale Integration; LSI; Maths Co-processor; Microprocessor; Motherboard; Parallel Processor; PCB; PCMCIA; Personal Computer Memory Card International Association; Printed Circuit Board; Processor; Semiconductor; Silicon Chip; Solid State; Sound Chip; Transistor; UART; Universal Asynchronous Receiver/Transmitter; Very Large Scale Integration; Video Card; VLSI;*

Archive
(1) Data which has been retained on a storage medium. (2) The process of retaining that data.
See Also: *3.5 Inch; 5.25 Inch; Backing Store; Backup; CD-RW Drive; COM; Compressed File; Computer Output Microfilm; DAT; Data; Data Element; Data Entity; Data Item; Deck; Digital Audio Tape; Disk; Disk Drive; Disk Pack; Disk Storage; Diskette; Drive; Export; FDD; Fiche; File; Five and a quarter; Fixed Disk Drive; Floppy Disk; Floppy Disk Drive; Folder; Grandfather, Father, Son; Hard Disk Drive; HDD; Information; Mag Tape; Magnetic Disk; Magnetic Tape; Mass Storage; Microfiche; Microfilm; Optical Drive; Output; Pack; Paper Tape; R/W; Read/Write; Record; Recording; Recording Device; Recording Medium; Restore; Save; Security; Storage; Store; Streamer; Tape Deck; Tape Streamer; Three and a Half; Unzip; Winchester Disk; Write; Zip; Zip Drive;*

Arithmetic and Logic Unit
(ALU). The part of a central processing unit which performs arithmetic and logical operations.
See Also: *286; 386; 486; ALU; AND gate; Application Specific Integrated Circuits; ASICS; Boolean Algebra; Central Processing Unit; Chip; Chipset; Clock Speed; Co-processor; CPU; FL; Flip Flop; Fuzzy Logic; IC; Integrated Circuit; I-OR gate; Large Scale Integration; Logic Gate; LSI; Maths Co-processor; Microprocessor; Motherboard; NAND gate; NEQ gate; NOR gate; NOT gate; Operator; OR gate; Parallel Processor; Processor; Silicon Chip; Transistor; Very Large Scale Integration; VLSI; X-OR gate;*

Array
A list of items set up in the computers memory by a program and used for processing in that program. Arrays can be a single list (one dimensional), double list (two dimensional) and more. Each item in the list is referenced using a subscript.
See Also: *Block; Bubble Sort; Conventional Memory; Core; Core Dump; Data; Data Element; Data Entity; Data Item; Disk Cache; Entity; Field; Flash Memory; Information; Magnetic Core; Memory; Null; Stack; Store; Subscript; Table; Working Storage; Workspace;*

Artificial Intelligence
(AI). A computer science which attempts to computerise human learning and reasoning.
See Also: *AI; Analogue; Application; EDS; Electronic Data System; Expert System; FL; Fuzzy Logic; Information Technology; IT; Leading*

Edge; Package; Software Package; Software System; State of the Art; Virtual Reality; VR;

ASCII

American Standard Code for Information Interchange. A standard 8-bit format in which data is stored as a character that makes it compatible across different hardware and software systems. Pronounced "askey".

See Also: *8 Bit; American Standard Code for Information Interchange; ASCII Files; Binary Digit; Bit; Bit Pattern; Byte; Character; Data; Data Type; EBCDIC; Eight Bit; Extended Binary Coded Decimal Interchange Code; Format; Hex; Hexadecimal; Information; Least Significant Bit; LSB; Most Significant Bit; MSB; Octal;*

ASCII Files

ASCII files are alphanumeric text files. Pronounced "askey".

See Also: *American Standard Code for Information Interchange; ASCII; Attachment; Batch File; Beginning of File; BOF; Character; Data; Document; EBCDIC; End of File; EOF; Extended Binary Coded Decimal Interchange Code; Extension; File; File Conversion; Filename Extension; Fragmentation; Index Sequential File; Information; Log File; Random File; Rich Text Format; RTF; Sequential File; Serial File; Tag File; Temp File;*

ASICS

Application Specific Integrated Circuits. Chips designed for specific tasks. e.g. controlling a washing machine.

See Also: *286; 386; 486; ALU; Analogue; Application Specific Integrated Circuits; Arithmetic and Logic Unit; Central Processing Unit; Chip; Chipset; Clock Speed; Co-processor; CPU; Graphics Card; IC; Integrated Circuit; Large Scale Integration; LSI; Maths Co-processor; Microprocessor; Motherboard; Parallel Processor; PCB; PCMCIA; Personal Computer Memory Card International Association; Printed Circuit Board; Processor; Semiconductor; Silicon Chip; Solid State; Sound Chip; Transistor; UART; Universal Asynchronous Receiver/Transmitter; Very Large Scale Integration; Video Card; VLSI;*

Assembler

A program which converts assembly code into machine code.

See Also: *Assembly Code; BCD; Binary; Binary Coded Decimal; Code; Code Generator; Compiler; Compiling; Conversion; High Level Language; Instruction Set; Interpreter; Language; Low Level Language; Machine Code; Machine Language; Object Code; Program; Programming Language; Software; Source Code;*

Assembly Code
A low level computer programming language very similar to machine code.
See Also: *Assembler; Code; Code Generator; Compiler; Compiling; High Level Language; Instruction Set; Language; Low Level Language; Machine Code; Machine Language; Module; Object Code; Program; Programming Language; Software;*

Asymmetric Digital Subscriber Line
(ADSL). A digital connection to the Internet using an ordinary telephone line instead of a modem which allows for fast data transfers.
See Also: *ADN; ADSL; Advanced Digital Network; Asynchronous; Asynchronous Transfer Mode; ATM; Bandwidth; Baud Rate; Binary Digit; Bit; Bits Per Second; BPS; Broadband; CCITT; CCTA; Characters Per Second; Communications; Consultative Committee International Telegraph and Telephone; CPS; Data Communications; Data Parity; Data Transmission; Datacoms; Dial In; Dial Up; Digital; Direct Connection; Duplex Transmission; FDDI; Fibre Distributed Data Interface; Fibre Optics; Full Duplex; Gbps; Half Duplex; HD; Information Superhighway; Integrated Services Digital Network; ISDN; Kbps; Leased Line; Mbps; Multiplex; Multiplexer; Narrowband; Open Systems Interconnect; Optical Fibre; OSI; Parallel Transmission; Parity Bit; Serial Interface; Serial Transmission; Simplex Transmission; Synchronous; T-1; T-3; Telecommunication; Telecoms; Teleprocessing System; TPS; Transfer Rate; Transmit; V90;*

Asymmetrical Modem
A modem which supports separate channels and transmits information simultaneously at different baud rates.
See Also: *Acoustic Coupler; ADN; Advanced Digital Network; Asynchronous; Asynchronous Transfer Mode; ATM; Bandwidth; Baud Rate; Black Box; Broadband; Channel; Characters Per Second; Communications; CPS; Data Communications; Data Parity; Data Transmission; Datacoms; Dial In; Dial Up; Duplex Transmission; Equipment; FDDI; Fibre Distributed Data Interface; Fibre Optics; Full Duplex; Half Duplex; Hardware; HD; Integrated Services Digital Network; ISDN; Kbps; Kit; Modem; Modulator Demodulator; Multiplex; Multiplexer; Narrowband; Open Systems Interconnect; Optical Fibre; OSI; Parallel Transmission; Parity Bit; Serial Interface; Serial Transmission; Simplex Transmission; Synchronous; T-1; T-3; Telecommunication; Telecoms; Teleprocessing System; TPS; Transfer Rate; Transmission Channel; Transmit; V90;*

Asynchronous
Abbreviated to Async. Transmission mode in which data is transmitted serially and simultaneously from one device to another. Characters are transmitted singly at irregular intervals of time.
See Also: *ACK; Acoustic Coupler; ADN; ADSL; Advanced Digital Network; Asymmetric Digital Subscriber Line; Asymmetrical Modem; Asynchronous Transfer Mode; ATM; Bandwidth; Baud Rate; Bits Per Second; BPS; Broadband; CCITT; CCTA; Characters Per Second; Communications; Consultative Committee International Telegraph and Telephone; CPS; Data Communications; Data Parity; Data Transmission; Datacoms; Dial In; Dial Up; Digital; Direct Connection; Duplex Transmission; FDDI; Fibre Distributed Data Interface; Fibre Optics; Full Duplex; Gbps; Half Duplex; HD; Information Superhighway; Integrated Services Digital Network; ISDN; Kbps; Leased Line; Mbps; Multiplex; Multiplexer; Narrowband; Open Systems Interconnect; Optical Fibre; OSI; Packet; Packet Switching; Parallel Transmission; Parity Bit; Serial Interface; Serial Transmission; Simplex Transmission; Synchronous; T-1; T-3; Telecommunication; Telecoms; Teleprocessing System; TPS; Transmit; V90;*

Asynchronous Transfer Mode
(ATM). A communication standard that allows large quantities of voice, video and other multimedia data to be transferred in real time.
See Also: *ADN; ADSL; Advanced Digital Network; AMR; Asymmetric Digital Subscriber Line; Asymmetrical Modem; Asynchronous; ATM; Automatic Message Routing; Bandwidth; Baud Rate; Bits Per Second; BPS; Broadband; CCITT; CCTA; Characters Per Second; Communications; Consultative Committee International Telegraph and Telephone; CPS; Data Communications; Data Parity; Data Transmission; Datacoms; Dial In; Dial Up; Digital; Direct Connection; Duplex Transmission; FDDI; Fibre Distributed Data Interface; Fibre Optics; Firewire; Full Duplex; Gbps; Half Duplex; HD; Integrated Services Digital Network; International Standards Organisation; ISDN; ISO; Kbps; Leased Line; Mbps; Multiplex; Multiplexer; Narrowband; Open Systems Interconnect; Optical Fibre; OSI; Parallel Transmission; Parity Bit; Serial Transmission; Simplex Transmission; Synchronous; T-1; T-3; Telecommunication; Telecoms; Teleprocessing System; TPS; Transfer Rate; Transmit; V90; WAP; Wireless Application Protocol;*

AT

Advanced Technology. The basis in which some personal computers were designed which used a 286 chip.

See Also: *16 Bit; 1st Generation; 286; 2nd Generation; 386; 3rd Generation; 486; 4th Generation; Advanced Technology; Analogue Computer; Chip; Chipset; Computer; Cross Platform; Desktop; Digital Computer; EDS; Electronic Data System; Environment; Equipment; Extended Technology; Hardware; IBM (tm) Compatible; Installation; Kit; Laptop; Machine; Micro; Microcomputer; Multi Platform; Notebook; OEM; Original Equipment Manufacturer; Palmtop Computer; PC; Personal Computer; Platform; Portable; Reduced Instruction Set Computing; RISC; Silicon Chip; Sixteen Bit; Standalone; Tower Computer; Turnkey; XT;*

ATAPI

Attachment Packet Interface. An upgrade to the hard disk drive which allows the disk controller to control CD drives as well.

See Also: *3.5 Inch; 5.25 Inch; Attachment Packet Interface; CD-ROM Drive; CD-RW Drive; Configuring; Device Driver; Digital Versatile Disk; Disk; Disk Drive; Disk Pack; Disk Storage; Diskette; Drive; Driver; DVD; EIDE; Enhanced Intelligent Drive Electronics; FDD; Five and a quarter; Fixed Disk Drive; Floppy Disk; Floppy Disk Drive; Hard Disk Drive; HDD; IDE; Integrated Drive Electronics; Interface; Magnetic Disk; Optical Drive; Pack; Self Monitoring Analysis and Reporting Technology; SMART; Software Driver; Storage; Three and a Half; Winchester Disk;*

ATM

Asynchronous Transfer Mode. A communication standard that allows large quantities of voice, video and other multimedia data to be transferred in real time.

See Also: *ADN; ADSL; Advanced Digital Network; AMR; Asymmetric Digital Subscriber Line; Asymmetrical Modem; Asynchronous; Asynchronous Transfer Mode; Automatic Message Routing; Bandwidth; Baud Rate; Bits Per Second; BPS; Broadband; CCITT; CCTA; Characters Per Second; Communications; Consultative Committee International Telegraph and Telephone; CPS; Data Communications; Data Parity; Data Transmission; Datacoms; Dial In; Dial Up; Digital; Direct Connection; Duplex Transmission; FDDI; Fibre Distributed Data Interface; Fibre Optics; Firewire; Full Duplex; Gbps; Half Duplex; HD; Integrated Services Digital Network; International Standards Organisation; ISDN; ISO; Kbps; Leased Line; Mbps; Multiplex; Multiplexer; Narrowband; Open Systems Interconnect; Optical Fibre;*

OSI; Parallel Transmission; Parity Bit; Serial Transmission; Simplex Transmission; Synchronous; T-1; T-3; Telecommunication; Telecoms; Teleprocessing System; TPS; Transfer Rate; Transmit; V90; WAP; Wireless Application Protocol;

Attachment
Any file that is attached to an e-mail, e.g. text, graphics.
See Also: *ASCII Files; Beginning of File; BitMaP; BMP; Body; BOF; Compressed File; Document; Download; Electronic Mail; E-mail; End of File; EOF; Extension; File; Filename Extension; GIF; Graphical Interchange Format; Index Sequential File; Joint Photographic Experts Group; JPEG; JPG; Log File; MIME; Motion Picture Experts Group; MP3; MPEG; MPG; Multipurpose Internet Mail Extensions; PDF; Portable Document Format; Random File; Rich Text Format; RTF; Sequential File; Serial File; Signature; Spam; Tag File; Tag Image File Format; Temp File; Thread; TIFF; Upload; Zip;*

Attachment Packet Interface
(ATAPI). An upgrade to the hard disk drive which allows the disk controller to control CD drives as well.
See Also: *3.5 Inch; 5.25 Inch; ATAPI; CD-ROM Drive; CD-RW Drive; Configuring; Device Driver; Digital Versatile Disk; Disk; Disk Drive; Disk Pack; Disk Storage; Diskette; Drive; Driver; DVD; EIDE; Enhanced Intelligent Drive Electronics; FDD; Five and a quarter; Fixed Disk Drive; Floppy Disk; Floppy Disk Drive; Hard Disk Drive; HDD; IDE; Integrated Drive Electronics; Interface; Magnetic Disk; Optical Drive; Pack; Self Monitoring Analysis and Reporting Technology; SMART; Software Driver; Storage; Three and a Half; Winchester Disk;*

Audit Trail
The path of procedures which traces the processing of transactions.
See Also: *Batch Processing; Computation; Compute; Data Flow; Data Flow Diagram; Data Model; Data Processing; Debug; Debugger; DFD; DP; EDP; Electronic Data Processing; Event; Flowchart; Function; Information System; IS; JCL; Job; Job Control Language; Log File; Logical Design; Macro; Path; Physical Design; Process; Processing; Real Time; Reengineering; Restore; Roll Back; Script; Security; Trace; Transaction Processing; Walkthrough;*

AUP

Acceptable User Policy. Rules provided by an Internet Service Provider detailing the use of their services.

See Also: *Acceptable User Policy; American National Standard Institute; Anonymous FTP; ANSI; CCITT; CCTA; CERN; Conseil Europeen pour la Recherche Nucleaire; Consultative Committee International Telegraph and Telephone; File Transfer Protocol; FTP; Host; International Standards Organisation; Internet; Internet Protocol; Internet Service Provider; IP; ISO; ISP; MP3; Net; Netiquette; Newbie; Point Of Presence; Point to Point Protocol; POP; PPP; Protocol; Provider; Service Provider; Simple Mail Transfer Protocol; Site; SMTP; TCP/IP; The Net; The Web; Transmission Control Protocol/Internet Protocol; WAP; Wap Internet Service Provider; Website; Wireless Application Protocol; WISP; World Wide Web; WWW;*

AUTOEXEC.BAT

A file on a Personal Computer containing set up procedures which are executed when the computer is switched on or reset. e.g. setting the format of the screen prompt.

See Also: *Batch File; Batch Processing; Boot; Boot Disk; Bootstrap; C Prompt; Call; Chain; Cold Start; Command; CONFIG.SYS; Configuring; Execute; File; Instruction; Instruction Set; Invoke; JCL; Job; Job Control Language; Process; Re-boot; Registry; Warm Start;*

Automatic Message Routing

(AMR). A procedure in which an electronic device automatically routs messages depending on the information contained in them.

See Also: *ACK; ADN; Advanced Digital Network; AMR; Analogue Digital Converter; AND gate; Asynchronous Transfer Mode; ATM; Black Box; Boolean Algebra; Client Server; Communications; Data Communications; Data Parity; Data Transmission; Datacoms; Dial In; Dial Up; Direct Connection; Distributed System/Network; Duplex Transmission; EFT; EFTPOS; Electronic Fund Transfer; Electronic Fund Transfer Point of Sales; Ethernet; FDDI; Fibre Distributed Data Interface; Fibre Optics; FL; Flip Flop; Full Duplex; Fuzzy Logic; Gateway; Half Duplex; HD; Integrated Services Digital Network; Intranet; I-OR gate; ISDN; LAN; Leased Line; Local Area Network; Logic Gate; Modem; Modulator Demodulator; Multiplex; Multiplexer; NAND gate; NEQ gate; Network; Node; NOR gate; NOT gate; Optical Fibre; OR gate; Parallel Transmission; Parity Bit; Protocol; Ring Network; Serial Transmission; Server; Simplex Transmission; Star Cluster; Star Network; Telecommunication; Telecoms; Teleprocessing*

System; Token Ring; TPS; V90; Very Large Scale Integration; VLSI; WAN; Wide Area Network; X-OR gate;

B/A
Business Analyst. A person with the knowledge and experience of a particular industry or application, who analyses, designs and documents that application.
See Also: *A/P; Analyst; Analyst Programmer; Business Analyst; Contractor; Data Base Analyst; Data Flow Diagram; Data Model; Data Processing Manager; DBA; Design; Development; DFD; DPM; Flowchart; Full Project Life Cycle; Hand Holding; Logical Design; Model; O & M; Object Oriented Analysis; Object Oriented Design; Object Oriented Programming; OOA; OOD; OOP; Organisation & Methods; Physical Design; Process Model; Programmer; Project Life Cycle; S/A; S/P; Software Development Cycle; Software House; Specification; Structured Design; System Analysis; System Analyst; Systems Programmer; Technical Author; Walkthrough;*

Backbone
The primary path of a network used to transmit data between network stations.
See Also: *Ethernet; Intranet; LAN; LAN Port; Local Area Network; Network; Network Information Centre; NIC; Ring Network; Star Cluster; Star Network; Token Ring; Transmission Channel; Transmit; WAN; Wide Area Network;*

Backing Store
(1) A storage device attached to a computer, e.g. disk or tape unit. (2) The storage medium used on the units, e.g. floppy disk.
See Also: *3.5 Inch; 5.25 Inch; Archive; Backup; CD-RW Drive; COM; Computer Output Microfilm; Computer Power; Configuration; DAT; Deck; Device; Digital Audio Tape; Disk; Disk Drive; Disk Pack; Disk Size; Disk Storage; Diskette; Drive; Environment; Equipment; FDD; Fiche; File; Five and a quarter; Fixed Disk Drive; Floppy Disk; Floppy Disk Drive; Grandfather, Father, Son; Hard Disk Drive; Hardware; HDD; Kit; Mag Tape; Magnetic Disk; Magnetic Tape; Mass Storage; Medium; Microfiche; Microfilm; Optical Drive; Pack; Paper Tape; Peripheral; Power; Recording; Recording Device; Recording Medium; Save; Security; Storage; Store; Streamer; System; Tape Deck; Tape Streamer; Three and a Half; Volume; Winchester Disk; Zip; Zip Drive;*

Backup

(1) A copy of data or programs on a storage medium. (2) The securing of information by recording it onto an external device. e.g. tape.

See Also: *3.5 Inch; 5.25 Inch; Archive; Backing Store; CD-RW Drive; COM; Computer Output Microfilm; DAT; Deck; Digital Audio Tape; Disk; Disk Drive; Disk Pack; Disk Storage; Diskette; Drive; Event; FDD; Fiche; File; Five and a quarter; Fixed Disk Drive; Floppy Disk; Floppy Disk Drive; Grandfather, Father, Son; Hard Disk Drive; HDD; Mag Tape; Magnetic Disk; Magnetic Tape; Mass Storage; Medium; Microfiche; Microfilm; Optical Drive; Output; Pack; Paper Tape; R/W; Read/Write; Record; Recording; Recording Device; Recording Medium; Roll Back; Save; Security; Storage; Store; Streamer; Tape Deck; Tape Streamer; Three and a Half; Unzip; Volume; Winchester Disk; Write; Zip; Zip Drive;*

Bandwidth

The volume of data that can be transmitted over a network at a given time, e.g. voice or data signals.

See Also: *ADN; ADSL; Advanced Digital Network; Asymmetric Digital Subscriber Line; Asymmetrical Modem; Asynchronous; Asynchronous Transfer Mode; ATM; Baud Rate; Binary Digit; Bit; Bits Per Second; BPS; Broadband; CCITT; CCTA; Characters Per Second; Communications; Consultative Committee International Telegraph and Telephone; CPS; Data; Data Communications; Data Parity; Data Transmission; Data Type; Datacoms; Dial In; Dial Up; Direct Connection; Duplex Transmission; Ethernet; FDDI; Fibre Distributed Data Interface; Fibre Optics; Full Duplex; Gbps; Half Duplex; HD; Information Superhighway; Integrated Services Digital Network; Internet; Intranet; ISDN; Kbps; LAN; Leased Line; Local Area Network; Mbps; Multiplex; Multiplexer; Narrowband; Net; Network; Open Systems Interconnect; Optical Fibre; OSI; Packet; Packet Switching; Parallel Transmission; Parity Bit; Protocol; Ring Network; Serial Interface; Serial Line Internet Protocol; Serial Transmission; Simplex Transmission; SLIP; Star Cluster; Star Network; Synchronous; T-1; T-3; TCP/IP; Telecommunication; Telecoms; Teleprocessing System; The Net; Token Ring; TPS; Transfer Rate; Transmission Control Protocol/Internet Protocol; Transmit; V90; WAN; WAP; Wide Area Network; Wireless Application Protocol;*

Bar Chart

A graphical representation showing the breakdown of percentages or amounts where each breakdown is represented by a bar.

See Also: *Bar Code; Graphics; Image Map; Image Processing;*

Bar Code
A graphical code in the format of dark vertical lines of varying widths representing data which can be optically read into a computer.
See Also: *Bar Chart; Graphics; Image Map; Image Processing;*

Barrel Printer
A line printer whose mechanism includes a barrel shaped component with characters, numbers and symbols embossed on the outside. Next to the barrel is an ink ribbon and paper. Print hammers hit the paper resulting in printed characters being transferred to the paper from the barrel through the ink ribbon.
See Also: *Bubble Jet; Configuration; Daisywheel; Device; Dot Matrix; Drum Printer; Duplex Printing; Environment; Equipment; Hard Copy; Hardware; Inkjet; Installation; Kit; Laser Jet; Laser Printer; LCD Printer; Line Printer; Lines Per Minute; Liquid Crystal Display Printer; Lpm; LPT Port; Matrix Printer; Page Printer; Pages Per Minute; Peripheral; PPM; Printer; Printer Driver; Printout; Simplex Printing; Thermal Printer;*

BASIC
Beginners All purpose Symbolic Instruction Code. A high level computer programming language. It can be interpretive (translated and executed at run time) or compiled (converted to machine code).
See Also: *3GL; 4GL; ADA; ALGOL; APL; C or C++; CLIPPER; COBOL; Code; Code Generator; Compiler; Compiling; CORAL; FORTH; FORTRAN; Fourth Generation Language; High Level Language; Instruction Set; Interpreter; JAVA; JAVASCRIPT; Language; LISP; LOGO; Module; NATURAL; PASCAL; PERL; PICK; PILOT; PL/1; Practical Extraction and Reporting Language; Program; Programming Language; PROLOG; RPG; Software; Source Code; Structured Program; Syntax; Third Generation Language; Visual Basic;*

Basic Input Output System
(BIOS). A collection of Read Only Memory (ROM) resident programs which communicates between the hardware and the operating system, and controls the fundamental processes of a computer.
See Also: *BIOS; Boot; Bootstrap; CMOS; Complementary Metal Oxide Semiconductor Memory; Disk Operating System; DOS; EEROM; Electrically Erasable Read Only Memory; Electronically Programmed Read Only Memory; EMS; Environment; EPROM; Erasable Programmable Read Only Memory; Expanded Memory; Expanded Memory Specification; Extended Memory; Firmware; High Memory; Linux; Operating System; OS; OS/2; Programmable Read Only Memory;*

PROM; RAM; RAM Disk; Rambus Dynamic Random Access Memory; Random Access Memory; RDRAM; Read Only Memory; Re-boot; ROM; ROM Resident; SDRAM; Self Monitoring Analysis and Reporting Technology; Shadow RAM Memory; SIMM; Single Inline Memory Modules; Single Inline Package; SIP; SMART; Synchronous Dynamic Random Access Memory; System Software;

Batch File
A file which is processed in background mode. i.e. not interactive with the screen. It can be a set of instructions to be carried out or a file of transactions to be processed.
See Also: *Application; ASCII Files; AUTOEXEC.BAT; Batch Processing; Beginning of File; BOF; Command; CONFIG.SYS; End of File; EOF; Extension; File; Filename Extension; Function; Index Sequential File; Macro; Registry; Script; Sequential File; Serial File; Temp File; Trailer;*

Batch Processing
Processing performed in background mode. i.e. not interactive with the screen. It can be a set of instructions to be carried out or a file of transactions to be processed.
See Also: *Abort; Application; Audit Trail; AUTOEXEC.BAT; Batch File; Bespoke; Call; Chain; Command; Computation; Compute; Data Processing; DP; EDP; Electronic Data Processing; End of File; End of Job; End of Tape; EOF; EOJ; EOT; Event; Execute; File Conversion; Function; Garbage In, Garbage Out; Housekeeping; Information System; Information Technology; Integrated; Integrated Systems; Invoke; IS; IT; Job; Macro; Mail Merge; Merge; Meta-Search Engine; Multitasking; Office Information System; OIS; Outsourcing; Print Spooler; Process; Processing; Recovery; Restore; Roll Back; Run; Run Time; Script; Search Engine; Spell Check; Spider; Spooler; Transaction Processing;*

Baud Rate
The speed at which data is transferred along a transmission line. The rate in bits per second varies depending on the line and equipment.
See Also: *Access Time; ADN; ADSL; Advanced Digital Network; Asymmetric Digital Subscriber Line; Asymmetrical Modem; Asynchronous; Asynchronous Transfer Mode; ATM; Bandwidth; Bits Per Second; BPS; Broadband; CCITT; CCTA; Communications; Consultative Committee International Telegraph and Telephone; Data; Data Communications; Data Parity; Data Transmission; Datacoms; Dial In; Dial Up; Duplex Transmission; FDDI; Fibre Distributed Data Interface; Fibre Optics; Full Duplex; Gbps; GHz; Gigahertz; Half Duplex; HD;*

Integrated Services Digital Network; ISDN; Kbps; KHz; Kilohertz; Mbps; Microsecond; Million Instructions Per Second; Millisecond; MIPS; Ms; Multiplex; Multiplexer; Nanosecond; Narrowband; Ns; Open Systems Interconnect; Optical Fibre; OSI; Parallel Transmission; Parity Bit; Pico Second; Serial Transmission; Simplex Transmission; Synchronous; T-1; T-3; Telecommunication; Telecoms; Teleprocessing System; TPS; Transfer Rate; Transmit; V90;

BBS

Bulletin Board System. A facility which you can connect to via your computer, modem and telephone line that enables you to access software databases in order for you to purchase and download software.

See Also: *Anchor; Application; Browser; Bulletin Board System; Cybercafe; Cyberspace; Database; DB; Distributed System/Network; Download; EDS; Electronic Data System; Ethernet; Freeware; FTP Site; FTPmail; Gopher; Internet; Intranet; LAN; Local Area Network; Mirror Site; Net; Network; Public Domain; Ring Network; Search Engine; Shareware; Software; Spider; Star Cluster; Star Network; T-1; T-3; The Net; Token Ring; Upload; WAN; Wide Area Network;*

BCD

Binary Coded Decimal. A method to convert the numbers 0 to 9 into binary notation using 4 binary digits. e.g. 9 = 1001 in binary.

See Also: *Assembler; Binary; Binary Coded Decimal; Binary Digit; Bit; Conversion; Convert; Denary; Hex; Hexadecimal; Least Significant Bit; LSB; Machine Code; Machine Language; Most Significant Bit; MSB; Object Code; Octal;*

BCS

The British Computer Society.

See Also: *American National Standard Institute; ANSI; CCITT; CCTA; CERN; Conseil Europeen pour la Recherche Nucleaire; Consultative Committee International Telegraph and Telephone; IEE; International Standards Organisation; ISO; NCC; User Group;*

Beginning of File

(BOF). A notation to indicate the start of a file.

See Also: *ASCII Files; Attachment; Batch File; BOF; Compressed File; Database; DB; Delimiter; Direct Access; Document; End of File; End of Tape; EOF; EOT; File; Header; Index Sequential File; Log File; Random Access; Random File; RDB; Relational Database; Sequential File; Serial File; Tag File; Temp File; Trailer;*

Bespoke
Software or hardware systems developed to match the user requirements exactly.
See Also: *Application; Batch Processing; CAD; CADCAM; CADMAT; CAE; CAI; CAM; CBT; Computer Aided Design; Computer Aided Design and Manufacturing; Computer Aided Design Manufacture and Test; Computer Aided Engineering; Computer Aided Instruction; Computer Aided Manufacturing; Computer Based Training; Configuring; Data Base Management System; Data Processing; DBMS; Desk Top Publishing; Development; DP; DTP; EDP; EDS; EFT; EFTPOS; Electronic Data Processing; Electronic Data System; Electronic Fund Transfer; Electronic Fund Transfer Point of Sales; Equipment; Expert System; Geographical Information System; GIS; Hardware; Implementation; Information System; Information Technology; In-house; IS; IT; Job; Kit; Logical Design; Physical Design; Processing; RDBMS/RDMS; Relational Database Management System; Releases; Software; Software Development Cycle; Software System; System; Turnkey; WYSIWYG;*

Bi Directional
Printing done on a matrix or inkjet printer where the print head moves in both directions.
See Also: *Bubble Jet; Daisywheel; Dot Matrix; Duplex Printing; Hard Copy; Inkjet; Landscape; Letter Quality; Lines Per Minute; Lpm; LQ; Matrix Printer; Near Letter Quality; NLQ; Plotter; Portrait; Postscript; Printer; Printer Driver; Printout; Simplex Printing; Thermal Printer;*

Binary
A numerical system which has a base of 2. Zero (0) and one (1) are the only two digits used to notate a binary number and each notation from the right has double the value of the preceding notation if set to 1. e.g. in a binary notation of 1101, the 1 furthest to the right has a value of 1, the 0 has no value, the next 1 has a value of 4 and the next 1 a value of 8, totalling 13.
See Also: *16 Bit; 32 Bit; 64 Bit; 8 Bit; AND gate; Assembler; BCD; Binary Coded Decimal; Binary Digit; Bit; Bit Pattern; Bits Per Inch; Bits Per Second; Boolean Algebra; BPI; BPS; Bubble Memory; Byte; Data Parity; Digital; Eight Bit; Gbps; Hex; Hexadecimal; I-OR gate; Kbps; Least Significant Bit; Logic Gate; LSB; Machine Code; Machine Language; Mbps; Most Significant Bit; MSB; NAND gate; NEQ gate; NOR gate; NOT gate; Object Code; Octal; OR gate; Parity Bit; Sixteen Bit; Sixty Four Bit; Thirty Two Bit; Toggle; Word; X-OR gate;*

Binary Coded Decimal
(BCD). A method to convert the numbers 0 to 9 into binary notation using 4 binary digits. e.g. 9 = 1001 in binary.
See Also: *Assembler; BCD; Binary; Binary Digit; Bit; Conversion; Convert; Denary; Hex; Hexadecimal; Least Significant Bit; LSB; Machine Code; Machine Language; Most Significant Bit; MSB; Object Code; Octal;*

Binary Digit
(BiT). The smallest piece of information recognised by a computer in binary notation of 0 or 1. A combination of bits can represent alphabetic characters, special characters or numeric digits.
See Also: *16 Bit; 32 Bit; 64 Bit; 8 Bit; Address; Address Bus; ADN; ADSL; Advanced Digital Network; American Standard Code for Information Interchange; AND gate; ASCII; Asymmetric Digital Subscriber Line; Bandwidth; BCD; Binary; Binary Coded Decimal; Bit; Bit Pattern; Bits Per Inch; Bits Per Second; Boolean Algebra; BPI; BPS; Broadband; Bubble Memory; Byte; Data; Data Bus; Data Parity; Data Type; Digital; Eight Bit; Gbps; I-OR gate; Kbps; Least Significant Bit; Logic Gate; LSB; Machine Code; Machine Language; Mbps; Most Significant Bit; MSB; NAND gate; Narrowband; NEQ gate; NOR gate; NOT gate; Object Code; OR gate; Parity Bit; Sixteen Bit; Sixty Four Bit; Thirty Two Bit; Toggle; Word; X-OR gate;*

BIOS
Basic Input Output System. A collection of Read Only Memory (ROM) resident programs which communicates between the hardware and the operating system, and controls the fundamental processes of a computer.
See Also: *Basic Input Output System; Boot; Bootstrap; CMOS; Complementary Metal Oxide Semiconductor Memory; Disk Operating System; DOS; EEROM; Electrically Erasable Read Only Memory; Electronically Programmed Read Only Memory; EMS; Environment; EPROM; Erasable Programmable Read Only Memory; Expanded Memory; Expanded Memory Specification; Extended Memory; Firmware; High Memory; Linux; Operating System; OS; OS/2; Programmable Read Only Memory; PROM; RAM; RAM Disk; Rambus Dynamic Random Access Memory; Random Access Memory; RDRAM; Read Only Memory; Re-boot; ROM; ROM Resident; SDRAM; Self Monitoring Analysis and Reporting Technology; Shadow RAM Memory; SIMM; Single Inline Memory Modules; Single Inline Package; SIP; SMART; Synchronous Dynamic Random Access Memory; System Software;*

Bit

BInary digiT. The smallest piece of information recognised by a computer in binary notation of 0 or 1. A combination of bits can represent alphabetic characters, special characters or numeric digits.

See Also: *16 Bit; 32 Bit; 64 Bit; 8 Bit; Address; Address Bus; ADN; ADSL; Advanced Digital Network; American Standard Code for Information Interchange; AND gate; ASCII; Asymmetric Digital Subscriber Line; Bandwidth; BCD; Binary; Binary Coded Decimal; Binary Digit; Bit Pattern; Bits Per Inch; Bits Per Second; Boolean Algebra; BPI; BPS; Broadband; Bubble Memory; Byte; Data; Data Bus; Data Parity; Data Type; Digital; Eight Bit; Gbps; I-OR gate; Kbps; Least Significant Bit; Logic Gate; LSB; Machine Code; Machine Language; Mbps; Most Significant Bit; MSB; NAND gate; Narrowband; NEQ gate; NOR gate; NOT gate; Object Code; OR gate; Parity Bit; Sixteen Bit; Sixty Four Bit; Thirty Two Bit; Toggle; Word; X-OR gate;*

Bit Pattern

The format of bits which make up a character. e.g. a binary bit pattern of 01000001 = upper case character 'A'.

See Also: *American Standard Code for Information Interchange; ASCII; Binary; Binary Digit; Bit; Bits Per Inch; BPI; Byte; Character; Data; Data Type; Digital; Least Significant Bit; LSB; Most Significant Bit; MSB; Word;*

BitMaP

(BMP). An image format made by a pattern of pixels and whose file extension is '.bmp'.

See Also: *Attachment; BMP; Clip Art; Display; Extension; Filename Extension; Format; GIF; Graphical Interchange Format; Graphics; Image Map; Image Processing; Joint Photographic Experts Group; JPEG; JPG; MIME; Multipurpose Internet Mail Extensions; PDF; Pixel; Portable Document Format; Resolution; Rich Text Format; RTF; Sprite; Tag Image File Format; TIFF;*

Bits Per Inch

(BPI). The density in which data is recorded on a medium.

See Also: *3.5 Inch; 5.25 Inch; Binary; Binary Digit; Bit; Bit Pattern; BPI; CD-ROM; DAT; Density; Digital Audio Tape; Digital Versatile Disk; Disk; Disk Pack; Disk Storage; Diskette; Double Density; DVD; Five and a quarter; Floppy Disk; High Density; Mag Tape; Magnetic Disk; Magnetic Tape; Medium; Optical Disk; Pack; Recording; Recording Medium; Sector; Storage; Store; Streamer; Tape Streamer; Three and a Half; Track; Volume;*

Bits Per Second
(BPS). A measure of speed at which data is transferred.
See Also: *16 Bit; 32 Bit; 64 Bit; 8 Bit; Access Time; Acoustic Coupler; Address Bus; ADN; ADSL; Advanced Digital Network; Asymmetric Digital Subscriber Line; Asynchronous; Asynchronous Transfer Mode; ATM; Bandwidth; Baud Rate; Binary; Binary Digit; Bit; BPS; Broadband; Bus; CCITT; CCTA; Characters Per Second; Communications; Consultative Committee International Telegraph and Telephone; CPS; Data Bus; Data Communications; Data Parity; Data Transmission; Datacoms; Dial In; Dial Up; Duplex Transmission; Eight Bit; FDDI; Fibre Distributed Data Interface; Fibre Optics; Full Duplex; Gbps; GHz; Gigahertz; Half Duplex; HD; Integrated Services Digital Network; ISDN; Kbps; KHz; Kilohertz; Local Bus; Mbps; Microsecond; Million Instructions Per Second; Millisecond; MIPS; Ms; Multiplex; Multiplexer; Nanosecond; Narrowband; Ns; Optical Fibre; Parallel Transmission; Parity Bit; Pico Second; Serial Transmission; Simplex Transmission; Sixteen Bit; Sixty Four Bit; Synchronous; System Bus; T-1; T-3; Telecommunication; Telecoms; Thirty Two Bit; Transfer Rate; Transmit; V90;*

Black Box
Any electronic device whose workings need not be known to use it.
See Also: *AMR; Asymmetrical Modem; Automatic Message Routing; CCD; Charge Coupled Device; Device; Dongle; Environment; Equipment; Hardware; Installation; Kit; Module; Peripheral;*

Bloatware
Software perceived as being unnecessarily large and which uses more system resources than it needs.
See Also: *Configuration; Defragment; Downsizing; Program; Reengineering; Software; Swapping; Working Storage; Workspace; Zip;*

Block
A size of area in a computer's memory or on a storage medium where data is stored and is identified by a number.
See Also: *3.5 Inch; 5.25 Inch; Absolute Address; Address; Array; Bubble Memory; Buffer; Cache Memory; CD-ROM; Cluster; Conventional Memory; Core; Core Dump; Cylinder; DAT; Digital Audio Tape; Disk; Disk Cache; Disk Pack; Disk Storage; Diskette; Dump; EMS; Expanded Memory; Expanded Memory Specification; Fiche; Five and a quarter; Flash Memory; Floppy Disk; High Memory; Mag Tape; Magnetic Core; Magnetic Disk; Magnetic Tape; Medium; Memory; Microfiche; Operand; Optical Disk; Pack; Paper Tape; Recording Medium; Relative Address;*

Sector; Storage; Store; Streamer; Tape Streamer; Three and a Half; Track; Upper Memory; Video Random Access Memory; Virtual Memory; VM; Volatile Memory; Volume; VRAM; Working Storage; Workspace;

Bluetooth (tm)
Shortrange wireless connectivity between computers, mobile telephones, portable handheld devices and connection to the Internet.
See Also: *Access; Communications; Data Communications; Data Transmission; Interface; Internet Protocol; IP; Protocol; Telecommunication; Telecoms; Transmit; WAP; Wi-Fi; Wireless Application Protocol; Wireless Fidelity;*

BMP
BitMaP. An image format made by a pattern of pixels and whose file extension is '.bmp'.
See Also: *Attachment; BitMaP; Clip Art; Display; Extension; Filename Extension; Format; GIF; Graphical Interchange Format; Graphics; Image Map; Image Processing; Joint Photographic Experts Group; JPEG; JPG; MIME; Multipurpose Internet Mail Extensions; PDF; Pixel; Portable Document Format; Resolution; Rich Text Format; RTF; Sprite; Tag Image File Format; TIFF;*

Body
The section of an e-mail message containing the most content, i.e. not the header/subject.
See Also: *Attachment; Electronic Mail; E-mail; Encryption; Hyperlink; Hypertext; IM; Instant Messaging; Mailbox; Mailing List; POP; Post Office Protocol; Signature; Simple Mail Transfer Protocol; SMTP; Spam; Thread;*

BOF
Beginning of File. A notation to indicate the start of a file.
See Also: *ASCII Files; Attachment; Batch File; Beginning of File; Compressed File; Database; DB; Delimiter; Direct Access; Document; End of File; End of Tape; EOF; EOT; File; Header; Index Sequential File; Log File; Random Access; Random File; RDB; Relational Database; Sequential File; Serial File; Tag File; Temp File; Trailer;*

Bookmark
A reference pointer to a website or URL to enable easy access to that site in the future.
See Also: *Address; Browser; Cookie; E-mail Address; Home Page; HTTP; Hyperlink; Hypertext; Hypertext Transfer Protocol; Internet;*

Internet Protocol; Internet Protocol Address; IP; IP Address; Meta Tag; Meta-Search Engine; Net; Search Engine; Site; Spider; Surfing; Tag; The Net; The Web; Thumbnail; Universal/Uniform Resource Locator; URL; Webring; Website; World Wide Web; WWW;

Boolean Algebra
A logical system in which algebraic notation is used to express logical relationships.
See Also: *ALU; AMR; AND gate; Arithmetic and Logic Unit; Automatic Message Routing; Binary; Binary Digit; Bit; FL; Flip Flop; Fuzzy Logic; I-OR gate; Logic Gate; Logical Design; NAND gate; NEQ gate; NOR gate; NOT gate; Operator; OR gate; X-OR gate;*

Boot
Abbr. of Bootstrap. A procedure using a set of instructions to initialise a computer when switched on or reset.
See Also: *AUTOEXEC.BAT; Basic Input Output System; BIOS; Boot Disk; Bootstrap; CMOS; Cold Start; Complementary Metal Oxide Semiconductor Memory; CONFIG.SYS; Disk Operating System; DOS; Instruction; Linux; Memory Resident; Operating System; OS; OS/2; Re-boot; Recovery; Registry; ROM Resident; System Software; UNIX; Warm Start;*

Boot Disk
A floppy disk containing a copy of the operating system that would be used to start the computer if it doesn't start normally.
See Also: *3.5 Inch; 5.25 Inch; AUTOEXEC.BAT; Boot; Bootstrap; CD-ROM; Cold Start; Disk; Disk Operating System; Disk Pack; Disk Storage; Diskette; DOS; Five and a quarter; Floppy Disk; Linux; Magnetic Disk; Operating System; Optical Disk; OS; OS/2; Pack; Re-boot; Recording Medium; Storage; Three and a Half; Warm Start; Winchester Disk;*

Bootstrap
A procedure using a set of instructions to initialise a computer when switched on or reset.
See Also: *AUTOEXEC.BAT; Basic Input Output System; BIOS; Boot; Boot Disk; CMOS; Cold Start; Complementary Metal Oxide Semiconductor Memory; CONFIG.SYS; Disk Operating System; DOS; Instruction; Linux; Memory Resident; Operating System; OS; OS/2; Re-boot; Recovery; Registry; ROM Resident; System Software; UNIX; Warm Start;*

BPI

Bits Per Inch. The density in which data is recorded on a medium.

See Also: *3.5 Inch; 5.25 Inch; Binary; Binary Digit; Bit; Bit Pattern; Bits Per Inch; CD-ROM; DAT; Density; Digital Audio Tape; Digital Versatile Disk; Disk; Disk Pack; Disk Storage; Diskette; Double Density; DVD; Five and a quarter; Floppy Disk; High Density; Mag Tape; Magnetic Disk; Magnetic Tape; Medium; Optical Disk; Pack; Recording; Recording Medium; Sector; Storage; Store; Streamer; Tape Streamer; Three and a Half; Track; Volume;*

BPS

Bits Per Second. A measure of speed at which data is transferred.

See Also: *16 Bit; 32 Bit; 64 Bit; 8 Bit; Access Time; Acoustic Coupler; Address Bus; ADN; ADSL; Advanced Digital Network; Asymmetric Digital Subscriber Line; Asynchronous; Asynchronous Transfer Mode; ATM; Bandwidth; Baud Rate; Binary; Binary Digit; Bit; Bits Per Second; Broadband; Bus; CCITT; CCTA; Characters Per Second; Communications; Consultative Committee International Telegraph and Telephone; CPS; Data Bus; Data Communications; Data Parity; Data Transmission; Datacoms; Dial In; Dial Up; Duplex Transmission; Eight Bit; FDDI; Fibre Distributed Data Interface; Fibre Optics; Full Duplex; Gbps; GHz; Gigahertz; Half Duplex; HD; Integrated Services Digital Network; ISDN; Kbps; KHz; Kilohertz; Local Bus; Mbps; Microsecond; Million Instructions Per Second; Millisecond; MIPS; Ms; Multiplex; Multiplexer; Nanosecond; Narrowband; Ns; Optical Fibre; Parallel Transmission; Parity Bit; Pico Second; Serial Transmission; Simplex Transmission; Sixteen Bit; Sixty Four Bit; Synchronous; System Bus; T-1; T-3; Telecommunication; Telecoms; Thirty Two Bit; Transfer Rate; Transmit; V90;*

Broadband

Transmission of data, voice or video signals using a wide bandwidth like ADSL or cable with much faster speeds than an ordinary modem. Typical speeds are 512Kbits/sec but can go to 2Mbits/sec.

See Also: *ADN; ADSL; Advanced Digital Network; Asymmetric Digital Subscriber Line; Asymmetrical Modem; Asynchronous; Asynchronous Transfer Mode; ATM; Bandwidth; Baud Rate; Binary Digit; Bit; Bits Per Second; BPS; CCITT; CCTA; Characters Per Second; Communications; Consultative Committee International Telegraph and Telephone; CPS; Data; Data Communications; Data Parity; Data Transmission; Data Type; Datacoms; Dial In; Dial Up; Direct Connection; Duplex Transmission; Ethernet; FDDI; Fibre Distributed Data Interface; Fibre Optics; Full Duplex; Gbps; Half Duplex; HD; Information*

Superhighway; Integrated Services Digital Network; Internet; ISDN; Kbps; LAN; Leased Line; Local Area Network; Mbps; Multiplex; Multiplexer; Narrowband; Net; Network; Open Systems Interconnect; Optical Fibre; OSI; Packet; Packet Switching; Parallel Transmission; Parity Bit; Protocol; Ring Network; Serial Interface; Serial Line Internet Protocol; Serial Transmission; Simplex Transmission; SLIP; Star Cluster; Star Network; Synchronous; T-1; T-3; TCP/IP; Telecommunication; Telecoms; Teleprocessing System; The Net; Token Ring; TPS; Transfer Rate; Transmission Control Protocol/Internet Protocol; Transmit; V90; WAN; WAP; Wide Area Network; Wireless Application Protocol;

Browser
Software on your computer that allows you to surf the Internet and view World Wide Web pages.
See Also: *Anchor; Applet; BBS; Bookmark; Bulletin Board System; Chat; Chatroom; Cybercafe; Cyberspace; Display; Extensible Hypertext Markup Language; eXtensible Markup Language; Gopher; Graphical User Interface; Graphics; GUI; Hacker; Home Page; Host; HTML; HTTP; Hyperlink; Hypertext; Hypertext Mark-Up Language; Hypertext Transfer Protocol; Image Processing; Internet; Internet Service Provider; Intranet; ISP; JAVA; JAVASCRIPT; Marquee; Meta Tag; Meta-Search Engine; Net; Netiquette; Page; Portal; Provider; Search Engine; Service Provider; Site; Software; Spider; Surfing; The Net; The Web; Thumbnail; Universal/Uniform Resource Locator; URL; Webhost; Webring; Website; World Wide Web; WWW; XHTML; XML;*

Bubble Jet
A printer where ink forms as a bubble on the print head before being transferred to the paper on contact.
See Also: *Barrel Printer; Bi Directional; Configuration; Cut Sheet Feeder; Daisywheel; Device; DIP Switch; Dot Matrix; Drum Printer; Duplex Printing; Environment; Equipment; Font Cartridge; Hard Copy; Hardware; Inkjet; Installation; Kit; Landscape; Laser Jet; Laser Printer; LCD Printer; Letter Quality; Line Printer; Lines Per Minute; Liquid Crystal Display Printer; Lpm; LPT Port; LQ; Matrix Printer; Near Letter Quality; NLQ; Page Printer; Pages Per Minute; Peripheral; Portrait; Postscript; PPM; Printer; Printer Driver; Printout; Sheet Feeder; Simplex Printing; Thermal Printer;*

Bubble Memory
A computers memory where data is stored in magnetized areas as binary notation. 1 represents a bubble and 0 no bubble.
See Also: *Absolute Address; Address; Binary; Binary Digit; Bit; Block; Buffer; Cache Memory; Conventional Memory; Core; Core Dump; DDR SDRAM; DIMM; Direct Memory Access; Direct Random Access Memory; Disk Cache; DMA; Double Data Rate SDRAM; DRAM; Dual Inline Memory Module; Dump; Dynamic Memory; Dynamically; EEROM; Electrically Erasable Read Only Memory; Electronically Programmed Read Only Memory; EMS; EPROM; Erasable Programmable Read Only Memory; Expanded Memory; Expanded Memory Specification; Extended Memory; Flash Memory; High Memory; Load; Magnetic Core; Memory; Memory Board; Memory Caching; Memory Card; Memory Resident; Mix; Programmable Read Only Memory; PROM; RAM; RAM Disk; Rambus Dynamic Random Access Memory; Random Access Memory; RDRAM; Read Only Memory; Relative Address; ROM; SDRAM; Shadow RAM Memory; SIMM; Single Inline Memory Modules; Single Inline Package; SIP; Stack; Store; Swapping; Synchronous Dynamic Random Access Memory; Upper Memory; Video Random Access Memory; Virtual Memory; VM; Volatile Memory; VRAM;*

Bubble Sort
A procedure for sorting items within a program. Each item from the top of a list is compared with the next until it finds its correct place of order by moving the next item up. The procedure is repeated for each item until there is no movement in the list. Items rise up or 'bubble up' the list.
See Also: *Array; Data Element; Data Entity; Data Item; Dynamically; Program; Stack; Working Storage; Workspace;*

Buddy List
Names of people that are stored and regularly used when communicating with those people, e.g. as in Instant Messaging.
See Also: *Address; Chat; Chatroom; Cybercafe; Cyberspace; Data; Electronic Mail; E-mail; E-mail Address; IM; Instant Messaging; Mailing List; Newsgroup; User Group;*

Buffer
A memory storage area where data is stored for a short time before another process or before being transferred.
See Also: *Absolute Address; Address; Block; Bubble Memory; Cache Memory; Clipboard; Conventional Memory; Core; Core Dump; DDR SDRAM; DIMM; Direct Memory Access; Direct Random Access*

Memory; Disk Cache; DMA; Double Data Rate SDRAM; DRAM; Dual Inline Memory Module; Dump; Dynamic Memory; Dynamically; EEROM; Electrically Erasable Read Only Memory; Electronically Programmed Read Only Memory; EMS; EPROM; Erasable Programmable Read Only Memory; Expanded Memory; Expanded Memory Specification; Extended Memory; Flash Memory; High Memory; Magnetic Core; Memory; Memory Caching; Mix; Programmable Read Only Memory; PROM; RAM; RAM Disk; Rambus Dynamic Random Access Memory; Random Access Memory; RDRAM; Read Only Memory; Relative Address; ROM; SDRAM; Shadow RAM Memory; SIMM; Single Inline Memory Modules; Single Inline Package; SIP; Stack; Store; Swapping; Synchronous Dynamic Random Access Memory; Virtual Memory; VM; Volatile Memory;

Bug
An unknown error in a computer or computer program.
See Also: *Abort; Code; Crash; Debug; Debugger; Downtime; General Protection Fault; GPF; Hangs; Head Crash; Hung; Machine Crash; Program; Program Crash; System Hangs; Trojan; Virus; Virus Checker; Worm;*

Bulletin Board System
(BBS). A facility which you can connect to via your computer, modem and telephone line that enables you to access software databases in order for you to purchase and download software.
See Also: *Anchor; Application; BBS; Browser; Cybercafe; Cyberspace; Database; DB; Distributed System/Network; Download; EDS; Electronic Data System; Ethernet; Freeware; FTP Site; FTPmail; Gopher; Internet; Intranet; LAN; Local Area Network; Mirror Site; Net; Network; Public Domain; Ring Network; Search Engine; Shareware; Software; Spider; Star Cluster; Star Network; T-1; T-3; The Net; Token Ring; Upload; WAN; Wide Area Network;*

Bus
A communication path which carries signals or data between the central processing unit in a computer to other parts of the computer and to other devices.
See Also: *16 Bit; 32 Bit; 64 Bit; 8 Bit; Address Bus; Bits Per Second; BPS; Central Processing Unit; Channel; Characters Per Second; Co-processor; CPS; CPU; Data Bus; Digital; Duplex Transmission; Eight Bit; Full Duplex; Gbps; Half Duplex; HD; I/O; Industry Standard Architecture; Input/Output; ISA; Kbps; Local Bus; Maths Co-processor; Mbps; MCA; Micro Channel Architecture; Parallel Transmission; Serial*

Transmission; Simplex Transmission; Sixteen Bit; Sixty Four Bit; Synchronous; System Bus; Thirty Two Bit; Transfer Rate; Transmission Channel; Universal Serial Bus; USB;

Business Analyst
(B/A). A person with the knowledge and experience of a particular industry or application, who analyses, designs and documents that application.
See Also: *A/P; Analyst; Analyst Programmer; B/A; Contractor; Data Base Analyst; Data Flow Diagram; Data Model; Data Processing Manager; DBA; Design; Development; DFD; DPM; Flowchart; Full Project Life Cycle; Hand Holding; Logical Design; Model; O & M; Object Oriented Analysis; Object Oriented Design; Object Oriented Programming; OOA; OOD; OOP; Organisation & Methods; Physical Design; Process Model; Programmer; Project Life Cycle; S/A; S/P; Software Development Cycle; Software House; Specification; Structured Design; System Analysis; System Analyst; Systems Programmer; Technical Author; Walkthrough;*

Busy
A state when a terminal or computer is not ready to accept data.
See Also: *Dead Lock; Deadly Embrace; Off Line; PING; Polling; System Hangs; Timeout;*

Byte
A unit of computer memory or storage equivalent to a single character and is made up from 8 bits. e.g. 'A' or '3'.
See Also: *8 Bit; American Standard Code for Information Interchange; ASCII; Binary; Binary Digit; Bit; Bit Pattern; Character; Data; Data Type; Delimiter; Eight Bit; Gb; Gigabyte; Information; K; Kb; Kbyte; Kilobit; Kilobyte; Mb; Mbyte; Megabit; Megabyte; Terabyte; Word;*

C or C++
A high level computer programming language.
See Also: *3GL; 4GL; ADA; ALGOL; APL; BASIC; CLIPPER; COBOL; Code; Code Generator; Compiler; Compiling; CORAL; FORTH; FORTRAN; Fourth Generation Language; High Level Language; Instruction Set; JAVA; JAVASCRIPT; Language; LISP; LOGO; Module; NATURAL; PASCAL; PERL; PICK; PILOT; PL/1; Practical Extraction and Reporting Language; Program; Programming Language; PROLOG; RPG; Software; Source Code; Structured Program; Syntax; Third Generation Language; Visual Basic;*

C Prompt
A term referring to Personal Computers where the disk drive notated with the letter 'C' is the default drive the system points to when using DOS. The letter 'C' appears on the screen which allows programs to be executed from the 'C' drive.
See Also: *AUTOEXEC.BAT; Cursor; Directory; Disk Drive; Disk Operating System; DOS; Execute; FDD; Fixed Disk Drive; Floppy Disk Drive; Hard Disk Drive; HDD; Linux; Prompt; Root Directory;*

Cache Memory
The memory within a computer used as a buffer to store temporary and recently used data from the processor which may be required again, thus rapidly improving access between the processor and main memory.
See Also: *Absolute Address; Address; Block; Bubble Memory; Buffer; Conventional Memory; Core; Core Dump; DDR SDRAM; DIMM; Direct Memory Access; Direct Random Access Memory; Disk Cache; DMA; Double Data Rate SDRAM; DRAM; Dual Inline Memory Module; Dump; Dynamic Memory; Dynamically; EEROM; Electrically Erasable Read Only Memory; Electronically Programmed Read Only Memory; EMS; EPROM; Erasable Programmable Read Only Memory; Expanded Memory; Expanded Memory Specification; Extended Memory; Flash Memory; High Memory; Magnetic Core; Memory; Memory Caching; Mix; Programmable Read Only Memory; PROM; RAM; RAM Disk; Rambus Dynamic Random Access Memory; Random Access Memory; RDRAM; Read Only Memory; Relative Address; ROM; SDRAM; Shadow RAM Memory; SIMM; Single Inline Memory Modules; Single Inline Package; SIP; Stack; Store; Swapping; Synchronous Dynamic Random Access Memory; Virtual Memory; VM; Volatile Memory;*

CAD
Computer Aided Design. A system which allows computers to be used in the design of technical drawings, two-dimensional objects and the creation of designs.
See Also: *Application; Bespoke; CADCAM; CADMAT; CAE; CAM; Computer Aided Design; Computer Aided Design and Manufacturing; Computer Aided Design Manufacture and Test; Computer Aided Engineering; Computer Aided Manufacturing; Data Processing; Desk Top Publishing; DP; DTP; EDP; EDS; Electronic Data Processing; Electronic Data System; Expert System; Freeware; Information System; Information Technology; IS; IT; Package; Processing; Shareware; Software; Software Package; Software System; Turnkey; Vertical Market;*

CADCAM
Computer Aided Design and Manufacturing. A procedure where computers are used in both the design and manufacture of products.
See Also: *Application; Bespoke; CAD; CADMAT; CAE; CAM; Computer Aided Design; Computer Aided Design and Manufacturing; Computer Aided Design Manufacture and Test; Computer Aided Engineering; Computer Aided Manufacturing; Data Processing; Desk Top Publishing; DP; DTP; EDP; EDS; Electronic Data Processing; Electronic Data System; Expert System; Freeware; Information System; Information Technology; IS; IT; Package; Processing; Shareware; Software; Software Package; Software System; Turnkey; Vertical Market;*

CADMAT
Computer Aided Design Manufacture and Test. A procedure where computers are used in the design, manufacture and testing of products.
See Also: *Application; Bespoke; CAD; CADCAM; CAE; CAM; Computer Aided Design; Computer Aided Design and Manufacturing; Computer Aided Design Manufacture and Test; Computer Aided Engineering; Computer Aided Manufacturing; Data Processing; Desk Top Publishing; DP; DTP; EDP; EDS; Electronic Data Processing; Electronic Data System; Expert System; Freeware; Information System; Information Technology; IS; IT; Package; Processing; Shareware; Software; Software Package; Software System; Turnkey; Vertical Market;*

CAE
Computer Aided Engineering. A computer system which is used to simulate processes and check the design of computer aided design systems.
See Also: *Application; Bespoke; CAD; CADCAM; CADMAT; CAM; Computer Aided Design; Computer Aided Design and Manufacturing; Computer Aided Design Manufacture and Test; Computer Aided Engineering; Computer Aided Manufacturing; Data Processing; Desk Top Publishing; DP; DTP; EDP; EDS; Electronic Data Processing; Electronic Data System; Expert System; Freeware; Information System; Information Technology; IS; IT; Package; Processing; Shareware; Software; Software Package; Software System; Turnkey; Vertical Market;*

CAI
Computer Aided Instruction. An application used on a computer to assist in training. There is dialogue between the user and computer to inform the user of any mistakes.
See Also: *Application; Bespoke; CBT; Computer Aided Instruction; Computer Based Training; Data Processing; Desk Top Publishing; DP;*

DTP; EDP; EDS; Electronic Data Processing; Electronic Data System; Expert System; Freeware; Information System; Information Technology; IS; IT; Package; Processing; Shareware; Software; Software Package; Software System; Turnkey; Vertical Market;

Call
A program command which executes another program or subroutine.
See Also: *Applet; AUTOEXEC.BAT; Batch Processing; Chain; Command; DLL; Dynamic Link Library; Enter; Event; EXE; Execute; Instruction; Instruction Set; Invoke; Load; Program; Run; Run Time; Subroutine;*

CAM
Computer Aided Manufacturing. A procedure which uses computers in manufacturing products.
See Also: *Application; Bespoke; CAD; CADCAM; CADMAT; CAE; Computer Aided Design; Computer Aided Design and Manufacturing; Computer Aided Design Manufacture and Test; Computer Aided Engineering; Computer Aided Manufacturing; Data Processing; Desk Top Publishing; DP; DTP; EDP; EDS; Electronic Data Processing; Electronic Data System; Expert System; Freeware; Information System; Information Technology; IS; IT; Package; Processing; Shareware; Software; Software Package; Software System; Turnkey; Vertical Market;*

Carriage Return
The control characters which enables a printer or the cursor on a screen to begin a new line.
See Also: *Command; Cursor; Enter; Input; Instruction; Interactive; Keyboard; Return;*

CASE
Computer Aided Software Engineering. A methodology which enables designing or programming to be easily done in a structured and controlled way.
See Also: *Application; Case Tool; Code Generator; Computer Aided Software Engineering; Data Flow; Data Flow Diagram; Data Model; Design; Development; DFD; Flowchart; Logical Design; Model; Modular; O & M; Organisation & Methods; Physical Design; Process Model; Reengineering; Specification; Top Down Technique; Wizard;*

Case Tool
A designing system or a program which enables design and programming to be easily done in a structured and controlled way.
See Also: *Application; CASE; Code Generator; Computer Aided Software Engineering; Data Flow; Data Flow Diagram; Data Model; Design; Development; DFD; Flowchart; Logical Design; Model; Modular; O & M; Organisation & Methods; Package; Physical Design; Process Model; Reengineering; Software Package; Specification; Top Down Technique; Wizard;*

Cathode Ray Tube
(CRT). The tube in the monitor which displays the screen.
See Also: *Analogue Monitor; Anti Glare Screen; CGA; Colour Graphics Adaptor; CRT; Device; Digital Monitor; Display; EGA; Enhanced Graphic Adaptor; Equipment; Extended Video Array; Graphics Card; Hardware; High Resolution; Installation; Intelligent Terminal; Interlaced; Kit; LCD; Liquid Crystal Display; Low Resolution; Monitor; Monochrome; Paint Screen; Peripheral; Plasma Screen; Prompt; Resolution; Screen; Screen Burn; Split Screen; Super Twist LCD; Super VGA; Super Video Graphics Array; SVGA; Terminal; TFT; Thin-Film Transistor; Touch Screen; Twip; VDT; VDU; VGA; Video Card; Video Display Terminal; Video Graphics Array; Video Random Access Memory; Visual Display Terminal; Visual Display Unit; VRAM; XGA;*

CBT
Computer Based Training. Training done by the use of computers and software.
See Also: *Application; Bespoke; CAI; Computer Aided Instruction; Computer Based Training; Data Processing; Desk Top Publishing; DP; DTP; EDP; EDS; Electronic Data Processing; Electronic Data System; Expert System; Freeware; Information System; Information Technology; IS; IT; Package; Processing; Shareware; Software; Software Package; Software System; Turnkey; Vertical Market;*

CCD
Charge Coupled Device. The component in a scanner which copies the image.
See Also: *Black Box; Charge Coupled Device; Device; Drum; Flatbed Scanner; Image Processing; OCR; OMR; Optical Character Reader; Optical Character Recognition; Optical Mark Recognition; Optical Scanner; Peripheral; Scanner;*

CCITT

Consultative Committee International Telegraph and Telephone. An international telecommunications body which determines data transmission and connection standards.

See Also: *Acceptable User Policy; Acoustic Coupler; ADN; ADSL; Advanced Digital Network; American National Standard Institute; ANSI; Asymmetric Digital Subscriber Line; Asynchronous; Asynchronous Transfer Mode; ATM; AUP; Bandwidth; Baud Rate; BCS; Bits Per Second; BPS; Broadband; CCTA; CERN; Characters Per Second; Client Server Protocol; Communications; Conseil Europeen pour la Recherche Nucleaire; Consultative Committee International Telegraph and Telephone; CPS; Data Communications; Data Parity; Data Transmission; Datacoms; Dial In; Dial Up; Direct Connection; Duplex Transmission; FDDI; Fibre Distributed Data Interface; Fibre Optics; Full Duplex; Gbps; Half Duplex; HD; IEE; Integrated Services Digital Network; International Standards Organisation; ISDN; ISO; Kbps; Leased Line; Mbps; Multiplex; Multiplexer; Narrowband; NCC; Open Systems Interconnect; Optical Fibre; OSI; Parallel Transmission; Parity Bit; Serial Interface; Serial Transmission; Simplex Transmission; Synchronous; Telecommunication; Telecoms; Teleprocessing System; TPS; Transfer Rate; Transmit; V90;*

CCTA

The Central Computer and Telecommunications Agency.

See Also: *Acceptable User Policy; Acoustic Coupler; ADN; ADSL; Advanced Digital Network; American National Standard Institute; ANSI; Asymmetric Digital Subscriber Line; Asynchronous; Asynchronous Transfer Mode; ATM; AUP; Bandwidth; Baud Rate; BCS; Bits Per Second; BPS; Broadband; CCITT; Characters Per Second; Communications; Consultative Committee International Telegraph and Telephone; CPS; Data Communications; Data Parity; Data Transmission; Datacoms; Dial In; Dial Up; Direct Connection; Duplex Transmission; FDDI; Fibre Distributed Data Interface; Fibre Optics; Full Duplex; Gbps; Half Duplex; HD; IEE; Integrated Services Digital Network; International Standards Organisation; ISDN; ISO; Kbps; Leased Line; Mbps; Multiplex; Multiplexer; Narrowband; NCC; Open Systems Interconnect; Optical Fibre; OSI; Parallel Transmission; Parity Bit; Serial Interface; Serial Transmission; Simplex Transmission; Synchronous; Telecommunication; Telecoms; Teleprocessing System; TPS; Transfer Rate; Transmit; V90;*

CD-ROM
Compact Disk-Read Only Memory. A compact disc on which information or programs are optically stored using a strong laser. A less strong laser is used to read the disc.
See Also: *Bits Per Inch; Block; Boot Disk; BPI; CD-ROM Drive; CD-RW Drive; Digital Versatile Disk; Directory; DVD; Medium; Optical Disk; Optical Drive; Recording Medium; Root Directory; Sub Directory;*

CD-ROM Drive
A peripheral device where information is optically stored on a compact disc.
See Also: *ATAPI; Attachment Packet Interface; CD-ROM; CD-RW Drive; Configuration; Device; Digital Versatile Disk; Drive; DVD; EIDE; Enhanced Intelligent Drive Electronics; Environment; Equipment; Hardware; IDE; Installation; Integrated Drive Electronics; Kit; Optical Disk; Optical Drive; Peripheral;*

CD-RW Drive
Compact Disk-ReWriter. A compact disk drive that can read as well as write data to the CD.
See Also: *Archive; ATAPI; Attachment Packet Interface; Backing Store; Backup; CD-ROM; CD-ROM Drive; Configuration; Device; Digital Versatile Disk; Drive; DVD; EIDE; Enhanced Intelligent Drive Electronics; Environment; Equipment; Hardware; Heads; IDE; Installation; Integrated Drive Electronics; Kit; Mass Storage; Optical Disk; Optical Drive; Peripheral; Read/Write Head; Recording; Recording Device; Save; Storage; Store; Write; Write Protect;*

Central Processing Unit
(CPU or Processor). The central area of a computer which controls the entire operation of the computer. It contains the memory and executes program instructions.
See Also: *286; 386; 486; ALU; Application Specific Integrated Circuits; Arithmetic and Logic Unit; ASICS; Bus; Chip; Chipset; Clock Speed; Computer Power; Conventional Memory; Co-processor; CPU; EISA; Enhanced Industry Standard Architecture; Expansion Card; Flash Memory; IC; Industry Standard Architecture; Integrated Circuit; Interrupt Request; IRQ; ISA; Local Bus; Maths Co-processor; MCA; Megahertz; Memory; Memory Caching; MHz; Micro Channel Architecture; Microprocessor; Mix; Parallel Processor; Power; Processor; Silicon Chip; System; System Bus; Zero Wait State;*

CERN
Conseil Européen pour la Recherche Nucléaire. An organisation in Geneva, Switzerland, where the World Wide Web was first developed.
See Also: *Acceptable User Policy; American National Standard Institute; ANSI; AUP; BCS; CCITT; Conseil Europeen pour la Recherche Nucleaire; Consultative Committee International Telegraph and Telephone; Cyberspace; DNS; Domain Name; Domain Name System; Home Page; IEE; International Standards Organisation; Internet; ISO; NCC; Net; Site; The Net; The Web; Universal/Uniform Resource Locator; URL; Website; World Wide Web; WWW;*

CGA
Colour Graphics Adaptor. An early standard of monitor design which has 4 colours and a resolution of 640x200 dots.
See Also: *Analogue Monitor; Anti Glare Screen; Cathode Ray Tube; Colour Graphics Adaptor; CRT; Device; Digital Monitor; Display; EGA; Enhanced Graphic Adaptor; Environment; Equipment; Extended Video Array; Graphics Card; Hardware; High Resolution; Installation; Intelligent Terminal; Interlaced; Kit; LCD; Liquid Crystal Display; Low Resolution; Monitor; Monochrome; Paint Screen; Peripheral; Plasma Screen; Prompt; Resolution; Screen; Screen Burn; Split Screen; Super Twist LCD; Super VGA; Super Video Graphics Array; SVGA; Terminal; TFT; Thin-Film Transistor; Touch Screen; Twip; VDT; VDU; VGA; Video Card; Video Display Terminal; Video Graphics Array; Video Random Access Memory; Visual Display Terminal; Visual Display Unit; VRAM; XGA;*

CGI
Common Gateway Interface. The method with which an HTTP server communicates with server gateway applications, i.e. the way Web programs processes the user requirements.
See Also: *Client Server; Client Server Protocol; Common Gateway Interface; Domain Name Server; File Server; File Transfer Protocol; Firewall; FTP; Gateway; HTTP; Hyperlink; Hypertext Transfer Protocol; Internet; Internet Protocol; Internet Service Provider; IP; ISP; Net; Page; PERL; Point Of Presence; POP; Portal; Practical Extraction and Reporting Language; Provider; Proxy Server; Secure Socket Layer; Serial Line Internet Protocol; Server; Service Provider; Site; SLIP; SSL; The Net; The Web; Universal/Uniform Resource Locator; URL; Webhost; Website; World Wide Web; WWW;*

Chain
A program command to execute or run another program.
See Also: *Applet; AUTOEXEC.BAT; Batch Processing; Call; Command; DLL; Dynamic Link Library; Enter; Event; EXE; Execute; Instruction; Instruction Set; Invoke; Load; Program; Run; Run Time; Subroutine;*

Channel
A path between a computer and its peripherals along which data is transferred.
See Also: *16 Bit; 32 Bit; 64 Bit; 8 Bit; Access; Address Bus; Asymmetrical Modem; Bus; Characters Per Second; Communications; CPS; Data Bus; Data Communications; Data Parity; Data Transmission; Datacoms; Digital; Direct Connection; Duplex Transmission; Eight Bit; FDDI; Fibre Distributed Data Interface; Fibre Optics; Firewire; Full Duplex; Half Duplex; HD; I/O; Industry Standard Architecture; Input/Output; ISA; Kbps; Leased Line; Local Bus; MCA; Micro Channel Architecture; Node; Optical Fibre; Parallel Transmission; Parity Bit; SCSI; Serial Transmission; Simplex Transmission; Sixteen Bit; Sixty Four Bit; Small Computer System Interface; System Bus; Thirty Two Bit; Transfer Rate; Transmission Channel; Transmit; Universal Serial Bus; USB;*

Character
Any letter, number or symbol which a computer stores as one byte.
See Also: *American Standard Code for Information Interchange; ASCII; ASCII Files; Bit Pattern; Byte; Characters Per Inch; Characters Per Second; Concatenate; Constant; CPI; CPS; Data; Data Type; Delimiter; Dots Per Inch; DPI; EBCDIC; Emoticons; Entity; Extended Binary Coded Decimal Interchange Code; Field; Font; Gb; Gigabyte; Hex; Hexadecimal; Information; Kilobit; Literal; Magnetic Ink Character Recognition; Megabit; MICR; OCR; Octal; OMR; Optical Character Reader; Optical Character Recognition; Optical Mark Recognition; Scalable Fonts; Smileys; String; Subscript; Terabyte; Variable; Wildcard; Word;*

Characters Per Inch
(CPI). The number of characters which can fit into an inch when printed or displayed. It depends on the font size and pitch of the characters.
See Also: *Character; CPI; Dots Per Inch; DPI; Font; Font Cartridge; Landscape; Letter Quality; LQ; Near Letter Quality; NLQ; Output; Portrait; Printer; Printout; Scalable Fonts;*

Characters Per Second
(CPS). A measurement of the speed that text information is transferred.
See Also: *Access Time; ADN; ADSL; Advanced Digital Network; Asymmetric Digital Subscriber Line; Asymmetrical Modem; Asynchronous; Asynchronous Transfer Mode; ATM; Bandwidth; Bits Per Second; BPS; Broadband; Bus; CCITT; CCTA; Channel; Character; Communications; Consultative Committee International Telegraph and Telephone; CPS; Data Communications; Data Parity; Data Transmission; Datacoms; Dial In; Dial Up; Duplex Transmission; ECP; Enhanced Parallel Port; EPP; Extended Capabilities Port; FDDI; Fibre Distributed Data Interface; Fibre Optics; Full Duplex; Gbps; GHz; Gigahertz; Half Duplex; HD; Integrated Services Digital Network; ISDN; Kbps; KHz; Kilohertz; Mbps; Microsecond; Million Instructions Per Second; Millisecond; MIPS; Ms; Multiplex; Multiplexer; Nanosecond; Narrowband; Ns; Open Systems Interconnect; Optical Fibre; OSI; Parallel Transmission; Parity Bit; Pico Second; Serial Transmission; Simplex Transmission; Synchronous; System Bus; T-1; T-3; Telecommunication; Telecoms; Transfer Rate; Transmission Channel; Transmit; V90;*

Charge Coupled Device
(CCD). The component in a scanner which copies the image.
See Also: *Black Box; CCD; Device; Drum; Flatbed Scanner; Image Processing; OCR; OMR; Optical Character Reader; Optical Character Recognition; Optical Mark Recognition; Optical Scanner; Peripheral; Scanner;*

Chat
Online communication between Internet users.
See Also: *Browser; Buddy List; Chatroom; Cybercafe; Cyberspace; Electronic Mail; E-mail; Emoticons; Flame; Forum; IM; Instant Messaging; Interactive; Internet; Internet Relay Chat; IRC; Net; Netiquette; Newbie; Newsgroup; Online; Point to Point Protocol; PPP; Smileys; Spam; The Net; Thread; User Group; Webcam;*

Chatroom
Internet locations where users can exchange typed chat.
See Also: *Browser; Buddy List; Chat; Cybercafe; Cyberspace; Electronic Mail; E-mail; Emoticons; Flame; Forum; IM; Instant Messaging; Interactive; Internet; Internet Relay Chat; IRC; Message Boards; Net; Netiquette; Newbie; Newsgroup; Online; Point to Point Protocol; PPP; Smileys; Spam; The Net; Thread; User Group; Webcam;*

Check Box
A field on a screen form that the user may select or deselect by clicking the box. The selection results in a tick or an X in the box and used as criteria for the task being performed.
See Also: *Click; Data; Data Element; Data Entity; Data Item; Data Type; Entity; Field; Input; Interactive; Toggle;*

Chip
An integrated circuit designed on a semiconductor material, normally silicon. It can be a memory chip or a chip designed for a specific task.
See Also: *286; 386; 486; Advanced Technology; ALU; AND gate; Application Specific Integrated Circuits; Arithmetic and Logic Unit; ASICS; AT; Central Processing Unit; Chipset; Clock Speed; Computer Power; Co-processor; CPU; Extended Technology; Flip Flop; GHz; Gigahertz; IC; Integrated Circuit; I-OR gate; KHz; Kilohertz; Large Scale Integration; Logic Gate; LSI; Maths Co-processor; Megahertz; Memory Board; Memory Card; MHz; Microprocessor; Motherboard; NAND gate; NEQ gate; NOR gate; NOT gate; OR gate; Parallel Processor; PCB; Power; Printed Circuit Board; Processor; Semiconductor; Silicon Chip; Solid State; Sound Chip; Transistor; UART; Universal Asynchronous Receiver/Transmitter; Very Large Scale Integration; VLSI; X-OR gate; XT;*

Chipset
Micro electronic chips located on printed circuit cards which provide the basic functionality for a device in which they are used.
See Also: *286; 386; 486; Advanced Technology; ALU; AND gate; Application Specific Integrated Circuits; Arithmetic and Logic Unit; ASICS; AT; Central Processing Unit; Chip; Clock Speed; Computer Power; Co-processor; CPU; Extended Technology; Fax Card; Flip Flop; GHz; Gigahertz; IC; Integrated Circuit; I-OR gate; KHz; Kilohertz; Large Scale Integration; Logic Gate; LSI; Maths Co-processor; Megahertz; Memory Board; Memory Card; MHz; Microprocessor; Motherboard; NAND gate; NEQ gate; NOR gate; NOT gate; OR gate; Parallel Processor; PCB; PCMCIA; Personal Computer Memory Card International Association; Power; Printed Circuit Board; Processor; Semiconductor; Silicon Chip; Solid State; Sound Card; Sound Chip; Transistor; UART; Universal Asynchronous Receiver/Transmitter; Very Large Scale Integration; VLSI; X-OR gate; XT;*

Click
The pressing of a mouse button or icon on the screen to select an item or carry out an action.
See Also: *Check Box; Command; Cursor; Drag; Drop-Down Menu; Execute; Menu; Mouse; Pop Up Menu; Pull Down Menu; Radio Button; Toolbar;*

Client Server
Hardware and software which control the sharing of devices and data files for computers connected together in a network.
See Also: *Access; AMR; Anonymous FTP; Automatic Message Routing; CGI; Client Server Protocol; Common Gateway Interface; Configuration; Database; DB; Device; Distributed System/Network; Domain Name Server; Environment; Equipment; Ethernet; File Server; File Sharing; Firewall; Front End Processor; Gateway; Handshake; Hardware; Host Processor; Installation; Intranet; Kit; LAN; LAN Port; Local Area Network; Locking; Mailserver; Multi User; Multitasking; Network; Network Information Centre; Network Operating System; NIC; Node; NOS; Open Systems Interconnect; OSI; Peripheral; Polling; Proxy Server; Record Locking; Remote Device; Ring Network; Server; Software; Star Cluster; Star Network; System; Time Share; Time Slice; Token Ring; WAN; Wide Area Network;*

Client Server Protocol
A communication protocol by which a computer requests the services of a server computer.
See Also: *Anonymous FTP; CCITT; CGI; Client Server; Common Gateway Interface; Communications; Consultative Committee International Telegraph and Telephone; Data Communications; Data Transmission; Datacoms; Dial In; Dial Up; Direct Connection; Distributed System/Network; Domain Name Server; Ethernet; FDDI; Fibre Distributed Data Interface; Fibre Optics; File Server; File Transfer Protocol; FTP; Gateway; Handshake; Host Processor; HTTP; Hypertext Transfer Protocol; International Standards Organisation; Internet; Internet Protocol; Internet Protocol Address; Intranet; IP; IP Address; ISO; LAN; Leased Line; Local Area Network; Mailserver; MIME; Multipurpose Internet Mail Extensions; Net; Network; Network Information Centre; Network Operating System; NIC; NOS; Open Systems Interconnect; Optical Fibre; OSI; Point to Point Protocol; PPP; Protocol; Proxy Server; Ring Network; Serial Line Internet Protocol; Server; Simple Mail Transfer Protocol; SLIP; SMTP; Star Cluster; Star Network; TCP/IP; Telecommunication; Telecoms; The Net; Token Ring; Transmission Control Protocol/Internet Protocol; WAN; WAP; Wide*

Area Network; Wireless Application Protocol; XMODEM; YMODEM; ZMODEM;

Clip Art
A collection of graphical images that can be inserted and used on a screen or web page.
See Also: *BitMaP; BMP; Desk Top Publishing; DTP; GIF; Graphical Interchange Format; Graphics; Icon; Image Map; Image Processing; Joint Photographic Experts Group; JPEG; JPG; Motion Picture Experts Group; MPEG; MPG; Pixel; Sprite; Tag Image File Format; TIFF; Twip; WIMP; Windows Icons Mice and Pull-down menus;*

Clipboard
A storage area in the computer which is temporarily used for data items that are 'cut' or 'copied'.
See Also: *Buffer; Conventional Memory; Core; Core Dump; Disk Cache; Flash Memory; Magnetic Core; Memory; Stack; Volatile Memory;*

CLIPPER
A high level computer programming language.
See Also: *3GL; 4GL; ADA; ALGOL; APL; BASIC; C or C++; COBOL; Code; Code Generator; Compiler; Compiling; CORAL; FORTH; FORTRAN; Fourth Generation Language; High Level Language; Instruction Set; JAVA; JAVASCRIPT; Language; LISP; LOGO; Module; NATURAL; PASCAL; PERL; PICK; PILOT; PL/1; Practical Extraction and Reporting Language; Program; Programming Language; PROLOG; RPG; Software; Source Code; Structured Program; Syntax; Third Generation Language; Visual Basic;*

Clock Speed
The speed at which the main processing chip in a computer operates. e.g. 450 MHz. It is based on an electronic device which provides a pulse at fixed intervals of time.
See Also: *286; 386; 486; ALU; Application Specific Integrated Circuits; Arithmetic and Logic Unit; ASICS; Central Processing Unit; Chip; Chipset; Computer Power; Co-processor; CPU; GHz; Gigahertz; IC; Integrated Circuit; KHz; Kilohertz; Maths Co-processor; MCA; Megahertz; MHz; Micro Channel Architecture; Microprocessor; Microsecond; Million Instructions Per Second; Millisecond; MIPS; Ms; Nanosecond; Ns; Pico Second; Power; Processor; Silicon Chip;*

Cluster
Small physical areas on a disk in which data is stored. Data can be spread across a number of clusters.
See Also: *3.5 Inch; 5.25 Inch; Block; Data; Disk; Disk Map; Disk Pack; Disk Storage; Diskette; Five and a quarter; Floppy Disk; Magnetic Disk; Pack; Sector; Storage; Three and a Half; Track; Volume; Winchester Disk;*

CMOS
Complementary Metal Oxide Semiconductor memory. A battery packed RAM (Random Access Memory) which stores the configuration information for a computer.
See Also: *Basic Input Output System; BIOS; Boot; Bootstrap; Cold Start; Complementary Metal Oxide Semiconductor Memory; CONFIG.SYS; Configuration; Configuring; Conventional Memory; DDR SDRAM; DIMM; Direct Random Access Memory; Double Data Rate SDRAM; DRAM; Dual Inline Memory Module; Dynamic Memory; EEROM; Electrically Erasable Read Only Memory; Electronically Programmed Read Only Memory; EMS; EPROM; Erasable Programmable Read Only Memory; Expanded Memory; Expanded Memory Specification; Extended Memory; Firmware; Flash Memory; High Memory; Memory; Programmable Read Only Memory; PROM; RAM; RAM Disk; Rambus Dynamic Random Access Memory; Random Access Memory; RDRAM; Read Only Memory; Re-boot; Registry; ROM; ROM Resident; SDRAM; Shadow RAM Memory; SIMM; Single Inline Memory Modules; Single Inline Package; SIP; Store; Synchronous Dynamic Random Access Memory; Tuning; Tweaking; Upper Memory; Volatile Memory; Warm Start;*

COBOL
COmmon Business Oriented Language. A high level computer programming language mainly used in commercial applications.
See Also: *3GL; 4GL; ADA; ALGOL; APL; BASIC; C or C++; CLIPPER; CODASYL; Code; Code Generator; Compiler; Compiling; Conference On DAta SYstems Languages; CORAL; FORTH; FORTRAN; Fourth Generation Language; High Level Language; Instruction Set; JAVA; JAVASCRIPT; Language; LISP; LOGO; Module; NATURAL; PASCAL; PERL; PICK; PILOT; PL/1; Practical Extraction and Reporting Language; Program; Programming Language; PROLOG; RPG; Software; Source Code; Structured Program; Syntax; Third Generation Language; Visual Basic;*

CODASYL

Conference On DAta SYstems Languages. A body responsible for developing and maintaining the COBOL programming language.

See Also: *3GL; 4GL; American National Standard Institute; ANSI; COBOL; Code; Compiler; Conference On DAta SYstems Languages; Fourth Generation Language; High Level Language; Language; NATURAL; Programming Language; Syntax; Third Generation Language;*

Code

(1) The lines of instructions in a program. (2) The process of coding a program.

See Also: *3GL; 4GL; A/P; Abort; ADA; ALGOL; Analyst Programmer; API; APL; Application Program Interface; Assembler; Assembly Code; BASIC; Bug; C or C++; CLIPPER; COBOL; CODASYL; Code Generator; CODEC; Command; Compiler; Compiling; COmpressor DECompressor; Conference On DAta SYstems Languages; CORAL; Debugger; Development; Device Driver; DLL; Driver; Dynamic Link Library; EXE; Extensible Hypertext Markup Language; eXtensible Markup Language; FORTH; FORTRAN; Fourth Generation Language; High Level Language; HTML; Hypertext Mark-Up Language; Instruction; Instruction Set; Interpreter; JAVA; JAVASCRIPT; JCL; Job Control Language; Language; LISP; LOGO; Loop; Low Level Language; Macro; Module; NATURAL; Page Description Language; PASCAL; Patch; PDL; PERL; PICK; Picture; PILOT; PL/1; Practical Extraction and Reporting Language; Program; Programmer; Programming Language; PROLOG; Query Language; RPG; S/P; Script; Shareware; Software; Software Development Cycle; Software Driver; Software House; Software System; SQL; Structured Program; Structured Query Language; Subroutine; Syntax; Systems Programmer; Terminate and Stay Resident; Third Generation Language; TSR; Utility; Visual Basic; XHTML; XML;*

Code Generator

Software which generates machine code from high-level designs or programs.

See Also: *3GL; 4GL; ADA; ALGOL; APL; Assembler; Assembly Code; BASIC; C or C++; CASE; Case Tool; CLIPPER; COBOL; Code; Compiler; Compiling; Computer Aided Software Engineering; Conversion; CORAL; FORTH; FORTRAN; Fourth Generation Language; High Level Language; Instruction Set; JAVA; JAVASCRIPT; Language; LISP; LOGO; Low Level Language; Machine Code; Machine Language; NATURAL; Object Code; PASCAL; PERL; PICK; PILOT;*

PL/1; Practical Extraction and Reporting Language; Program; Programming Language; PROLOG; Query Language; RPG; Software; Source Code; SQL; Structured Query Language; Third Generation Language; Visual Basic;

CODEC
COmpressor/DECompressor. Programming code that instructs the computer how to decode multimedia information.
See Also: *Code; COmpressor DECompressor; Configuring; Device Driver; Display; DLL; Driver; Dynamic Link Library; Graphical User Interface; GUI; MIME; Motion Picture Experts Group; MP3; MPEG; MPG; Multimedia; Multipurpose Internet Mail Extensions; Program; Software; Software Driver; Stream; Utility;*

Cold Start
The initial turning on of a computer at the mains or at the computer's on/off switch. The computer then initialises itself.
See Also: *AUTOEXEC.BAT; Boot; Boot Disk; Bootstrap; CMOS; Complementary Metal Oxide Semiconductor Memory; CONFIG.SYS; Disk Operating System; DOS; Linux; Load; Operating System; OS; OS/2; Re-boot; Registry; Warm Start;*

Colour Graphics Adaptor
(CGA). An early standard of monitor design which has 4 colours and a resolution of 640x200 dots.
See Also: *Analogue Monitor; Anti Glare Screen; Cathode Ray Tube; CGA; CRT; Device; Digital Monitor; Display; EGA; Enhanced Graphic Adaptor; Environment; Equipment; Extended Video Array; Graphics Card; Hardware; High Resolution; Installation; Intelligent Terminal; Interlaced; Kit; LCD; Liquid Crystal Display; Low Resolution; Monitor; Monochrome; Paint Screen; Peripheral; Plasma Screen; Prompt; Resolution; Screen; Screen Burn; Split Screen; Super Twist LCD; Super VGA; Super Video Graphics Array; SVGA; Terminal; TFT; Thin-Film Transistor; Touch Screen; Twip; VDT; VDU; VGA; Video Card; Video Display Terminal; Video Graphics Array; Video Random Access Memory; Visual Display Terminal; Visual Display Unit; VRAM; XGA;*

COM
Computer Output Microfilm. The process of recording data in a reduced size on plastic film.
See Also: *Archive; Backing Store; Backup; Computer Output Microfilm; Fiche; Grandfather, Father, Son; Mass Storage; Medium; Microfiche; Microfilm; Recording Medium; Save;*

Comma Separated Values
(CSV). Data items in a record separated from each other by commas, which identify the start and end of each data field.
See Also: *CSV; Data; Data Element; Data Entity; Data Item; Data Type; Database; DB; Field; Format; Information; Key; RDB; Record; Relational Database; Sequential File; Serial File; String; Table; Tag; Trailer; Transaction; Variable;*

Command
An instruction to the computer to perform a specific task.
See Also: *AUTOEXEC.BAT; Batch File; Batch Processing; Call; Carriage Return; Chain; Click; Code; CONFIG.SYS; Enter; Esc; Escape; Execute; Function; Function Key; Instruction; Instruction Set; Invoke; JCL; Job; Job Control Language; Load; Macro; Program; Registry; Return; Script; Subroutine; Syntax; System Software; Toolbar;*

Common Gateway Interface
(CGI). The method with which an HTTP server communicates with server gateway applications, i.e. the way Web programs processes the user requirements.
See Also: *CGI; Client Server; Client Server Protocol; Domain Name Server; File Server; File Transfer Protocol; Firewall; FTP; Gateway; HTTP; Hyperlink; Hypertext Transfer Protocol; Internet; Internet Protocol; Internet Service Provider; IP; ISP; Net; Page; PERL; Point Of Presence; POP; Portal; Practical Extraction and Reporting Language; Provider; Proxy Server; Secure Socket Layer; Serial Line Internet Protocol; Server; Service Provider; Site; SLIP; SSL; The Net; The Web; Universal/Uniform Resource Locator; URL; Webhost; Website; World Wide Web; WWW;*

Communications
Abbreviated to Comms. The process by which data is transmitted between two or more devices.
See Also: *ACK; Acoustic Coupler; ADN; ADSL; Advanced Digital Network; AMR; Asymmetric Digital Subscriber Line; Asymmetrical Modem; Asynchronous; Asynchronous Transfer Mode; ATM; Automatic Message Routing; Bandwidth; Baud Rate; Bits Per Second; Bluetooth (tm); BPS; Broadband; CCITT; CCTA; Channel; Characters Per Second; Client Server Protocol; Consultative Committee International Telegraph and Telephone; CPS; Data Communications; Data Parity; Data Transmission; Datacoms; Dial In; Dial Up; Digital; Direct Connection; Duplex Transmission; ECP; Enhanced Parallel Port; EPP; Extended Capabilities Port; FDDI; Fibre Distributed Data Interface; Fibre Optics;*

Firewire; Full Duplex; Gbps; GHz; Gigahertz; Half Duplex; HD; Integrated Services Digital Network; ISDN; Kbps; KHz; Kilohertz; Leased Line; Mbps; Modem; Modulator Demodulator; Multiplex; Multiplexer; Narrowband; Node; Open Systems Interconnect; Optical Fibre; OSI; Packet; Packet Switching; Parallel Transmission; Parity Bit; Protocol; Serial Transmission; Simplex Transmission; Synchronous; Telecommunication; Telecoms; Teleprocessing System; TPS; Transfer Rate; Transmission Channel; Transmit; V90; Wi-Fi; Wireless Fidelity;

Compatible
A term used when computers, devices, peripherals and software work together or can be connected to each other without change.
See Also: *Computer; Cross Platform; Desktop; Device; Digital Analog Converter; Digital Computer; DIP Switch; EBCDIC; Extended Binary Coded Decimal Interchange Code; Handshake; IBM (tm) Compatible; Integrated Systems; Laptop; Machine; Midrange System; Minicomputer; Multi Platform; Notebook; OEM; Open Systems Interconnect; Original Equipment Manufacturer; OSI; Palmtop Computer; PC; Peripheral; Personal Computer; Platform; Plug and Play; Plug Compatible; Portable; Protocol; TCP/IP; Tower Computer; Transmission Control Protocol/Internet Protocol;*

Compiler
A program which converts high level computer program languages into machine code while checking for syntax errors.
See Also: *3GL; 4GL; ADA; ALGOL; APL; Assembler; Assembly Code; BASIC; C or C++; CLIPPER; COBOL; CODASYL; Code; Code Generator; Compiling; Conference On DAta SYstems Languages; CORAL; FORTH; FORTRAN; Fourth Generation Language; High Level Language; Interpreter; LISP; LOGO; Low Level Language; Machine Code; Machine Language; NATURAL; Object Code; PASCAL; PERL; PICK; PILOT; PL/1; Practical Extraction and Reporting Language; PROLOG; RPG; Source Code; Syntax; Third Generation Language;*

Compiling
The process of converting program code into machine code and is performed by a compiler.
See Also: *3GL; 4GL; ADA; ALGOL; APL; Assembler; Assembly Code; BASIC; C or C++; CLIPPER; COBOL; Code; Code Generator; Compiler; CORAL; FORTH; FORTRAN; Fourth Generation Language; High Level Language; Interpreter; LISP; LOGO; Low Level Language; Machine Code; Machine Language; NATURAL; Object Code; PASCAL;*

PERL; PICK; PILOT; PL/1; Practical Extraction and Reporting Language; PROLOG; RPG; Source Code; Third Generation Language;

Complementary Metal Oxide Semiconductor Memory
(CMOS). A battery packed RAM which stores the configuration information for a computer.
See Also: *Basic Input Output System; BIOS; Boot; Bootstrap; CMOS; Cold Start; CONFIG.SYS; Configuration; Configuring; Conventional Memory; DDR SDRAM; DIMM; Direct Random Access Memory; Double Data Rate SDRAM; DRAM; Dual Inline Memory Module; Dynamic Memory; EEROM; Electrically Erasable Read Only Memory; Electronically Programmed Read Only Memory; EMS; EPROM; Erasable Programmable Read Only Memory; Expanded Memory; Expanded Memory Specification; Extended Memory; Firmware; Flash Memory; High Memory; Memory; Programmable Read Only Memory; PROM; RAM; RAM Disk; Rambus Dynamic Random Access Memory; Random Access Memory; RDRAM; Read Only Memory; Re-boot; Registry; ROM; ROM Resident; SDRAM; Shadow RAM Memory; SIMM; Single Inline Memory Modules; Single Inline Package; SIP; Store; Synchronous Dynamic Random Access Memory; Tuning; Tweaking; Upper Memory; Volatile Memory; Warm Start;*

Compressed File
A file whose data has been compressed to be stored in a smaller area. The data needs to be decompressed before it can be used.
See Also: *Archive; Attachment; Beginning of File; BOF; Compression; Conversion; Convert; Data Compression; Decompression; End of File; EOF; File; File Conversion; Packed Data; PKZIP; Random File; Self Extracting File; Storage; Unzip; Zip;*

Compression
The process where data is reduced in size to take up a smaller area when stored or transmitted.
See Also: *Compressed File; Conversion; Convert; Data; Data Compression; Data Type; Decompression; Density; Double Density; File Conversion; High Density; Packed Data; PKZIP; Self Extracting File; Unzip; Zip;*

COmpressor DECompressor
(CODEC). Programming code that instructs the computer how to decode multimedia information.
See Also: *Code; CODEC; Configuring; Device Driver; Display; DLL; Driver; Dynamic Link Library; Graphical User Interface; GUI; MIME;*

Motion Picture Experts Group; MP3; MPEG; MPG; Multimedia; Multipurpose Internet Mail Extensions; Program; Software; Software Driver; Stream; Utility;

Computation
The processes performed by a computer. e.g. calculations, processing of data.
See Also: *Audit Trail; Batch Processing; Compute; Data Processing; DP; EDP; EDS; EFT; EFTPOS; Electronic Data Processing; Electronic Data System; Electronic Fund Transfer; Electronic Fund Transfer Point of Sales; Expert System; Facilities Management; FM; Geographical Information System; GIS; Housekeeping; Information Technology; Integrated Systems; IT; Job; Multitasking; Office Information System; OIS; Process; Processing; Software System; Spreadsheet; Teleprocessing System; TPS; Vertical Market; Word Processor; WP;*

Compute
To use a computer to calculate and to process data.
See Also: *Audit Trail; Batch Processing; Computation; Data Processing; DP; EDP; EDS; EFT; EFTPOS; Electronic Data Processing; Electronic Data System; Electronic Fund Transfer; Electronic Fund Transfer Point of Sales; Expert System; Facilities Management; FM; Geographical Information System; GIS; Information Technology; Integrated Systems; IT; Job; Multitasking; Office Information System; OIS; Operator; Process; Processing; Software System; Spreadsheet; Teleprocessing System; TPS; Vertical Market; Word Processor; WP;*

Computer
An electronic machine which inputs, processes, stores and outputs data using programs to perform the tasks.
See Also: *1st Generation; 2nd Generation; 3rd Generation; 4th Generation; Advanced Technology; Analogue Computer; AT; Compatible; Computer Power; Configuration; Cross Platform; Desktop; Digital Computer; Distributed System/Network; Downsizing; EDS; Electronic Data System; Emulate; Emulation; Environment; Equipment; Extended Technology; Front End Processor; Hardware; Host Processor; IBM (tm) Compatible; Information System; Information Technology; Installation; IS; IT; Kit; Laptop; Leading Edge; Machine; Mailserver; Mainframe; Micro; Microcomputer; Midrange System; Minicomputer; Multi Platform; Multimedia; Node; Notebook; Number Cruncher; OEM; Original Equipment Manufacturer; Palmtop Computer; PC; PDA; Personal Computer; Personal Digital Assistant; Platform; Portable;*

Power; Standalone; State of the Art; System; Tower Computer; Turnkey; Voice Activated; XT;

Computer Aided Design

(CAD). A system which allows computers to be used in the design of technical drawings, two dimensional objects and the creation of designs.
See Also: *Application; Bespoke; CAD; CADCAM; CADMAT; CAE; CAM; Computer Aided Design and Manufacturing; Computer Aided Design Manufacture and Test; Computer Aided Engineering; Computer Aided Manufacturing; Data Processing; Desk Top Publishing; DP; DTP; EDP; EDS; Electronic Data Processing; Electronic Data System; Expert System; Freeware; Information System; Information Technology; IS; IT; Package; Processing; Shareware; Software; Software Package; Software System; Turnkey; Vertical Market;*

Computer Aided Design and Manufacturing

(CADCAM). A procedure where computers are used in both the design and manufacture of a product.
See Also: *Application; Bespoke; CAD; CADCAM; CADMAT; CAE; CAM; Computer Aided Design; Computer Aided Design Manufacture and Test; Computer Aided Engineering; Computer Aided Manufacturing; Data Processing; Desk Top Publishing; DP; DTP; EDP; EDS; Electronic Data Processing; Electronic Data System; Expert System; Freeware; Information System; Information Technology; IS; IT; Package; Processing; Shareware; Software; Software Package; Software System; Turnkey; Vertical Market;*

Computer Aided Design Manufacture and Test

(CADMAT). A procedure where computers are used in the design, manufacture and testing of products.
See Also: *Application; Bespoke; CAD; CADCAM; CADMAT; CAE; CAM; Computer Aided Design; Computer Aided Design and Manufacturing; Computer Aided Engineering; Computer Aided Manufacturing; Data Processing; Desk Top Publishing; DP; DTP; EDP; EDS; Electronic Data Processing; Electronic Data System; Expert System; Freeware; Information System; Information Technology; IS; IT; Package; Processing; Shareware; Software; Software Package; Software System; Turnkey; Vertical Market;*

Computer Aided Engineering
(CAE). A computer system which is used to simulate processes and check the design of computer aided design systems.
See Also: *Application; Bespoke; CAD; CADCAM; CADMAT; CAE; CAM; Computer Aided Design; Computer Aided Design and Manufacturing; Computer Aided Design Manufacture and Test; Computer Aided Manufacturing; Data Processing; Desk Top Publishing; DP; DTP; EDP; EDS; Electronic Data Processing; Electronic Data System; Expert System; Freeware; Information System; Information Technology; IS; IT; Package; Processing; Shareware; Software; Software Package; Software System; Turnkey; Vertical Market;*

Computer Aided Instruction
(CAI). An application used on a computer to assist in training. There is dialogue between the user and computer to inform the user of any mistakes.
See Also: *Application; Bespoke; CAI; CBT; Computer Based Training; Data Processing; Desk Top Publishing; DP; DTP; EDP; EDS; Electronic Data Processing; Electronic Data System; Expert System; Freeware; Information System; Information Technology; IS; IT; Package; Processing; Shareware; Software; Software Package; Software System; Turnkey; Vertical Market;*

Computer Aided Manufacturing
(CAM). A procedure which uses computers in manufacturing products.
See Also: *Application; Bespoke; CAD; CADCAM; CADMAT; CAE; CAM; Computer Aided Design; Computer Aided Design and Manufacturing; Computer Aided Design Manufacture and Test; Computer Aided Engineering; Data Processing; Desk Top Publishing; DP; DTP; EDP; EDS; Electronic Data Processing; Electronic Data System; Expert System; Freeware; Information System; Information Technology; IS; IT; Package; Processing; Shareware; Software; Software Package; Software System; Turnkey; Vertical Market;*

Computer Aided Software Engineering
(CASE). A methodology which enables designing or programming to be easily done in a structured and controlled way.
See Also: *Application; CASE; Case Tool; Code Generator; Data Flow; Data Flow Diagram; Data Model; Design; Development; DFD; Flowchart; Logical Design; Model; Modular; O & M; Organisation & Methods; Physical Design; Process Model; Reengineering; Specification; Top Down Technique; Wizard;*

Computer Based Training
(CBT). Training done by the use of computers and software.
See Also: *Application; Bespoke; CAI; CBT; Computer Aided Instruction; Data Processing; Desk Top Publishing; DP; DTP; EDP; EDS; Electronic Data Processing; Electronic Data System; Expert System; Freeware; Information System; Information Technology; IS; IT; Package; Processing; Shareware; Software; Software Package; Software System; Turnkey; Vertical Market;*

Computer Output Microfilm
(COM). The process of recording data in a reduced size on a plastic film.
See Also: *Archive; Backing Store; Backup; COM; Fiche; Grandfather, Father, Son; Mass Storage; Medium; Microfiche; Microfilm; Recording Medium; Save;*

Computer Power
The speed and size of a computer, in particular the chip processing speed, the disk access speed, the size of memory and the storage capacities.
See Also: *286; 3.5 Inch; 32 Bit; 386; 486; 5.25 Inch; Backing Store; Central Processing Unit; Chip; Chipset; Clock Speed; Computer; Conventional Memory; Co-processor; Core; Core Dump; CPU; Cross Platform; DDR SDRAM; Desktop; Digital Computer; Digital Versatile Disk; DIMM; Direct Random Access Memory; Disk; Disk Cache; Disk Drive; Disk Pack; Disk Size; Disk Storage; Diskette; Double Data Rate SDRAM; DRAM; Drive; Dual Inline Memory Module; DVD; Dynamic Memory; EEROM; Electrically Erasable Read Only Memory; Electronically Programmed Read Only Memory; EMS; EPROM; Erasable Programmable Read Only Memory; Expanded Memory; Expanded Memory Specification; Extended Memory; FDD; Five and a quarter; Fixed Disk Drive; Flash Memory; Floppy Disk; Floppy Disk Drive; GHz; Gigahertz; Hard Disk Drive; HDD; High Memory; IBM (tm) Compatible; Kbps; KHz; Kilohertz; Laptop; Machine; Magnetic Core; Magnetic Disk; Mass Storage; Maths Co-processor; Megabyte; Megahertz; Memory; MHz; Microprocessor; Midrange System; Million Instructions Per Second; Minicomputer; MIPS; Notebook; Pack; Palmtop Computer; Parallel Processor; PC; Personal Computer; Platform; Portable; Power; Processor; Programmable Read Only Memory; PROM; RAM; RAM Disk; Rambus Dynamic Random Access Memory; Random Access Memory; RDRAM; Read Only Memory; ROM; SDRAM; Shadow RAM Memory; Silicon Chip; SIMM; Single Inline Memory Modules; Single Inline Package; SIP; Storage; Store; Synchronous Dynamic Random Access Memory; System; Thirty Two Bit; Three and a Half; Tower Computer;*

Concatenate
The merging of two or more items into one item. The second following the first etc. e.g. the words doc1, doc2, and doc3 concatenated would be doc1doc2doc3.
See Also: *Character; Data; Data Element; Data Entity; Data Item; Data Type; Defragment; String;*

Conference On DAta SYstems Languages
(CODASYL). A body responsible for developing and maintaining the COBOL programming language.
See Also: *3GL; 4GL; American National Standard Institute; ANSI; COBOL; CODASYL; Code; Compiler; Fourth Generation Language; High Level Language; Language; NATURAL; Programming Language; Syntax; Third Generation Language;*

CONFIG.SYS
A file on a Personal Computer containing configuration instructions that are executed when the computer is switched on or reset. e.g. set the number of files that can be open at any one time.
See Also: *AUTOEXEC.BAT; Batch File; Boot; Bootstrap; CMOS; Cold Start; Command; Complementary Metal Oxide Semiconductor Memory; Configuration; Configuring; Instruction; Instruction Set; Re-boot; Registry; Tuning; Tweaking; Warm Start;*

Configuration
The hardware and software that make up a computer system.
See Also: *3.5 Inch; 5.25 Inch; Application; Backing Store; Barrel Printer; Bloatware; Bubble Jet; CD-ROM Drive; CD-RW Drive; Client Server; CMOS; Complementary Metal Oxide Semiconductor Memory; Computer; CONFIG.SYS; Configuring; Cross Platform; Daisywheel; DAT; Desktop; Device; Digital Audio Tape; Digital Computer; Digital Versatile Disk; Disk; Disk Drive; Disk Operating System; Disk Pack; Disk Size; Disk Storage; Diskette; DOS; Dot Matrix; Drive; Drum Printer; DVD; Environment; Equipment; FDD; File Server; Firewall; Firmware; Five and a quarter; Fixed Disk Drive; Flatbed Scanner; Floppy Disk; Floppy Disk Drive; Front End Processor; Hand Held Device; Hard Disk Drive; Hardware; HDD; IBM (tm) Compatible; Information System; Inkjet; Installation; Intelligent Terminal; IS; Keyboard; Kit; Laptop; Laser Jet; Laser Printer; LCD Printer; Light Pen; Line Printer; Linux; Liquid Crystal Display Printer; Machine; Mag Tape; Magnetic Disk; Magnetic Tape; Mainframe; Mass Storage; Matrix Printer; Micro; Microcomputer; Midrange System; Minicomputer; Mouse; Multi Platform; Multi User; Multimedia; Notebook; Number*

Cruncher; OCR; OMR; Open System; Operating System; Optical Character Reader; Optical Character Recognition; Optical Drive; Optical Mark Recognition; Optical Scanner; OS; OS/2; Pack; Page Printer; Palmtop Computer; PC; Peripheral; Personal Computer; Platform; Plotter; Plug and Play; Plug Compatible; Portable; Printer; Program; Recording Device; Registry; Remote Device; Scanner; Server; Software; Software System; Storage; Store; Streamer; System; System Software; Tape Deck; Tape Streamer; Terminal; TFT; Thermal Printer; Thin-Film Transistor; Three and a Half; Tower Computer; Turnkey; UNIX; Utility; VDT; VDU; VGA; Video Display Terminal; Video Graphics Array; Visual Display Terminal; Visual Display Unit; Winchester Disk; Zip Drive;

Configuring
The preparation of computer equipment and programs to suit your work methods, and to make your system compatible with other equipment and software.
See Also: *ATAPI; Attachment Packet Interface; AUTOEXEC.BAT; Bespoke; CMOS; CODEC; Complementary Metal Oxide Semiconductor Memory; COmpressor DECompressor; CONFIG.SYS; Configuration; Device Driver; Dongle; Driver; Emulate; Emulation; Going Live; Hand Holding; Implementation; Install; Installation; Multi User; Plug and Play; Plug Compatible; Printer Driver; Registry; Software Driver; System; Tuning; Tweaking; Upgrade;*

Conseil Européen pour la Recherche Nucléaire
(CERN). An organisation in Geneva, Switzerland, where the World Wide Web was first developed.
See Also: *Acceptable User Policy; American National Standard Institute; ANSI; AUP; BCS; CCITT; CERN; Consultative Committee International Telegraph and Telephone; Cyberspace; DNS; Domain Name; Domain Name System; Home Page; IEE; International Standards Organisation; Internet; ISO; NCC; Net; Site; The Net; The Web; Universal/Uniform Resource Locator; URL; Website; World Wide Web; WWW;*

Constant
A value in a program which remains unchanged during the execution of the program.
See Also: *Character; Data; Data Element; Data Entity; Data Item; Data Type; Entity; Field; Group; Information; Literal; Null;*

Consultative Committee International Telegraph and Telephone
(CCITT). An international telecommunications body which determines data transmission and connection standards.
See Also: *Acceptable User Policy; Acoustic Coupler; ADN; ADSL; Advanced Digital Network; American National Standard Institute; ANSI; Asymmetric Digital Subscriber Line; Asynchronous; Asynchronous Transfer Mode; ATM; AUP; Bandwidth; Baud Rate; BCS; Bits Per Second; BPS; Broadband; CCITT; CCTA; CERN; Characters Per Second; Client Server Protocol; Communications; Conseil Europeen pour la Recherche Nucleaire; CPS; Data Communications; Data Parity; Data Transmission; Datacoms; Dial In; Dial Up; Direct Connection; Duplex Transmission; FDDI; Fibre Distributed Data Interface; Fibre Optics; Full Duplex; Gbps; Half Duplex; HD; IEE; Integrated Services Digital Network; International Standards Organisation; ISDN; ISO; Kbps; Leased Line; Mbps; Multiplex; Multiplexer; Narrowband; NCC; Open Systems Interconnect; Optical Fibre; OSI; Parallel Transmission; Parity Bit; Serial Interface; Serial Transmission; Simplex Transmission; Synchronous; Telecommunication; Telecoms; Teleprocessing System; TPS; Transfer Rate; Transmit; V90;*

Contractor
People who sub contract their professional services, normally through a Limited Company.
See Also: *A/P; Analyst; Analyst Programmer; B/A; Business Analyst; Data Base Analyst; Data Processing Manager; DBA; Development; DPM; Operator; Programmer; S/A; S/P; System Analyst; Systems Programmer; Technical Author;*

Conventional Memory
The first megabyte of memory of which 640k is made available to the operating system.
See Also: *Absolute Address; Address; Array; Block; Bubble Memory; Buffer; Cache Memory; Central Processing Unit; Clipboard; CMOS; Complementary Metal Oxide Semiconductor Memory; Computer Power; Core; Core Dump; CPU; DDR SDRAM; DIMM; Direct Memory Access; Direct Random Access Memory; Disk Cache; DMA; Double Data Rate SDRAM; DRAM; Dual Inline Memory Module; Dump; Dynamic Memory; Dynamically; EEROM; Electrically Erasable Read Only Memory; Electronically Programmed Read Only Memory; EMS; EPROM; Erasable Programmable Read Only Memory; Expanded Memory; Expanded Memory Specification; Extended Memory; Flash Memory; High Memory; Load; Magnetic Core; Memory; Memory Board; Memory Caching; Memory Card; Memory Resident; Mix; Overlay;*

Power; Programmable Read Only Memory; PROM; RAM; RAM Disk; Rambus Dynamic Random Access Memory; Random Access Memory; RDRAM; Read Only Memory; Relative Address; ROM; SDRAM; Shadow RAM Memory; SIMM; Single Inline Memory Modules; Single Inline Package; SIP; Store; Synchronous Dynamic Random Access Memory; Upper Memory; Video Random Access Memory; Volatile Memory; VRAM; Working Storage; Workspace;

Conversion
The process of converting data or programs from one format or protocol to another.
See Also: *Assembler; BCD; Binary Coded Decimal; Code Generator; Compressed File; Compression; Convert; Data Compression; Decompression; Digital Analog Converter; File Conversion; Maintenance; Packed Data;*

Convert
(1) The process of converting data from one format or protocol to another.
(2) The upgrading of hardware or software.
See Also: *BCD; Binary Coded Decimal; Compressed File; Compression; Conversion; Data Compression; Decompression; Digital Analog Converter; File Conversion; Packed Data; Plug and Play; Upgrade;*

Cookie
Software sent by your server which records information about you and your browsing habits. The information is used by the server to process your requests.
See Also: *Anchor; Anonymous FTP; API; Applet; Application Program Interface; Bookmark; Host; Internet Service Provider; ISP; Provider; Proxy Server; Service Provider; Software;*

Co-processor
A separate processor in a computer used by specialised applications with complex calculations. It is also known as a math's co-processor.
See Also: *286; 386; 486; ALU; Application Specific Integrated Circuits; Arithmetic and Logic Unit; ASICS; Bus; Central Processing Unit; Chip; Chipset; Clock Speed; Computer Power; CPU; Floating Point; IC; Industry Standard Architecture; Integrated Circuit; Interrupt Request; IRQ; ISA; Local Bus; Maths Co-processor; MCA; Megahertz; MHz; Micro Channel Architecture; Microprocessor; Parallel Processor; Power; Processor; Silicon Chip; System Bus;*

CORAL
COmmon Real time Application Language. A high level computer programming language used mainly in real time applications.
See Also: *3GL; 4GL; ADA; ALGOL; APL; BASIC; C or C++; CLIPPER; COBOL; Code; Code Generator; Compiler; Compiling; FORTH; FORTRAN; Fourth Generation Language; High Level Language; Instruction Set; JAVA; JAVASCRIPT; Language; LISP; LOGO; Module; NATURAL; PASCAL; PERL; PICK; PILOT; PL/1; Practical Extraction and Reporting Language; Program; Programming Language; PROLOG; RPG; Software; Source Code; Structured Program; Syntax; Third Generation Language; Visual Basic;*

Core
The computer's memory before solid-state memories were invented. It consists of rows and columns of ferrite rings which can be magnetised and demagnetised to give binary storage.
See Also: *Absolute Address; Address; Array; Block; Bubble Memory; Buffer; Cache Memory; Clipboard; Computer Power; Conventional Memory; Core Dump; DDR SDRAM; DIMM; Direct Memory Access; Direct Random Access Memory; Disk Cache; DMA; Double Data Rate SDRAM; DRAM; Dual Inline Memory Module; Dump; Dynamic Memory; Dynamically; EEROM; Electrically Erasable Read Only Memory; Electronically Programmed Read Only Memory; EMS; EPROM; Erasable Programmable Read Only Memory; Expanded Memory; Expanded Memory Specification; Extended Memory; Flash Memory; High Memory; Magnetic Core; Memory; Memory Caching; Memory Resident; Mix; Overlay; Power; Programmable Read Only Memory; PROM; RAM; RAM Disk; Rambus Dynamic Random Access Memory; Random Access Memory; RDRAM; Read Only Memory; Relative Address; ROM; SDRAM; Shadow RAM Memory; SIMM; Single Inline Memory Modules; Single Inline Package; SIP; Store; Synchronous Dynamic Random Access Memory; System; Upper Memory; Video Random Access Memory; Volatile Memory; VRAM; Working Storage; Workspace;*

Core Dump
A display or printout of the computers memory.
See Also: *Absolute Address; Address; Array; Block; Bubble Memory; Buffer; Cache Memory; Clipboard; Computer Power; Conventional Memory; Core; DDR SDRAM; DIMM; Direct Random Access Memory; Disk Cache; Double Data Rate SDRAM; DRAM; Dual Inline Memory Module; Dump; Dynamic Memory; Dynamically; EEROM; Electrically Erasable Read Only Memory; Electronically Programmed Read Only*

Memory; EMS; EPROM; Erasable Programmable Read Only Memory; Expanded Memory; Expanded Memory Specification; Extended Memory; Flash Memory; High Memory; Magnetic Core; Memory; Memory Resident; Mix; Power; Printout; Programmable Read Only Memory; PROM; RAM; RAM Disk; Rambus Dynamic Random Access Memory; Random Access Memory; RDRAM; Read Only Memory; Relative Address; ROM; SDRAM; Shadow RAM Memory; SIMM; Single Inline Memory Modules; Single Inline Package; SIP; Store; Synchronous Dynamic Random Access Memory; Upper Memory; Video Random Access Memory; Volatile Memory; VRAM; Working Storage; Workspace;

CPI

Characters Per Inch. The numbers of characters which can fit into an inch when printed or displayed. It depends on the font size and pitch of the characters.

See Also: *Character; Characters Per Inch; Dots Per Inch; DPI; Font; Font Cartridge; Landscape; Letter Quality; LQ; Near Letter Quality; NLQ; Output; Portrait; Printer; Printout; Scalable Fonts;*

CPS

Characters Per Second. A measurement of the speed that text information is transferred.

See Also: *Access Time; ADN; ADSL; Advanced Digital Network; Asymmetric Digital Subscriber Line; Asymmetrical Modem; Asynchronous; Asynchronous Transfer Mode; ATM; Bandwidth; Bits Per Second; BPS; Broadband; Bus; CCITT; CCTA; Channel; Character; Characters Per Second; Communications; Consultative Committee International Telegraph and Telephone; Data Communications; Data Parity; Data Transmission; Datacoms; Dial In; Dial Up; Duplex Transmission; ECP; Enhanced Parallel Port; EPP; Extended Capabilities Port; FDDI; Fibre Distributed Data Interface; Fibre Optics; Full Duplex; Gbps; GHz; Gigahertz; Half Duplex; HD; Integrated Services Digital Network; ISDN; Kbps; KHz; Kilohertz; Mbps; Microsecond; Million Instructions Per Second; Millisecond; MIPS; Ms; Multiplex; Multiplexer; Nanosecond; Narrowband; Ns; Open Systems Interconnect; Optical Fibre; OSI; Parallel Transmission; Parity Bit; Pico Second; Serial Transmission; Simplex Transmission; Synchronous; System Bus; T-1; T-3; Telecommunication; Telecoms; Transfer Rate; Transmission Channel; Transmit; V90;*

CPU
Central Processing Unit. The central area of a computer which controls the entire operation of a computer. It contains the memory and executes program instructions.
See Also: *286; 386; 486; ALU; Application Specific Integrated Circuits; Arithmetic and Logic Unit; ASICS; Bus; Central Processing Unit; Chip; Chipset; Clock Speed; Computer Power; Conventional Memory; Co-processor; EISA; Enhanced Industry Standard Architecture; Expansion Card; Flash Memory; IC; Industry Standard Architecture; Integrated Circuit; Interrupt Request; IRQ; ISA; Local Bus; Maths Co-processor; MCA; Megahertz; Memory; Memory Caching; MHz; Micro Channel Architecture; Microprocessor; Mix; Parallel Processor; Power; Processor; Silicon Chip; System; System Bus; Zero Wait State;*

Crash
(1) Mechanical failure of the read/write heads or dirt on the heads in a storage unit. (2) A state when a program stops running due to a bug in the program or the computer system.
See Also: *3.5 Inch; 5.25 Inch; Abort; Bug; Debug; Debugger; Died; Disk; Disk Drive; Disk Pack; Disk Storage; Diskette; Downtime; FDD; Five and a quarter; Fixed Disk Drive; Floppy Disk; Floppy Disk Drive; General Protection Fault; GPF; Hangs; Hard Disk Drive; HDD; Head Crash; Heads; Hung; Machine Crash; Magnetic Disk; Pack; Program Crash; Read/Write Head; System Hangs; Three and a Half;*

Cross Platform
A term used when different makes of computers with similar designs allow the same software to work on the different makes.
See Also: *Advanced Technology; Analogue Computer; AT; Compatible; Computer; Computer Power; Configuration; Desktop; Digital Computer; Downsizing; EDS; Electronic Data System; Emulate; Emulation; Environment; Equipment; Extended Technology; Hardware; IBM (tm) Compatible; Information System; Information Technology; Installation; IS; IT; Kit; Laptop; Leading Edge; Machine; Mainframe; Micro; Microcomputer; Midrange System; Minicomputer; Multi Platform; Node; Notebook; Number Cruncher; Open System; Palmtop Computer; PC; Personal Computer; Platform; Portable; Power; Standalone; State of the Art; System; Tower Computer; Turnkey; Voice Activated; XT;*

CRT
Cathode Ray Tube. The tube in the monitor which displays the screen.
See Also: *Analogue Monitor; Anti Glare Screen; Cathode Ray Tube; CGA; Colour Graphics Adaptor; Device; Digital Monitor; Display;*

EGA; Enhanced Graphic Adaptor; Equipment; Extended Video Array; Graphics Card; Hardware; High Resolution; Installation; Intelligent Terminal; Interlaced; Kit; LCD; Liquid Crystal Display; Low Resolution; Monitor; Monochrome; Paint Screen; Peripheral; Plasma Screen; Prompt; Resolution; Screen; Screen Burn; Split Screen; Super Twist LCD; Super VGA; Super Video Graphics Array; SVGA; Terminal; TFT; Thin-Film Transistor; Touch Screen; Twip; VDT; VDU; VGA; Video Card; Video Display Terminal; Video Graphics Array; Video Random Access Memory; Visual Display Terminal; Visual Display Unit; VRAM; XGA;

CSV
Comma Separated Values. Data items in a record separated from each other by commas, which identify the start and end of each data field.
See Also: *Comma Separated Values; Data; Data Element; Data Entity; Data Item; Data Type; Database; DB; Field; Format; Information; Key; RDB; Record; Relational Database; Sequential File; Serial File; String; Table; Tag; Trailer; Transaction; Variable;*

Cursor
A pointer which blinks on the visual display unit screen and indicates a specific position on the screen.
See Also: *C Prompt; Carriage Return; Click; Display; Graphics; Icon; Image Processing; Pixel; Prompt; Scroll; Sprite; Twip;*

Cut Sheet Feeder
A device attached to a printer which allows for single sheets of paper to be fed to the printer.
See Also: *Bubble Jet; Daisywheel; Device; Dot Matrix; Equipment; Hard Copy; Inkjet; Kit; Matrix Printer; Peripheral; Printer; Sheet Feeder; Thermal Printer;*

Cybercafe
An establishment, like a cafe, where you can use their computer equipment to access the World Wide Web.
See Also: *Anchor; BBS; Browser; Buddy List; Bulletin Board System; Chat; Chatroom; Cyberspace; DNS; Domain Name; Domain Name Server; Domain Name System; Electronic Mail; E-mail; E-mail Address; End User; IM; Instant Messaging; Internet; Mailbox; Message Boards; Net; Netiquette; Newbie; Newsgroup; Point to Point Protocol; PPP; Public Domain; The Net; The Web; Thread; User; User Group; World Wide Web; WWW;*

Cyberspace
The Internet where users interact with each other electronically.
See Also: *Anchor; Applet; BBS; Browser; Buddy List; Bulletin Board System; CERN; Chat; Chatroom; Conseil Europeen pour la Recherche Nucleaire; Cybercafe; DNS; Domain Name; Domain Name Server; Domain Name System; E-commerce; EDI; Electronic Data Interchange; Electronic Mail; E-mail; E-mail Address; File Transfer Protocol; FTP; FTP Site; FTPmail; Gopher; Hit; Home Page; Host; Host Processor; HTTP; Hyperlink; Hypertext; Hypertext Transfer Protocol; IM; Information Superhighway; Instant Messaging; Internet; Internet Protocol; Internet Protocol Address; Internet Relay Chat; Internet Service Provider; IP; IP Address; IRC; ISP; Link; Mailbox; Mailing List; Mailserver; Message Boards; Meta Tag; Meta-Search Engine; Mirror Site; Net; Netiquette; Newbie; Newsgroup; Online; PING; Point Of Presence; Point to Point Protocol; POP; Portal; PPP; Provider; Proxy Server; Public Domain; Search Engine; Secure Socket Layer; Serial Line Internet Protocol; Service Provider; Simple Mail Transfer Protocol; Site; SLIP; SMTP; Spam; Spider; SSL; Surfing; The Net; The Web; Thread; WAP; Wap Internet Service Provider; Webcam; Webhost; Webring; Website; Wireless Application Protocol; WISP; World Wide Web; WWW;*

Cylinder
A set of concentric tracks on different surfaces of a disk pack.
See Also: *3.5 Inch; 5.25 Inch; Block; Disk; Disk Pack; Disk Size; Disk Storage; Diskette; Five and a quarter; Floppy Disk; Magnetic Disk; Medium; Pack; Recording Medium; Sector; Storage; Three and a Half; Track;*

Daemon
A program that remains dormant in the computer until such time that it is needed to perform a task.
See Also: *Applet; DLL; Dynamic Link Library; Job; Module; Program; ROM Resident; Trojan; Utility; Virus; Virus Checker; Worm;*

Daisywheel
(1) The print head attached to a printer in the shape of a daisy and has characters, numbers and symbols at the end of its 'petals' which is used for printing. (2) A printer which uses a daisy wheel print head.
See Also: *Barrel Printer; Bi Directional; Bubble Jet; Configuration; Cut Sheet Feeder; Device; DIP Switch; Dot Matrix; Drum Printer; Duplex Printing; Environment; Equipment; Font Cartridge; Hard Copy; Hardware; Inkjet; Installation; Kit; Landscape; Laser Jet; Laser Printer; LCD Printer; Letter Quality; Line Printer; Lines Per Minute; Liquid*

Crystal Display Printer; Lpm; LPT Port; LQ; Matrix Printer; Near Letter Quality; NLQ; Page Printer; Pages Per Minute; Peripheral; Portrait; PPM; Printer; Printer Driver; Printout; Sheet Feeder; Simplex Printing; Thermal Printer;

DAT
Digital Audio Tape. A recording unit and also the medium on which information is digitally recorded in a high density.
See Also: *Archive; Backing Store; Backup; Bits Per Inch; Block; BPI; Configuration; Deck; Density; Device; Digital Audio Tape; Double Density; Drive; End of Tape; Environment; EOT; Equipment; Grandfather, Father, Son; Hardware; High Density; Installation; Kit; Mag Tape; Magnetic Tape; Mass Storage; Medium; Peripheral; Recording; Recording Device; Recording Medium; Save; Storage; Store; Tape Deck; Tape Streamer; Zip Drive;*

Data
Another word meaning information.
See Also: *8 Bit; American Standard Code for Information Interchange; Archive; Array; ASCII; ASCII Files; Bandwidth; Baud Rate; Binary Digit; Bit; Bit Pattern; Broadband; Buddy List; Byte; Character; Check Box; Cluster; Comma Separated Values; Compression; Concatenate; Constant; CSV; Data Dictionary; Data Element; Data Entity; Data Flow; Data Flow Diagram; Data Item; Data Model; Data Protection Act; Data Type; Database; DB; Decompression; DFD; Digital; EBCDIC; Eight Bit; Encryption; Entity; Extended Binary Coded Decimal Interchange Code; Field; Garbage In, Garbage Out; Gb; Gigabyte; Group; Hex; Hexadecimal; I/O; Information; Information Technology; Input; Input/Output; IT; K; Kb; Kbyte; Key; Kilobit; Kilobyte; Literal; Mb; Mbyte; Megabit; Megabyte; Narrowband; Null; Octal; Operand; Packet; Packet Switching; Parameter; Patch; Radio Button; Record; Recording; Sector; String; Swapping; Table; Terabyte; Track; Transaction; Variable; Word; Write;*

Data Base Analyst
(DBA). A person who designs and maintains databases.
See Also: *A/P; Analyst; Analyst Programmer; B/A; Business Analyst; Contractor; Data Base Management System; Data Processing Manager; Database; DB; DBA; DBMS; Design; Development; DPM; Model; Process Model; Programmer; RDB; RDBMS/RDMS; Relational Database; Relational Database Management System; S/A; S/P; System Analyst; Systems Programmer; Technical Author;*

Data Base Management System
(DBMS). Software to set up and process a database.
See Also: *Bespoke; Data Base Analyst; Data Dictionary; Data Processing; Database; DB; DBA; DBMS; DP; Information System; Information Technology; IS; IT; Package; Processing; RDB; RDBMS/RDMS; Relational Database; Relational Database Management System; Roll Back; Software; Software Package; Software System; System;*

Data Bus
A communication path in which data within a computer is carried from one point to another. e.g. by 8, 16 or 32 bits.
See Also: *16 Bit; 32 Bit; 64 Bit; 8 Bit; Address Bus; Binary Digit; Bit; Bits Per Second; BPS; Bus; Channel; Digital; Eight Bit; Expansion Card; Gbps; I/O; Input/Output; Kbps; Local Bus; Mbps; Sixteen Bit; Sixty Four Bit; System Bus; Thirty Two Bit; Transmission Channel;*

Data Centre
A place where data processing is done. It can be within an organisation either integral to the building or at a different location. It can also be a company in their own right who provide data processing to others.
See Also: *Data Processing; Distributed System/Network; DP; EDP; EDS; Electronic Data Processing; Electronic Data System; Environment; Facilities Management; FM; Information Technology; In-house; Installation; IT; Software House;*

Data Communications
Abbreviated to Data Comms. The process by which data is transmitted between two or more devices.
See Also: *ACK; Acoustic Coupler; ADN; ADSL; Advanced Digital Network; AMR; Asymmetric Digital Subscriber Line; Asymmetrical Modem; Asynchronous; Asynchronous Transfer Mode; ATM; Automatic Message Routing; Bandwidth; Baud Rate; Bits Per Second; Bluetooth (tm); BPS; Broadband; CCITT; CCTA; Channel; Characters Per Second; Client Server Protocol; Communications; Consultative Committee International Telegraph and Telephone; CPS; Data Parity; Data Transmission; Datacoms; Dial In; Dial Up; Digital; Direct Connection; Duplex Transmission; ECP; Enhanced Parallel Port; EPP; Extended Capabilities Port; FDDI; Fibre Distributed Data Interface; Fibre Optics; Firewire; Full Duplex; Gbps; GHz; Gigahertz; Half Duplex; HD; Integrated Services Digital Network; ISDN; Kbps; KHz; Kilohertz; Leased Line; Mbps; Modem; Modulator Demodulator; Multiplex; Multiplexer; Narrowband; Node; Open Systems Interconnect; Optical*

Fibre; OSI; Packet; Packet Switching; Parallel Transmission; Parity Bit; Protocol; Serial Transmission; Simplex Transmission; Synchronous; Telecommunication; Telecoms; Teleprocessing System; TPS; Transfer Rate; Transmission Channel; Transmit; V90; Wi-Fi; Wireless Fidelity;

Data Compression
The process when data is reduced in size to take up a smaller area for storage or transmission.
See Also: *Compressed File; Compression; Conversion; Convert; Decompression; Packed Data; PKZIP; Unzip; Zip;*

Data Dictionary
A retention area defining data items in a database where the data items are recorded and tracked by the database system.
See Also: *Data; Data Base Management System; Data Element; Data Entity; Data Item; Data Type; Database; DB; DBMS; Entity; Field; File; Group; Information; RDB; RDBMS/RDMS; Relational Database; Relational Database Management System;*

Data Element
An item or field which represents a piece of data. e.g. telephone number.
See Also: *Archive; Array; Bubble Sort; Check Box; Comma Separated Values; Concatenate; Constant; CSV; Data; Data Dictionary; Data Entity; Data Flow; Data Flow Diagram; Data Item; Data Model; Data Protection Act; Data Type; Database; DB; DFD; Digital; EBCDIC; Entity; Extended Binary Coded Decimal Interchange Code; Field; Group; Information; Input; Key; Literal; Null; Parameter; Radio Button; Record; Recording; String; Subscript; Table; Transaction; Variable; Word;*

Data Entity
One item of data or a group item which may have more than one item of data. In each case it has its own meaning and relationships to other entities.
See Also: *Archive; Array; Bubble Sort; Check Box; Comma Separated Values; Concatenate; Constant; CSV; Data; Data Dictionary; Data Element; Data Flow; Data Flow Diagram; Data Item; Data Model; Data Type; Database; DB; DFD; Digital; EBCDIC; Entity; Extended Binary Coded Decimal Interchange Code; Field; Group; Information; Input; Key; Literal; Null; Parameter; Radio Button; RDB; Record; Recording; Relational Database; String; Table; Transaction; Variable; Word;*

Data Flow

A representation, normally in graphical form, of data and the processes the data is used in.

See Also: *Audit Trail; CASE; Case Tool; Computer Aided Software Engineering; Data; Data Element; Data Entity; Data Flow Diagram; Data Item; Data Model; Data Type; Design; Development; DFD; Event; Key; Model; Modular; O & M; Organisation & Methods; Process Model; Structured Design; Top Down Technique;*

Data Flow Diagram

(DFD). A graphical representation of data and the processes performed on the data.

See Also: *Analyst; Audit Trail; B/A; Business Analyst; CASE; Case Tool; Computer Aided Software Engineering; Data; Data Element; Data Entity; Data Flow; Data Item; Data Model; Data Type; Design; Development; DFD; Event; Key; Model; Modular; O & M; Organisation & Methods; Process Model; S/A; Structured Design; Top Down Technique;*

Data Item

An item which represents a piece of data. e.g. name.

See Also: *Archive; Array; Bubble Sort; Check Box; Comma Separated Values; Concatenate; Constant; CSV; Data; Data Dictionary; Data Element; Data Entity; Data Flow; Data Flow Diagram; Data Model; Data Protection Act; Data Type; Database; DB; DFD; Digital; EBCDIC; Entity; Extended Binary Coded Decimal Interchange Code; Field; Group; Information; Input; Key; Literal; Null; Parameter; Radio Button; Record; Recording; String; Subscript; Table; Transaction; Variable; Word;*

Data Model

A graphical design representing the data within an organisation and the relationships between one item of information with another.

See Also: *Analyst; Audit Trail; B/A; Business Analyst; CASE; Case Tool; Computer Aided Software Engineering; Data; Data Element; Data Entity; Data Flow; Data Flow Diagram; Data Item; Data Type; Design; Development; DFD; Entity; Event; Key; Model; Modular; O & M; Organisation & Methods; Process Model; S/A; Structured Design; Top Down Technique;*

Data Parity
An extra bit attached to a set of binary digits and used to check that all the other bits were transferred from one point to another correctly.
See Also: *ADN; ADSL; Advanced Digital Network; AMR; Asymmetric Digital Subscriber Line; Asymmetrical Modem; Asynchronous; Asynchronous Transfer Mode; ATM; Automatic Message Routing; Bandwidth; Baud Rate; Binary; Binary Digit; Bit; Bits Per Second; BPS; Broadband; CCITT; CCTA; Channel; Characters Per Second; Communications; Consultative Committee International Telegraph and Telephone; CPS; Data Communications; Data Transmission; Datacoms; Dial In; Dial Up; Digital; Direct Connection; Duplex Transmission; FDDI; Fibre Distributed Data Interface; Fibre Optics; Full Duplex; Gbps; Half Duplex; HD; Integrated Services Digital Network; ISDN; Leased Line; Mbps; Multiplex; Multiplexer; Narrowband; Open Systems Interconnect; Optical Fibre; OSI; Packet; Packet Switching; Parallel Transmission; Parity Bit; Serial Transmission; Simplex Transmission; Synchronous; Telecommunication; Telecoms; Transmission Channel; Transmit; V90;*

Data Processing
(DP). The manipulation, analysis and storage of data on a computer.
See Also: *Audit Trail; Batch Processing; Bespoke; CAD; CADCAM; CADMAT; CAE; CAI; CAM; CBT; Computation; Compute; Computer Aided Design; Computer Aided Design and Manufacturing; Computer Aided Design Manufacture and Test; Computer Aided Engineering; Computer Aided Instruction; Computer Aided Manufacturing; Computer Based Training; Data Base Management System; Data Centre; DBMS; Desk Top Publishing; Distributed System/Network; DP; DTP; E-commerce; EDI; EDP; EFT; EFTPOS; Electronic Data Interchange; Electronic Data Processing; Electronic Fund Transfer; Electronic Fund Transfer Point of Sales; Expert System; Facilities Management; FM; Geographical Information System; GIS; Information System; Information Technology; IS; IT; Job; Multitasking; Office Information System; OIS; Outsourcing; Processing; RDBMS/RDMS; Relational Database Management System; Run; Run Time; Software System; Spreadsheet; Teleprocessing System; TPS; Vertical Market; Word Processor; WP;*

Data Processing Manager
(DPM). A person who manages a computer department.
See Also: *A/P; Analyst; Analyst Programmer; B/A; Business Analyst; Contractor; Data Base Analyst; DBA; DPM; Programmer; S/A; S/P; System Analyst; Systems Programmer; Technical Author;*

Data Protection Act
An Act of Parliament by which anybody who holds personal data on individuals has to be registered. The Act is intended to protect the rights of those individuals about whom personal data is recorded.
See Also: *Data; Data Element; Data Item; Data Type; International Standards Organisation; ISO;*

Data Transmission
The process when data is transferred along communication lines or through the air from one computer or device to another.
See Also: *ACK; Acoustic Coupler; ADN; ADSL; Advanced Digital Network; AMR; Asymmetric Digital Subscriber Line; Asymmetrical Modem; Asynchronous; Asynchronous Transfer Mode; ATM; Automatic Message Routing; Bandwidth; Baud Rate; Bits Per Second; Bluetooth (tm); BPS; Broadband; CCITT; CCTA; Channel; Characters Per Second; Client Server Protocol; Communications; Consultative Committee International Telegraph and Telephone; CPS; Data Communications; Data Parity; Datacoms; Dial In; Dial Up; Digital; Direct Connection; Duplex Transmission; ECP; Enhanced Parallel Port; EPP; Extended Capabilities Port; FDDI; Fibre Distributed Data Interface; Fibre Optics; Full Duplex; Gbps; GHz; Gigahertz; Half Duplex; HD; Integrated Services Digital Network; ISDN; Kbps; KHz; Kilohertz; Leased Line; Mbps; Modem; Modulator Demodulator; Multiplex; Multiplexer; Narrowband; Node; Open Systems Interconnect; Optical Fibre; OSI; Packet; Packet Switching; Parallel Transmission; Parity Bit; Serial Transmission; Simplex Transmission; Synchronous; Telecommunication; Telecoms; Teleprocessing System; TPS; Transfer Rate; Transmission Channel; Transmit; V90; Wi-Fi; Wireless Fidelity;*

Data Type
The classification of an item of data. e.g. numeric, alphanumeric.
See Also: *8 Bit; American Standard Code for Information Interchange; ASCII; Bandwidth; Binary Digit; Bit; Bit Pattern; Broadband; Byte; Character; Check Box; Comma Separated Values; Compression; Concatenate; Constant; CSV; Data; Data Dictionary; Data Element; Data Entity; Data Flow; Data Flow Diagram; Data Item; Data Model; Data Protection Act; Database; DB; Decompression; DFD; Digital; EBCDIC; Eight Bit; Entity; Extended Binary Coded Decimal Interchange Code; Field; Group; Hex; Hexadecimal; Information; Key; Literal; Narrowband; Null; Octal; Parameter; Radio Button; Record; String; Table; Transaction; Variable; Word;*

Database
(DB). A collection of files and records relating to each other which can be accessed in many ways by a database management system.
See Also: *BBS; Beginning of File; BOF; Bulletin Board System; Client Server; Comma Separated Values; CSV; Data; Data Base Analyst; Data Base Management System; Data Dictionary; Data Element; Data Entity; Data Item; Data Type; DB; DBA; DBMS; Direct Access; End of File; Entity; EOF; Field; File; Index Sequential File; Information; Key; Random Access; Random File; RDB; RDBMS/RDMS; Record; Relational Database; Relational Database Management System; Sequential File; Serial File; Server; Table; Tag File; Transaction;*

Datacoms
A term for data transferred along communication lines or through the air.
See Also: *ACK; Acoustic Coupler; ADN; ADSL; Advanced Digital Network; AMR; Asymmetric Digital Subscriber Line; Asymmetrical Modem; Asynchronous; Asynchronous Transfer Mode; ATM; Automatic Message Routing; Bandwidth; Baud Rate; Bits Per Second; BPS; Broadband; CCITT; CCTA; Channel; Characters Per Second; Client Server Protocol; Communications; Consultative Committee International Telegraph and Telephone; CPS; Data Communications; Data Parity; Data Transmission; Dial In; Dial Up; Digital; Direct Connection; Duplex Transmission; ECP; Enhanced Parallel Port; EPP; Extended Capabilities Port; FDDI; Fibre Distributed Data Interface; Fibre Optics; Full Duplex; Gbps; GHz; Gigahertz; Half Duplex; HD; Integrated Services Digital Network; ISDN; Kbps; KHz; Kilohertz; Leased Line; Mbps; Modem; Modulator Demodulator; Multiplex; Multiplexer; Narrowband; Node; Open Systems Interconnect; Optical Fibre; OSI; Packet; Packet Switching; Parallel Transmission; Parity Bit; Serial Transmission; Simplex Transmission; Synchronous; Telecommunication; Telecoms; Teleprocessing System; TPS; Transfer Rate; Transmission Channel; Transmit; V90;*

DB
Database. A collection of files and records relating to each other which can be accessed in many ways by a database management system.
See Also: *BBS; Beginning of File; BOF; Bulletin Board System; Client Server; Comma Separated Values; CSV; Data; Data Base Analyst; Data Base Management System; Data Dictionary; Data Element; Data Entity; Data Item; Data Type; Database; DBA; DBMS; Direct Access; End of File; Entity; EOF; Field; File; Index Sequential File; Information; Key; Random Access; Random File; RDB; RDBMS/RDMS; Record; Relational*

Database; Relational Database Management System; Sequential File; Serial File; Server; Table; Tag File; Transaction;

DBA

Data Base Analyst. A person who designs and maintains databases.

See Also: *A/P; Analyst; Analyst Programmer; B/A; Business Analyst; Contractor; Data Base Analyst; Data Base Management System; Data Processing Manager; Database; DB; DBMS; Design; Development; DPM; Model; Process Model; Programmer; RDB; RDBMS/RDMS; Relational Database; Relational Database Management System; S/A; S/P; System Analyst; Systems Programmer; Technical Author;*

DBMS

Data Base Management System. Software to set up and process a database.

See Also: *Bespoke; Data Base Analyst; Data Base Management System; Data Dictionary; Data Processing; Database; DB; DBA; DP; Information System; Information Technology; IS; IT; Package; Processing; RDB; RDBMS/RDMS; Relational Database; Relational Database Management System; Roll Back; Software; Software Package; Software System; System;*

DDR SDRAM

Double Data Rate SDRAM. Very fast memory that reads and writes at the rising and falling edges of the system clock thus doubling data throughput.

See Also: *Bubble Memory; Buffer; Cache Memory; CMOS; Complementary Metal Oxide Semiconductor Memory; Computer Power; Conventional Memory; Core; Core Dump; DIMM; Direct Memory Access; Direct Random Access Memory; Disk Cache; DMA; Double Data Rate SDRAM; DRAM; Dual Inline Memory Module; Dynamic Memory; Dynamically; EEROM; Electrically Erasable Read Only Memory; Electronically Programmed Read Only Memory; EMS; EPROM; Erasable Programmable Read Only Memory; Expanded Memory; Expanded Memory Specification; Extended Memory; Flash Memory; High Memory; Magnetic Core; Memory; Memory Board; Memory Caching; Memory Card; Memory Resident; Mix; Power; Programmable Read Only Memory; PROM; RAM; RAM Disk; Rambus Dynamic Random Access Memory; Random Access Memory; RDRAM; Read Only Memory; ROM; SDRAM; Shadow RAM Memory; SIMM; Single Inline Memory Modules; Single Inline Package; SIP; Stack; Store; Swapping; Synchronous Dynamic Random Access Memory; Upper Memory; Video Random Access Memory; VRAM; Working Storage; Workspace;*

Dead Lock
A state which occurs when two or more users are trying to access the same item of data and none can get access to it.
See Also: *Access; Busy; Deadly Embrace; Died; End User; File; File Sharing; General Protection Fault; GPF; Hangs; Hung; Locking; R/W; Read; Read/Write; Record Locking; System Hangs; User; Write;*

Deadly Embrace
A state which arises when two or more programs are trying to update the same data record at the same time and one of the programs already has the record locked for updating.
See Also: *Access; Busy; Dead Lock; Died; End User; File; File Sharing; General Protection Fault; GPF; Hangs; Hung; Locking; R/W; Read; Read/Write; Record Locking; System Hangs; User; Write;*

Debug
The process of finding and correcting errors in a computer system or program.
See Also: *Abort; Audit Trail; Bug; Crash; Debugger; Downtime; General Protection Fault; GPF; Hangs; Head Crash; Hung; Machine Crash; Program Crash; System Hangs; Trace;*

Debugger
A program used as an aid to locate errors in other program code, by monitoring that other code during development.
See Also: *Abort; Audit Trail; Bug; Code; Crash; Debug; Development; Downtime; General Protection Fault; GPF; Hangs; Head Crash; Hung; Machine Crash; Program; Program Crash; Software System; System Hangs;*

Deck
A tape unit which uses magnetic tape to store information.
See Also: *Archive; Backing Store; Backup; DAT; Device; Digital Audio Tape; Drive; Environment; Equipment; Hardware; Installation; Kit; Mag Tape; Magnetic Tape; Mass Storage; Peripheral; Recording Device; Save; Storage; Store; Streamer; System; Tape Deck; Tape Streamer;*

Decompression
The process when compressed data is restored to its normal format for processing.
See Also: *Compressed File; Compression; Conversion; Convert; Data; Data Compression; Data Type; Density; Double Density; File*

Conversion; High Density; Packed Data; PKZIP; Self Extracting File; Unzip; Zip;

Defragment
The process where parts of file that are stored in different locations of a disk are combined so that the whole file can be stored in one location.
See Also: *3.5 Inch; 5.25 Inch; Bloatware; Concatenate; Disk; Disk Map; Disk Pack; Disk Storage; Diskette; File; Five and a quarter; Floppy Disk; Fragmentation; Housekeeping; Magnetic Disk; Maintenance; Pack; Three and a Half; Volume; Winchester Disk;*

Delimiter
A character which is used to mark the beginning and ending of a piece of data.
See Also: *Beginning of File; BOF; Byte; Character; End of File; End of Tape; EOF; EOT;*

Denary
A numerical system with a base of 10. This is our normal decimal system using numbers 0 - 9.
See Also: *BCD; Binary Coded Decimal; Digital; EBCDIC; Extended Binary Coded Decimal Interchange Code; Hex; Hexadecimal; Octal;*

Density
A term referring to the volume of information which can be stored on magnetic storage media. e.g. single density, double density and high density.
See Also: *3.5 Inch; 5.25 Inch; Bits Per Inch; BPI; Compression; DAT; Decompression; Digital Audio Tape; Disk; Disk Pack; Disk Size; Disk Storage; Diskette; Double Density; Five and a quarter; Floppy Disk; High Density; Mag Tape; Magnetic Disk; Magnetic Tape; Mass Storage; Medium; Pack; Packed Data; Recording Medium; Storage; Streamer; Tape Streamer; Three and a Half; Volume; Winchester Disk;*

Design
(1) A specification of a computer hardware or software system. (2) The process of preparing the hardware or software specification.
See Also: *A/P; Analyst; Analyst Programmer; B/A; Business Analyst; CASE; Case Tool; Computer Aided Software Engineering; Data Base Analyst; Data Flow; Data Flow Diagram; Data Model; DBA; Development; DFD; Flowchart; Full Project Life Cycle; Logical Design; Model; Modular; Physical Design; Process Model; Program Specification; Programmer; Project Life Cycle; S/A; S/P; Specification;*

System Analysis; System Analyst; Systems Programmer; Top Down Technique; Wizard;

Desk Top Publishing
(DTP). Software which is used to produce professional looking documentation with graphic designs.
See Also: *Application; Bespoke; CAD; CADCAM; CADMAT; CAE; CAI; CAM; CBT; Clip Art; Computer Aided Design; Computer Aided Design and Manufacturing; Computer Aided Design Manufacture and Test; Computer Aided Engineering; Computer Aided Instruction; Computer Aided Manufacturing; Computer Based Training; Data Processing; DP; DTP; EDP; EDS; Electronic Data Processing; Electronic Data System; Graphics; Image Map; Image Processing; Information System; Information Technology; IS; IT; Office Information System; OIS; Package; Program; Shareware; Software; Software Package; Software System; Turnkey; Vertical Market; Word Processor; WP;*

Desktop
A computer which sits on top of a desk as opposed to a laptop. Refers normally to personal computers.
See Also: *1st Generation; 2nd Generation; 3rd Generation; 4th Generation; Advanced Technology; Analogue Computer; AT; Compatible; Computer; Computer Power; Configuration; Cross Platform; Digital Computer; Downsizing; EDS; Electronic Data System; Environment; Equipment; Extended Technology; Hardware; IBM (tm) Compatible; Information System; Information Technology; Installation; IS; IT; Kit; Laptop; Machine; Micro; Microcomputer; Multi Platform; Notebook; OEM; Original Equipment Manufacturer; Palmtop Computer; PC; Personal Computer; Platform; Portable; Power; Standalone; System; Tower Computer; Turnkey; Voice Activated; XT;*

Development
The analysis, design, programming and testing of computer hardware and software systems.
See Also: *A/P; Analyst; Analyst Programmer; B/A; Bespoke; Business Analyst; CASE; Case Tool; Code; Computer Aided Software Engineering; Contractor; Data Base Analyst; Data Flow; Data Flow Diagram; Data Model; DBA; Debugger; Design; DFD; Flowchart; Full Project Life Cycle; Implementation; In-house; Leading Edge; Live; Logical Design; Modular; Module; O & M; Object Oriented Analysis; Object Oriented Design; Object Oriented Programming; OOA; OOD; OOP; Organisation & Methods; Physical Design; Program; Program Specification; Programmer; Project Life Cycle; Reengineering; S/A; S/P;*

Software; Software Development Cycle; Software House; Software System; Specification; State of the Art; Structured Design; Structured Program; Syntax; System Analysis; System Analyst; System Software; Systems Programmer; Top Down Technique; Upgrade; Walkthrough; Wizard; Working Storage; Workspace;

Device

A hardware unit which is interfaced to a computer. e.g. disk or printer.

See Also: *3.5 Inch; 5.25 Inch; Access; Access Time; Acoustic Coupler; Analogue; Analogue Digital Converter; Analogue Monitor; Anti Glare Screen; Backing Store; Barrel Printer; Black Box; Bubble Jet; Cathode Ray Tube; CCD; CD-ROM Drive; CD-RW Drive; CGA; Charge Coupled Device; Client Server; Colour Graphics Adaptor; Compatible; Configuration; CRT; Cut Sheet Feeder; Daisywheel; DAT; Deck; Device Driver; Digital Analog Converter; Digital Audio Tape; Digital Monitor; Digital Versatile Disk; Disk; Disk Drive; Disk Pack; Disk Size; Disk Storage; Diskette; Display; Dongle; Dot Matrix; Drive; Drum Printer; DVD; EGA; Emulate; Emulation; Enhanced Graphic Adaptor; Environment; Equipment; Extended Video Array; FDD; Firewire; Five and a quarter; Fixed Disk Drive; Flatbed Scanner; Floppy Disk; Floppy Disk Drive; Front End Processor; Hand Held Device; Hard Disk Drive; Hardware; HDD; Inkjet; Intelligent Terminal; Interface; Keyboard; Kit; Laser Jet; Laser Printer; LCD; LCD Printer; Leading Edge; LED; Light Emitting Diode; Light Pen; Line Printer; Liquid Crystal Display; Liquid Crystal Display Printer; Load; Mag Tape; Magnetic Disk; Magnetic Tape; Mass Storage; Matrix Printer; Modem; Modulator Demodulator; Monitor; Monochrome; Mouse; OCR; OMR; Optical Character Reader; Optical Character Recognition; Optical Drive; Optical Mark Recognition; Optical Scanner; Pack; Page Printer; PDA; Peripheral; Personal Digital Assistant; Plasma Screen; Plotter; Plug and Play; Plug Compatible; Printer; Recording Device; Remote Device; Scanner; Screen; Server; Sheet Feeder; State of the Art; Storage; Store; Streamer; Super Twist LCD; Super VGA; Super Video Graphics Array; SVGA; System; Tape Deck; Tape Streamer; Terminal; TFT; Thermal Printer; Thin-Film Transistor; Three and a Half; Touch Screen; Tracker Ball; VDT; VDU; VGA; Video Display Terminal; Video Graphics Array; Visual Display Terminal; Visual Display Unit; Webcam; Winchester Disk; XGA; Zip Drive;*

Device Driver
A program which converts another program commands into those used by a peripheral device. e.g. printer driver.
See Also: *API; Application Program Interface; ATAPI; Attachment Packet Interface; Code; CODEC; COmpressor DECompressor; Configuring; Device; DLL; Driver; Dynamic Link Library; EXE; Freeware; Function; Instruction Set; Macro; Module; Peripheral; Printer Driver; Program; Recording Device; Remote Device; Script; Software; Software Driver; System Software; Utility;*

DFD
Data Flow Diagram. A graphical representation of data and the processes performed on the data.
See Also: *Analyst; Audit Trail; B/A; Business Analyst; CASE; Case Tool; Computer Aided Software Engineering; Data; Data Element; Data Entity; Data Flow; Data Flow Diagram; Data Item; Data Model; Data Type; Design; Development; Event; Key; Model; Modular; O & M; Organisation & Methods; Process Model; S/A; Structured Design; Top Down Technique;*

Dial In
The process where a computer is dialled up by another computer or by a person to enable the transfer of data from one to the other via communication lines and modems.
See Also: *Access; Acoustic Coupler; ADN; ADSL; Advanced Digital Network; AMR; Anonymous FTP; Asymmetric Digital Subscriber Line; Asymmetrical Modem; Asynchronous; Asynchronous Transfer Mode; ATM; Automatic Message Routing; Bandwidth; Baud Rate; Bits Per Second; BPS; Broadband; CCITT; CCTA; Characters Per Second; Client Server Protocol; Communications; Consultative Committee International Telegraph and Telephone; CPS; Data Communications; Data Parity; Data Transmission; Datacoms; Dial Up; Digital; Duplex Transmission; ECP; Enhanced Parallel Port; EPP; Extended Capabilities Port; FDDI; Fibre Distributed Data Interface; Fibre Optics; Full Duplex; Gbps; Half Duplex; Handshake; HD; IM; Instant Messaging; Integrated Services Digital Network; ISDN; Kbps; Mbps; Modem; Modulator Demodulator; Multiplex; Multiplexer; Narrowband; Node; Online; Open Systems Interconnect; Optical Fibre; OSI; Parallel Transmission; Parity Bit; Serial Transmission; Simplex Transmission; Synchronous; Telecommunication; Telecoms; Teleprocessing System; TPS; Transfer Rate; Transmit; V90;*

Dial Up
The process where a computer is dialled up by another computer or by a person to enable the transfer of data from one to the other via communication lines and modems.
See Also: *Access; Acoustic Coupler; ADN; ADSL; Advanced Digital Network; AMR; Anonymous FTP; Asymmetric Digital Subscriber Line; Asymmetrical Modem; Asynchronous; Asynchronous Transfer Mode; ATM; Automatic Message Routing; Bandwidth; Baud Rate; Bits Per Second; BPS; Broadband; CCITT; CCTA; Characters Per Second; Client Server Protocol; Communications; Consultative Committee International Telegraph and Telephone; CPS; Data Communications; Data Parity; Data Transmission; Datacoms; Dial In; Digital; Duplex Transmission; ECP; Enhanced Parallel Port; EPP; Extended Capabilities Port; FDDI; Fibre Distributed Data Interface; Fibre Optics; Full Duplex; Gbps; Half Duplex; Handshake; HD; IM; Instant Messaging; Integrated Services Digital Network; ISDN; Kbps; Mbps; Modem; Modulator Demodulator; Multiplex; Multiplexer; Narrowband; Node; Online; Open Systems Interconnect; Optical Fibre; OSI; Parallel Transmission; Parity Bit; Serial Transmission; Simplex Transmission; Synchronous; Telecommunication; Telecoms; Teleprocessing System; TPS; Transfer Rate; Transmit; V90;*

Died
A term used when a computer system powers off for some reason or if the software has a fault and no longer runs.
See Also: *Abort; Crash; Dead Lock; Deadly Embrace; Downtime; General Protection Fault; GPF; Hangs; Head Crash; Hung; Machine Crash; Program Crash; System Hangs; Timeout;*

Digital
The representation, processing or transmission of data in a numerical form, usually binary.
See Also: *16 Bit; 32 Bit; 64 Bit; 8 Bit; Address Bus; ADN; ADSL; Advanced Digital Network; Analogue Digital Converter; Asymmetric Digital Subscriber Line; Asynchronous; Asynchronous Transfer Mode; ATM; Binary; Binary Digit; Bit; Bit Pattern; Bus; Channel; Communications; Data; Data Bus; Data Communications; Data Element; Data Entity; Data Item; Data Parity; Data Transmission; Data Type; Datacoms; Denary; Dial In; Dial Up; Digital Analog Converter; Digital Versatile Disk; Digital Video Interface; Direct Connection; Duplex Transmission; DVD; DVI; Eight Bit; FDDI; Fibre Distributed Data Interface; Fibre Optics; Full Duplex; Half Duplex; HD; Image Processing; Integrated Services Digital Network; ISDN; Leading Edge;*

Leased Line; Least Significant Bit; Local Bus; LSB; MIDI; Most Significant Bit; MSB; Multiplex; Multiplexer; Musical Instrument Digital Interface; Optical Fibre; Parallel Transmission; Parity Bit; Serial Transmission; Simplex Transmission; Sixteen Bit; Sixty Four Bit; State of the Art; Synchronous; System Bus; Thirty Two Bit; Transmission Channel; Transmit; V90;

Digital Analog Converter
A device which converts digital signals into analogue signals.
See Also: *Analogue; Analogue Digital Converter; Compatible; Conversion; Convert; Device; Digital; Equipment; Hardware; Kit; Peripheral; Printer;*

Digital Audio Tape
(DAT). A recording unit and also the medium on which information is digitally recorded in a high density.
See Also: *Archive; Backing Store; Backup; Bits Per Inch; Block; BPI; Configuration; DAT; Deck; Density; Device; Double Density; Drive; End of Tape; Environment; EOT; Equipment; Grandfather, Father, Son; Hardware; High Density; Installation; Kit; Mag Tape; Magnetic Tape; Mass Storage; Medium; Peripheral; Recording; Recording Device; Recording Medium; Save; Storage; Store; Tape Deck; Tape Streamer; Zip Drive;*

Digital Computer
A computer which operates with input converted to digital format.
See Also: *1st Generation; 2nd Generation; 3rd Generation; 4th Generation; Advanced Technology; Analogue Computer; AT; Compatible; Computer; Computer Power; Configuration; Cross Platform; Desktop; Distributed System/Network; Downsizing; EDS; Electronic Data System; Environment; Equipment; Extended Technology; Hardware; IBM (tm) Compatible; Information System; Information Technology; Installation; IS; IT; Kit; Laptop; Machine; Mainframe; Micro; Microcomputer; Midrange System; Minicomputer; Multi Platform; Notebook; Number Cruncher; OEM; Original Equipment Manufacturer; Palmtop Computer; PC; Personal Computer; Platform; Portable; Power; Standalone; Tower Computer; Turnkey; Voice Activated; XT;*

Digital Monitor
A visual display unit, terminal or screen which supports a fixed number of colours.
See Also: *Analogue Monitor; Anti Glare Screen; Cathode Ray Tube; CGA; Colour Graphics Adaptor; CRT; Device; Digital Video Interface; Display; DVI; EGA; Enhanced Graphic Adaptor; Environment; Equipment; Extended Video Array; Graphics Card; Hardware; High Resolution; Installation; Intelligent Terminal; Interlaced; Kit; LCD; Liquid Crystal Display; Low Resolution; Monitor; Monochrome; Paint Screen; Peripheral; Plasma Screen; Prompt; Resolution; Screen; Screen Burn; Split Screen; Super Twist LCD; Super VGA; Super Video Graphics Array; SVGA; Terminal; TFT; Thin-Film Transistor; Touch Screen; Twip; VDT; VDU; VGA; Video Card; Video Display Terminal; Video Graphics Array; Video Random Access Memory; Visual Display Terminal; Visual Display Unit; VRAM; XGA;*

Digital Versatile Disk
(DVD). A high speed, high capacity type of CD-ROM. Also refers to the drive that uses the disk.
See Also: *ATAPI; Attachment Packet Interface; Bits Per Inch; BPI; CD-ROM; CD-ROM Drive; CD-RW Drive; Computer Power; Configuration; Device; Digital; Drive; DVD; Equipment; Hardware; Heads; Installation; Kit; Mass Storage; Medium; Optical Disk; Optical Drive; Peripheral; Power; Read/Write Head; Recording Device; Recording Medium; Storage; Store;*

Digital Video Interface
(DVI). A digital interface between some TFT monitors and PCs which gives a better quality image on the screen.
See Also: *Accelerated Graphics Port; Advanced Graphics Port; AGP; Digital; Digital Monitor; Display; DVI; Graphics Card; High Resolution; Image Processing; Interface; Monitor; Screen; Video Card;*

DIMM
Dual Inline Memory Module. Two SD-RAM chips on the PC motherboard. The SD-RAM has 168 pins and the DDR-SD-RAM has 184 pins.
See Also: *Bubble Memory; Buffer; Cache Memory; CMOS; Complementary Metal Oxide Semiconductor Memory; Computer Power; Conventional Memory; Core; Core Dump; DDR SDRAM; Direct Memory Access; Direct Random Access Memory; Disk Cache; DMA; Double Data Rate SDRAM; DRAM; Dual Inline Memory Module; Dynamic Memory; Dynamically; EEROM; Electrically Erasable Read Only Memory;*

Electronically Programmed Read Only Memory; EMS; EPROM; Erasable Programmable Read Only Memory; Expanded Memory; Expanded Memory Specification; Expansion Card; Extended Memory; Flash Memory; High Memory; Magnetic Core; Memory; Memory Board; Memory Caching; Memory Card; Memory Resident; Mix; Power; Programmable Read Only Memory; PROM; RAM; RAM Disk; Rambus Dynamic Random Access Memory; Random Access Memory; RDRAM; Read Only Memory; ROM; SDRAM; Shadow RAM Memory; SIMM; Single Inline Memory Modules; Single Inline Package; SIP; Stack; Store; Swapping; Synchronous Dynamic Random Access Memory; Upper Memory; Video Random Access Memory; VRAM; Working Storage; Workspace;

DIP Switch
A series of switches on a peripheral device used to configure the device to specific settings. e.g. UK printing format on a printer.
See Also: *Bubble Jet; Compatible; Daisywheel; Dot Matrix; Inkjet; Letter Quality; LQ; Matrix Printer; Near Letter Quality; NLQ; Peripheral; Toggle;*

Direct Access
The procedure in which a record is read or written directly from/to a file using a key.
See Also: *Access; Access Time; Beginning of File; BOF; Database; DB; End of File; EOF; File; Index Sequential File; Indexed Sequential Access Method; ISAM; Key; Keyed Sequential Access Method; KSAM; R/W; Random Access; Random File; Read; Read/Write; Tag; Tag File; Write;*

Direct Connection
A direct connection to another computer or the Internet as opposed to a dialled-up connection.
See Also: *ADN; ADSL; Advanced Digital Network; AMR; Asymmetric Digital Subscriber Line; Asynchronous; Asynchronous Transfer Mode; ATM; Automatic Message Routing; Bandwidth; Broadband; CCITT; CCTA; Channel; Client Server Protocol; Communications; Consultative Committee International Telegraph and Telephone; Data Communications; Data Parity; Data Transmission; Datacoms; Digital; Duplex Transmission; ECP; Enhanced Parallel Port; EPP; Extended Capabilities Port; FDDI; Fibre Distributed Data Interface; Fibre Optics; Firewire; Full Duplex; Half Duplex; Handshake; HD; Integrated Services Digital Network; ISDN; Leased Line; Multiplex; Multiplexer; Narrowband; Node; Open Systems Interconnect; Optical Fibre; OSI; Parallel Transmission; Parity Bit; Serial Transmission; Simplex*

Transmission; Synchronous; Telecommunication; Telecoms; Teleprocessing System; TPS; Transmission Channel; Transmit; V90;

Direct Memory Access
(DMA). A process where data is retrieved from a storage device and transferred to the computer's memory without using the processor.
See Also: *Access; Bubble Memory; Buffer; Cache Memory; Conventional Memory; Core; DDR SDRAM; DIMM; Direct Random Access Memory; Disk Cache; DMA; Double Data Rate SDRAM; DRAM; Drive; Dual Inline Memory Module; Dynamic Memory; EEROM; EIDE; EISA; Electrically Erasable Read Only Memory; Electronically Programmed Read Only Memory; EMS; Enhanced Industry Standard Architecture; Enhanced Intelligent Drive Electronics; EPROM; Erasable Programmable Read Only Memory; Expanded Memory; Expanded Memory Specification; Extended Memory; Flash Memory; High Memory; Magnetic Core; Memory; Memory Caching; Programmable Read Only Memory; PROM; RAM; RAM Disk; Rambus Dynamic Random Access Memory; Random Access Memory; RDRAM; Read Only Memory; ROM; SDRAM; Shadow RAM Memory; SIMM; Single Inline Memory Modules; Single Inline Package; SIP; Storage; Store; Synchronous Dynamic Random Access Memory; Volatile Memory; Working Storage; Workspace; Zero Wait State;*

Direct Random Access Memory
(DRAM). Memory in which data is transferred to and from directly using an Input/Output channel.
See Also: *Bubble Memory; Buffer; Cache Memory; CMOS; Complementary Metal Oxide Semiconductor Memory; Computer Power; Conventional Memory; Core; Core Dump; DDR SDRAM; DIMM; Direct Memory Access; Disk Cache; DMA; Double Data Rate SDRAM; DRAM; Dual Inline Memory Module; Dynamic Memory; Dynamically; EEROM; Electrically Erasable Read Only Memory; Electronically Programmed Read Only Memory; EMS; EPROM; Erasable Programmable Read Only Memory; Expanded Memory; Expanded Memory Specification; Extended Memory; Flash Memory; High Memory; Magnetic Core; Memory; Memory Board; Memory Caching; Memory Card; Memory Resident; Mix; Power; Programmable Read Only Memory; PROM; RAM; RAM Disk; Rambus Dynamic Random Access Memory; Random Access Memory; RDRAM; Read Only Memory; ROM; SDRAM; Shadow RAM Memory; SIMM; Single Inline Memory Modules; Single Inline Package; SIP; Stack; Store; Swapping; Synchronous Dynamic Random Access Memory; Upper Memory; Video Random Access Memory; VRAM; Working Storage; Workspace;*

Directory
An index of files on a storage medium.
See Also: *3.5 Inch; 5.25 Inch; C Prompt; CD-ROM; Disk; Disk Pack; Disk Storage; Diskette; FAT; Fiche; File; File Allocation Table; Five and a quarter; Floppy Disk; Folder; Magnetic Disk; Microfiche; Optical Disk; Pack; Path; Recording Medium; Root Directory; Storage; Sub Directory; Three and a Half; Volume;*

Disk
(1) The storage medium whose surfaces are covered with a magnetic material on which information is recorded. (2) The device in which the storage medium is used.
See Also: *3.5 Inch; 5.25 Inch; Archive; ATAPI; Attachment Packet Interface; Backing Store; Backup; Bits Per Inch; Block; Boot Disk; BPI; Cluster; Computer Power; Configuration; Crash; Cylinder; Defragment; Density; Device; Directory; Disk Drive; Disk Map; Disk Operating System; Disk Pack; Disk Size; Disk Storage; Diskette; DOS; Double Density; Drive; EIDE; EISA; Enhanced Industry Standard Architecture; Enhanced Intelligent Drive Electronics; Equipment; FDD; Five and a quarter; Fixed Disk Drive; Floppy Disk; Floppy Disk Drive; Format; Fragmentation; Grandfather, Father, Son; Hard Disk Drive; Hardware; HDD; Head Crash; Heads; High Density; IDE; Indexed Sequential Access Method; Integrated Drive Electronics; ISAM; Keyed Sequential Access Method; Kit; KSAM; Machine Crash; Magnetic Disk; Mass Storage; Medium; Pack; Path; Peripheral; Power; Read/Write Head; Recording; Recording Device; Recording Medium; Root Directory; Save; Sector; Seek Time; Storage; Store; Sub Directory; Three and a Half; Track; Volume; Winchester Disk; Wipe; Write; Write Protect;*

Disk Cache
The memory within a computer used as a buffer to improve the speed of data transfer to and from disk devices and the processor.
See Also: *Absolute Address; Address; Array; Block; Bubble Memory; Buffer; Cache Memory; Clipboard; Computer Power; Conventional Memory; Core; Core Dump; DDR SDRAM; DIMM; Direct Memory Access; Direct Random Access Memory; DMA; Double Data Rate SDRAM; DRAM; Dual Inline Memory Module; Dynamic Memory; Dynamically; EEROM; Electrically Erasable Read Only Memory; Electronically Programmed Read Only Memory; EMS; EPROM; Erasable Programmable Read Only Memory; Expanded Memory; Expanded Memory Specification; Extended Memory; Flash Memory; High Memory; Magnetic Core; Memory; Memory Caching; Memory Resident; Mix; Power; Programmable Read Only Memory; PROM;*

RAM; RAM Disk; Rambus Dynamic Random Access Memory; Random Access Memory; RDRAM; Read Only Memory; Relative Address; ROM; SDRAM; Shadow RAM Memory; SIMM; Single Inline Memory Modules; Single Inline Package; SIP; Store; Synchronous Dynamic Random Access Memory; Upper Memory; Video Random Access Memory; Volatile Memory; VRAM; Working Storage; Workspace;

Disk Drive

A storage device which uses magnetic disk that can be of a fixed or exchangeable type.

See Also: *3.5 Inch; 5.25 Inch; Archive; ATAPI; Attachment Packet Interface; Backing Store; Backup; C Prompt; Computer Power; Configuration; Crash; Device; Disk; Disk Pack; Disk Size; Disk Storage; Diskette; Drive; EIDE; EISA; Enhanced Industry Standard Architecture; Enhanced Intelligent Drive Electronics; Equipment; FDD; Five and a quarter; Fixed Disk Drive; Floppy Disk; Floppy Disk Drive; Hard Disk Drive; Hardware; HDD; Head Crash; Heads; I/O; IDE; Input/Output; Integrated Drive Electronics; Kit; Machine Crash; Magnetic Disk; Mass Storage; Pack; Peripheral; Power; Read/Write Head; Recording; Recording Device; Save; Seek Time; Storage; Store; Three and a Half; Winchester Disk; Write; Write Protect;*

Disk Map

A graphical representation of the areas allocated on a disk showing used, unused and bad areas.

See Also: *3.5 Inch; 5.25 Inch; Cluster; Defragment; Disk; Disk Pack; Disk Storage; Diskette; Five and a quarter; Floppy Disk; Format; Fragmentation; Graphics; Image Map; Image Processing; Magnetic Disk; Pack; Three and a Half; Volume;*

Disk Operating System

(DOS). An operating system for a computer where the operating system programs reside on disk. Some of the programs are loaded into memory when the computer is switched on or reset.

See Also: *API; Application Program Interface; Basic Input Output System; BIOS; Boot; Boot Disk; Bootstrap; C Prompt; Cold Start; Configuration; Disk; Disk Pack; Diskette; DOS; Environment; FAT; File Allocation Table; Floppy Disk; Graphical User Interface; GUI; High Memory; Housekeeping; Installation; Linux; Magnetic Disk; Network Operating System; NOS; Open System; Operating System; OS; OS/2; Pack; Re-boot; Software; System Software; UNIX; Upper Memory; Warm Start;*

Disk Pack

The exchangeable magnetic disk used in a disk drive.

See Also: *3.5 Inch; 5.25 Inch; Archive; ATAPI; Attachment Packet Interface; Backing Store; Backup; Bits Per Inch; Block; Boot Disk; BPI; Cluster; Computer Power; Configuration; Crash; Cylinder; Defragment; Density; Device; Directory; Disk; Disk Drive; Disk Map; Disk Operating System; Disk Size; Disk Storage; Diskette; DOS; Double Density; Drive; Equipment; FDD; Five and a quarter; Fixed Disk Drive; Floppy Disk; Floppy Disk Drive; Format; Fragmentation; Grandfather, Father, Son; Hard Disk Drive; Hardware; HDD; Head Crash; Heads; High Density; Indexed Sequential Access Method; ISAM; Keyed Sequential Access Method; Kit; KSAM; Machine Crash; Magnetic Disk; Mass Storage; Medium; Pack; Peripheral; Power; Read/Write Head; Recording; Recording Device; Recording Medium; Root Directory; Save; Sector; Seek Time; Storage; Store; Sub Directory; Three and a Half; Track; Volume; Winchester Disk; Wipe; Write; Write Protect;*

Disk Size

(1) The volume of information which can be stored on a disk. e.g. 1.2Mb. (2) The physical size of the storage medium or unit. e.g. 3.5 inch.

See Also: *3.5 Inch; 5.25 Inch; Backing Store; Computer Power; Configuration; Cylinder; Density; Device; Disk; Disk Drive; Disk Pack; Disk Storage; Diskette; Double Density; FDD; Five and a quarter; Fixed Disk Drive; Floppy Disk; Floppy Disk Drive; Hard Disk Drive; HDD; High Density; Magnetic Disk; Mass Storage; Medium; Pack; Peripheral; Power; Recording Medium; Storage; Store; Three and a Half; Volume; Winchester Disk;*

Disk Storage

(1) The medium on which information is recorded. (2) The device in which the medium is used.

See Also: *3.5 Inch; 5.25 Inch; Archive; ATAPI; Attachment Packet Interface; Backing Store; Backup; Bits Per Inch; Block; Boot Disk; BPI; Cluster; Computer Power; Configuration; Crash; Cylinder; Defragment; Density; Device; Directory; Disk; Disk Drive; Disk Map; Disk Pack; Disk Size; Diskette; Double Density; Drive; EIDE; EISA; Enhanced Industry Standard Architecture; Enhanced Intelligent Drive Electronics; Equipment; FDD; Five and a quarter; Fixed Disk Drive; Floppy Disk; Floppy Disk Drive; Format; Fragmentation; Grandfather, Father, Son; Hard Disk Drive; Hardware; HDD; Head Crash; Heads; High Density; IDE; Indexed Sequential Access Method; Integrated Drive Electronics; ISAM; Keyed Sequential Access Method; Kit; KSAM; Machine Crash; Magnetic Disk; Mass Storage; Medium; Pack; Peripheral; Power;*

Read/Write Head; Recording; Recording Device; Recording Medium; Remote Device; Root Directory; Save; Sector; Security; Seek Time; Storage; Store; Sub Directory; System; Three and a Half; Track; Volume; Winchester Disk; Wipe; Write; Write Protect;

Diskette

A floppy disk. The recording medium used in disk drives.

See Also: *3.5 Inch; 5.25 Inch; Archive; ATAPI; Attachment Packet Interface; Backing Store; Backup; Bits Per Inch; Block; Boot Disk; BPI; Cluster; Computer Power; Configuration; Crash; Cylinder; Defragment; Density; Device; Directory; Disk; Disk Drive; Disk Map; Disk Operating System; Disk Pack; Disk Size; Disk Storage; DOS; Double Density; EIDE; Enhanced Intelligent Drive Electronics; Equipment; FDD; Five and a quarter; Fixed Disk Drive; Floppy Disk; Floppy Disk Drive; Format; Fragmentation; Grandfather, Father, Son; Hard Disk Drive; Hardware; HDD; Head Crash; Heads; High Density; Indexed Sequential Access Method; ISAM; Keyed Sequential Access Method; Kit; KSAM; Machine Crash; Magnetic Disk; Mass Storage; Medium; Pack; Peripheral; Power; Read/Write Head; Recording; Recording Device; Recording Medium; Root Directory; Save; Sector; Seek Time; Storage; Store; Sub Directory; Three and a Half; Track; Volume; Winchester Disk; Wipe; Write; Write Protect;*

Display

(1) A visual display unit, monitor or terminal. (2) The data displayed on the screen.

See Also: *Analogue Monitor; Anti Glare Screen; BitMaP; BMP; Browser; Cathode Ray Tube; CGA; CODEC; Colour Graphics Adaptor; COmpressor DECompressor; CRT; Cursor; Device; Digital Monitor; Digital Video Interface; Drop-Down Menu; Dump; DVI; EGA; Enhanced Graphic Adaptor; Environment; Equipment; Extended Video Array; Frame Rate; GIF; Graphical Interchange Format; Graphical User Interface; Graphics; Graphics Card; GUI; Hardware; High Resolution; Image Processing; Installation; Intelligent Terminal; Interlaced; Joint Photographic Experts Group; JPEG; JPG; Kit; LCD; Liquid Crystal Display; Low Resolution; Marquee; Menu; Monitor; Monochrome; Output; Paint Screen; Peripheral; Pixel; Plasma Screen; Pop Up Menu; Prompt; Pull Down Menu; Resolution; Screen; Screen Burn; Screen Dump; Scroll; Split Screen; Sprite; Super Twist LCD; Super VGA; Super Video Graphics Array; SVGA; Terminal; TFT; Thin-Film Transistor; Toolbar; Touch Screen; Twip; VDT; VDU; VGA; Video Card; Video Display Terminal; Video Graphics Array; Video Random Access*

Memory; Visual Display Terminal; Visual Display Unit; VRAM; WIMP; Windows Icons Mice and Pull-down menus; WYSIWYG; XGA;

Distributed System/Network
A computer system which has remote computers connected to a main processing unit. Each remote computer can have their own remote computers connected to them thus making a distributed system/network.
See Also: *AMR; Analogue Computer; Automatic Message Routing; BBS; Bulletin Board System; Client Server; Client Server Protocol; Computer; Data Centre; Data Processing; Digital Computer; DP; EDP; EDS; Electronic Data Processing; Electronic Data System; Environment; Equipment; Ethernet; File Server; Front End Processor; Gateway; Hardware; Host Processor; Information System; Information Technology; Intranet; IS; IT; Kit; LAN; Local Area Network; Machine; Micro; Microcomputer; Midrange System; Minicomputer; Multi Platform; Network; Network Information Centre; Network Operating System; NIC; Node; NOS; Open System; Point of Sales; POS; Remote Device; Ring Network; Server; Star Cluster; Star Network; System; Teleprocessing System; Token Ring; TPS; Turnkey; WAN; Wide Area Network;*

DLL
Dynamic Link Library. A program that has common processes which can be used by different applications. It remains as a separate program module and used when required.
See Also: *API; Applet; Application Program Interface; Call; Chain; Code; CODEC; COmpressor DECompressor; Daemon; Device Driver; Driver; Dynamic Link Library; EXE; Firmware; Freeware; Function; Instruction; Instruction Set; Invoke; Macro; Module; Nesting; Program; Script; Software Driver; Subroutine; System Software; Terminate and Stay Resident; TSR; Utility;*

DMA
Direct Memory Access. A process where data is retrieved from a storage device and transferred to the computer's memory without using the processor.
See Also: *Access; Bubble Memory; Buffer; Cache Memory; Conventional Memory; Core; DDR SDRAM; DIMM; Direct Memory Access; Direct Random Access Memory; Disk Cache; Double Data Rate SDRAM; DRAM; Drive; Dual Inline Memory Module; Dynamic Memory; EEROM; EIDE; EISA; Electrically Erasable Read Only Memory; Electronically Programmed Read Only Memory; EMS; Enhanced Industry Standard Architecture; Enhanced Intelligent Drive Electronics; EPROM; Erasable*

Programmable Read Only Memory; Expanded Memory; Expanded Memory Specification; Extended Memory; Flash Memory; High Memory; Magnetic Core; Memory; Memory Caching; Programmable Read Only Memory; PROM; RAM; RAM Disk; Rambus Dynamic Random Access Memory; Random Access Memory; RDRAM; Read Only Memory; ROM; SDRAM; Shadow RAM Memory; SIMM; Single Inline Memory Modules; Single Inline Package; SIP; Storage; Store; Synchronous Dynamic Random Access Memory; Volatile Memory; Working Storage; Workspace; Zero Wait State;

DNS

Domain Name System. A system that translates a domain name into an IP Address which is used by the Internet to access that address.

See Also: *Address; Anchor; CERN; Conseil Europeen pour la Recherche Nucleaire; Cybercafe; Cyberspace; Domain Name; Domain Name Server; Domain Name System; E-mail Address; Hit; Home Page; Host; Internet; Internet Protocol Address; Internet Service Provider; IP Address; ISP; Net; Provider; Service Provider; Site; The Net; The Web; Universal/Uniform Resource Locator; URL; Webhost; Webring; Website; World Wide Web; WWW;*

Document

A file recorded in a word processing system containing text. e.g. a letter.

See Also: *ASCII Files; Attachment; Beginning of File; BOF; Edit; End of File; EOF; File; Mail Merge; Spell Check;*

Domain Name

The unique name that identifies an Internet site. The last part of the name after the dot indicates a logical or geographical location, e.g. .gov=government dept, .uk=United Kingdom.

See Also: *Address; Anchor; CERN; Conseil Europeen pour la Recherche Nucleaire; Cybercafe; Cyberspace; DNS; Domain Name Server; Domain Name System; E-mail Address; Hit; Home Page; Host; Internet; Internet Protocol Address; Internet Service Provider; IP Address; ISP; Net; Provider; Service Provider; Site; The Net; The Web; Universal/Uniform Resource Locator; URL; Webhost; Webring; Website; World Wide Web; WWW;*

Domain Name Server

Computers connected to the Internet which track and convert Domain Names to the equivalent numeric IP Addresses.

See Also: *Address; CGI; Client Server; Client Server Protocol; Common Gateway Interface; Cybercafe; Cyberspace; DNS; Domain Name;*

Domain Name System; Host; Host Processor; Internet; Internet Protocol; Internet Protocol Address; Internet Service Provider; IP; IP Address; ISP; Net; Provider; Proxy Server; Server; Service Provider; Site; The Net; The Web; Universal/Uniform Resource Locator; URL; Webhost; Webring; Website; World Wide Web; WWW;

Domain Name System
(DNS). A system that translates a domain name into an IP Address which is used by the Internet to access that address.
See Also: *Address; Anchor; CERN; Conseil Europeen pour la Recherche Nucleaire; Cybercafe; Cyberspace; DNS; Domain Name; Domain Name Server; E-mail Address; Hit; Home Page; Host; Internet; Internet Protocol Address; Internet Service Provider; IP Address; ISP; Net; Provider; Service Provider; Site; The Net; The Web; Universal/Uniform Resource Locator; URL; Webhost; Webring; Website; World Wide Web; WWW;*

Dongle
An electronic device which is connected to one of the computer ports, normally the printer port, and is programmed to allow the authorised use of software which only runs when the dongle is installed.
See Also: *Black Box; Configuring; Device; Parallel Port; Peripheral; Port; Security; Serial Port;*

DOS
Disk Operating System. An operating system for a computer where the operating system programs reside on disk. Some of the programs are loaded into memory when the computer is initialised.
See Also: *API; Application Program Interface; Basic Input Output System; BIOS; Boot; Boot Disk; Bootstrap; C Prompt; Cold Start; Configuration; Disk; Disk Operating System; Disk Pack; Diskette; Environment; FAT; File Allocation Table; Floppy Disk; Graphical User Interface; GUI; High Memory; Housekeeping; Installation; Linux; Magnetic Disk; Network Operating System; NOS; Open System; Operating System; OS; OS/2; Pack; Re-boot; Software; System Software; UNIX; Upper Memory; Warm Start;*

Dot
The full stop in an Internet address.
See Also: *Address; E-mail Address; Internet; Net; The Net; Universal/Uniform Resource Locator; URL;*

Dot Matrix
A printer in which printing is achieved by a matrix of pins on the print head that form the characters. The characters are transferred to paper by the pins pushing against a ribbon.
See Also: *Barrel Printer; Bi Directional; Bubble Jet; Configuration; Cut Sheet Feeder; Daisywheel; Device; DIP Switch; Dots Per Inch; DPI; Drum Printer; Duplex Printing; Environment; Equipment; Font Cartridge; Hard Copy; Hardware; Inkjet; Installation; Kit; Landscape; Laser Jet; Laser Printer; LCD Printer; Letter Quality; Line Printer; Lines Per Minute; Liquid Crystal Display Printer; Lpm; LPT Port; LQ; Matrix Printer; Near Letter Quality; NLQ; Page Printer; Pages Per Minute; Peripheral; Portrait; Postscript; PPM; Printer; Printer Driver; Printout; Sheet Feeder; Simplex Printing; Thermal Printer;*

Dots Per Inch
(DPI). The number of dots per inch which make up printed characters, pictures or graphics.
See Also: *Character; Characters Per Inch; CPI; Dot Matrix; DPI; Format; Letter Quality; LQ; Matrix Printer; Near Letter Quality; NLQ; Output;*

Double Data Rate SDRAM
(DDR SDRAM). Very fast memory that reads and writes at the rising and falling edges of the system clock thus doubling data throughput.
See Also: *Bubble Memory; Buffer; Cache Memory; CMOS; Complementary Metal Oxide Semiconductor Memory; Computer Power; Conventional Memory; Core; Core Dump; DDR SDRAM; DIMM; Direct Memory Access; Direct Random Access Memory; Disk Cache; DMA; DRAM; Dual Inline Memory Module; Dynamic Memory; Dynamically; EEROM; Electrically Erasable Read Only Memory; Electronically Programmed Read Only Memory; EMS; EPROM; Erasable Programmable Read Only Memory; Expanded Memory; Expanded Memory Specification; Extended Memory; Flash Memory; High Memory; Magnetic Core; Memory; Memory Board; Memory Caching; Memory Card; Memory Resident; Mix; Power; Programmable Read Only Memory; PROM; RAM; RAM Disk; Rambus Dynamic Random Access Memory; Random Access Memory; RDRAM; Read Only Memory; ROM; SDRAM; Shadow RAM Memory; SIMM; Single Inline Memory Modules; Single Inline Package; SIP; Stack; Store; Swapping; Synchronous Dynamic Random Access Memory; Upper Memory; Video Random Access Memory; VRAM; Working Storage; Workspace;*

Double Density
A disk medium which can record twice as much information in the same area as a single density disk.
See Also: *3.5 Inch; 5.25 Inch; Bits Per Inch; BPI; Compression; DAT; Decompression; Density; Digital Audio Tape; Disk; Disk Pack; Disk Size; Disk Storage; Diskette; Five and a quarter; Floppy Disk; High Density; Mag Tape; Magnetic Disk; Magnetic Tape; Mass Storage; Medium; Pack; Packed Data; Recording Medium; Storage; Streamer; Tape Streamer; Three and a Half; Volume; Winchester Disk;*

Download
The transfer of data or files from a remote computer to a local computer.
See Also: *Acoustic Coupler; Attachment; BBS; Bulletin Board System; EFT; EFTPOS; Electronic Fund Transfer; Electronic Fund Transfer Point of Sales; File Server; MP3; Point of Sales; POS; Stream; TCP/IP; Telecommunication; Telecoms; Transmission Control Protocol/Internet Protocol; Transmit; Upload;*

Downsizing
A term used when organisations reduce their computer processing power by changing to less powerful equipment and software. In some cases to achieve the same results.
See Also: *Bloatware; Computer; Cross Platform; Desktop; Digital Computer; Equipment; Facilities Management; FM; Hand Held Device; Hardware; IBM (tm) Compatible; In-house; Kit; Laptop; Machine; Micro; Microcomputer; Midrange System; Minicomputer; Notebook; Outsourcing; Palmtop Computer; PC; Personal Computer; Platform; Portable; Standalone; Tower Computer; Turnkey;*

Downtime
The period of time when a computer is not in operation due to failure or maintenance.
See Also: *Abort; Bug; Crash; Debug; Debugger; Died; General Protection Fault; GPF; Head Crash; Machine Crash; Maintenance; Mean Time Between Failure; MTBF; Off Line; Program Crash; System Hangs; Third Party Maintenance;*

DP
Data Processing. The manipulation, analysis and storage of data on a computer.
See Also: *Audit Trail; Batch Processing; Bespoke; CAD; CADCAM; CADMAT; CAE; CAI; CAM; CBT; Computation; Compute; Computer Aided Design; Computer Aided Design and Manufacturing; Computer*

Aided Design Manufacture and Test; Computer Aided Engineering; Computer Aided Instruction; Computer Aided Manufacturing; Computer Based Training; Data Base Management System; Data Centre; Data Processing; DBMS; Desk Top Publishing; Distributed System/Network; DTP; E-commerce; EDI; EDP; EFT; EFTPOS; Electronic Data Interchange; Electronic Data Processing; Electronic Fund Transfer; Electronic Fund Transfer Point of Sales; Expert System; Facilities Management; FM; Geographical Information System; GIS; Information System; Information Technology; IS; IT; Job; Multitasking; Office Information System; OIS; Outsourcing; Processing; RDBMS/RDMS; Relational Database Management System; Run; Run Time; Software System; Spreadsheet; Teleprocessing System; TPS; Vertical Market; Word Processor; WP;

DPI
Dots Per Inch. The number of dots per inch which make up printed characters, pictures or graphics.
See Also: *Character; Characters Per Inch; CPI; Dot Matrix; Dots Per Inch; Format; Letter Quality; LQ; Matrix Printer; Near Letter Quality; NLQ; Output;*

DPM
Data Processing Manager. A person who manages a computer department.
See Also: *A/P; Analyst; Analyst Programmer; B/A; Business Analyst; Contractor; Data Base Analyst; Data Processing Manager; DBA; Programmer; S/A; S/P; System Analyst; Systems Programmer; Technical Author;*

Drag
The process of moving an object on the screen from one location to another by clicking on it with the mouse button and moving the mouse while keeping the mouse button depressed.
See Also: *Click; Floating Toolbar; Graphics; Icon; Image Processing; Mouse; Scroll; Sprite; Toolbar;*

DRAM
Direct Random Access Memory. Memory in which data is transferred to and from directly using an Input/Output channel.
See Also: *Bubble Memory; Buffer; Cache Memory; CMOS; Complementary Metal Oxide Semiconductor Memory; Computer Power; Conventional Memory; Core; Core Dump; DDR SDRAM; DIMM; Direct Memory Access; Direct Random Access Memory; Disk Cache; DMA;*

Double Data Rate SDRAM; Dual Inline Memory Module; Dynamic Memory; Dynamically; EEROM; Electrically Erasable Read Only Memory; Electronically Programmed Read Only Memory; EMS; EPROM; Erasable Programmable Read Only Memory; Expanded Memory; Expanded Memory Specification; Extended Memory; Flash Memory; High Memory; Magnetic Core; Memory; Memory Board; Memory Caching; Memory Card; Memory Resident; Mix; Power; Programmable Read Only Memory; PROM; RAM; RAM Disk; Rambus Dynamic Random Access Memory; Random Access Memory; RDRAM; Read Only Memory; ROM; SDRAM; Shadow RAM Memory; SIMM; Single Inline Memory Modules; Single Inline Package; SIP; Stack; Store; Swapping; Synchronous Dynamic Random Access Memory; Upper Memory; Video Random Access Memory; VRAM; Working Storage; Workspace;

Drive
A peripheral device used for recording or retrieving information. e.g. disk or tape.
See Also: *3.5 Inch; 5.25 Inch; Access; Archive; ATAPI; Attachment Packet Interface; Backing Store; Backup; CD-ROM Drive; CD-RW Drive; Computer Power; Configuration; DAT; Deck; Device; Digital Audio Tape; Digital Versatile Disk; Direct Memory Access; Disk; Disk Drive; Disk Pack; Disk Storage; DMA; DVD; EIDE; EISA; Enhanced Industry Standard Architecture; Enhanced Intelligent Drive Electronics; Equipment; FDD; Five and a quarter; Fixed Disk Drive; Floppy Disk Drive; Hard Disk Drive; Hardware; HDD; IDE; Integrated Drive Electronics; Kit; Magnetic Disk; Optical Drive; Pack; Peripheral; Power; Recording Device; Remote Device; Save; Storage; Store; Streamer; Tape Deck; Tape Streamer; Three and a Half; Winchester Disk; Zip Drive;*

Driver
A program used by the operating system which converts another program's commands into those used by a hardware device. e.g. printer.
See Also: *API; Application Program Interface; ATAPI; Attachment Packet Interface; Code; CODEC; COmpressor DECompressor; Configuring; Device Driver; DLL; Dynamic Link Library; EXE; Freeware; Function; Instruction Set; Macro; Module; Printer Driver; Program; Software; Software Driver; System Software; Utility;*

Drop-Down Menu
A list of items on the screen from which to choose. It is activated by entering specific control codes from the keyboard or with a mouse.
See Also: *Click; Display; Hot Key; Instruction; Keyboard; Menu; Mouse; Pop Up Menu; Pull Down Menu; Toolbar; User Friendly;*

Drum
The drum unit in a laser printer which is positively charged by a beam of light to build up the print format before it is transferred to the paper.
See Also: *CCD; Charge Coupled Device; Flatbed Scanner; Optical Scanner; Scanner;*

Drum Printer
A line printer whose mechanism includes a barrel shaped component with characters, numbers and symbols embossed on the outside. Next to the barrel is an ink ribbon and paper. Print hammers hit the paper resulting in printed characters being transferred to the paper from the barrel through the ink ribbon.
See Also: *Barrel Printer; Bubble Jet; Configuration; Daisywheel; Device; Dot Matrix; Duplex Printing; Environment; Equipment; Hard Copy; Hardware; Inkjet; Installation; Kit; Laser Jet; Laser Printer; LCD Printer; Line Printer; Lines Per Minute; Liquid Crystal Display Printer; Lpm; LPT Port; Matrix Printer; Page Printer; Pages Per Minute; Peripheral; PPM; Printer; Printer Driver; Printout; Simplex Printing; Thermal Printer;*

DTP
Desk Top Publishing. Software which is used to produce professional looking documentation with graphic designs.
See Also: *Application; Bespoke; CAD; CADCAM; CADMAT; CAE; CAI; CAM; CBT; Clip Art; Computer Aided Design; Computer Aided Design and Manufacturing; Computer Aided Design Manufacture and Test; Computer Aided Engineering; Computer Aided Instruction; Computer Aided Manufacturing; Computer Based Training; Data Processing; Desk Top Publishing; DP; EDP; EDS; Electronic Data Processing; Electronic Data System; Graphics; Image Map; Image Processing; Information System; Information Technology; IS; IT; Office Information System; OIS; Package; Program; Shareware; Software; Software Package; Software System; Turnkey; Vertical Market; Word Processor; WP;*

Dual Inline Memory Module
(DIMM). Two SD-RAM chips on the PC motherboard. The SD-RAM has 168 pins and the DDR-SD-RAM has 184 pins.
See Also: *Bubble Memory; Buffer; Cache Memory; CMOS; Complementary Metal Oxide Semiconductor Memory; Computer Power; Conventional Memory; Core; Core Dump; DDR SDRAM; DIMM; Direct Memory Access; Direct Random Access Memory; Disk Cache; DMA; Double Data Rate SDRAM; DRAM; Dynamic Memory; Dynamically; EEROM; Electrically Erasable Read Only Memory; Electronically Programmed Read Only Memory; EMS; EPROM; Erasable Programmable Read Only Memory; Expanded Memory; Expanded Memory Specification; Expansion Card; Extended Memory; Flash Memory; High Memory; Magnetic Core; Memory; Memory Board; Memory Caching; Memory Card; Memory Resident; Mix; Power; Programmable Read Only Memory; PROM; RAM; RAM Disk; Rambus Dynamic Random Access Memory; Random Access Memory; RDRAM; Read Only Memory; ROM; SDRAM; Shadow RAM Memory; SIMM; Single Inline Memory Modules; Single Inline Package; SIP; Stack; Store; Swapping; Synchronous Dynamic Random Access Memory; Upper Memory; Video Random Access Memory; VRAM; Working Storage; Workspace;*

Dump
(1) A display or printout of the computers memory. (2) To dump the computer's memory onto a screen or printout.
See Also: *Address; Block; Bubble Memory; Buffer; Cache Memory; Conventional Memory; Core; Core Dump; Display; Flash Memory; Magnetic Core; Memory; Operand; Printout; Screen Dump; Store;*

Duplex Printing
Printing on both sides of the paper.
See Also: *Barrel Printer; Bi Directional; Bubble Jet; Daisywheel; Dot Matrix; Drum Printer; Hard Copy; Inkjet; Laser Jet; Laser Printer; LCD Printer; Letter Quality; Line Printer; Liquid Crystal Display Printer; LQ; Matrix Printer; Near Letter Quality; NLQ; Output; Page Printer; Pages Per Minute; PPM; Printer; Printer Driver; Printout; Simplex Printing; Thermal Printer;*

Duplex Transmission
The simultaneous transmission of data in both directions along a communication line.
See Also: *ACK; Acoustic Coupler; ADN; ADSL; Advanced Digital Network; AMR; Asymmetric Digital Subscriber Line; Asymmetrical*

Modem; Asynchronous; Asynchronous Transfer Mode; ATM; Automatic Message Routing; Bandwidth; Baud Rate; Bits Per Second; BPS; Broadband; Bus; CCITT; CCTA; Channel; Characters Per Second; Communications; Consultative Committee International Telegraph and Telephone; CPS; Data Communications; Data Parity; Data Transmission; Datacoms; Dial In; Dial Up; Digital; Direct Connection; FDDI; Fibre Distributed Data Interface; Fibre Optics; Firewire; Full Duplex; Gbps; Half Duplex; HD; Integrated Services Digital Network; ISDN; Kbps; Leased Line; Mbps; Modem; Modulator Demodulator; Multiplex; Multiplexer; Narrowband; Open Systems Interconnect; Optical Fibre; OSI; Packet; Packet Switching; Parallel Transmission; Parity Bit; Serial Interface; Serial Transmission; Simplex Transmission; Synchronous; Telecommunication; Telecoms; Transfer Rate; Transmission Channel; Transmit; V90;

DVD

Digital Versatile Disk. (1) A high speed, high capacity CD-ROM. (2) A high speed, type of CD-ROM drive. Also refers to the drive that uses the disk.

See Also: *ATAPI; Attachment Packet Interface; Bits Per Inch; BPI; CD-ROM; CD-ROM Drive; CD-RW Drive; Computer Power; Configuration; Device; Digital; Digital Versatile Disk; Drive; Equipment; Hardware; Heads; Installation; Kit; Mass Storage; Medium; Optical Disk; Optical Drive; Peripheral; Power; Read/Write Head; Recording Device; Recording Medium; Storage; Store;*

DVI

Digital Video Interface. A digital interface between some TFT monitors and PCs which gives a better quality image on the screen.

See Also: *Accelerated Graphics Port; Advanced Graphics Port; AGP; Digital; Digital Monitor; Digital Video Interface; Display; Graphics Card; High Resolution; Image Processing; Interface; Monitor; Screen; Video Card;*

Dynamic Link Library

(DLL). A program that has common processes which can be used by different applications. It remains as a separate program module and used when required.

See Also: *API; Applet; Application Program Interface; Call; Chain; Code; CODEC; COmpressor DECompressor; Daemon; Device Driver; DLL; Driver; EXE; Firmware; Freeware; Function; Instruction; Instruction Set; Invoke; Macro; Module; Nesting; Program; Script;*

Software Driver; Subroutine; System Software; Terminate and Stay Resident; TSR; Utility;

Dynamic Memory
Memory used on a temporary basis where data stored is re-read almost immediately for further processing. The contents of the memory disappear in a short period of time.
See Also: *Bubble Memory; Buffer; Cache Memory; CMOS; Complementary Metal Oxide Semiconductor Memory; Computer Power; Conventional Memory; Core; Core Dump; DDR SDRAM; DIMM; Direct Memory Access; Direct Random Access Memory; Disk Cache; DMA; Double Data Rate SDRAM; DRAM; Dual Inline Memory Module; Dynamically; EEROM; Electrically Erasable Read Only Memory; Electronically Programmed Read Only Memory; EMS; EPROM; Erasable Programmable Read Only Memory; Expanded Memory; Expanded Memory Specification; Extended Memory; Flash Memory; High Memory; Magnetic Core; Memory; Memory Board; Memory Caching; Memory Card; Memory Resident; Mix; Power; Programmable Read Only Memory; PROM; RAM; RAM Disk; Rambus Dynamic Random Access Memory; Random Access Memory; RDRAM; Read Only Memory; ROM; SDRAM; Shadow RAM Memory; SIMM; Single Inline Memory Modules; Single Inline Package; SIP; Stack; Store; Swapping; Synchronous Dynamic Random Access Memory; Upper Memory; Video Random Access Memory; VRAM; Working Storage; Workspace;*

Dynamically
A state where data is transferred from one program to another or where operations are performed on data in memory.
See Also: *Bubble Memory; Bubble Sort; Buffer; Cache Memory; Conventional Memory; Core; Core Dump; DDR SDRAM; DIMM; Direct Random Access Memory; Disk Cache; Double Data Rate SDRAM; DRAM; Dual Inline Memory Module; Dynamic Memory; EEROM; Electrically Erasable Read Only Memory; Electronically Programmed Read Only Memory; EMS; EPROM; Erasable Programmable Read Only Memory; Expanded Memory; Expanded Memory Specification; Extended Memory; Flash Memory; High Memory; Magnetic Core; Memory; Memory Caching; Memory Resident; Processing; Programmable Read Only Memory; PROM; RAM; RAM Disk; Rambus Dynamic Random Access Memory; Random Access Memory; RDRAM; Read Only Memory; ROM; SDRAM; Shadow RAM Memory; SIMM; Single Inline Memory Modules; Single Inline Package; SIP; Store; Synchronous Dynamic Random Access Memory; Terminate and Stay Resident; TSR; Upper Memory; Virtual Memory; VM; Volatile Memory;*

EBCDIC

Extended Binary Coded Decimal Interchange Code. A format in which data is stored which makes it compatible for use by other programs or computers. Pronounced "ebbsedic".

See Also: *American National Standard Institute; American Standard Code for Information Interchange; ANSI; ASCII; ASCII Files; Character; Compatible; Data; Data Element; Data Entity; Data Item; Data Type; Denary; Extended Binary Coded Decimal Interchange Code; Field; Format; Group; International Standards Organisation; ISO; Literal; Null; String;*

E-commerce

Buying and selling products using the Internet.

See Also: *Cyberspace; Data Processing; DP; EDI; EFT; EFTPOS; Electronic Data Interchange; Electronic Fund Transfer; Electronic Fund Transfer Point of Sales; Firewall; Internet Service Provider; ISP; Provider; Service Provider;*

ECP

Extended Capabilities Port. Also known as Enhanced Parallel Port. An upgraded parallel port on the computer which can transfer data bi-directionally at rates of over 2 Mb/sec.

See Also: *Characters Per Second; Communications; CPS; Data Communications; Data Transmission; Datacoms; Dial In; Dial Up; Direct Connection; Enhanced Parallel Port; EPP; Extended Capabilities Port; FDDI; Fibre Distributed Data Interface; Fibre Optics; Leased Line; Optical Fibre; Parallel Interface; Parallel Port; Parallel Transmission; Port; Serial Port; Transfer Rate; Transmit;*

EDI

Electronic Data Interchange. A system which allows companies to transfer documents such as orders, invoices, payments, electronically using computers and communication lines instead of paper format.

See Also: *Cyberspace; Data Processing; DP; E-commerce; EFT; EFTPOS; Electronic Data Interchange; Electronic Fund Transfer; Electronic Fund Transfer Point of Sales; Firewall; Internet Service Provider; ISP; Point of Sales; POS; Provider; Real Time; Service Provider;*

Edit
The process of creating or updating a program, document or file using a text editor or word processor.
See Also: *Document; File; Line Editor; Page Editor; Program; Spell Check; Word Processor; Word Wrap; WP;*

EDP
Electronic Data Processing. The manipulation, analysis and storage of data on a computer.
See Also: *Audit Trail; Batch Processing; Bespoke; CAD; CADCAM; CADMAT; CAE; CAI; CAM; CBT; Computation; Compute; Computer Aided Design; Computer Aided Design and Manufacturing; Computer Aided Design Manufacture and Test; Computer Aided Engineering; Computer Aided Instruction; Computer Aided Manufacturing; Computer Based Training; Data Centre; Data Processing; Desk Top Publishing; Distributed System/Network; DP; DTP; Electronic Data Processing; Expert System; Facilities Management; FM; Geographical Information System; GIS; Information System; Information Technology; Integrated Systems; IS; IT; Magnetic Ink Character Recognition; MICR; Outsourcing; Software System;*

EDS
Electronic Data System. A computer hardware and software system.
See Also: *1st Generation; 2nd Generation; 3rd Generation; 4th Generation; Advanced Technology; AI; Analogue Computer; Application; Artificial Intelligence; AT; BBS; Bespoke; Bulletin Board System; CAD; CADCAM; CADMAT; CAE; CAI; CAM; CBT; Computation; Compute; Computer; Computer Aided Design; Computer Aided Design and Manufacturing; Computer Aided Design Manufacture and Test; Computer Aided Engineering; Computer Aided Instruction; Computer Aided Manufacturing; Computer Based Training; Cross Platform; Data Centre; Desk Top Publishing; Desktop; Digital Computer; Distributed System/Network; DTP; EFT; EFTPOS; Electronic Data System; Electronic Fund Transfer; Electronic Fund Transfer Point of Sales; Environment; Equipment; Expert System; Extended Technology; Geographical Information System; GIS; Hardware; IBM (tm) Compatible; Information System; Installation; Integrated Systems; IS; Kit; Laptop; Leading Edge; Machine; Mainframe; Micro; Microcomputer; Midrange System; Minicomputer; Multi Platform; Notebook; Number Cruncher; Office Information System; OIS; Outsourcing; Package; Palmtop Computer; PC; Personal Computer; Platform; Portable; Processing; Software; Software Package; Software*

System; Standalone; State of the Art; System; Third Party Maintenance; Tower Computer; Turnkey; Vertical Market; Word Processor; WP; XT;

EEROM

Electrically Erasable Read Only Memory. A ROM chip whose contents can be programmed and reprogrammed using a special device.

See Also: *Basic Input Output System; BIOS; Bubble Memory; Buffer; Cache Memory; CMOS; Complementary Metal Oxide Semiconductor Memory; Computer Power; Conventional Memory; Core; Core Dump; DDR SDRAM; DIMM; Direct Memory Access; Direct Random Access Memory; Disk Cache; DMA; Double Data Rate SDRAM; DRAM; Dual Inline Memory Module; Dynamic Memory; Dynamically; Electrically Erasable Read Only Memory; Electronically Programmed Read Only Memory; EMS; EPROM; Erasable Programmable Read Only Memory; Expanded Memory; Expanded Memory Specification; Extended Memory; Flash Memory; High Memory; Magnetic Core; Memory; Memory Board; Memory Caching; Memory Card; Memory Resident; Mix; Power; Programmable Read Only Memory; PROM; RAM; RAM Disk; Rambus Dynamic Random Access Memory; Random Access Memory; RDRAM; Read Only Memory; ROM; ROM Resident; SDRAM; Shadow RAM Memory; SIMM; Single Inline Memory Modules; Single Inline Package; SIP; Stack; Store; Swapping; Synchronous Dynamic Random Access Memory; Upper Memory; Video Random Access Memory; VRAM; Working Storage; Workspace;*

EFT

Electronic Fund Transfer. The process by which financial transactions are transferred via communication lines to be debited or credited at the receiving end.

See Also: *AMR; Automatic Message Routing; Bespoke; Computation; Compute; Data Processing; Download; DP; E-commerce; EDI; EDS; EFTPOS; Electronic Data Interchange; Electronic Data System; Electronic Fund Transfer; Electronic Fund Transfer Point of Sales; Point of Sales; POS; Real Time; Secure Socket Layer; SSL; Teleprocessing System; TPS; Upload;*

EFTPOS

Electronic Fund Transfer Point of Sales. The process by which money transactions are transferred via communication lines to be debited or credited. It refers to Point of Sales transactions in a retail outlet where bank or credit cards are used for purchasing.

See Also: *AMR; Automatic Message Routing; Bespoke; Computation; Compute; Data Processing; Download; DP; E-commerce; EDI; EDS;*

EFT; Electronic Data Interchange; Electronic Data System; Electronic Fund Transfer; Electronic Fund Transfer Point of Sales; Point of Sales; POS; Real Time; Secure Socket Layer; SSL; Teleprocessing System; TPS; Upload;

EGA

Enhanced Graphic Adaptor. A visual display unit which can use up to 64 colours and has a resolution of 640x350 dots.

See Also: *Analogue Monitor; Anti Glare Screen; Cathode Ray Tube; CGA; Colour Graphics Adaptor; CRT; Device; Digital Monitor; Display; Enhanced Graphic Adaptor; Environment; Equipment; Extended Video Array; Graphics Card; Hardware; High Resolution; Installation; Intelligent Terminal; Interlaced; Kit; LCD; Liquid Crystal Display; Low Resolution; Monitor; Monochrome; Paint Screen; Peripheral; Plasma Screen; Prompt; Resolution; Screen; Screen Burn; Split Screen; Super Twist LCD; Super VGA; Super Video Graphics Array; SVGA; Terminal; TFT; Thin-Film Transistor; Touch Screen; Twip; VDT; VDU; VGA; Video Card; Video Display Terminal; Video Graphics Array; Video Random Access Memory; Visual Display Terminal; Visual Display Unit; VRAM; XGA;*

EIDE

Enhanced Intelligent Drive Electronics. An interface between the PC's motherboard and storage devices, e.g. disk drives. This is an upgrade to IDE.

See Also: *3.5 Inch; 5.25 Inch; ATAPI; Attachment Packet Interface; CD-ROM Drive; CD-RW Drive; Direct Memory Access; Disk; Disk Drive; Disk Storage; Diskette; DMA; Drive; EISA; Enhanced Industry Standard Architecture; Enhanced Intelligent Drive Electronics; FDD; Firewire; Five and a quarter; Fixed Disk Drive; Floppy Disk; Floppy Disk Drive; Hard Disk Drive; HDD; IDE; Industry Standard Architecture; Integrated Drive Electronics; Interface; ISA; Magnetic Disk; MCA; Micro Channel Architecture; Motherboard; Optical Drive; PCMCIA; Personal Computer Memory Card International Association; SCSI; Self Monitoring Analysis and Reporting Technology; Small Computer System Interface; SMART; Store; Three and a Half; Ultra DMA; Winchester Disk;*

Eight Bit
(8 bit). A term describing the architecture of a computer in which data is stored in 8 bit registers, or transferred from one part of a computer to another in an 8 bit wide data bus.
See Also: *16 Bit; 32 Bit; 64 Bit; 8 Bit; Address; Address Bus; American Standard Code for Information Interchange; Analogue Computer; ASCII; Binary; Binary Digit; Bit; Bits Per Second; BPS; Bus; Byte; Channel; Data; Data Bus; Data Type; Digital; Gbps; Least Significant Bit; Local Bus; LSB; Mbps; Most Significant Bit; MSB; Register; Sixteen Bit; Sixty Four Bit; System Bus; Thirty Two Bit; Transmission Channel;*

EISA
Enhanced Industry Standard Architecture. A system design which speeds up the processing between the processor and hard disk or visual display unit while allowing for the use of existing technology with future upgrades.
See Also: *Central Processing Unit; CPU; Direct Memory Access; Disk; Disk Drive; Disk Storage; DMA; Drive; EIDE; Enhanced Industry Standard Architecture; Enhanced Intelligent Drive Electronics; FDD; Fixed Disk Drive; Floppy Disk Drive; Hard Disk Drive; HDD; IDE; Industry Standard Architecture; Integrated Drive Electronics; Interface; ISA; Magnetic Disk; MCA; Micro Channel Architecture; SCSI; Self Monitoring Analysis and Reporting Technology; Small Computer System Interface; SMART; Store; Ultra DMA; Winchester Disk;*

Electrically Erasable Read Only Memory
(EEROM). A ROM chip whose contents can be programmed and reprogrammed using a special device.
See Also: *Basic Input Output System; BIOS; Bubble Memory; Buffer; Cache Memory; CMOS; Complementary Metal Oxide Semiconductor Memory; Computer Power; Conventional Memory; Core; Core Dump; DDR SDRAM; DIMM; Direct Memory Access; Direct Random Access Memory; Disk Cache; DMA; Double Data Rate SDRAM; DRAM; Dual Inline Memory Module; Dynamic Memory; Dynamically; EEROM; Electronically Programmed Read Only Memory; EMS; EPROM; Erasable Programmable Read Only Memory; Expanded Memory; Expanded Memory Specification; Extended Memory; Flash Memory; High Memory; Magnetic Core; Memory; Memory Board; Memory Caching; Memory Card; Memory Resident; Mix; Power; Programmable Read Only Memory; PROM; RAM; RAM Disk; Rambus Dynamic Random Access Memory; Random Access Memory; RDRAM; Read Only Memory; ROM; ROM Resident; SDRAM; Shadow RAM Memory; SIMM; Single Inline Memory Modules; Single Inline Package; SIP; Stack; Store;*

Swapping; Synchronous Dynamic Random Access Memory; Upper Memory; Video Random Access Memory; VRAM; Working Storage; Workspace;

Electronic Data Interchange
(EDI). A system which allows companies to transfer documents such as orders, invoices, payments, electronically using computers and communication lines instead of paper format.
See Also: *Cyberspace; Data Processing; DP; E-commerce; EDI; EFT; EFTPOS; Electronic Fund Transfer; Electronic Fund Transfer Point of Sales; Firewall; Internet Service Provider; ISP; Point of Sales; POS; Provider; Real Time; Service Provider;*

Electronic Data Processing
(EDP). The manipulation, analysis and storage of data on a computer.
See Also: *Audit Trail; Batch Processing; Bespoke; CAD; CADCAM; CADMAT; CAE; CAI; CAM; CBT; Computation; Compute; Computer Aided Design; Computer Aided Design and Manufacturing; Computer Aided Design Manufacture and Test; Computer Aided Engineering; Computer Aided Instruction; Computer Aided Manufacturing; Computer Based Training; Data Centre; Data Processing; Desk Top Publishing; Distributed System/Network; DP; DTP; EDP; Expert System; Facilities Management; FM; Geographical Information System; GIS; Information System; Information Technology; Integrated Systems; IS; IT; Magnetic Ink Character Recognition; MICR; Outsourcing; Software System;*

Electronic Data System
(EDS). A computer hardware and software system.
See Also: *1st Generation; 2nd Generation; 3rd Generation; 4th Generation; Advanced Technology; AI; Analogue Computer; Application; Artificial Intelligence; AT; BBS; Bespoke; Bulletin Board System; CAD; CADCAM; CADMAT; CAE; CAI; CAM; CBT; Computation; Compute; Computer; Computer Aided Design; Computer Aided Design and Manufacturing; Computer Aided Design Manufacture and Test; Computer Aided Engineering; Computer Aided Instruction; Computer Aided Manufacturing; Computer Based Training; Cross Platform; Data Centre; Desk Top Publishing; Desktop; Digital Computer; Distributed System/Network; DTP; EDS; EFT; EFTPOS; Electronic Fund Transfer; Electronic Fund Transfer Point of Sales; Environment; Equipment; Expert System; Extended Technology; Geographical Information System; GIS; Hardware; IBM (tm) Compatible; Information System; Installation; Integrated Systems; IS; Kit; Laptop; Leading Edge; Machine; Mainframe; Micro;*

Microcomputer; Midrange System; Minicomputer; Multi Platform; Notebook; Number Cruncher; Office Information System; OIS; Outsourcing; Package; Palmtop Computer; PC; Personal Computer; Platform; Portable; Processing; Software; Software Package; Software System; Standalone; State of the Art; System; Third Party Maintenance; Tower Computer; Turnkey; Vertical Market; Word Processor; WP; XT;

Electronic Fund Transfer
(EFT). The process by which financial transactions are transferred via communication lines to be debited or credited at the receiving end.
See Also: *AMR; Automatic Message Routing; Bespoke; Computation; Compute; Data Processing; Download; DP; E-commerce; EDI; EDS; EFT; EFTPOS; Electronic Data Interchange; Electronic Data System; Electronic Fund Transfer Point of Sales; Point of Sales; POS; Real Time; Secure Socket Layer; SSL; Teleprocessing System; TPS; Upload;*

Electronic Fund Transfer Point of Sales
(EFTPOS). The process by which money transactions are transferred via communication lines to be debited or credited. It refers to Point of Sales transactions in a retail outlet where bank or credit cards are used for purchasing.
See Also: *AMR; Automatic Message Routing; Bespoke; Computation; Compute; Data Processing; Download; DP; E-commerce; EDI; EDS; EFT; EFTPOS; Electronic Data Interchange; Electronic Data System; Electronic Fund Transfer; Point of Sales; POS; Real Time; Secure Socket Layer; SSL; Teleprocessing System; TPS; Upload;*

Electronic Mail
E-mail, where messages and data files can be sent to other computers around the world.
See Also: *Address; Attachment; Body; Buddy List; Chat; Chatroom; Cybercafe; Cyberspace; E-mail; E-mail Address; Flame; Footer; Forum; FTPmail; Header; IM; Instant Messaging; Internet Relay Chat; IRC; Mailbox; Mailing List; Mailserver; Message Boards; MIME; Multipurpose Internet Mail Extensions; POP; Post Office Protocol; Signature; Simple Mail Transfer Protocol; SMTP; Snail Mail; Spam; Thread;*

Electronically Programmed Read Only Memory
(EPROM). A ROM chip whose contents can be programmed and reprogrammed using a special device.
See Also: *Basic Input Output System; BIOS; Bubble Memory; Buffer; Cache Memory; CMOS; Complementary Metal Oxide Semiconductor*

Memory; Computer Power; Conventional Memory; Core; Core Dump; DDR SDRAM; DIMM; Direct Memory Access; Direct Random Access Memory; Disk Cache; DMA; Double Data Rate SDRAM; DRAM; Dual Inline Memory Module; Dynamic Memory; Dynamically; EEROM; Electrically Erasable Read Only Memory; EMS; EPROM; Erasable Programmable Read Only Memory; Expanded Memory; Expanded Memory Specification; Extended Memory; Flash Memory; High Memory; Magnetic Core; Memory; Memory Board; Memory Caching; Memory Card; Memory Resident; Mix; Power; Programmable Read Only Memory; PROM; RAM; RAM Disk; Rambus Dynamic Random Access Memory; Random Access Memory; RDRAM; Read Only Memory; ROM; ROM Resident; SDRAM; Shadow RAM Memory; SIMM; Single Inline Memory Modules; Single Inline Package; SIP; Stack; Store; Swapping; Synchronous Dynamic Random Access Memory; Upper Memory; Video Random Access Memory; VRAM; Working Storage; Workspace;

E-mail
Electronic mail, where messages and data files can be sent to other computers around the world.
See Also: *Address; Attachment; Body; Buddy List; Chat; Chatroom; Cybercafe; Cyberspace; Electronic Mail; E-mail Address; Flame; Footer; Forum; FTPmail; Header; IM; Instant Messaging; Internet Relay Chat; IRC; Mailbox; Mailing List; Mailserver; Message Boards; MIME; Multipurpose Internet Mail Extensions; POP; Post Office Protocol; Signature; Simple Mail Transfer Protocol; SMTP; Snail Mail; Spam; Thread;*

E-mail Address
A private Internet address to which e-mails are sent.
See Also: *Address; Anchor; Anonymous FTP; Bookmark; Buddy List; Cybercafe; Cyberspace; DNS; Domain Name; Domain Name System; Dot; Electronic Mail; E-mail; Internet Protocol Address; IP Address; Mailbox; Mailing List; Mailserver; Universal/Uniform Resource Locator; URL;*

Emoticons
Characters that make up a facial emotion when viewed sideways, e.g. :-) represents a smile.
See Also: *Character; Chat; Chatroom; Forum; Graphics; IM; Instant Messaging; Nerd; Netiquette; Newbie; Newsgroup; Signature; Smileys;*

EMS
Expanded Memory Specification. A system design which allows access to a large bank of memory by switching between sections of it.
See Also: *Basic Input Output System; BIOS; Block; Bubble Memory; Buffer; Cache Memory; CMOS; Complementary Metal Oxide Semiconductor Memory; Computer Power; Conventional Memory; Core; Core Dump; DDR SDRAM; DIMM; Direct Memory Access; Direct Random Access Memory; Disk Cache; DMA; Double Data Rate SDRAM; DRAM; Dual Inline Memory Module; Dynamic Memory; Dynamically; EEROM; Electrically Erasable Read Only Memory; Electronically Programmed Read Only Memory; EPROM; Erasable Programmable Read Only Memory; Expanded Memory; Expanded Memory Specification; Extended Memory; Flash Memory; High Memory; Magnetic Core; Memory; Memory Board; Memory Caching; Memory Card; Memory Resident; Mix; Overlay; Power; Programmable Read Only Memory; PROM; RAM; RAM Disk; Rambus Dynamic Random Access Memory; Random Access Memory; RDRAM; Read Only Memory; ROM; SDRAM; Shadow RAM Memory; SIMM; Single Inline Memory Modules; Single Inline Package; SIP; Stack; Store; Swapping; Synchronous Dynamic Random Access Memory; Upper Memory; Video Random Access Memory; VRAM; Working Storage; Workspace;*

Emulate
A state where a computer or peripheral device performs similar to another computer or device it is intending to copy.
See Also: *Computer; Configuring; Cross Platform; Device; Emulation; Environment; Equipment; Hardware; IBM (tm) Compatible; Kit; Machine; Midrange System; Minicomputer; Peripheral; Platform;*

Emulation
The process where a computer or peripheral device performs similar to another computer or device it is intending to copy.
See Also: *Computer; Configuring; Cross Platform; Device; Emulate; Environment; Equipment; Hardware; IBM (tm) Compatible; Kit; Machine; Midrange System; Minicomputer; Peripheral; Platform;*

Encryption
A system that converts messages and data into a secret code for security protection.
See Also: *Body; Data; Secure Socket Layer; Security; SSL;*

End of File
(EOF). A notation to indicate the end of a data file.
See Also: *ASCII Files; Attachment; Batch File; Batch Processing; Beginning of File; BOF; Compressed File; Database; DB; Delimiter; Direct Access; Document; End of Tape; EOF; EOT; File; Index Sequential File; Log File; Random Access; RDB; Relational Database; Sequential File; Serial File; Tag File; Temp File; Trailer;*

End of Job
(EOJ). A notation to indicate the end of a job or task on a computer.
See Also: *Batch Processing; EOJ; JCL; Job; Job Control Language; Log In/Off; Process;*

End of Tape
(EOT). A notation to indicate that end of tape has been reached.
See Also: *Batch Processing; Beginning of File; BOF; DAT; Delimiter; Digital Audio Tape; End of File; EOF; EOT; Mag Tape; Magnetic Tape; Paper Tape; Tape Deck; Tape Streamer; Zip Drive;*

End User
A person who uses a computer. Refers normally to people in large organisations where software and hardware are designed and prepared for those people to use.
See Also: *Cybercafe; Dead Lock; Deadly Embrace; Hand Holding; Hands On; Help Desk; Log In/Off; Multi User; User; User Friendly; User Group; User Guide; User Manual;*

Enhanced Graphic Adaptor
(EGA). A visual display unit which can use up to 64 colours and has a resolution of 640x350 dots.
See Also: *Analogue Monitor; Anti Glare Screen; Cathode Ray Tube; CGA; Colour Graphics Adaptor; CRT; Device; Digital Monitor; Display; EGA; Environment; Equipment; Extended Video Array; Graphics Card; Hardware; High Resolution; Installation; Intelligent Terminal; Interlaced; Kit; LCD; Liquid Crystal Display; Low Resolution; Monitor; Monochrome; Paint Screen; Peripheral; Plasma Screen; Prompt; Resolution; Screen; Screen Burn; Split Screen; Super Twist LCD; Super VGA; Super Video Graphics Array; SVGA; Terminal; TFT; Thin-Film Transistor; Touch Screen; Twip; VDT; VDU; VGA; Video Card; Video Display Terminal; Video Graphics Array; Video Random Access Memory; Visual Display Terminal; Visual Display Unit; VRAM; XGA;*

Enhanced Industry Standard Architecture
(EISA). A system design which speeds up the processing between the processor and hard disk or visual display unit while allowing for the use of existing technology with future upgrades.
See Also: *Central Processing Unit; CPU; Direct Memory Access; Disk; Disk Drive; Disk Storage; DMA; Drive; EIDE; EISA; Enhanced Intelligent Drive Electronics; FDD; Fixed Disk Drive; Floppy Disk Drive; Hard Disk Drive; HDD; IDE; Industry Standard Architecture; Integrated Drive Electronics; Interface; ISA; Magnetic Disk; MCA; Micro Channel Architecture; SCSI; Self Monitoring Analysis and Reporting Technology; Small Computer System Interface; SMART; Store; Ultra DMA; Winchester Disk;*

Enhanced Intelligent Drive Electronics
(EIDE). An interface between the PC's motherboard and storage devices, e.g. disk drives. This is an upgrade to IDE.
See Also: *3.5 Inch; 5.25 Inch; ATAPI; Attachment Packet Interface; CD-ROM Drive; CD-RW Drive; Direct Memory Access; Disk; Disk Drive; Disk Storage; Diskette; DMA; Drive; EIDE; EISA; Enhanced Industry Standard Architecture; FDD; Firewire; Five and a quarter; Fixed Disk Drive; Floppy Disk; Floppy Disk Drive; Hard Disk Drive; HDD; IDE; Industry Standard Architecture; Integrated Drive Electronics; Interface; ISA; Magnetic Disk; MCA; Micro Channel Architecture; Motherboard; Optical Drive; PCMCIA; Personal Computer Memory Card International Association; SCSI; Self Monitoring Analysis and Reporting Technology; Small Computer System Interface; SMART; Store; Three and a Half; Ultra DMA; Winchester Disk;*

Enhanced Parallel Port
(EPP). Also known as Extended Capabilities Port. An upgraded parallel port on the computer which can transfer data bi-directionally at rates of over 2 Mb/sec.
See Also: *Characters Per Second; Communications; CPS; Data Communications; Data Transmission; Datacoms; Dial In; Dial Up; Direct Connection; ECP; EPP; Extended Capabilities Port; FDDI; Fibre Distributed Data Interface; Fibre Optics; Leased Line; Optical Fibre; Parallel Interface; Parallel Port; Parallel Transmission; Port; Serial Port; Transfer Rate; Transmit;*

Enter

A key on the keyboard which is used to get the typed information into a computer when depressed. Also know as the RETURN key.

See Also: *Call; Carriage Return; Chain; Command; Input; Instruction; Invoke; Keyboard; Return;*

Entity

One item of data or a group item which may have more than one item of data. In each case it has its own meaning and relationships with other entities.

See Also: *Array; Character; Check Box; Constant; Data; Data Dictionary; Data Element; Data Entity; Data Item; Data Model; Data Type; Database; DB; Field; Group; Information; Key; Literal; Null; Parameter; RDB; Relational Database; Subscript; Variable;*

Environment

(1) A computer installation with all its computers and peripheral devices.
(2) The procedures, operating system and software within a computer in which programs operate.

See Also: *1st Generation; 2nd Generation; 3rd Generation; 4th Generation; Advanced Technology; Analogue Computer; Analogue Monitor; AT; Backing Store; Barrel Printer; Basic Input Output System; BIOS; Black Box; Bubble Jet; CD-ROM Drive; CD-RW Drive; CGA; Client Server; Colour Graphics Adaptor; Computer; Configuration; Cross Platform; Daisywheel; DAT; Data Centre; Deck; Desktop; Device; Digital Audio Tape; Digital Computer; Digital Monitor; Disk Operating System; Display; Distributed System/Network; DOS; Dot Matrix; Drum Printer; EDS; EGA; Electronic Data System; Emulate; Emulation; Enhanced Graphic Adaptor; Equipment; Ethernet; Extended Technology; Extended Video Array; File Server; Flatbed Scanner; Front End Processor; Global; Graphical User Interface; GUI; Hand Held Device; Hardware; Host; IBM (tm) Compatible; Inkjet; Installation; Integrated Systems; Intelligent Terminal; Keyboard; Kit; LAN; Laptop; Laser Jet; Laser Printer; LCD; LCD Printer; Line Printer; Linux; Liquid Crystal Display; Liquid Crystal Display Printer; Local Area Network; Machine; Mag Tape; Magnetic Tape; Mainframe; Matrix Printer; Micro; Microcomputer; Midrange System; Minicomputer; Monitor; Monochrome; Mouse; Multi Platform; Multi User; Multimedia; Network; Notebook; Number Cruncher; Open System; Operating System; Optical Drive; Optical Scanner; OS; OS/2; Page Printer; Palmtop Computer; Paper Tape; PC; Peripheral; Personal Computer; Plasma Screen; Platform; Plotter; Portable; Printer; Recording Device; Remote Device; Ring Network; Scanner; Screen; Server; Standalone; Star Cluster; Star*

Network; Super Twist LCD; Super VGA; Super Video Graphics Array; SVGA; System; Tape Deck; Tape Streamer; Terminal; TFT; Thermal Printer; Thin-Film Transistor; Token Ring; Touch Screen; Tower Computer; Turnkey; UNIX; VDT; VDU; VGA; Video Display Terminal; Video Graphics Array; Visual Display Terminal; Visual Display Unit; WAN; Wide Area Network; WIMP; Winchester Disk; Windows Icons Mice and Pull-down menus; XGA; XT;

EOF

End of File. A notation to indicate the end of a data file.

See Also: *ASCII Files; Attachment; Batch File; Batch Processing; Beginning of File; BOF; Compressed File; Database; DB; Delimiter; Direct Access; Document; End of File; End of Tape; EOT; File; Index Sequential File; Log File; Random Access; RDB; Relational Database; Sequential File; Serial File; Tag File; Temp File; Trailer;*

EOJ

End of Job. A notation to indicate the end of a job or task on a computer.

See Also: *Batch Processing; End of Job; JCL; Job; Job Control Language; Log In/Off; Process;*

EOT

End of Tape. A notation to indicate that end of tape has been reached.

See Also: *Batch Processing; Beginning of File; BOF; DAT; Delimiter; Digital Audio Tape; End of File; End of Tape; EOF; Mag Tape; Magnetic Tape; Paper Tape; Tape Deck; Tape Streamer; Zip Drive;*

EPP

Enhanced Parallel Port. Also known as Extended Capabilities Port. An upgraded parallel port on the computer which can transfer data bi-directionally at rates of over 2 Mb/sec.

See Also: *Characters Per Second; Communications; CPS; Data Communications; Data Transmission; Datacoms; Dial In; Dial Up; Direct Connection; ECP; Enhanced Parallel Port; Extended Capabilities Port; FDDI; Fibre Distributed Data Interface; Fibre Optics; Leased Line; Optical Fibre; Parallel Interface; Parallel Port; Parallel Transmission; Port; Serial Port; Transfer Rate; Transmit;*

EPROM
Electronically Programmed Read Only Memory OR Erasable Programmable Read Only Memory. A ROM chip whose contents can be programmed and reprogrammed using a special device.
See Also: *Basic Input Output System; BIOS; Bubble Memory; Buffer; Cache Memory; CMOS; Complementary Metal Oxide Semiconductor Memory; Computer Power; Conventional Memory; Core; Core Dump; DDR SDRAM; DIMM; Direct Memory Access; Direct Random Access Memory; Disk Cache; DMA; Double Data Rate SDRAM; DRAM; Dual Inline Memory Module; Dynamic Memory; Dynamically; EEROM; Electrically Erasable Read Only Memory; Electronically Programmed Read Only Memory; EMS; Erasable Programmable Read Only Memory; Expanded Memory; Expanded Memory Specification; Extended Memory; Flash Memory; High Memory; Magnetic Core; Memory; Memory Board; Memory Caching; Memory Card; Memory Resident; Mix; Power; Programmable Read Only Memory; PROM; RAM; RAM Disk; Rambus Dynamic Random Access Memory; Random Access Memory; RDRAM; Read Only Memory; ROM; ROM Resident; SDRAM; Shadow RAM Memory; SIMM; Single Inline Memory Modules; Single Inline Package; SIP; Stack; Store; Swapping; Synchronous Dynamic Random Access Memory; Upper Memory; Video Random Access Memory; VRAM; Working Storage; Workspace;*

Equipment
The computer hardware.
See Also: *1st Generation; 2nd Generation; 3.5 Inch; 3rd Generation; 4th Generation; 5.25 Inch; Acoustic Coupler; Advanced Technology; Analogue Computer; Analogue Digital Converter; Analogue Monitor; Anti Glare Screen; Asymmetrical Modem; AT; Backing Store; Barrel Printer; Bespoke; Black Box; Bubble Jet; Cathode Ray Tube; CD-ROM Drive; CD-RW Drive; CGA; Client Server; Colour Graphics Adaptor; Computer; Configuration; Cross Platform; CRT; Cut Sheet Feeder; Daisywheel; DAT; Deck; Desktop; Device; Digital Analog Converter; Digital Audio Tape; Digital Computer; Digital Monitor; Digital Versatile Disk; Disk; Disk Drive; Disk Pack; Disk Storage; Diskette; Display; Distributed System/Network; Dot Matrix; Downsizing; Drive; Drum Printer; DVD; EDS; EGA; Electronic Data System; Emulate; Emulation; Enhanced Graphic Adaptor; Environment; Extended Technology; Extended Video Array; FDD; File Server; Five and a quarter; Fixed Disk Drive; Flatbed Scanner; Floppy Disk; Floppy Disk Drive; Global; Hand Held Device; Hard Disk Drive; Hardware; HDD; Host Processor; IBM (tm) Compatible; Inkjet; Installation; Integrated Systems; Intelligent Terminal; Keyboard; Kit; Laptop; Laser Jet; Laser Printer; LCD; LCD*

Printer; Leading Edge; LED; Light Emitting Diode; Light Pen; Line Printer; Liquid Crystal Display; Liquid Crystal Display Printer; Machine; Mag Tape; Magnetic Disk; Magnetic Tape; Mailserver; Mainframe; Mass Storage; Matrix Printer; Micro; Microcomputer; Midrange System; Minicomputer; Modem; Modulator Demodulator; Monitor; Monochrome; Mouse; Multi Platform; Node; Notebook; Number Cruncher; OCR; OMR; Optical Character Reader; Optical Character Recognition; Optical Drive; Optical Mark Recognition; Optical Scanner; Pack; Page Printer; Palmtop Computer; PC; PDA; Peripheral; Personal Computer; Personal Digital Assistant; Plasma Screen; Platform; Plotter; Plug Compatible; Portable; Printer; Recording Device; Remote Device; Scanner; Screen; Server; Sheet Feeder; Standalone; State of the Art; Storage; Store; Streamer; Super Twist LCD; Super VGA; Super Video Graphics Array; SVGA; System; Tape Deck; Tape Streamer; Terminal; TFT; Thermal Printer; Thin-Film Transistor; Third Party Maintenance; Three and a Half; Touch Screen; Tower Computer; Tracker Ball; Turnkey; VDT; VDU; VGA; Video Display Terminal; Video Graphics Array; Visual Display Terminal; Visual Display Unit; Volume; Webcam; Winchester Disk; XGA; XT; Zip Drive;

Erasable Programmable Read Only Memory
(EPROM). A ROM chip which can be programmed using a special device and whose contents can be reprogrammed.
See Also: *Basic Input Output System; BIOS; Bubble Memory; Buffer; Cache Memory; CMOS; Complementary Metal Oxide Semiconductor Memory; Computer Power; Conventional Memory; Core; Core Dump; DDR SDRAM; DIMM; Direct Memory Access; Direct Random Access Memory; Disk Cache; DMA; Double Data Rate SDRAM; DRAM; Dual Inline Memory Module; Dynamic Memory; Dynamically; EEROM; Electrically Erasable Read Only Memory; Electronically Programmed Read Only Memory; EMS; EPROM; Expanded Memory; Expanded Memory Specification; Extended Memory; Flash Memory; High Memory; Magnetic Core; Memory; Memory Board; Memory Caching; Memory Card; Memory Resident; Mix; Power; Programmable Read Only Memory; PROM; RAM; RAM Disk; Rambus Dynamic Random Access Memory; Random Access Memory; RDRAM; Read Only Memory; ROM; ROM Resident; SDRAM; Shadow RAM Memory; SIMM; Single Inline Memory Modules; Single Inline Package; SIP; Stack; Store; Swapping; Synchronous Dynamic Random Access Memory; Upper Memory; Video Random Access Memory; VRAM; Working Storage; Workspace;*

Esc

Abbr. of Escape. (1) The key on a keyboard when activated allows you to cancel processing and return to a previous function. (2) A command used in many internal computer statements to carry out an instruction.

See Also: *Abort; Command; Escape; Hot Key; Instruction; Interrupt; Interrupt Request; IRQ; Keyboard;*

Escape

(1) The key on a keyboard when activated allows you to cancel processing and return to a previous function. (2) A command used in many internal computer statements to carry out an instruction.

See Also: *Abort; Command; Esc; Hot Key; Instruction; Interrupt; Interrupt Request; IRQ; Keyboard;*

Ethernet

A local area networking system linking a number of computers together to use shared devices and data files.

See Also: *AMR; Anonymous FTP; Automatic Message Routing; Backbone; Bandwidth; BBS; Broadband; Bulletin Board System; Client Server; Client Server Protocol; Distributed System/Network; Environment; File Server; File Sharing; Gateway; Host Processor; Intranet; LAN; LAN Port; Local Area Network; Multi User; Multitasking; Narrowband; Network; Network Information Centre; Network Operating System; NIC; Node; NOS; Open Systems Interconnect; OSI; Ring Network; Server; Star Cluster; Star Network; TCP/IP; Token Ring; Transmission Control Protocol/Internet Protocol; WAN; Wide Area Network;*

Event

Something that happens to a data item. e.g. a set of procedures to validate the item.

See Also: *Audit Trail; Backup; Batch Processing; Call; Chain; Data Flow; Data Flow Diagram; Data Model; DFD; Execute; Function; Instruction; Invoke; Job; Macro; Nesting; Save; Script;*

EXE

Abbr. of EXEcutable. A program file which has a file suffix of '.exe'.

See Also: *Call; Chain; Code; Device Driver; DLL; Driver; Dynamic Link Library; Execute; Firmware; Freeware; Function; Instruction; Instruction Set; Invoke; Job; Load; Machine Code; Machine Language; Macro; Module; Object Code; Program; Run; Run Time; Script; Shareware; Software; Software Driver; Utility;*

Execute
To run a computer program or perform an instruction, statement or command.
See Also: *AUTOEXEC.BAT; Batch Processing; C Prompt; Call; Chain; Click; Command; Event; EXE; Firmware; Format; Function; Instruction; Invoke; Load; Macro; Program; Run; Run Time; Script; Voice Activated;*

Expanded Memory
Memory which is allocated in 64k chunks at a time that may be required by programs if they need to use a large amount of memory.
See Also: *Basic Input Output System; BIOS; Block; Bubble Memory; Buffer; Cache Memory; CMOS; Complementary Metal Oxide Semiconductor Memory; Computer Power; Conventional Memory; Core; Core Dump; DDR SDRAM; DIMM; Direct Memory Access; Direct Random Access Memory; Disk Cache; DMA; Double Data Rate SDRAM; DRAM; Dual Inline Memory Module; Dynamic Memory; Dynamically; EEROM; Electrically Erasable Read Only Memory; Electronically Programmed Read Only Memory; EMS; EPROM; Erasable Programmable Read Only Memory; Expanded Memory Specification; Extended Memory; Flash Memory; High Memory; Magnetic Core; Memory; Memory Board; Memory Caching; Memory Card; Memory Resident; Mix; Overlay; Power; Programmable Read Only Memory; PROM; RAM; RAM Disk; Rambus Dynamic Random Access Memory; Random Access Memory; RDRAM; Read Only Memory; ROM; SDRAM; Shadow RAM Memory; SIMM; Single Inline Memory Modules; Single Inline Package; SIP; Stack; Store; Swapping; Synchronous Dynamic Random Access Memory; Upper Memory; Video Random Access Memory; VRAM; Working Storage; Workspace;*

Expanded Memory Specification
(EMS). A system design which allows access to a large bank of memory by switching between sections of it.
See Also: *Basic Input Output System; BIOS; Block; Bubble Memory; Buffer; Cache Memory; CMOS; Complementary Metal Oxide Semiconductor Memory; Computer Power; Conventional Memory; Core; Core Dump; DDR SDRAM; DIMM; Direct Memory Access; Direct Random Access Memory; Disk Cache; DMA; Double Data Rate SDRAM; DRAM; Dual Inline Memory Module; Dynamic Memory; Dynamically; EEROM; Electrically Erasable Read Only Memory; Electronically Programmed Read Only Memory; EMS; EPROM; Erasable Programmable Read Only Memory; Expanded Memory; Extended Memory; Flash Memory; High Memory; Magnetic Core; Memory; Memory Board; Memory Caching; Memory Card; Memory Resident;*

Mix; Overlay; Power; Programmable Read Only Memory; PROM; RAM; RAM Disk; Rambus Dynamic Random Access Memory; Random Access Memory; RDRAM; Read Only Memory; ROM; SDRAM; Shadow RAM Memory; SIMM; Single Inline Memory Modules; Single Inline Package; SIP; Stack; Store; Swapping; Synchronous Dynamic Random Access Memory; Upper Memory; Video Random Access Memory; VRAM; Working Storage; Workspace;

Expansion Card
A printed circuit board which allows the central processor to transfer data to and from a peripheral device using a larger data bus.
See Also: *Central Processing Unit; CPU; Data Bus; DIMM; Dual Inline Memory Module; Expansion Slot; Fax Card; Maths Co-processor; Motherboard; PCB; PCI; PCMCIA; Peripheral Component Interconnect; Personal Computer Memory Card International Association; Printed Circuit Board; Slot; Sound Card;*

Expansion Slot
A location within a computer which allows printed circuit boards or cards to be slotted in for upgrades to the system.
See Also: *Accelerated Graphics Port; Advanced Graphics Port; AGP; AGP Slot; Expansion Card; Fax Card; Memory Board; Memory Card; Motherboard; PCB; PCI; PCMCIA; Peripheral Component Interconnect; Personal Computer Memory Card International Association; Port; Printed Circuit Board; Slot; Sound Card;*

Expert System
A computer package capable of performing the functions of a human expert. It is a knowledge based system which asks questions and then makes decisions depending on the answers entered.
See Also: *AI; AND gate; Application; Artificial Intelligence; Bespoke; CAD; CADCAM; CADMAT; CAE; CAI; CAM; CBT; Computation; Compute; Computer Aided Design; Computer Aided Design and Manufacturing; Computer Aided Design Manufacture and Test; Computer Aided Engineering; Computer Aided Instruction; Computer Aided Manufacturing; Computer Based Training; Data Processing; DP; EDP; EDS; Electronic Data Processing; Electronic Data System; FL; Fuzzy Logic; I-OR gate; Logic Gate; Logical Design; NAND gate; NEQ gate; NOR gate; NOT gate; OR gate; Package; Software Package; Virtual Reality; VR; X-OR gate;*

Export
The transfer of data or a file from a computer system.
See Also: *Archive; Import; Output;*

Extended Binary Coded Decimal Interchange Code
(EBCDIC). A format in which data is stored which makes it compatible for use by other programs or computers. Pronounced "ebbsedic".
See Also: *American National Standard Institute; American Standard Code for Information Interchange; ANSI; ASCII; ASCII Files; Character; Compatible; Data; Data Element; Data Entity; Data Item; Data Type; Denary; EBCDIC; Field; Format; Group; International Standards Organisation; ISO; Literal; Null; String;*

Extended Capabilities Port
(ECP). Also known as Enhanced Parallel Port. An upgraded parallel port on the computer which can transfer data bi-directionally at rates of over 2 Mb/sec.
See Also: *Characters Per Second; Communications; CPS; Data Communications; Data Transmission; Datacoms; Dial In; Dial Up; Direct Connection; ECP; Enhanced Parallel Port; EPP; FDDI; Fibre Distributed Data Interface; Fibre Optics; Leased Line; Optical Fibre; Parallel Interface; Parallel Port; Parallel Transmission; Port; Serial Port; Transfer Rate; Transmit;*

Extended Memory
Installed memory which is greater than the basic 1Mb of conventional memory.
See Also: *Basic Input Output System; BIOS; Bubble Memory; Buffer; Cache Memory; CMOS; Complementary Metal Oxide Semiconductor Memory; Computer Power; Conventional Memory; Core; Core Dump; DDR SDRAM; DIMM; Direct Memory Access; Direct Random Access Memory; Disk Cache; DMA; Double Data Rate SDRAM; DRAM; Dual Inline Memory Module; Dynamic Memory; Dynamically; EEROM; Electrically Erasable Read Only Memory; Electronically Programmed Read Only Memory; EMS; EPROM; Erasable Programmable Read Only Memory; Expanded Memory; Expanded Memory Specification; Flash Memory; High Memory; Magnetic Core; Memory; Memory Board; Memory Caching; Memory Card; Memory Resident; Mix; Overlay; Power; Programmable Read Only Memory; PROM; RAM; RAM Disk; Rambus Dynamic Random Access Memory; Random Access Memory; RDRAM; Read Only Memory; ROM; SDRAM; Shadow RAM Memory; SIMM; Single Inline Memory Modules; Single Inline Package; SIP; Stack; Store; Swapping; Synchronous Dynamic Random Access Memory;*

Upper Memory; Video Random Access Memory; VRAM; Working Storage; Workspace;

Extended Technology
(XT). The basis in which some personal computers were designed before the 286 chip was developed. Internally the processor can handle 16 bit data transfer but only communicates with external devices using 8 bit data transfer.
See Also: *16 Bit; 1st Generation; 286; 2nd Generation; 386; 3rd Generation; 486; 4th Generation; Advanced Technology; Analogue Computer; AT; Chip; Chipset; Computer; Cross Platform; Desktop; Digital Computer; EDS; Electronic Data System; Environment; Equipment; Front End Processor; Hardware; IBM (tm) Compatible; Installation; Kit; Laptop; Machine; Micro; Microcomputer; Multi Platform; Notebook; OEM; Original Equipment Manufacturer; Palmtop Computer; PC; Personal Computer; Platform; Portable; Reduced Instruction Set Computing; RISC; Silicon Chip; Sixteen Bit; Standalone; Tower Computer; Turnkey; XT;*

Extended Video Array
(XGA). A standard of visual display unit design which allows faster speeds, a better resolution and more colours.
See Also: *Analogue Monitor; Anti Glare Screen; Cathode Ray Tube; CGA; Colour Graphics Adaptor; CRT; Device; Digital Monitor; Display; EGA; Enhanced Graphic Adaptor; Environment; Equipment; Graphics Card; Hardware; High Resolution; Installation; Intelligent Terminal; Interlaced; Kit; LCD; Liquid Crystal Display; Low Resolution; Monitor; Monochrome; Paint Screen; Peripheral; Plasma Screen; Prompt; Resolution; Screen; Screen Burn; Split Screen; Super Twist LCD; Super VGA; Super Video Graphics Array; SVGA; Terminal; TFT; Thin-Film Transistor; Touch Screen; Twip; VDT; VDU; VGA; Video Card; Video Display Terminal; Video Graphics Array; Video Random Access Memory; Visual Display Terminal; Visual Display Unit; VRAM; XGA;*

Extensible Hypertext Markup Language
(XHTML). A web page programming language that is a hybrid between HTML and XML.
See Also: *Anchor; Applet; Browser; Code; eXtensible Markup Language; High Level Language; HTML; Hyperlink; Hypertext; Hypertext Mark-Up Language; Instruction Set; JAVA; JAVASCRIPT; Language; Meta Tag; Module; Page; Page Description Language; PDL; Programming Language; Source Code; The Web; World Wide Web; WWW; XHTML; XML;*

eXtensible Markup Language
(XML). A programming language used to create a website or web pages.
See Also: *Anchor; Applet; Browser; Code; Extensible Hypertext Markup Language; High Level Language; HTML; Hyperlink; Hypertext; Hypertext Mark-Up Language; Instruction Set; JAVA; JAVASCRIPT; Language; Meta Tag; Module; Page; Page Description Language; PDL; Programming Language; Source Code; The Web; World Wide Web; WWW; XHTML; XML;*

Extension
The three or four letter suffix after the end of a file name which denotes the type of file. It is separated from the filename with a dot, e.g. '.doc' = document file, '.jpg' = graphics file.
See Also: *ASCII Files; Attachment; Batch File; BitMaP; BMP; File; Filename Extension; GIF; Graphical Interchange Format; Joint Photographic Experts Group; JPEG; JPG; Motion Picture Experts Group; MPEG; MPG; PDF; Portable Document Format; Rich Text Format; RTF; Tag Image File Format; TIFF; WAV; Waveform Audio;*

Facilities Management
(FM). A service provided to companies by outside organisations who take over the data processing on behalf of the company.
See Also: *Computation; Compute; Data Centre; Data Processing; Downsizing; DP; EDP; Electronic Data Processing; FM; Installation; Integrated Systems; Outsourcing; Processing; Software House; Software System; Third Party Maintenance;*

FAQ
Frequently Asked Questions. A list of frequently asked questions and answers relating to a particular subject.
See Also: *Forum; Frequently Asked Questions; Newsgroup;*

FAT
File Allocation Table. A type of file index on the hard disk used by the operating system.
See Also: *Directory; Disk Operating System; DOS; File Allocation Table; Linux; Operating System; OS; OS/2; Root Directory; Sub Directory;*

Fax Card

A printed circuit board which allows a facsimile (Fax) to be sent and received by a computer.

See Also: *Accelerated Graphics Port; Advanced Graphics Port; AGP; AGP Slot; Chipset; Expansion Card; Expansion Slot; Graphics Card; Memory Board; Memory Card; Motherboard; PCB; PCI; PCMCIA; Peripheral Component Interconnect; Personal Computer Memory Card International Association; Printed Circuit Board; Slot; Sound Card; Video Card;*

FDD

Floppy Disk Drive. A device which is integral or attached to a computer and used with a floppy disk to record information.

See Also: *3.5 Inch; 5.25 Inch; Archive; ATAPI; Attachment Packet Interface; Backing Store; Backup; C Prompt; Computer Power; Configuration; Crash; Device; Disk; Disk Drive; Disk Pack; Disk Size; Disk Storage; Diskette; Drive; EIDE; EISA; Enhanced Industry Standard Architecture; Enhanced Intelligent Drive Electronics; Equipment; Five and a quarter; Fixed Disk Drive; Floppy Disk; Floppy Disk Drive; Hard Disk Drive; Hardware; HDD; Head Crash; Heads; IDE; Integrated Drive Electronics; Kit; Machine Crash; Magnetic Disk; Mass Storage; Pack; Peripheral; Power; Read/Write Head; Recording; Recording Device; Save; Seek Time; Storage; Store; Three and a Half; Winchester Disk; Write; Write Protect;*

FDDI

Fibre Distributed Data Interface. A standard for data transmission through optical fibres at rates of about 100 million bps.

See Also: *Acoustic Coupler; ADN; ADSL; Advanced Digital Network; AMR; Asymmetric Digital Subscriber Line; Asymmetrical Modem; Asynchronous; Asynchronous Transfer Mode; ATM; Automatic Message Routing; Bandwidth; Baud Rate; Bits Per Second; BPS; Broadband; CCITT; CCTA; Channel; Characters Per Second; Client Server Protocol; Communications; Consultative Committee International Telegraph and Telephone; CPS; Data Communications; Data Parity; Data Transmission; Datacoms; Dial In; Dial Up; Digital; Direct Connection; Duplex Transmission; ECP; Enhanced Parallel Port; EPP; Extended Capabilities Port; Fibre Distributed Data Interface; Fibre Optics; Full Duplex; Gbps; Half Duplex; Handshake; HD; Integrated Services Digital Network; ISDN; Kbps; Leased Line; Mbps; Modem; Modulator Demodulator; Multiplex; Multiplexer; Narrowband; Open Systems Interconnect; Optical Fibre; OSI; Packet; Packet Switching; Parallel Transmission; Parity Bit; Serial Transmission; Simplex Transmission;*

Synchronous; Telecommunication; Telecoms; Teleprocessing System; TPS; Transfer Rate; Transmission Channel; Transmit; V90;

Fibre Distributed Data Interface

(FDDI). A standard for data transmission through optical fibres at rates of about 100 million bps.

See Also: *Acoustic Coupler; ADN; ADSL; Advanced Digital Network; AMR; Asymmetric Digital Subscriber Line; Asymmetrical Modem; Asynchronous; Asynchronous Transfer Mode; ATM; Automatic Message Routing; Bandwidth; Baud Rate; Bits Per Second; BPS; Broadband; CCITT; CCTA; Channel; Characters Per Second; Client Server Protocol; Communications; Consultative Committee International Telegraph and Telephone; CPS; Data Communications; Data Parity; Data Transmission; Datacoms; Dial In; Dial Up; Digital; Direct Connection; Duplex Transmission; ECP; Enhanced Parallel Port; EPP; Extended Capabilities Port; FDDI; Fibre Optics; Full Duplex; Gbps; Half Duplex; Handshake; HD; Integrated Services Digital Network; ISDN; Kbps; Leased Line; Mbps; Modem; Modulator Demodulator; Multiplex; Multiplexer; Narrowband; Open Systems Interconnect; Optical Fibre; OSI; Packet; Packet Switching; Parallel Transmission; Parity Bit; Serial Transmission; Simplex Transmission; Synchronous; Telecommunication; Telecoms; Teleprocessing System; TPS; Transfer Rate; Transmission Channel; Transmit; V90;*

Fibre Optics

Very thin glass or plastic fibres which use light to transmit data along the fibres.

See Also: *Acoustic Coupler; ADN; ADSL; Advanced Digital Network; AMR; Asymmetric Digital Subscriber Line; Asymmetrical Modem; Asynchronous; Asynchronous Transfer Mode; ATM; Automatic Message Routing; Bandwidth; Baud Rate; Bits Per Second; BPS; Broadband; CCITT; CCTA; Channel; Characters Per Second; Client Server Protocol; Communications; Consultative Committee International Telegraph and Telephone; CPS; Data Communications; Data Parity; Data Transmission; Datacoms; Dial In; Dial Up; Digital; Direct Connection; Duplex Transmission; ECP; Enhanced Parallel Port; EPP; Extended Capabilities Port; FDDI; Fibre Distributed Data Interface; Full Duplex; Gbps; Half Duplex; HD; Integrated Services Digital Network; ISDN; Kbps; Leased Line; Mbps; Modem; Modulator Demodulator; Multiplex; Multiplexer; Narrowband; Open Systems Interconnect; Optical Fibre; OSI; Packet; Packet Switching; Parallel Transmission; Parity Bit; Serial Transmission; Simplex Transmission; Synchronous; Telecommunication;*

Telecoms; Teleprocessing System; TPS; Transfer Rate; Transmission Channel; Transmit; V90;

Fiche
A recording medium where data is reduced in size and printed onto a piece of plastic the size of a post card. A microfiche reader is needed to view the data on the fiche.
See Also: *Archive; Backing Store; Backup; Block; COM; Computer Output Microfilm; Directory; Medium; Microfiche; Microfilm; Output; Recording Medium; Root Directory; Save; Sub Directory;*

Field
An item of data. A number of fields make a record.
See Also: *Array; Character; Check Box; Comma Separated Values; Constant; CSV; Data; Data Dictionary; Data Element; Data Entity; Data Item; Data Type; Database; DB; EBCDIC; Entity; Extended Binary Coded Decimal Interchange Code; Group; Information; Key; Literal; Null; Radio Button; Record; Subscript; Transaction; Variable; Word;*

File
A stored collection of records in some possible order.
See Also: *Access; Archive; ASCII Files; Attachment; AUTOEXEC.BAT; Backing Store; Backup; Batch File; Beginning of File; BOF; Compressed File; Data Dictionary; Database; DB; Dead Lock; Deadly Embrace; Defragment; Direct Access; Directory; Document; Edit; End of File; EOF; Extension; File Conversion; File Server; File Sharing; File Transfer Protocol; Filename Extension; Folder; Fragmentation; FTP; FTP Site; Grandfather, Father, Son; Header; Index Sequential File; Indexed Sequential Access Method; Information; ISAM; Keyed Sequential Access Method; KSAM; Log File; Mirror Site; Random Access; Random File; RDB; RDBMS/RDMS; Relational Database; Relational Database Management System; Root Directory; Save; Self Extracting File; Sequential File; Serial File; Sub Directory; Table; Tag File; Temp File;*

File Allocation Table
(FAT). A type of file index on the hard disk used by the operating system.
See Also: *Directory; Disk Operating System; DOS; FAT; Linux; Operating System; OS; OS/2; Root Directory; Sub Directory;*

File Conversion
The process of converting a file from one format to another.
See Also: *ASCII Files; Batch Processing; Compressed File; Compression; Conversion; Convert; Decompression; File; Maintenance;*

File Server
Hardware and software, which control the sharing of data files for computers connected together in a network.
See Also: *Access; CGI; Client Server; Client Server Protocol; Common Gateway Interface; Configuration; Distributed System/Network; Download; Environment; Equipment; Ethernet; File; File Sharing; Gateway; Hardware; Host Processor; Installation; Intranet; Kit; LAN; LAN Port; Local Area Network; Mailserver; Multi User; Multitasking; Network; Network Information Centre; Network Operating System; NIC; Node; NOS; Open Systems Interconnect; OSI; Remote Device; Ring Network; Server; Star Cluster; Star Network; TCP/IP; Teleprocessing System; Token Ring; TPS; Transmission Control Protocol/Internet Protocol; Upload; WAN; Wide Area Network; XMODEM; YMODEM; ZMODEM;*

File Sharing
A procedure where more than one program can share in the use of the same file(s) with control not allowing any program to update a record if it is currently being updated by another program.
See Also: *Access; Client Server; Dead Lock; Deadly Embrace; Ethernet; File; File Server; Integrated; Integrated Systems; Intranet; LAN; Local Area Network; Locking; Multi User; Multitasking; Network; Record Locking; Ring Network; Server; Star Cluster; Star Network; Token Ring; WAN; Wide Area Network;*

File Transfer Protocol
(FTP). Rules or ways of transferring files via the Internet.
See Also: *Acceptable User Policy; Anonymous FTP; AUP; CGI; Client Server Protocol; Common Gateway Interface; Cyberspace; File; FTP; FTP Site; FTPmail; Gateway; Handshake; International Standards Organisation; ISO; Mirror Site; MP3; Protocol; TCP/IP; Transmission Control Protocol/Internet Protocol;*

Filename Extension
The three or four letter suffix after the end of a file name which denotes the type of file. It is separated from the filename with a dot, e.g. '.doc' = document file, '.jpg' = graphics file.
See Also: *ASCII Files; Attachment; Batch File; BitMaP; BMP; Extension; File; GIF; Graphical Interchange Format; Joint Photographic Experts Group; JPEG; JPG; Motion Picture Experts Group; MPEG; MPG; PDF; Portable Document Format; Rich Text Format; RTF; Tag Image File Format; TIFF; WAV; Waveform Audio;*

Firewall
Computer hardware/software used as security to restrict access to a computer or network.
See Also: *CGI; Client Server; Common Gateway Interface; Configuration; E-commerce; EDI; Electronic Data Interchange; Gateway; Hacker; Network Information Centre; NIC; Secure Socket Layer; Security; Server; Software System; SSL; Virus; Virus Checker;*

Firewire
A connection between a PC and devices which provides for fast transmission of data.
See Also: *ADN; Advanced Digital Network; Asynchronous Transfer Mode; ATM; Channel; Communications; Data Communications; Device; Direct Connection; Duplex Transmission; EIDE; Enhanced Intelligent Drive Electronics; Full Duplex; IDE; Integrated Drive Electronics; Interface; Leased Line; MCA; Micro Channel Architecture; Multiplexer; PC; Personal Computer; SCSI; Serial Interface; Simplex Transmission; Small Computer System Interface; Transmission Channel; V90;*

Firmware
Programs which are stored in read only memory (ROM) and are not lost when the computer is turned off or reset.
See Also: *Basic Input Output System; BIOS; CMOS; Complementary Metal Oxide Semiconductor Memory; Configuration; DLL; Dynamic Link Library; EXE; Execute; Instruction; Memory Resident; Program; ROM Resident; System Software;*

Five and a quarter
(1) A floppy disk, which is 5.25 inches in diameter with storage capacities that vary from 360k to 1.2Mb. (2) The disk drive to take a 5.25 inch disk.
See Also: *3.5 Inch; 5.25 Inch; Archive; ATAPI; Attachment Packet Interface; Backing Store; Backup; Bits Per Inch; Block; Boot Disk; BPI; Cluster; Computer Power; Configuration; Crash; Cylinder; Defragment; Density; Device; Directory; Disk; Disk Drive; Disk Map; Disk Pack; Disk Size; Disk Storage; Diskette; Double Density; Drive; EIDE; Enhanced Intelligent Drive Electronics; Equipment; FDD; Fixed Disk Drive; Floppy Disk; Floppy Disk Drive; Format; Fragmentation; Grandfather, Father, Son; Hard Disk Drive; Hardware; HDD; Head Crash; Heads; High Density; IDE; Indexed Sequential Access Method; Integrated Drive Electronics; ISAM; Keyed Sequential Access Method; Kit; KSAM; Machine Crash; Magnetic Disk; Mass Storage; Medium; Pack; Peripheral; Power; Read/Write Head; Recording; Recording Device; Recording Medium; Root Directory; Save; Sector; Seek Time;*

Storage; Store; Sub Directory; Three and a Half; Track; Volume; Winchester Disk; Wipe; Write; Write Protect;

Fixed Disk Drive
A magnetic storage device enclosed in a sealed unit.
See Also: *3.5 Inch; 5.25 Inch; Archive; ATAPI; Attachment Packet Interface; Backing Store; Backup; C Prompt; Computer Power; Configuration; Crash; Device; Disk; Disk Drive; Disk Pack; Disk Size; Disk Storage; Diskette; Drive; EIDE; EISA; Enhanced Industry Standard Architecture; Enhanced Intelligent Drive Electronics; Equipment; FDD; Five and a quarter; Floppy Disk; Floppy Disk Drive; Hard Disk Drive; Hardware; HDD; Head Crash; Heads; IDE; Integrated Drive Electronics; Kit; Machine Crash; Magnetic Disk; Mass Storage; Pack; Peripheral; Power; Read/Write Head; Recording; Recording Device; Save; Seek Time; Storage; Store; Three and a Half; Winchester Disk; Write; Write Protect;*

FL
Fuzzy Logic. A logic system where a percentage factor is allocated to the logical operations which makes for a different procedure path through the logic each time.
See Also: *AI; ALU; AMR; AND gate; Arithmetic and Logic Unit; Artificial Intelligence; Automatic Message Routing; Boolean Algebra; Expert System; Flip Flop; Fuzzy Logic; I-OR gate; Logic Gate; NAND gate; NEQ gate; NOR gate; NOT gate; OR gate; X-OR gate;*

Flame
A derogatory message sent by e-mail as reprimand for not adhering to netiquette.
See Also: *Chat; Chatroom; Electronic Mail; E-mail; Hacker; Mailbox; Mailing List; Netiquette; Signature;*

Flash Memory
Memory that can be updated by software.
See Also: *Absolute Address; Address; Array; Block; Bubble Memory; Buffer; Cache Memory; Central Processing Unit; Clipboard; CMOS; Complementary Metal Oxide Semiconductor Memory; Computer Power; Conventional Memory; Core; Core Dump; CPU; DDR SDRAM; DIMM; Direct Memory Access; Direct Random Access Memory; Disk Cache; DMA; Double Data Rate SDRAM; DRAM; Dual Inline Memory Module; Dump; Dynamic Memory; Dynamically; EEROM; Electrically Erasable Read Only Memory; Electronically Programmed Read Only Memory; EMS; EPROM; Erasable Programmable Read Only Memory; Expanded*

Memory; Expanded Memory Specification; Extended Memory; High Memory; Magnetic Core; Maths Co-processor; Memory; Memory Board; Memory Caching; Memory Card; Memory Resident; Mix; Power; Programmable Read Only Memory; PROM; RAM; RAM Disk; Rambus Dynamic Random Access Memory; Random Access Memory; RDRAM; Read Only Memory; Relative Address; ROM; SDRAM; Shadow RAM Memory; SIMM; Single Inline Memory Modules; Single Inline Package; SIP; Store; Synchronous Dynamic Random Access Memory; Upper Memory; Video Random Access Memory; Volatile Memory; VRAM; Working Storage; Workspace;

Flatbed Scanner
A flat device like a photocopier which optically reads a document into the computer by recognising the shapes of characters or graphics when the document is scanned.
See Also: *Analogue Digital Converter; CCD; Charge Coupled Device; Configuration; Device; Drum; Environment; Equipment; Hardware; Installation; Kit; OCR; OMR; Optical Character Reader; Optical Character Recognition; Optical Mark Recognition; Optical Scanner; Peripheral; Scanner;*

Flip Flop
Part of a processor or printed circuit capable of being in an 'on/off' or 'open/shut' state.
See Also: *ALU; AMR; AND gate; Arithmetic and Logic Unit; Automatic Message Routing; Boolean Algebra; Chip; Chipset; FL; Fuzzy Logic; I-OR gate; Large Scale Integration; Logic Gate; LSI; NAND gate; NEQ gate; NOR gate; NOT gate; OR gate; Processor; Silicon Chip; Sound Chip; Toggle; Transistor; Very Large Scale Integration; VLSI; X-OR gate;*

Floating Point
A mathematical notation which allows large numbers with a decimal point to be stored. The decimal point is not in its correct position and is stored with a number indicating where the point should be.
See Also: *Co-processor; Maths Co-processor;*

Floating Toolbar
A collection of icons that can be moved to anywhere on the screen.
See Also: *Drag; Graphics; Icon; Image Map; Image Processing; Sprite; Toolbar;*

Floppy Disk

A disk of a flexible material which has magnetic surfaces on which data is recorded.

See Also: *3.5 Inch; 5.25 Inch; Archive; ATAPI; Attachment Packet Interface; Backing Store; Backup; Bits Per Inch; Block; Boot Disk; BPI; Cluster; Computer Power; Configuration; Crash; Cylinder; Defragment; Density; Device; Directory; Disk; Disk Drive; Disk Map; Disk Operating System; Disk Pack; Disk Size; Disk Storage; Diskette; DOS; Double Density; EIDE; Enhanced Intelligent Drive Electronics; Equipment; FDD; Five and a quarter; Fixed Disk Drive; Floppy Disk Drive; Format; Fragmentation; Grandfather, Father, Son; Hard Disk Drive; Hardware; HDD; Head Crash; Heads; High Density; Indexed Sequential Access Method; ISAM; Keyed Sequential Access Method; Kit; KSAM; Machine Crash; Magnetic Disk; Mass Storage; Medium; Pack; Peripheral; Power; Read/Write Head; Recording; Recording Device; Recording Medium; Root Directory; Save; Sector; Seek Time; Storage; Store; Sub Directory; Three and a Half; Track; Volume; Winchester Disk; Wipe; Write; Write Protect;*

Floppy Disk Drive

(FDD). A device which is integral or attached to a computer and used with a floppy disk to record information.

See Also: *3.5 Inch; 5.25 Inch; Archive; ATAPI; Attachment Packet Interface; Backing Store; Backup; C Prompt; Computer Power; Configuration; Crash; Device; Disk; Disk Drive; Disk Pack; Disk Size; Disk Storage; Diskette; Drive; EIDE; EISA; Enhanced Industry Standard Architecture; Enhanced Intelligent Drive Electronics; Equipment; FDD; Five and a quarter; Fixed Disk Drive; Floppy Disk; Hard Disk Drive; Hardware; HDD; Head Crash; Heads; IDE; Integrated Drive Electronics; Kit; Machine Crash; Magnetic Disk; Mass Storage; Pack; Peripheral; Power; Read/Write Head; Recording; Recording Device; Save; Seek Time; Storage; Store; Three and a Half; Winchester Disk; Write; Write Protect;*

Flowchart

A graphical representation showing the flow of a process, a series of processes or a program.

See Also: *Analyst; Audit Trail; B/A; Business Analyst; CASE; Case Tool; Computer Aided Software Engineering; Design; Development; Logical Design; Model; Modular; O & M; Organisation & Methods; Physical Design; Process Model; Program Specification; S/A; Specification;*

FM
Facilities Management. A service provided to companies by outside organisations who take over the data processing on behalf of the company.
See Also: *Computation; Compute; Data Centre; Data Processing; Downsizing; DP; EDP; Electronic Data Processing; Facilities Management; Installation; Integrated Systems; Outsourcing; Processing; Software House; Software System; Third Party Maintenance;*

Folder
A logical area on a disk in which files are stored and organised. There may be sub folders within folders.
See Also: *Archive; Directory; File; Path; Root Directory; Sub Directory;*

Font
A collection of characters and symbols of the same typeface.
See Also: *Character; Characters Per Inch; CPI; Font Cartridge; Format; Letter Quality; LQ; Near Letter Quality; NLQ; OCR; OMR; Optical Character Reader; Optical Character Recognition; Optical Mark Recognition; Postscript; Scalable Fonts; WYSIWYG;*

Font Cartridge
A cartridge which plugs into a printer and holds different font types for printing.
See Also: *Bubble Jet; Characters Per Inch; CPI; Daisywheel; Dot Matrix; Font; Inkjet; Laser Jet; Laser Printer; LCD Printer; Letter Quality; Liquid Crystal Display Printer; LQ; Matrix Printer; Near Letter Quality; NLQ; Page Printer; Postscript; Printer; Scalable Fonts; Thermal Printer;*

Footer
An area at the bottom of a printed page reserved for document details.
See Also: *Electronic Mail; E-mail; Header; Page;*

Format
(1) The characteristics of text or graphics. (2) A command to initialise a disk for use.
See Also: *3.5 Inch; 5.25 Inch; American Standard Code for Information Interchange; ASCII; BitMaP; BMP; Comma Separated Values; CSV; Disk; Disk Map; Disk Pack; Disk Storage; Diskette; Dots Per Inch; DPI; EBCDIC; Execute; Extended Binary Coded Decimal Interchange Code; Five and a quarter; Floppy Disk; Font; Fragmentation; GIF; Graphical Interchange Format; Joint Photographic Experts Group; JPEG; JPG;*

Landscape; Letter Quality; LQ; Magnetic Disk; Matrix; Motion Picture Experts Group; MPEG; MPG; Near Letter Quality; NLQ; Pack; PDF; Portable Document Format; Portrait; Postscript; Record; Rich Text Format; RTF; Scalable Fonts; Tag Image File Format; Three and a Half; TIFF; Utility; WYSIWYG;

FORTH
A high level computer programming language.
See Also: *3GL; 4GL; ADA; ALGOL; APL; BASIC; C or C++; CLIPPER; COBOL; Code; Code Generator; Compiler; Compiling; CORAL; FORTRAN; Fourth Generation Language; High Level Language; Instruction Set; JAVA; JAVASCRIPT; Language; LISP; LOGO; Module; NATURAL; PASCAL; PERL; PICK; PILOT; PL/1; Practical Extraction and Reporting Language; Program; Programming Language; PROLOG; RPG; Software; Source Code; Structured Program; Syntax; Third Generation Language; Visual Basic;*

FORTRAN
A high-level computer programming language used for mathematical and scientific applications.
See Also: *3GL; 4GL; ADA; ALGOL; APL; BASIC; C or C++; CLIPPER; COBOL; Code; Code Generator; Compiler; Compiling; CORAL; FORTH; Fourth Generation Language; High Level Language; Instruction Set; JAVA; JAVASCRIPT; Language; LISP; LOGO; Module; NATURAL; PASCAL; PERL; PICK; PILOT; PL/1; Practical Extraction and Reporting Language; Program; Programming Language; PROLOG; RPG; Software; Source Code; Structured Program; Syntax; Third Generation Language; Visual Basic;*

Forum
An area on a website where users can read or write messages and take part in a debate electronically.
See Also: *Chat; Chatroom; Electronic Mail; E-mail; Emoticons; FAQ; Frequently Asked Questions; IM; Instant Messaging; Interactive; Internet Relay Chat; IRC; Mailbox; Nerd; Netiquette; Newbie; Newsgroup; Online; Real Time; Site; Smileys; Surfing; The Web; Thread; User Group; Webring; Website; World Wide Web; WWW;*

Fourth Generation Language
A fourth generation high level computer programming language.
See Also: *3GL; 4GL; 4th Generation; ADA; ALGOL; APL; BASIC; C or C++; CLIPPER; COBOL; CODASYL; Code; Code Generator; Compiler; Compiling; Conference On DAta SYstems Languages;*

CORAL; FORTH; FORTRAN; High Level Language; Instruction Set; Interpreter; LISP; LOGO; NATURAL; PASCAL; PERL; PICK; PILOT; PL/1; Practical Extraction and Reporting Language; Program; PROLOG; RPG; Software; Software System; Source Code; Syntax; System; System Software; Third Generation Language; Visual Basic;

Fragmentation
The efficient use by the operating system to store files in many available areas on the disk even though they may not be next to each other.
See Also: *3.5 Inch; 5.25 Inch; ASCII Files; Defragment; Disk; Disk Map; Disk Pack; Disk Storage; Diskette; File; Five and a quarter; Floppy Disk; Format; Housekeeping; Index Sequential File; Log File; Magnetic Disk; Pack; Random File; Serial File; Storage; Tag File; Temp File; Three and a Half; Volume; Winchester Disk;*

Frame Rate
The number of frames displayed over a period of time to show movement on the screen. A higher rate shows a faster action than a slow rate.
See Also: *Display; Graphics; Graphics Card; Image Processing; Interlaced; Low Resolution; Monitor; Paint Screen; Resolution; Screen; Sprite; TFT; Thin-Film Transistor; Twip; VDU; Video Card; Visual Display Unit;*

Freeware
Software supplied free of charge attained through magazines or downloaded from the Internet.
See Also: *Application; BBS; Bulletin Board System; CAD; CADCAM; CADMAT; CAE; CAI; CAM; CBT; Computer Aided Design; Computer Aided Design and Manufacturing; Computer Aided Design Manufacture and Test; Computer Aided Engineering; Computer Aided Instruction; Computer Aided Manufacturing; Computer Based Training; Device Driver; DLL; Driver; Dynamic Link Library; EXE; Module; Package; Program; Public Domain; Software; Software Driver; Software Package; Software System;*

Frequently Asked Questions
(FAQ). A list of frequently asked questions and answers relating to a particular subject.
See Also: *FAQ; Forum; Newsgroup;*

Front End Processor
A device which interfaces and communicates with the main processor. Usually a computer that processes input data before passing it to the main computer.
See Also: *Analogue Digital Converter; Client Server; Computer; Configuration; Device; Distributed System/Network; Environment; Extended Technology; Hand Held Device; IBM (tm) Compatible; Installation; Integrated; Machine; Micro; Microcomputer; Midrange System; Minicomputer; Peripheral; Point of Sales; POS; Remote Device; Server; Turnkey; XT;*

FTP
File Transfer Protocol. Rules or ways of transferring files via the Internet.
See Also: *Acceptable User Policy; Anonymous FTP; AUP; CGI; Client Server Protocol; Common Gateway Interface; Cyberspace; File; File Transfer Protocol; FTP Site; FTPmail; Gateway; Handshake; International Standards Organisation; ISO; Mirror Site; MP3; Protocol; TCP/IP; Transmission Control Protocol/Internet Protocol;*

FTP Site
A website used as a depository for files which users may download.
See Also: *Anonymous FTP; BBS; Bulletin Board System; Cyberspace; File; File Transfer Protocol; FTP; FTPmail; Mirror Site; Network Information Centre; NIC; Site; The Web; Webring; Website; World Wide Web; WWW;*

FTPmail
The process when e-mail is used to access FTP sites.
See Also: *Anonymous FTP; BBS; Bulletin Board System; Cyberspace; Electronic Mail; E-mail; File Transfer Protocol; FTP; FTP Site; Mirror Site; Site; Website;*

Full Duplex
A transmission system along a communication line which allows devices to communicate with each other at the same time.
See Also: *ACK; Acoustic Coupler; ADN; ADSL; Advanced Digital Network; AMR; Asymmetric Digital Subscriber Line; Asymmetrical Modem; Asynchronous; Asynchronous Transfer Mode; ATM; Automatic Message Routing; Bandwidth; Baud Rate; Bits Per Second; BPS; Broadband; Bus; CCITT; CCTA; Channel; Characters Per Second; Communications; Consultative Committee International Telegraph and Telephone; CPS; Data Communications; Data Parity; Data Transmission; Datacoms; Dial In; Dial Up; Digital; Direct Connection;*

Duplex Transmission; FDDI; Fibre Distributed Data Interface; Fibre Optics; Firewire; Gbps; Half Duplex; HD; Integrated Services Digital Network; ISDN; Kbps; Leased Line; Mbps; Modem; Modulator Demodulator; Multiplex; Multiplexer; Narrowband; Optical Fibre; Parallel Transmission; Parity Bit; Serial Interface; Serial Transmission; Simplex Transmission; Synchronous; Telecommunication; Telecoms; Teleprocessing System; TPS; Transfer Rate; Transmission Channel; Transmit; V90;

Full Project Life Cycle
All aspects in the development of a project for both hardware and software systems.
See Also: *A/P; Analyst; Analyst Programmer; B/A; Business Analyst; Design; Development; Going Live; Hand Holding; Live; Logical Design; Model; Modular; Physical Design; Process Model; Program Specification; Programmer; Project Life Cycle; Reengineering; S/A; S/P; Software Development Cycle; Software House; Specification; Structured Design; System Analysis; System Analyst; Systems Programmer; Technical Author; Upgrade; Walkthrough;*

Function
A set procedure of instructions to carry out a specific task.
See Also: *Applet; Audit Trail; Batch File; Batch Processing; Command; Device Driver; DLL; Driver; Dynamic Link Library; Event; EXE; Execute; Function Key; Instruction Set; JCL; Job; Job Control Language; Macro; Module; Nesting; Program; Run; Run Time; Script; Software Driver; Subroutine; System Software; Toggle; Utility;*

Function Key
One of a set of keys on the keyboard used for different functions by programs and allows commands to be done easily and quickly. They can also be programmed to carry out a function.
See Also: *Command; Function; Hot Key; Instruction; Keyboard; Macro; Script;*

Fuzzy Logic
(FL). A logic system where a percentage factor is allocated to the logical operations which makes for a different procedure path through the logic each time.
See Also: *AI; ALU; AMR; AND gate; Arithmetic and Logic Unit; Artificial Intelligence; Automatic Message Routing; Boolean Algebra; Expert System; FL; Flip Flop; I-OR gate; Logic Gate; NAND gate; NEQ gate; NOR gate; NOT gate; OR gate; X-OR gate;*

Garbage In, Garbage Out
Information put into and taken out of a computer. Information used within a computer or output from a computer is only as good as the information put in.
See Also: *Batch Processing; Data; Information; Input;*

Gateway
The computer hardware and software, which allows the connection from one network to another where there are two opposing protocols.
See Also: *Access; AMR; Automatic Message Routing; CGI; Client Server; Client Server Protocol; Common Gateway Interface; Distributed System/Network; Ethernet; File Server; File Transfer Protocol; Firewall; FTP; Handshake; Intranet; LAN; LAN Port; Local Area Network; Mailserver; Network; Network Information Centre; Network Operating System; NIC; Node; NOS; Open Systems Interconnect; OSI; Protocol; Ring Network; Secure Socket Layer; Serial Line Internet Protocol; Server; SLIP; Software; SSL; Star Cluster; Star Network; TCP/IP; Token Ring; Transmission Control Protocol/Internet Protocol; WAN; Wide Area Network; XMODEM; YMODEM; ZMODEM;*

Gb
Gigabyte. 1024 megabytes or one thousand million bytes (1,000,000,000). One byte equals one character.
See Also: *Byte; Character; Data; Gigabyte; K; Kb; Kbyte; Kilobit; Kilobyte; Mb; Mbyte; Megabit; Megabyte; Terabyte;*

Gbps
Giga (billion) bits per second. Represents a data transfer speed.
See Also: *16 Bit; 32 Bit; 64 Bit; 8 Bit; Access Time; Acoustic Coupler; Address Bus; ADN; ADSL; Advanced Digital Network; Asymmetric Digital Subscriber Line; Asynchronous; Asynchronous Transfer Mode; ATM; Bandwidth; Baud Rate; Binary; Binary Digit; Bit; Bits Per Second; BPS; Broadband; Bus; CCITT; CCTA; Characters Per Second; Communications; Consultative Committee International Telegraph and Telephone; CPS; Data Bus; Data Communications; Data Parity; Data Transmission; Datacoms; Dial In; Dial Up; Duplex Transmission; Eight Bit; FDDI; Fibre Distributed Data Interface; Fibre Optics; Full Duplex; GHz; Gigahertz; Half Duplex; HD; Integrated Services Digital Network; ISDN; Kbps; KHz; Kilohertz; Local Bus; Mbps; Microsecond; Million Instructions Per Second; Millisecond; MIPS; Ms; Multiplex; Multiplexer; Nanosecond; Narrowband; Ns; Optical Fibre; Parallel Transmission; Parity Bit; Pico Second; Serial Transmission; Simplex Transmission; Sixteen Bit; Sixty Four Bit; Synchronous; System Bus; T-1; T-3;*

Telecommunication; Telecoms; Thirty Two Bit; Transfer Rate; Transmit; V90;

General Protection Fault

(GPF). An error that occurs when a program is trying to use memory that is already used by another program.

See Also: *Bug; Crash; Dead Lock; Deadly Embrace; Debug; Debugger; Died; Downtime; GPF; Head Crash; Machine Crash; Program Crash; Recovery; System Hangs; Upper Memory;*

Geographical Information System

(GIS). A computer system where data is mapped or recorded by location. When mapped across a wide area the data can be manipulated or analysed to produce geographical information by location and comparison with other locations.

See Also: *Application; Bespoke; Computation; Compute; Data Processing; DP; EDP; EDS; Electronic Data Processing; Electronic Data System; GIS; Information System; Information Technology; IS; IT; Package; Processing; Shareware; Software; Software Package; Software System; Vertical Market;*

GHz

Gigahertz. A measure of the processor's chip speed. It is the measure of speed at which the system clock operates in a computer. e.g. 1 GHz = 1000 Mhz.

See Also: *Baud Rate; Bits Per Second; BPS; Characters Per Second; Chip; Chipset; Clock Speed; Communications; Computer Power; CPS; Data Communications; Data Transmission; Datacoms; Gbps; Gigahertz; Kbps; KHz; Kilohertz; Mbps; Megahertz; MHz; Power; Processor; Silicon Chip; Telecommunication; Telecoms; Transmit;*

GIF

Graphical Interchange Format. A file format for the storage of display images. The graphical files have a file extension of '.gif'.

See Also: *Attachment; BitMaP; BMP; Clip Art; Display; Extension; Filename Extension; Format; Graphical Interchange Format; Graphics; Image Processing; Joint Photographic Experts Group; JPEG; JPG; MIME; Multipurpose Internet Mail Extensions; PDF; Pixel; Portable Document Format; Resolution; Rich Text Format; RTF; Sprite; Tag Image File Format; Thumbnail; TIFF;*

Gigabyte
(Gb). 1024 megabytes or one thousand million bytes (1,000,000,000). One byte equals one character.
See Also: *Byte; Character; Data; Gb; K; Kb; Kbyte; Kilobit; Kilobyte; Mb; Mbyte; Megabit; Megabyte; Terabyte;*

Gigahertz
(GHz). A measure of the processor's chip speed. It is the measure of speed at which the system clock operates in a computer. e.g. 1 GHz = 1000 Mhz.
See Also: *Baud Rate; Bits Per Second; BPS; Characters Per Second; Chip; Chipset; Clock Speed; Communications; Computer Power; CPS; Data Communications; Data Transmission; Datacoms; Gbps; GHz; Kbps; KHz; Kilohertz; Mbps; Megahertz; MHz; Power; Processor; Silicon Chip; Telecommunication; Telecoms; Transmit;*

GIS
Geographical Information System. A computer system where data is mapped or recorded by location. When mapped across a wide area the data can be manipulated or analysed to produce geographical information by location and comparison with other locations.
See Also: *Application; Bespoke; Computation; Compute; Data Processing; DP; EDP; EDS; Electronic Data Processing; Electronic Data System; Geographical Information System; Information System; Information Technology; IS; IT; Package; Processing; Shareware; Software; Software Package; Software System; Vertical Market;*

Global
A term relating to the overall aspect of hardware and/or software. It can apply to all or an individual item of hardware or software.
See Also: *Environment; Equipment; Hardware; Installation; Kit; Software; The Web; World Wide Web; WWW;*

Going Live
The point in time when a computer system is first used while not in testing mode.
See Also: *Configuring; Full Project Life Cycle; Hand Holding; Live; Project Life Cycle; Releases; Run Time; Upgrade;*

Gopher

A system used to search for data or files, e.g. Internet searches, where the system takes a request for information and searches for it.

See Also: *BBS; Browser; Bulletin Board System; Cyberspace; Interactive; Internet; Meta-Search Engine; Net; Program; Public Domain; Query Language; Search Engine; Spider; SQL; Structured Query Language; The Net; Utility; Worm;*

GPF

General Protection Fault. An error that occurs when a program is trying to use memory that is already used by another program.

See Also: *Bug; Crash; Dead Lock; Deadly Embrace; Debug; Debugger; Died; Downtime; General Protection Fault; Head Crash; Machine Crash; Program Crash; Recovery; System Hangs; Upper Memory;*

Grandfather, Father, Son

The procedure of backing up or retaining data by securing the last three copies.

See Also: *3.5 Inch; 5.25 Inch; Archive; Backing Store; Backup; COM; Computer Output Microfilm; DAT; Digital Audio Tape; Disk; Disk Pack; Disk Storage; Diskette; File; Five and a quarter; Floppy Disk; Mag Tape; Magnetic Disk; Magnetic Tape; Mass Storage; Microfilm; Pack; Paper Tape; Recording; Recording Device; Recording Medium; Recovery; Restore; Roll Back; Save; Security; Storage; Store; Streamer; Tape Deck; Tape Streamer; Three and a Half; Volume; Winchester Disk; Zip; Zip Drive;*

Graphical Interchange Format

(GIF). A file format for the storage of display images. The graphical files have a file extension of '.gif'.

See Also: *Attachment; BitMaP; BMP; Clip Art; Display; Extension; Filename Extension; Format; GIF; Graphics; Image Processing; Joint Photographic Experts Group; JPEG; JPG; MIME; Multipurpose Internet Mail Extensions; PDF; Pixel; Portable Document Format; Resolution; Rich Text Format; RTF; Sprite; Tag Image File Format; Thumbnail; TIFF;*

Graphical User Interface

(GUI). A system which allows computer users to work with graphical pictures or icons on the screen instead of text. It is an operating system environment. Pronounced "gooey".

See Also: *API; Application Program Interface; Browser; CODEC; COmpressor DECompressor; Disk Operating System; Display; DOS;*

Environment; Graphics; GUI; Image Map; Image Processing; Linux; Operating System; OS; OS/2; Program; Software System; System Software; User Friendly; WIMP; Windows Icons Mice and Pull-down menus;

Graphics

Input and output in graphical form as displayed on a PC screen.

See Also: *Accelerated Graphics Port; Advanced Graphics Port; AGP; AGP Slot; Bar Chart; Bar Code; BitMaP; BMP; Browser; Clip Art; Cursor; Desk Top Publishing; Disk Map; Display; Drag; DTP; Emoticons; Floating Toolbar; Frame Rate; GIF; Graphical Interchange Format; Graphical User Interface; Graphics Card; GUI; High Resolution; Hyperlink; Hypertext; Icon; Image Map; Image Processing; Joint Photographic Experts Group; JPEG; JPG; Low Resolution; Marquee; Motion Picture Experts Group; MPEG; MPG; Multimedia; PDF; Pie Chart; Pixel; Portable Document Format; Radio Button; Resolution; Screen Dump; Smileys; Sprite; Tag Image File Format; TIFF; Toolbar; Twip; Video Card; WIMP; Window; Windows Icons Mice and Pull-down menus; WYSIWYG;*

Graphics Card

The printed circuit board that controls the monitor allowing all the complexities of colour and designs we see on the screen.

See Also: *Accelerated Graphics Port; Advanced Graphics Port; AGP; AGP Slot; Analogue Monitor; Anti Glare Screen; Application Specific Integrated Circuits; ASICS; Cathode Ray Tube; CGA; Colour Graphics Adaptor; CRT; Digital Monitor; Digital Video Interface; Display; DVI; EGA; Enhanced Graphic Adaptor; Extended Video Array; Fax Card; Frame Rate; Graphics; High Resolution; IC; Image Processing; Integrated Circuit; Intelligent Terminal; Interlaced; LCD; Liquid Crystal Display; Low Resolution; Monitor; Monochrome; Motherboard; Paint Screen; PCB; PCI; PCMCIA; Peripheral Component Interconnect; Personal Computer Memory Card International Association; Plasma Screen; Printed Circuit Board; Resolution; Screen; Sound Card; Split Screen; Super Twist LCD; Super VGA; Super Video Graphics Array; SVGA; Terminal; TFT; Thin-Film Transistor; Touch Screen; VDT; VDU; VGA; Video Card; Video Display Terminal; Video Graphics Array; Video Random Access Memory; Visual Display Terminal; Visual Display Unit; VRAM; XGA;*

Group
Two or more data items or fields.
See Also: *Constant; Data; Data Dictionary; Data Element; Data Entity; Data Item; Data Type; EBCDIC; Entity; Extended Binary Coded Decimal Interchange Code; Field; Information; Literal; Null; Variable;*

GUI
Graphical User Interface. A system which allows computer users to work with graphical pictures or icons on the screen instead of text. It is an operating system environment. Pronounced "gooey".
See Also: *API; Application Program Interface; Browser; CODEC; COmpressor DECompressor; Disk Operating System; Display; DOS; Environment; Graphical User Interface; Graphics; Image Map; Image Processing; Linux; Operating System; OS; OS/2; Program; Software System; System Software; User Friendly; WIMP; Windows Icons Mice and Pull-down menus;*

Hacker
A person who does not have the authority to use or access a computer. They gain access by deciphering passwords and are normally at a different location to where the computer is located.
See Also: *Browser; Firewall; Flame; Log In/Off; Password; Pirate Copy; Spam; Surfing; Trojan; Virus; Virus Checker;*

Half Duplex
(HD). A transmission system in both directions along a communication line but not simultaneously.
See Also: *ACK; Acoustic Coupler; ADN; ADSL; Advanced Digital Network; AMR; Asymmetric Digital Subscriber Line; Asymmetrical Modem; Asynchronous; Asynchronous Transfer Mode; ATM; Automatic Message Routing; Bandwidth; Baud Rate; Bits Per Second; BPS; Broadband; Bus; CCITT; CCTA; Channel; Characters Per Second; Communications; Consultative Committee International Telegraph and Telephone; CPS; Data Communications; Data Parity; Data Transmission; Datacoms; Dial In; Dial Up; Digital; Direct Connection; Duplex Transmission; FDDI; Fibre Distributed Data Interface; Fibre Optics; Full Duplex; Gbps; HD; Integrated Services Digital Network; ISDN; Kbps; Leased Line; Mbps; Modem; Modulator Demodulator; Narrowband; Open Systems Interconnect; Optical Fibre; OSI; Parallel Transmission; Parity Bit; Serial Transmission; Simplex Transmission; Synchronous; Telecommunication; Telecoms; Transfer Rate; Transmission Channel; Transmit; V90;*

Hand Held Device
A device which is held in the hand and used remotely to capture and process data. It can then link with a computer to transfer the data.
See Also: *Analogue; Analogue Computer; Analogue Digital Converter; Configuration; Device; Downsizing; Environment; Equipment; Front End Processor; Hardware; Kit; Light Pen; Mouse; PDA; Peripheral; Personal Digital Assistant; Recording Device; Remote Device;*

Hand Holding
The helping of users who are not familiar with hardware or software systems.
See Also: *Analyst; B/A; Business Analyst; Configuring; End User; Full Project Life Cycle; Going Live; Hands On; Help Desk; Live; Project Life Cycle; Run Time; S/A; System Analyst; User; User Guide; User Manual; Walkthrough;*

Hands On
A term used when a person is physically using a computer.
See Also: *End User; Hand Holding; Interactive; Operator; User;*

Handshake
A signal which is compatible between two or more computers or pieces of equipment that informs about the communication status between each other. e.g. ready to transmit data.
See Also: *Access; ACK; Acoustic Coupler; Client Server; Client Server Protocol; Compatible; Dial In; Dial Up; Direct Connection; FDDI; Fibre Distributed Data Interface; File Transfer Protocol; FTP; Gateway; Integrated Services Digital Network; Interactive; Internet Protocol; Internet Service Provider; IP; ISDN; ISP; Leased Line; MIDI; MIME; Modem; Modulator Demodulator; Multipurpose Internet Mail Extensions; Musical Instrument Digital Interface; Node; Online; Open Systems Interconnect; OSI; PING; Point to Point Protocol; PPP; Protocol; Provider; Secure Socket Layer; Serial Line Internet Protocol; Server; Service Provider; SLIP; SSL; TCP/IP; Transmission Control Protocol/Internet Protocol; Wap Internet Service Provider; WISP; XMODEM; YMODEM; ZMODEM;*

Hangs
A term used when a computer hardware or software system stops in the middle of processing with no indication of the cause and does not allow the user to continue unless the system is re-initialised.
See Also: *Abort; Bug; Crash; Dead Lock; Deadly Embrace; Debug; Debugger; Died; Head Crash; Hung; Locking; Machine Crash; Off Line; Program Crash; Record Locking; System Hangs; Timeout;*

Hard Copy
The result of formatted information produced on paper output.
See Also: *Barrel Printer; Bi Directional; Bubble Jet; Cut Sheet Feeder; Daisywheel; Dot Matrix; Drum Printer; Duplex Printing; Inkjet; Landscape; Laser Jet; Laser Printer; LCD Printer; Letter Quality; Line Printer; Lines Per Minute; Liquid Crystal Display Printer; Lpm; LQ; Matrix Printer; Near Letter Quality; NLQ; Output; Page Printer; Pages Per Minute; Plotter; Portrait; Postscript; PPM; Printer; Printout; Sheet Feeder; Simplex Printing; Thermal Printer;*

Hard Disk Drive
(HDD). A peripheral device in which information is stored on a sealed magnetic disk.
See Also: *3.5 Inch; 5.25 Inch; Archive; ATAPI; Attachment Packet Interface; Backing Store; Backup; C Prompt; Computer Power; Configuration; Crash; Device; Disk; Disk Drive; Disk Pack; Disk Size; Disk Storage; Diskette; Drive; EIDE; EISA; Enhanced Industry Standard Architecture; Enhanced Intelligent Drive Electronics; Equipment; FDD; Five and a quarter; Fixed Disk Drive; Floppy Disk; Floppy Disk Drive; Hardware; HDD; Head Crash; Heads; IDE; Integrated Drive Electronics; Kit; Machine Crash; Magnetic Disk; Mass Storage; MCA; Micro Channel Architecture; Pack; Peripheral; Power; Read/Write Head; Recording; Recording Device; Save; Seek Time; Storage; Store; Three and a Half; Winchester Disk; Write; Write Protect;*

Hardware
The equipment which make up a computer system.
See Also: *1st Generation; 2nd Generation; 3.5 Inch; 3rd Generation; 4th Generation; 5.25 Inch; Acoustic Coupler; Advanced Technology; Analogue Computer; Analogue Digital Converter; Analogue Monitor; Anti Glare Screen; Asymmetrical Modem; AT; Backing Store; Barrel Printer; Bespoke; Black Box; Bubble Jet; Cathode Ray Tube; CD-ROM Drive; CD-RW Drive; CGA; Client Server; Colour Graphics Adaptor; Computer; Configuration; Cross Platform; CRT; Daisywheel; DAT; Deck; Desktop; Device; Digital Analog Converter; Digital Audio Tape;*

Digital Computer; Digital Monitor; Digital Versatile Disk; Disk; Disk Drive; Disk Pack; Disk Storage; Diskette; Display; Distributed System/Network; Dot Matrix; Downsizing; Drive; Drum Printer; DVD; EDS; EGA; Electronic Data System; Emulate; Emulation; Enhanced Graphic Adaptor; Environment; Equipment; Extended Technology; Extended Video Array; FDD; File Server; Five and a quarter; Fixed Disk Drive; Flatbed Scanner; Floppy Disk; Floppy Disk Drive; Global; Hand Held Device; Hard Disk Drive; HDD; Host Processor; IBM (tm) Compatible; Information System; Information Technology; Inkjet; Install; Installation; Integrated Systems; Intelligent Terminal; IS; IT; Keyboard; Kit; Laptop; Laser Jet; Laser Printer; LCD; LCD Printer; Leading Edge; Light Pen; Line Printer; Liquid Crystal Display; Liquid Crystal Display Printer; Machine; Mag Tape; Magnetic Disk; Magnetic Tape; Mailserver; Mainframe; Maintenance; Mass Storage; Matrix Printer; Micro; Microcomputer; Midrange System; Minicomputer; Modem; Modular; Modulator Demodulator; Monitor; Monochrome; Mouse; Multi Platform; Node; Notebook; Number Cruncher; OCR; OMR; Optical Character Reader; Optical Character Recognition; Optical Drive; Optical Mark Recognition; Optical Scanner; Pack; Page Printer; Palmtop Computer; PC; PDA; Peripheral; Personal Computer; Personal Digital Assistant; Plasma Screen; Platform; Plotter; Plug Compatible; Portable; Printer; Recording Device; Releases; Remote Device; Scanner; Screen; Server; Standalone; State of the Art; Storage; Store; Streamer; Super Twist LCD; Super VGA; Super Video Graphics Array; SVGA; System; Tape Deck; Tape Streamer; Terminal; TFT; Thermal Printer; Thin-Film Transistor; Third Party Maintenance; Three and a Half; Touch Screen; Tower Computer; Tracker Ball; Turnkey; VDT; VDU; VGA; Video Display Terminal; Video Graphics Array; Visual Display Terminal; Visual Display Unit; Volume; Webcam; Winchester Disk; XGA; XT; Zip Drive;

HD

Half Duplex. Transmission in both directions along a communications line but not simultaneously.

See Also: *ACK; Acoustic Coupler; ADN; ADSL; Advanced Digital Network; AMR; Asymmetric Digital Subscriber Line; Asymmetrical Modem; Asynchronous; Asynchronous Transfer Mode; ATM; Automatic Message Routing; Bandwidth; Baud Rate; Bits Per Second; BPS; Broadband; Bus; CCITT; CCTA; Channel; Characters Per Second; Communications; Consultative Committee International Telegraph and Telephone; CPS; Data Communications; Data Parity; Data Transmission; Datacoms; Dial In; Dial Up; Digital; Direct Connection; Duplex Transmission; FDDI; Fibre Distributed Data Interface; Fibre*

Optics; Full Duplex; Gbps; Half Duplex; Integrated Services Digital Network; ISDN; Kbps; Leased Line; Mbps; Modem; Modulator Demodulator; Narrowband; Open Systems Interconnect; Optical Fibre; OSI; Parallel Transmission; Parity Bit; Serial Transmission; Simplex Transmission; Synchronous; Telecommunication; Telecoms; Transfer Rate; Transmission Channel; Transmit; V90;

HDD

Hard Disk Drive. A peripheral device in which information is stored on a sealed magnetic disk.

See Also: *3.5 Inch; 5.25 Inch; Archive; ATAPI; Attachment Packet Interface; Backing Store; Backup; C Prompt; Computer Power; Configuration; Crash; Device; Disk; Disk Drive; Disk Pack; Disk Size; Disk Storage; Diskette; Drive; EIDE; EISA; Enhanced Industry Standard Architecture; Enhanced Intelligent Drive Electronics; Equipment; FDD; Five and a quarter; Fixed Disk Drive; Floppy Disk; Floppy Disk Drive; Hard Disk Drive; Hardware; Head Crash; Heads; IDE; Integrated Drive Electronics; Kit; Machine Crash; Magnetic Disk; Mass Storage; MCA; Micro Channel Architecture; Pack; Peripheral; Power; Read/Write Head; Recording; Recording Device; Save; Seek Time; Storage; Store; Three and a Half; Winchester Disk; Write; Write Protect;*

Head Crash

Mechanical failure of the read/write heads in a disk unit. Also, if the failure occurs due to dirt on the heads or between the head and disk surface.

See Also: *3.5 Inch; 5.25 Inch; Abort; Bug; Crash; Debug; Debugger; Died; Disk; Disk Drive; Disk Pack; Disk Storage; Diskette; Downtime; FDD; Five and a quarter; Fixed Disk Drive; Floppy Disk; Floppy Disk Drive; General Protection Fault; GPF; Hangs; Hard Disk Drive; HDD; Heads; Hung; Machine Crash; Magnetic Disk; Pack; Program Crash; Read/Write Head; System Hangs; Three and a Half;*

Header

(1) A record at the beginning of a file containing information on the data in the file. (2) An area at the top of a printed page or e-mail reserved for brief document/e-mail details.

See Also: *Beginning of File; BOF; Electronic Mail; E-mail; File; Footer; Page;*

Heads
The read/write heads on a peripheral device. e.g. disk or tape unit.
See Also: *3.5 Inch; 5.25 Inch; CD-RW Drive; Crash; Digital Versatile Disk; Disk; Disk Drive; Disk Pack; Disk Storage; Diskette; DVD; FDD; Five and a quarter; Fixed Disk Drive; Floppy Disk; Floppy Disk Drive; Hard Disk Drive; HDD; Head Crash; Machine Crash; Mag Tape; Magnetic Disk; Magnetic Tape; Optical Drive; Pack; R/W; Read; Read/Write; Read/Write Head; Recording Device; Storage; Store; Streamer; Tape Deck; Tape Streamer; Three and a Half; Winchester Disk; Write; Zip Drive;*

Help Desk
A facility provided by a company to its computer users which allows the users to get help to a problem they may have encountered while using the computer system. This is normally done by telephone.
See Also: *End User; Hand Holding; User; User Group; User Guide; User Manual; Walkthrough;*

Hex
Abbr. of Hexadecimal. A numerical system with a base of 16 using numbers 0 - 9 and the letters A - E representing ten to fifteen. Data can be represented in this format.
See Also: *American Standard Code for Information Interchange; ASCII; BCD; Binary; Binary Coded Decimal; Character; Data; Data Type; Denary; Hexadecimal; Octal;*

Hexadecimal
A numerical system with a base of 16 using numbers 0 - 9 and the letters A - E representing ten to fifteen. Data can be represented in this format.
See Also: *American Standard Code for Information Interchange; ASCII; BCD; Binary; Binary Coded Decimal; Character; Data; Data Type; Denary; Hex; Octal;*

High Density
A format in which data is stored on a peripheral device enabling more data to be stored in the same storage area as for normal density.
See Also: *3.5 Inch; 5.25 Inch; Bits Per Inch; BPI; Compression; DAT; Decompression; Density; Digital Audio Tape; Disk; Disk Pack; Disk Size; Disk Storage; Diskette; Double Density; Five and a quarter; Floppy Disk; Mag Tape; Magnetic Disk; Magnetic Tape; Mass Storage; Medium; Pack; Packed Data; Recording Medium; Storage; Streamer; Tape Streamer; Three and a Half; Volume; Winchester Disk;*

High Level Language
A computer programming language which is more similar to human language than machine code. Each statement is equivalent to many machine code statements.
See Also: *3GL; 4GL; ADA; ALGOL; APL; Assembler; Assembly Code; BASIC; C or C++; CLIPPER; COBOL; CODASYL; Code; Code Generator; Compiler; Compiling; Conference On DAta SYstems Languages; CORAL; Extensible Hypertext Markup Language; eXtensible Markup Language; FORTH; FORTRAN; Fourth Generation Language; HTML; Hypertext Mark-Up Language; Instruction Set; Interpreter; JAVA; JAVASCRIPT; JCL; Job Control Language; Language; LISP; LOGO; Low Level Language; NATURAL; Page Description Language; PASCAL; PDL; PERL; PICK; PILOT; PL/1; Practical Extraction and Reporting Language; Programming Language; PROLOG; Query Language; RPG; Software; SQL; Structured Query Language; Third Generation Language; Visual Basic; XHTML; XML;*

High Memory
A partition of the computer's main memory where the operating system and any program that remain resident are stored.
See Also: *Basic Input Output System; BIOS; Block; Bubble Memory; Buffer; Cache Memory; CMOS; Complementary Metal Oxide Semiconductor Memory; Computer Power; Conventional Memory; Core; Core Dump; DDR SDRAM; DIMM; Direct Memory Access; Direct Random Access Memory; Disk Cache; Disk Operating System; DMA; DOS; Double Data Rate SDRAM; DRAM; Dual Inline Memory Module; Dynamic Memory; Dynamically; EEROM; Electrically Erasable Read Only Memory; Electronically Programmed Read Only Memory; EMS; EPROM; Erasable Programmable Read Only Memory; Expanded Memory; Expanded Memory Specification; Extended Memory; Flash Memory; Linux; Load; Magnetic Core; Memory; Memory Board; Memory Caching; Memory Card; Memory Resident; Mix; Operating System; OS; OS/2; Overlay; Power; Programmable Read Only Memory; PROM; RAM; RAM Disk; Rambus Dynamic Random Access Memory; Random Access Memory; RDRAM; Read Only Memory; ROM; SDRAM; Shadow RAM Memory; SIMM; Single Inline Memory Modules; Single Inline Package; SIP; Stack; Store; Swapping; Synchronous Dynamic Random Access Memory; Terminate and Stay Resident; TSR; UNIX; Upper Memory; Video Random Access Memory; VRAM; Working Storage; Workspace;*

High Resolution
A screen made up of 640 pixels across and 480 down giving a clearer display of data or graphics.
See Also: *Analogue Monitor; Anti Glare Screen; Cathode Ray Tube; CGA; Colour Graphics Adaptor; CRT; Digital Monitor; Digital Video Interface; Display; DVI; EGA; Enhanced Graphic Adaptor; Extended Video Array; Graphics; Graphics Card; Image Processing; Interlaced; LCD; Liquid Crystal Display; Monitor; Monochrome; Pixel; Plasma Screen; Resolution; Screen; Screen Burn; Sprite; Super Twist LCD; Super VGA; Super Video Graphics Array; SVGA; Terminal; TFT; Thin-Film Transistor; Touch Screen; VDT; VDU; VGA; Video Card; Video Display Terminal; Video Graphics Array; Visual Display Terminal; Visual Display Unit; XGA;*

Hit
One occurrence of the number of times a website has been accessed.
See Also: *Address; Anchor; Cyberspace; DNS; Domain Name; Domain Name System; Home Page; HTTP; Hyperlink; Hypertext; Hypertext Transfer Protocol; Internet; Internet Protocol Address; Internet Service Provider; IP Address; ISP; Link; Net; Page; Provider; Search Engine; Service Provider; Site; Spider; Surfing; The Net; The Web; Universal/Uniform Resource Locator; URL; Website; World Wide Web; WWW;*

Home Page
This is normally the first and main page of a website from where other pages may be accessed.
See Also: *Address; Anchor; Bookmark; Browser; CERN; Conseil Europeen pour la Recherche Nucleaire; Cyberspace; DNS; Domain Name; Domain Name System; Hit; HTML; Hyperlink; Hypertext; Hypertext Mark-Up Language; Internet; Internet Service Provider; ISP; Link; Meta Tag; Meta-Search Engine; Net; Page; Portal; Provider; Service Provider; Site; Surfing; The Net; The Web; Universal/Uniform Resource Locator; URL; Webring; Website; World Wide Web; WWW;*

Host
The Internet Service Provider or a computer that administers websites.
See Also: *Acceptable User Policy; AUP; Browser; Cookie; Cyberspace; DNS; Domain Name; Domain Name Server; Domain Name System; Environment; Host Processor; HTTP; Hyperlink; Hypertext; Hypertext Transfer Protocol; Information Superhighway; Internet; Internet Protocol; Internet Protocol Address; Internet Relay Chat; Internet Service Provider; IP; IP Address; IRC; ISP; Mailserver; Net; Network*

Information Centre; NIC; Point Of Presence; Point to Point Protocol; POP; Portal; PPP; Provider; Search Engine; Service Provider; Site; Spider; Surfing; The Net; The Web; Universal/Uniform Resource Locator; URL; Wap Internet Service Provider; Webhost; Webring; Website; WISP; World Wide Web; WWW;

Host Processor

A computer attached to and controlling the processing of other computers.

See Also: *Client Server; Client Server Protocol; Computer; Cyberspace; Distributed System/Network; Domain Name Server; Equipment; Ethernet; File Server; Hardware; Host; Internet; Internet Service Provider; ISP; Kit; LAN; Local Area Network; Machine; Mailserver; Midrange System; Minicomputer; Net; Network; Point to Point Protocol; PPP; Provider; Proxy Server; Server; Service Provider; Star Cluster; Star Network; The Net; Token Ring; Webhost;*

Hot Key

A combination of key presses on the keyboard to carry out a command. Normally the CNTL or ALT key with another key.

See Also: *Drop-Down Menu; Esc; Escape; Function Key; Keyboard; Menu; Pop Up Menu; Pull Down Menu;*

Housekeeping

Procedures carried out by the computer's operating system in the background. e.g. automatic backup, reallocation of memory.

See Also: *Batch Processing; Computation; Defragment; Disk Operating System; DOS; Fragmentation; Job; Linux; Multitasking; Network Operating System; NOS; Operating System; OS; OS/2; Spooler; Swapping; System Software; UNIX; Virus Checker;*

HTML

Hypertext Mark-Up Language. A programming language used to create a website or web page and allows text to be linked to other pages by using hyperlinks.

See Also: *Anchor; Applet; Browser; Code; Extensible Hypertext Markup Language; eXtensible Markup Language; High Level Language; Home Page; Hyperlink; Hypertext; Hypertext Mark-Up Language; Instruction Set; Internet; JAVA; JAVASCRIPT; Language; Meta Tag; Module; Net; Page; Page Description Language; PDL; Programming Language; Site; The Net; The Web; Webring; Website; World Wide Web; WWW; XHTML; XML;*

HTTP
Hypertext Transfer Protocol. Instructions for communicating between a computer and the World Wide Web.
See Also: *Bookmark; Browser; CGI; Client Server Protocol; Common Gateway Interface; Cyberspace; Hit; Host; Hypertext Transfer Protocol; Information Superhighway; Internet; Internet Protocol; Internet Protocol Address; Internet Service Provider; IP; IP Address; ISP; Net; Point Of Presence; Point to Point Protocol; POP; PPP; Protocol; Provider; Service Provider; Site; TCP/IP; The Net; The Web; Transmission Control Protocol/Internet Protocol; WAP; Wap Internet Service Provider; Webhost; Webring; Website; Wireless Application Protocol; WISP; World Wide Web; WWW;*

Hung
The point when a program stops responding and cannot continue.
See Also: *Abort; Bug; Crash; Dead Lock; Deadly Embrace; Debug; Debugger; Died; Hangs; Head Crash; Locking; Machine Crash; Off Line; Program Crash; Record Locking; System Hangs; Timeout;*

Hyperlink
Highlighted text (Hypertext) on your Internet browser screen or in a document. It provides a link to another part of the website or document or to a different website or document.
See Also: *Address; Anchor; Body; Bookmark; Browser; CGI; Common Gateway Interface; Cyberspace; Extensible Hypertext Markup Language; eXtensible Markup Language; Graphics; Hit; Home Page; Host; HTML; Hypertext; Hypertext Mark-Up Language; Icon; Image Map; Image Processing; Internet; Internet Protocol Address; IP Address; Link; Meta Tag; Meta-Search Engine; Net; Site; Surfing; The Net; The Web; Thumbnail; Universal/Uniform Resource Locator; URL; Webring; Website; World Wide Web; WWW; XHTML; XML;*

Hypertext
Text or images on a web page or in a document that links (hyperlink) to other pages or documents when clicked.
See Also: *Address; Anchor; Body; Bookmark; Browser; Cyberspace; Extensible Hypertext Markup Language; eXtensible Markup Language; Graphics; Hit; Home Page; Host; HTML; Hyperlink; Hypertext Mark-Up Language; Icon; Image Map; Image Processing; Link; Page; The Web; Thumbnail; Universal/Uniform Resource Locator; URL; World Wide Web; WWW; XHTML; XML;*

Hypertext Mark-Up Language
(HTML). A programming language used to create a website or web page and allows text to be linked to other pages by using hyperlinks.
See Also: *Anchor; Applet; Browser; Code; Extensible Hypertext Markup Language; eXtensible Markup Language; High Level Language; Home Page; HTML; Hyperlink; Hypertext; Instruction Set; Internet; JAVA; JAVASCRIPT; Language; Meta Tag; Module; Net; Page; Page Description Language; PDL; Programming Language; Site; The Net; The Web; Webring; Website; World Wide Web; WWW; XHTML; XML;*

Hypertext Transfer Protocol
(HTTP). Instructions for communicating between a computer and the World Wide Web.
See Also: *Bookmark; Browser; CGI; Client Server Protocol; Common Gateway Interface; Cyberspace; Hit; Host; HTTP; Information Superhighway; Internet; Internet Protocol; Internet Protocol Address; Internet Service Provider; IP; IP Address; ISP; Net; Point Of Presence; Point to Point Protocol; POP; PPP; Protocol; Provider; Service Provider; Site; TCP/IP; The Net; The Web; Transmission Control Protocol/Internet Protocol; WAP; Wap Internet Service Provider; Webhost; Webring; Website; Wireless Application Protocol; WISP; World Wide Web; WWW;*

I/O
Input/Output. The process where data is input and output to/from a computer via I/O channels.
See Also: *Access; Bus; Channel; Data; Data Bus; Disk Drive; Import; Information; Information System; Input; Input/Output; Interactive; Interface; IS; Local Bus; R/W; Read; Read/Write; Recording Device; System Bus; Transmission Channel; UART; Universal Asynchronous Receiver/Transmitter; Write;*

IBM (tm) Compatible
Any personal computer which follows the design standard of an IBM PC.
See Also: *1st Generation; 2nd Generation; 3rd Generation; 4th Generation; Advanced Technology; Analogue Computer; AT; Compatible; Computer; Computer Power; Configuration; Cross Platform; Desktop; Digital Computer; Downsizing; EDS; Electronic Data System; Emulate; Emulation; Environment; Equipment; Extended Technology; Front End Processor; Hardware; Information System; Information Technology; Installation; IS; IT; Kit; Laptop; Machine; Mailserver; Micro; Microcomputer; Multi Platform; Notebook; OEM; Original Equipment Manufacturer; Palmtop Computer; PC; Personal*

Computer; Platform; Portable; Power; Standalone; Tower Computer; Turnkey; Voice Activated; XT;

IC
Integrated Circuit. A solid-state circuit made from a semiconductor material which has the design imprinted on it. e.g. a chip.
See Also: *286; 386; 486; ALU; Analogue; Application Specific Integrated Circuits; Arithmetic and Logic Unit; ASICS; Central Processing Unit; Chip; Chipset; Clock Speed; Co-processor; CPU; Graphics Card; Integrated Circuit; Large Scale Integration; LSI; Maths Co-processor; Memory Board; Memory Card; Microprocessor; Motherboard; Parallel Processor; PCB; Printed Circuit Board; Processor; Semiconductor; Silicon Chip; Solid State; Sound Chip; Transistor; UART; Universal Asynchronous Receiver/Transmitter; Very Large Scale Integration; Video Card; VLSI;*

Icon
A graphical representation on a screen of a command to run a program or execute a task.
See Also: *Clip Art; Cursor; Drag; Floating Toolbar; Graphics; Hyperlink; Hypertext; Image Map; Image Processing; Link; Sprite; Toolbar;*

IDE
Integrated Drive Electronics. An interface between the PC's motherboard and storage devices, e.g. disk drives.
See Also: *3.5 Inch; 5.25 Inch; ATAPI; Attachment Packet Interface; CD-ROM Drive; CD-RW Drive; Disk; Disk Drive; Disk Storage; Drive; EIDE; EISA; Enhanced Industry Standard Architecture; Enhanced Intelligent Drive Electronics; FDD; Firewire; Five and a quarter; Fixed Disk Drive; Floppy Disk Drive; Hard Disk Drive; HDD; Industry Standard Architecture; Integrated Drive Electronics; Interface; ISA; Magnetic Disk; MCA; Micro Channel Architecture; Motherboard; Optical Drive; PCMCIA; Personal Computer Memory Card International Association; Self Monitoring Analysis and Reporting Technology; SMART; Three and a Half; Ultra DMA; Winchester Disk;*

IEE
The Institute of Electrical Engineers.
See Also: *American National Standard Institute; ANSI; BCS; CCITT; CCTA; CERN; Conseil Europeen pour la Recherche Nucleaire; Consultative Committee International Telegraph and Telephone; International Standards Organisation; ISO; NCC;*

IM
Instant Messaging. The process where computer users connected to the Internet communicate with other users in Real Time by exchanging text messages.
See Also: *Body; Buddy List; Chat; Chatroom; Cybercafe; Cyberspace; Dial In; Dial Up; Electronic Mail; E-mail; Emoticons; Forum; Instant Messaging; Interactive; Internet; Internet Relay Chat; IRC; Message Boards; Nerd; Net; Netiquette; Newbie; Newsgroup; Real Time; Smileys; The Net; Thread; User;*

Image Map
An image split into different sections allowing each section to be selected as a hyperlink which connects to another web page.
See Also: *Bar Chart; Bar Code; BitMaP; BMP; Clip Art; Desk Top Publishing; Disk Map; DTP; Floating Toolbar; Graphical User Interface; Graphics; GUI; Hyperlink; Hypertext; Icon; Image Processing; Joint Photographic Experts Group; JPEG; JPG; Marquee; Multimedia; PDF; Pie Chart; Pixel; Portable Document Format; Radio Button; Sprite; Twip; WIMP; Window; Windows Icons Mice and Pull-down menus;*

Image Processing
The processing of a graphical picture which is in digital format.
See Also: *Bar Chart; Bar Code; BitMaP; BMP; Browser; CCD; Charge Coupled Device; Clip Art; Cursor; Desk Top Publishing; Digital; Digital Video Interface; Disk Map; Display; Drag; DTP; DVI; Floating Toolbar; Frame Rate; GIF; Graphical Interchange Format; Graphical User Interface; Graphics; Graphics Card; GUI; High Resolution; Hyperlink; Hypertext; Icon; Image Map; Joint Photographic Experts Group; JPEG; JPG; Low Resolution; Marquee; Motion Picture Experts Group; MPEG; MPG; PDF; Pie Chart; Pixel; Portable Document Format; Radio Button; Resolution; Sprite; Tag Image File Format; TIFF; Twip; Video Card; WIMP; Window; Windows Icons Mice and Pull-down menus;*

Implementation
The process of installing hardware and/or software and ensuring all the parts work with each other. It includes the setting up of data files and parameters to enable the system to operate.
See Also: *Bespoke; Configuring; Development; Import; Information Technology; In-house; Install; Installation; IT; Live; Upgrade;*

Import
The transfer of data or files into a computer system.
See Also: *Export; I/O; Implementation; Input; Input/Output; Install; Installation;*

Index Sequential File
A file created with an index which allows access to each record using the index and a key.
See Also: *ASCII Files; Attachment; Batch File; Beginning of File; BOF; Database; DB; Direct Access; End of File; EOF; File; Fragmentation; Indexed Sequential Access Method; Information; ISAM; Key; Keyed Sequential Access Method; KSAM; Log File; Random Access; Random File; RDB; Record; Relational Database; Sequential Access; Sequential File; Serial Access; Serial File; Tag File; Temp File;*

Indexed Sequential Access Method
(ISAM). A type of access to a disk file which allows reading and writing to the file using an index and a key.
See Also: *3.5 Inch; 5.25 Inch; Direct Access; Disk; Disk Pack; Disk Storage; Diskette; File; Five and a quarter; Floppy Disk; Index Sequential File; ISAM; Key; Keyed Sequential Access Method; KSAM; Magnetic Disk; Pack; R/W; Random Access; Read; Read/Write; Sequential Access; Serial Access; Three and a Half; Volume; Winchester Disk; Write;*

Industry Standard Architecture
(ISA). A Personal Computer design standard whose communication path between the processor and external devices has a transfer rate of 8 MHz.
See Also: *Bus; Central Processing Unit; Channel; Co-processor; CPU; EIDE; EISA; Enhanced Industry Standard Architecture; Enhanced Intelligent Drive Electronics; IDE; Integrated Drive Electronics; ISA; Local Bus; Maths Co-processor; MCA; Micro Channel Architecture; Microprocessor; Processor; SCSI; Small Computer System Interface; System Bus; Transmission Channel; Ultra DMA;*

Information
Data input, stored, manipulated and output from a computer.
See Also: *American Standard Code for Information Interchange; Archive; Array; ASCII; ASCII Files; Byte; Character; Comma Separated Values; Constant; CSV; Data; Data Dictionary; Data Element; Data Entity; Data Item; Data Type; Database; DB; Entity; Field; File; Garbage In, Garbage Out; Group; I/O; Index Sequential File;*

Information System; Information Technology; Input; Input/Output; IS; IT; Key; Literal; Parameter; Radio Button; Record; String; Table; Variable;

Information Superhighway
The connection to the Internet using high speed cables such as fibre optics.
See Also: *Access; ADN; ADSL; Advanced Digital Network; Anchor; Asymmetric Digital Subscriber Line; Asynchronous; Bandwidth; Broadband; Cyberspace; Host; HTTP; Hypertext Transfer Protocol; Integrated Services Digital Network; Internet; Internet Service Provider; ISDN; ISP; Modem; Modulator Demodulator; Narrowband; Net; Provider; Proxy Server; Service Provider; Surfing; Synchronous; The Net; The Web; Wap Internet Service Provider; Webhost; WISP; World Wide Web; WWW;*

Information System
(IS). Hardware and software which allow data to be input, manipulated, stored and output.
See Also: *Application; Audit Trail; Batch Processing; Bespoke; CAD; CADCAM; CADMAT; CAE; CAI; CAM; CBT; Computer; Computer Aided Design; Computer Aided Design and Manufacturing; Computer Aided Design Manufacture and Test; Computer Aided Engineering; Computer Aided Instruction; Computer Aided Manufacturing; Computer Based Training; Configuration; Cross Platform; Data Base Management System; Data Processing; DBMS; Desk Top Publishing; Desktop; Digital Computer; Distributed System/Network; DP; DTP; EDP; EDS; Electronic Data Processing; Electronic Data System; Geographical Information System; GIS; Hardware; I/O; IBM (tm) Compatible; Information; Information Technology; Input/Output; Integrated Systems; IS; IT; Kit; Laptop; Machine; Midrange System; Minicomputer; Notebook; Office Information System; OIS; Outsourcing; Package; Palmtop Computer; PC; Personal Computer; Platform; Portable; RDBMS/RDMS; Relational Database Management System; Software; Software Package; Software System; System; Tower Computer; Turnkey; Vertical Market;*

Information Technology
(IT). The manipulation, analysis and storage of data on a computer.
See Also: *AI; Analogue Computer; Artificial Intelligence; Batch Processing; Bespoke; CAD; CADCAM; CADMAT; CAE; CAI; CAM; CBT; Computation; Compute; Computer; Computer Aided Design; Computer Aided Design and Manufacturing; Computer Aided Design Manufacture and Test; Computer Aided Engineering; Computer Aided*

Instruction; Computer Aided Manufacturing; Computer Based Training; Cross Platform; Data; Data Base Management System; Data Centre; Data Processing; DBMS; Desk Top Publishing; Desktop; Digital Computer; Distributed System/Network; DP; DTP; EDP; Electronic Data Processing; Geographical Information System; GIS; Hardware; IBM (tm) Compatible; Implementation; Information; Information System; Installation; Integrated Systems; IS; IT; Kit; Laptop; Machine; Midrange System; Minicomputer; Notebook; Office Information System; OIS; Outsourcing; Palmtop Computer; PC; Personal Computer; Platform; Portable; Processing; Program; RDBMS/RDMS; Relational Database Management System; Software; Software System; Tower Computer;

In-house
A term used when projects, tasks or jobs are done within a company instead of using outside organisations.
See Also: *Bespoke; Data Centre; Development; Downsizing; Implementation; Job; Software Development Cycle; Software House; Software System; User;*

Inkjet
A type of printer which prints by exuding ink from nozzles on the print head to form the characters on the paper.
See Also: *Barrel Printer; Bi Directional; Bubble Jet; Configuration; Cut Sheet Feeder; Daisywheel; Device; DIP Switch; Dot Matrix; Drum Printer; Duplex Printing; Environment; Equipment; Font Cartridge; Hard Copy; Hardware; Installation; Kit; Landscape; Laser Jet; Laser Printer; LCD Printer; Letter Quality; Line Printer; Lines Per Minute; Liquid Crystal Display Printer; Lpm; LPT Port; LQ; Matrix Printer; Near Letter Quality; NLQ; Page Printer; Pages Per Minute; Peripheral; Portrait; Postscript; PPM; Printer; Printer Driver; Printout; Sheet Feeder; Simplex Printing; Thermal Printer;*

Input
Information fed into a computer.
See Also: *Carriage Return; Check Box; Data; Data Element; Data Entity; Data Item; Enter; Garbage In, Garbage Out; I/O; Import; Information; Input/Output; Light Pen; Parameter; Radio Button; String; Variable;*

Input/Output
(I/O). The process where data is input and output to/from a computer via I/O channels.
See Also: *Access; Bus; Channel; Data; Data Bus; Disk Drive; I/O; Import; Information; Information System; Input; Interactive; Interface; IS; Local Bus; R/W; Read; Read/Write; Recording Device; System Bus; Transmission Channel; UART; Universal Asynchronous Receiver/Transmitter; Write;*

Install
The procedure to set up hardware and/or software.
See Also: *Configuring; Hardware; Implementation; Import; Installation; Kit; Live; Releases; Software; Upgrade;*

Installation
(1) The process of installing hardware and/or software. (2) A computer site comprising all the equipment and software.
See Also: *Advanced Technology; Analogue Computer; Analogue Monitor; Anti Glare Screen; AT; Barrel Printer; Black Box; Bubble Jet; Cathode Ray Tube; CD-ROM Drive; CD-RW Drive; CGA; Client Server; Colour Graphics Adaptor; Computer; Configuration; Configuring; Cross Platform; CRT; Daisywheel; DAT; Data Centre; Deck; Desktop; Digital Audio Tape; Digital Computer; Digital Monitor; Digital Versatile Disk; Disk Operating System; Display; DOS; Dot Matrix; Drum Printer; DVD; EDS; EGA; Electronic Data System; Enhanced Graphic Adaptor; Environment; Equipment; Extended Technology; Extended Video Array; Facilities Management; File Server; Flatbed Scanner; FM; Front End Processor; Global; Hardware; IBM (tm) Compatible; Implementation; Import; Information Technology; Inkjet; Install; IT; Kit; Laptop; Laser Jet; Laser Printer; LCD; LCD Printer; Line Printer; Linux; Liquid Crystal Display; Liquid Crystal Display Printer; Live; Machine; Mag Tape; Magnetic Tape; Mainframe; Mass Storage; Matrix Printer; Micro; Microcomputer; Midrange System; Minicomputer; Monitor; Monochrome; Notebook; Number Cruncher; Operating System; Optical Drive; Optical Scanner; OS; OS/2; Page Printer; Palmtop Computer; PC; Personal Computer; Plasma Screen; Platform; Plotter; Portable; Printer; Releases; Scanner; Screen; Server; Software; Standalone; Storage; Store; Streamer; Super Twist LCD; Super VGA; Super Video Graphics Array; SVGA; System; Tape Deck; Tape Streamer; Terminal; TFT; Thermal Printer; Thin-Film Transistor; Touch Screen; Tower Computer; Turnkey; Upgrade; VDT; VDU; VGA; Video Display Terminal; Video Graphics Array; Visual Display Terminal; Visual Display Unit; Winchester Disk; XGA; XT; Zip Drive;*

Instant Messaging
(IM). The process where computer users connected to the Internet communicate with other users in Real Time by exchanging text messages.
See Also: *Body; Buddy List; Chat; Chatroom; Cybercafe; Cyberspace; Dial In; Dial Up; Electronic Mail; E-mail; Emoticons; Forum; IM; Interactive; Internet; Internet Relay Chat; IRC; Message Boards; Nerd; Net; Netiquette; Newbie; Newsgroup; Real Time; Smileys; The Net; Thread; User;*

Instruction
A command to a computer from a program or an operator.
See Also: *AUTOEXEC.BAT; Boot; Bootstrap; Call; Carriage Return; Chain; Code; Command; CONFIG.SYS; DLL; Drop-Down Menu; Dynamic Link Library; Enter; Esc; Escape; Event; EXE; Execute; Firmware; Function Key; Instruction Set; Interrupt Request; Invoke; IRQ; JCL; Job Control Language; Keyboard; Light Pen; Macro; Menu; Mouse; Parameter; Pop Up Menu; Program; Pull Down Menu; Re-boot; Return; Script; Syntax; System Software; Voice Activated;*

Instruction Set
A list of operations a computer performs. e.g. a program.
See Also: *3GL; 4GL; ADA; ALGOL; APL; Applet; Assembler; Assembly Code; AUTOEXEC.BAT; BASIC; C or C++; Call; Chain; CLIPPER; COBOL; Code; Code Generator; Command; CONFIG.SYS; CORAL; Device Driver; DLL; Driver; Dynamic Link Library; EXE; Extensible Hypertext Markup Language; eXtensible Markup Language; FORTH; FORTRAN; Fourth Generation Language; Function; High Level Language; HTML; Hypertext Mark-Up Language; Instruction; Invoke; JAVA; JAVASCRIPT; JCL; Job; Job Control Language; Language; LISP; LOGO; Low Level Language; Machine Code; Machine Language; Macro; Module; NATURAL; Nesting; Object Code; Page Description Language; PASCAL; PDL; PERL; PICK; PILOT; PL/1; Practical Extraction and Reporting Language; Process; Program; Programming Language; PROLOG; Query Language; Reduced Instruction Set Computing; RISC; ROM Resident; RPG; Run; Run Time; Script; Software; Software Driver; Source Code; SQL; Structured Query Language; Subroutine; Syntax; Third Generation Language; Utility; Visual Basic; XHTML; XML;*

Integrated
(1) A term used when peripheral devices are assembled within the same casing unit as the central processor. (2) Software systems that link with each other. e.g. payroll and general ledger.
See Also: *Batch Processing; File Sharing; Front End Processor; Integrated Systems; Modular; Multi User; Multitasking; Package; RDB; Relational Database; Software; Software Package; Software System; Turnkey;*

Integrated Circuit
(IC). A solid-state circuit made from a semiconductor material which has the design imprinted on it. e.g. a chip.
See Also: *286; 386; 486; ALU; Analogue; Application Specific Integrated Circuits; Arithmetic and Logic Unit; ASICS; Central Processing Unit; Chip; Chipset; Clock Speed; Co-processor; CPU; Graphics Card; IC; Large Scale Integration; LSI; Maths Co-processor; Memory Board; Memory Card; Microprocessor; Motherboard; Parallel Processor; PCB; Printed Circuit Board; Processor; Semiconductor; Silicon Chip; Solid State; Sound Chip; Transistor; UART; Universal Asynchronous Receiver/Transmitter; Very Large Scale Integration; Video Card; VLSI;*

Integrated Drive Electronics
(IDE). An interface between the PC's motherboard and storage devices, e.g. disk drives
See Also: *3.5 Inch; 5.25 Inch; ATAPI; Attachment Packet Interface; CD-ROM Drive; CD-RW Drive; Disk; Disk Drive; Disk Storage; Drive; EIDE; EISA; Enhanced Industry Standard Architecture; Enhanced Intelligent Drive Electronics; FDD; Firewire; Five and a quarter; Fixed Disk Drive; Floppy Disk Drive; Hard Disk Drive; HDD; IDE; Industry Standard Architecture; Interface; ISA; Magnetic Disk; MCA; Micro Channel Architecture; Motherboard; Optical Drive; PCMCIA; Personal Computer Memory Card International Association; Self Monitoring Analysis and Reporting Technology; SMART; Three and a Half; Ultra DMA; Winchester Disk;*

Integrated Services Digital Network
(ISDN). A network structure which allows for faster data transmission in digital format where a single network can carry or switch different telecommunication services. e.g. voice and pictures.
See Also: *ADN; ADSL; Advanced Digital Network; AMR; Asymmetric Digital Subscriber Line; Asymmetrical Modem; Asynchronous; Asynchronous Transfer Mode; ATM; Automatic Message Routing;*

Bandwidth; Baud Rate; Bits Per Second; BPS; Broadband; CCITT; CCTA; Characters Per Second; Communications; Consultative Committee International Telegraph and Telephone; CPS; Data Communications; Data Parity; Data Transmission; Datacoms; Dial In; Dial Up; Digital; Direct Connection; Duplex Transmission; FDDI; Fibre Distributed Data Interface; Fibre Optics; Full Duplex; Gbps; Half Duplex; Handshake; HD; Information Superhighway; ISDN; Kbps; Leased Line; Mbps; Modem; Modulator Demodulator; Multiplex; Multiplexer; Narrowband; Node; Open Systems Interconnect; Optical Fibre; OSI; Parallel Transmission; Parity Bit; Serial Interface; Serial Transmission; Simplex Transmission; Synchronous; T-1; T-3; Telecommunication; Telecoms; Teleprocessing System; TPS; Transfer Rate; Transmit; V90;

Integrated Systems
Software or hardware systems that link with each other in some way. e.g. invoicing with a general ledger.
See Also: *Application; Batch Processing; Compatible; Computation; Compute; EDP; EDS; Electronic Data Processing; Electronic Data System; Environment; Equipment; Facilities Management; File Sharing; FM; Hardware; Information System; Information Technology; Integrated; IS; IT; Kit; Office Information System; OIS; Package; Software Package; Software System; System; Turnkey; Vertical Market; Word Processor; WP;*

Intelligent Terminal
A terminal which has the ability to perform some form of processing.
See Also: *Analogue Monitor; Anti Glare Screen; Cathode Ray Tube; CGA; Colour Graphics Adaptor; Configuration; CRT; Device; Digital Monitor; Display; EGA; Enhanced Graphic Adaptor; Environment; Equipment; Extended Video Array; Graphics Card; Hardware; Interactive; Kit; LCD; Liquid Crystal Display; Low Resolution; Monitor; Monochrome; Paint Screen; Peripheral; Plasma Screen; Point of Sales; POS; Processing; Screen; Screen Burn; Split Screen; Super Twist LCD; Super VGA; Super Video Graphics Array; SVGA; Terminal; TFT; Thin-Film Transistor; Touch Screen; Twip; VDT; VDU; VGA; Video Display Terminal; Video Graphics Array; Visual Display Terminal; Visual Display Unit; XGA;*

Interactive
The communication between a user and a computer.
See Also: *Carriage Return; Chat; Chatroom; Check Box; Forum; Gopher; Hands On; Handshake; I/O; IM; Input/Output; Instant*

Messaging; Intelligent Terminal; Keyboard; Mouse; Newsgroup; Online; Real Time; Voice Activated;

Interface
The connection between two devices or two programs which enable data to be transferred from one to the other. e.g. computer to printer.
See Also: *Access; Acoustic Coupler; Analogue; Analogue Digital Converter; Anonymous FTP; API; Application Program Interface; ATAPI; Attachment Packet Interface; Bluetooth (tm); Device; Digital Video Interface; DVI; EIDE; EISA; Enhanced Industry Standard Architecture; Enhanced Intelligent Drive Electronics; Firewire; I/O; IDE; Input/Output; Integrated Drive Electronics; Internet Protocol; Internet Relay Chat; IP; IRC; MCA; Micro Channel Architecture; MIDI; Modem; Modulator Demodulator; Musical Instrument Digital Interface; Parallel Interface; Parallel Port; PCI; Peripheral; Peripheral Component Interconnect; Port; Proxy Server; PS/2; Remote Device; RS232; RS423; SCSI; Self Monitoring Analysis and Reporting Technology; Serial Interface; Serial Line Internet Protocol; Serial Port; SLIP; Small Computer System Interface; SMART; TCP/IP; Transmission Control Protocol/Internet Protocol; Universal Serial Bus; USB; WAP; Wi-Fi; Wireless Application Protocol; Wireless Fidelity; XMODEM; YMODEM; ZMODEM;*

Interlaced
A visual display unit design which allows some monitors to support high-resolution displays. The screen is displayed in two passes where odd lines are displayed first and even lines second.
See Also: *Analogue Monitor; Anti Glare Screen; Cathode Ray Tube; CGA; Colour Graphics Adaptor; CRT; Digital Monitor; Display; EGA; Enhanced Graphic Adaptor; Extended Video Array; Frame Rate; Graphics Card; High Resolution; LCD; Liquid Crystal Display; Low Resolution; Monitor; Monochrome; Paint Screen; Plasma Screen; Resolution; Screen; Super Twist LCD; Super VGA; Super Video Graphics Array; SVGA; Terminal; TFT; Thin-Film Transistor; Touch Screen; VDT; VDU; VGA; Video Display Terminal; Video Graphics Array; Visual Display Terminal; Visual Display Unit; XGA;*

International Standards Organisation
(ISO). An international body representing protocols and standards from different countries.
See Also: *Acceptable User Policy; American National Standard Institute; ANSI; Asynchronous Transfer Mode; ATM; AUP; BCS; CCITT; CCTA; CERN; Client Server Protocol; Conseil Europeen pour la Recherche*

Nucleaire; Consultative Committee International Telegraph and Telephone; Data Protection Act; EBCDIC; Extended Binary Coded Decimal Interchange Code; File Transfer Protocol; FTP; IEE; Internet Protocol; IP; ISO; NCC; Protocol;

Internet

The collection of inter-connected computers and networks around the world. Often referred to as "the net".

See Also: *Acceptable User Policy; Anchor; Applet; AUP; Bandwidth; BBS; Bookmark; Broadband; Browser; Bulletin Board System; CERN; CGI; Chat; Chatroom; Client Server Protocol; Common Gateway Interface; Conseil Europeen pour la Recherche Nucleaire; Cybercafe; Cyberspace; DNS; Domain Name; Domain Name Server; Domain Name System; Dot; Gopher; Hit; Home Page; Host; Host Processor; HTML; HTTP; Hyperlink; Hypertext Mark-Up Language; Hypertext Transfer Protocol; IM; Information Superhighway; Instant Messaging; Internet Protocol; Internet Protocol Address; Internet Relay Chat; Internet Service Provider; IP; IP Address; IRC; ISP; Link; Message Boards; Meta Tag; Meta-Search Engine; Narrowband; Net; Netiquette; Newbie; Newsgroup; Page; PING; Point Of Presence; Point to Point Protocol; POP; PPP; Provider; Proxy Server; Search Engine; Secure Socket Layer; Serial Line Internet Protocol; Service Provider; Simple Mail Transfer Protocol; Site; SLIP; SMTP; Spider; SSL; Stream; Surfing; T-1; T-3; TCP/IP; The Net; The Web; Transmission Control Protocol/Internet Protocol; WAP; Wap Internet Service Provider; Webhost; Webring; Website; Wireless Application Protocol; WISP; World Wide Web; Worm; WWW;*

Internet Protocol

(IP). The rules used on the Internet for computers to communicate with each other.

See Also: *Acceptable User Policy; Anchor; AUP; Bluetooth (tm); Bookmark; CGI; Client Server Protocol; Common Gateway Interface; Cyberspace; Domain Name Server; Handshake; Host; HTTP; Hypertext Transfer Protocol; Interface; International Standards Organisation; Internet; Internet Protocol Address; IP; IP Address; ISO; MIME; Multipurpose Internet Mail Extensions; Net; PING; Point to Point Protocol; PPP; Protocol; Secure Socket Layer; Serial Line Internet Protocol; Simple Mail Transfer Protocol; SLIP; SMTP; SSL; TCP/IP; The Net; Transmission Control Protocol/Internet Protocol; WAP; Wi-Fi; Wireless Application Protocol; Wireless Fidelity;*

Internet Protocol Address
(IP Address). Internet Protocol Address. Also known as IP Number. The unique number identifying each domain name on the Internet.
See Also: *Address; Anchor; Bookmark; Client Server Protocol; Cyberspace; DNS; Domain Name; Domain Name Server; Domain Name System; E-mail Address; Hit; Host; HTTP; Hyperlink; Hypertext Transfer Protocol; Internet; Internet Protocol; IP; IP Address; Net; Point Of Presence; Point to Point Protocol; POP; PPP; Protocol; Serial Line Internet Protocol; Simple Mail Transfer Protocol; SLIP; SMTP; The Net; WAP; Wireless Application Protocol;*

Internet Relay Chat
(IRC). An Internet program which allows users to communicate with other users in real time.
See Also: *Chat; Chatroom; Cyberspace; Electronic Mail; E-mail; Forum; Host; IM; Instant Messaging; Interface; Internet; Internet Service Provider; IRC; ISP; Mailserver; Net; Netiquette; Newbie; Newsgroup; Online; Point to Point Protocol; PPP; Program; Provider; Serial Line Internet Protocol; Service Provider; Simple Mail Transfer Protocol; SLIP; SMTP; The Net; Thread; Webhost;*

Internet Service Provider
(ISP). A company that provides access to the Internet for computer users.
See Also: *Acceptable User Policy; AUP; Browser; CGI; Common Gateway Interface; Cookie; Cyberspace; DNS; Domain Name; Domain Name Server; Domain Name System; E-commerce; EDI; Electronic Data Interchange; Handshake; Hit; Home Page; Host; Host Processor; HTTP; Hypertext Transfer Protocol; Information Superhighway; Internet; Internet Relay Chat; IRC; ISP; Mailserver; Net; Newsgroup; PING; Point Of Presence; Point to Point Protocol; POP; POP; Portal; Post Office Protocol; PPP; Provider; Proxy Server; Search Engine; Serial Line Internet Protocol; Service Provider; SLIP; Spider; Surfing; The Net; Wap Internet Service Provider; Webhost; WISP;*

Interpreter
A program which converts a high level computer language into machine code one line at a time during execution of the program and also checks for syntax errors at the same time.
See Also: *3GL; 4GL; Assembler; BASIC; Code; Compiler; Compiling; Fourth Generation Language; High Level Language; Software; Source Code; Syntax; Third Generation Language;*

Interrupt
A signal which tells the computer to halt processing until a later time.
See Also: *Abort; API; Application Program Interface; Esc; Escape; Interrupt Request; IRQ; Off Line; Terminate and Stay Resident; Time Share; Time Slice; TSR;*

Interrupt Request
(IRQ). A signal used by devices to interrupt the processor in order for an action to be undertaken, e.g. a keyboard entry or mouse click.
See Also: *API; Application Program Interface; Central Processing Unit; Co-processor; CPU; Esc; Escape; Instruction; Interrupt; IRQ; Maths Co-processor; Terminate and Stay Resident; TSR;*

Intranet
Computers connected together in a Local Area Network or Wide Area Network environment and using the Internet as the carrier of data.
See Also: *AMR; Automatic Message Routing; Backbone; Bandwidth; BBS; Browser; Bulletin Board System; Client Server; Client Server Protocol; Distributed System/Network; Ethernet; File Server; File Sharing; Gateway; LAN; Local Area Network; Network; Network Information Centre; Network Operating System; NIC; Node; NOS; Polling; Remote Device; Ring Network; Server; Star Cluster; Star Network; Token Ring; WAN; Wide Area Network;*

Invoke
The procedure to start a process or program.
See Also: *Applet; AUTOEXEC.BAT; Batch Processing; Call; Chain; Command; DLL; Dynamic Link Library; Enter; Event; EXE; Execute; Instruction; Instruction Set; Load; Program; Run; Run Time; Subroutine;*

I-OR gate
Inclusive OR gate. A logic gate on a chip which operates with binary digits where an output of logic value 1 occurs if any of the inputs have a logic value 1. e.g. Inp=0 and Inp=0 then Out=0, Inp=1 and Inp=0 then Out=1.
See Also: *ALU; AMR; AND gate; Arithmetic and Logic Unit; Automatic Message Routing; Binary; Binary Digit; Bit; Boolean Algebra; Chip; Chipset; Expert System; FL; Flip Flop; Fuzzy Logic; Large Scale Integration; Logic Gate; LSI; NAND gate; NEQ gate; NOR gate; NOT gate; OR gate; Silicon Chip; Transistor; Very Large Scale Integration; VLSI; X-OR gate;*

IP
Internet Protocol. The rules used on the Internet for computers to communicate with each other.
See Also: *Acceptable User Policy; Anchor; AUP; Bluetooth (tm); Bookmark; CGI; Client Server Protocol; Common Gateway Interface; Cyberspace; Domain Name Server; Handshake; Host; HTTP; Hypertext Transfer Protocol; Interface; International Standards Organisation; Internet; Internet Protocol; Internet Protocol Address; IP Address; ISO; MIME; Multipurpose Internet Mail Extensions; Net; PING; Point to Point Protocol; PPP; Protocol; Secure Socket Layer; Serial Line Internet Protocol; Simple Mail Transfer Protocol; SLIP; SMTP; SSL; TCP/IP; The Net; Transmission Control Protocol/Internet Protocol; WAP; Wi-Fi; Wireless Application Protocol; Wireless Fidelity;*

IP Address
Internet Protocol Address. Also known as IP Number. The unique number identifying each domain name on the Internet.
See Also: *Address; Anchor; Bookmark; Client Server Protocol; Cyberspace; DNS; Domain Name; Domain Name Server; Domain Name System; E-mail Address; Hit; Host; HTTP; Hyperlink; Hypertext Transfer Protocol; Internet; Internet Protocol; Internet Protocol Address; IP; Net; Point Of Presence; Point to Point Protocol; POP; PPP; Protocol; Serial Line Internet Protocol; Simple Mail Transfer Protocol; SLIP; SMTP; The Net; WAP; Wireless Application Protocol;*

IRC
Internet Relay Chat. An Internet program which allows users to communicate with other users in real time.
See Also: *Chat; Chatroom; Cyberspace; Electronic Mail; E-mail; Forum; Host; IM; Instant Messaging; Interface; Internet; Internet Relay Chat; Internet Service Provider; ISP; Mailserver; Net; Netiquette; Newbie; Newsgroup; Online; Point to Point Protocol; PPP; Program; Provider; Serial Line Internet Protocol; Service Provider; Simple Mail Transfer Protocol; SLIP; SMTP; The Net; Thread; Webhost;*

IRQ
Interrupt Request. A signal used by devices to interrupt the processor in order for an action to be undertaken, e.g. a keyboard entry or mouse click.
See Also: *API; Application Program Interface; Central Processing Unit; Co-processor; CPU; Esc; Escape; Instruction; Interrupt; Interrupt Request; Maths Co-processor; Terminate and Stay Resident; TSR;*

IS

Information System. Hardware and software which allow data to be input, manipulated, stored and output.

See Also: *Application; Audit Trail; Batch Processing; Bespoke; CAD; CADCAM; CADMAT; CAE; CAI; CAM; CBT; Computer; Computer Aided Design; Computer Aided Design and Manufacturing; Computer Aided Design Manufacture and Test; Computer Aided Engineering; Computer Aided Instruction; Computer Aided Manufacturing; Computer Based Training; Configuration; Cross Platform; Data Base Management System; Data Processing; DBMS; Desk Top Publishing; Desktop; Digital Computer; Distributed System/Network; DP; DTP; EDP; EDS; Electronic Data Processing; Electronic Data System; Geographical Information System; GIS; Hardware; I/O; IBM (tm) Compatible; Information; Information System; Information Technology; Input/Output; Integrated Systems; IT; Kit; Laptop; Machine; Midrange System; Minicomputer; Notebook; Office Information System; OIS; Outsourcing; Package; Palmtop Computer; PC; Personal Computer; Platform; Portable; RDBMS/RDMS; Relational Database Management System; Software; Software Package; Software System; System; Tower Computer; Turnkey; Vertical Market;*

ISA

Industry Standard Architecture. A Personal Computer design standard whose communication path between the processor and external devices has a transfer rate of 8 MHz.

See Also: *Bus; Central Processing Unit; Channel; Co-processor; CPU; EIDE; EISA; Enhanced Industry Standard Architecture; Enhanced Intelligent Drive Electronics; IDE; Industry Standard Architecture; Integrated Drive Electronics; Local Bus; Maths Co-processor; MCA; Micro Channel Architecture; Microprocessor; Processor; SCSI; Small Computer System Interface; System Bus; Transmission Channel; Ultra DMA;*

ISAM

Indexed Sequential Access Method. A type of access to a disk file which allows reading and writing to the file using an index as a key.

See Also: *3.5 Inch; 5.25 Inch; Direct Access; Disk; Disk Pack; Disk Storage; Diskette; File; Five and a quarter; Floppy Disk; Index Sequential File; Indexed Sequential Access Method; Key; Keyed Sequential Access Method; KSAM; Magnetic Disk; Pack; R/W; Random Access; Read; Read/Write; Sequential Access; Serial Access; Three and a Half; Volume; Winchester Disk; Write;*

ISDN

Integrated Services Digital Network. A network structure which allows for faster data transmission in digital format where a single network can carry or switch different telecommunication services. e.g. audio, video and data.

See Also: *ADN; ADSL; Advanced Digital Network; AMR; Asymmetric Digital Subscriber Line; Asymmetrical Modem; Asynchronous; Asynchronous Transfer Mode; ATM; Automatic Message Routing; Bandwidth; Baud Rate; Bits Per Second; BPS; Broadband; CCITT; CCTA; Characters Per Second; Communications; Consultative Committee International Telegraph and Telephone; CPS; Data Communications; Data Parity; Data Transmission; Datacoms; Dial In; Dial Up; Digital; Direct Connection; Duplex Transmission; FDDI; Fibre Distributed Data Interface; Fibre Optics; Full Duplex; Gbps; Half Duplex; Handshake; HD; Information Superhighway; Integrated Services Digital Network; Kbps; Leased Line; Mbps; Modem; Modulator Demodulator; Multiplex; Multiplexer; Narrowband; Node; Open Systems Interconnect; Optical Fibre; OSI; Parallel Transmission; Parity Bit; Serial Interface; Serial Transmission; Simplex Transmission; Synchronous; T-1; T-3; Telecommunication; Telecoms; Teleprocessing System; TPS; Transfer Rate; Transmit; V90;*

ISO

International Standards Organisation. An international body representing protocols and standards from different countries.

See Also: *Acceptable User Policy; American National Standard Institute; ANSI; Asynchronous Transfer Mode; ATM; AUP; BCS; CCITT; CCTA; CERN; Client Server Protocol; Conseil Europeen pour la Recherche Nucleaire; Consultative Committee International Telegraph and Telephone; Data Protection Act; EBCDIC; Extended Binary Coded Decimal Interchange Code; File Transfer Protocol; FTP; IEE; International Standards Organisation; Internet Protocol; IP; NCC; Protocol;*

ISP

Internet Service Provider. A company that provides access to the Internet for computer users.

See Also: *Acceptable User Policy; AUP; Browser; CGI; Common Gateway Interface; Cookie; Cyberspace; DNS; Domain Name; Domain Name Server; Domain Name System; E-commerce; EDI; Electronic Data Interchange; Handshake; Hit; Home Page; Host; Host Processor; HTTP; Hypertext Transfer Protocol; Information Superhighway; Internet; Internet Relay Chat; Internet Service Provider; IRC; Mailserver; Net;*

Newsgroup; PING; Point Of Presence; Point to Point Protocol; POP; POP; Portal; Post Office Protocol; PPP; Provider; Proxy Server; Search Engine; Serial Line Internet Protocol; Service Provider; SLIP; Spider; Surfing; The Net; Wap Internet Service Provider; Webhost; WISP;

IT

Information Technology. The manipulation, analysis and storage of data on a computer.

See Also: *AI; Analogue Computer; Artificial Intelligence; Batch Processing; Bespoke; CAD; CADCAM; CADMAT; CAE; CAI; CAM; CBT; Computation; Compute; Computer; Computer Aided Design; Computer Aided Design and Manufacturing; Computer Aided Design Manufacture and Test; Computer Aided Engineering; Computer Aided Instruction; Computer Aided Manufacturing; Computer Based Training; Cross Platform; Data; Data Base Management System; Data Centre; Data Processing; DBMS; Desk Top Publishing; Desktop; Digital Computer; Distributed System/Network; DP; DTP; EDP; Electronic Data Processing; Geographical Information System; GIS; Hardware; IBM (tm) Compatible; Implementation; Information; Information System; Information Technology; Installation; Integrated Systems; IS; Kit; Laptop; Machine; Midrange System; Minicomputer; Notebook; Office Information System; OIS; Outsourcing; Palmtop Computer; PC; Personal Computer; Platform; Portable; Processing; Program; RDBMS/RDMS; Relational Database Management System; Software; Software System; Tower Computer;*

JAVA

A programming language which supports multimedia effects and mainly used for Internet applications.

See Also: *ADA; ALGOL; APL; BASIC; Browser; C or C++; CLIPPER; COBOL; Code; Code Generator; CORAL; Extensible Hypertext Markup Language; eXtensible Markup Language; FORTH; FORTRAN; High Level Language; HTML; Hypertext Mark-Up Language; Instruction Set; JAVASCRIPT; Language; LISP; LOGO; Module; NATURAL; Page Description Language; PASCAL; PDL; PERL; PICK; PILOT; PL/1; Practical Extraction and Reporting Language; Program; Programming Language; PROLOG; RPG; Software; Source Code; Syntax; Visual Basic; XHTML; XML;*

JAVASCRIPT
A simple programming language mainly used for designing websites and Internet applications.
See Also: *ADA; ALGOL; APL; BASIC; Browser; C or C++; CLIPPER; COBOL; Code; Code Generator; CORAL; Extensible Hypertext Markup Language; eXtensible Markup Language; FORTH; FORTRAN; High Level Language; HTML; Hypertext Mark-Up Language; Instruction Set; JAVA; Language; LISP; LOGO; Module; NATURAL; Page Description Language; PASCAL; PDL; PERL; PICK; PILOT; PL/1; Practical Extraction and Reporting Language; Program; Programming Language; PROLOG; RPG; Software; Source Code; Syntax; Visual Basic; XHTML; XML;*

JCL
Job Control Language. A set of procedure instructions which enables a person to communicate the operating system in a computer.
See Also: *Audit Trail; AUTOEXEC.BAT; Code; Command; End of Job; EOJ; Function; High Level Language; Instruction; Instruction Set; Job; Job Control Language; Language; Macro; Nesting; Process; Programming Language; Script; Subroutine; Syntax;*

Job
A program or a series of programs which perform a specific task on a computer. e.g. invoicing.
See Also: *Abort; Audit Trail; AUTOEXEC.BAT; Batch Processing; Bespoke; Command; Computation; Compute; Daemon; Data Processing; DP; End of Job; EOJ; Event; EXE; Function; Housekeeping; In-house; Instruction Set; JCL; Job Control Language; Macro; Module; Multitasking; Nesting; Run; Run Time; Script; Utility;*

Job Control Language
(JCL). A set of procedure instructions or programming language which enables a person to communicate with the operating system.
See Also: *Audit Trail; AUTOEXEC.BAT; Code; Command; End of Job; EOJ; Function; High Level Language; Instruction; Instruction Set; JCL; Job; Language; Macro; Nesting; Process; Programming Language; Script; Subroutine; Syntax;*

Joint Photographic Experts Group
(JPEG or JPG). A file format in which display images are stored. File extensions of either '.jpg' or '.jpeg' are used for this type of file.
See Also: *Attachment; BitMaP; BMP; Clip Art; Display; Extension; Filename Extension; Format; GIF; Graphical Interchange Format;*

Graphics; Image Map; Image Processing; JPEG; JPG; MIME; Multipurpose Internet Mail Extensions; PDF; Pixel; Portable Document Format; Resolution; Rich Text Format; RTF; Sprite; Tag Image File Format; Thumbnail; TIFF;

JPEG
Joint Photographic Experts Group. A file format in which display images are stored. File extensions of either '.jpg' or '.jpeg' are used for this type of file. Also known as JPG.
See Also: *Attachment; BitMaP; BMP; Clip Art; Display; Extension; Filename Extension; Format; GIF; Graphical Interchange Format; Graphics; Image Map; Image Processing; Joint Photographic Experts Group; JPG; MIME; Multipurpose Internet Mail Extensions; PDF; Pixel; Portable Document Format; Resolution; Rich Text Format; RTF; Sprite; Tag Image File Format; Thumbnail; TIFF;*

JPG
Joint Photographic Experts Group. A file format in which display images are stored. File extensions of either '.jpg' or '.jpeg' are used for this type of file. Also known as JPEG.
See Also: *Attachment; BitMaP; BMP; Clip Art; Display; Extension; Filename Extension; Format; GIF; Graphical Interchange Format; Graphics; Image Map; Image Processing; Joint Photographic Experts Group; JPEG; MIME; Multipurpose Internet Mail Extensions; PDF; Pixel; Portable Document Format; Resolution; Rich Text Format; RTF; Sprite; Tag Image File Format; Thumbnail; TIFF;*

K
Kilobyte. 1024 bytes or characters. Sometimes referred to as 1K.
See Also: *Byte; Data; Gb; Gigabyte; Kb; Kbyte; Kilobit; Kilobyte; Mb; Mbyte; Megabit; Megabyte; Terabyte; Word;*

Kb
Kilobyte. 1024 bytes or characters. Sometimes referred to as 1K.
See Also: *Byte; Data; Gb; Gigabyte; K; Kbyte; Kilobit; Kilobyte; Mb; Mbyte; Megabit; Megabyte; Terabyte; Word;*

Kbps
Kilo (thousand) bits per second. Represents a data transfer speed.
See Also: *Access Time; Acoustic Coupler; Address Bus; ADN; ADSL; Advanced Digital Network; Asymmetric Digital Subscriber Line; Asymmetrical Modem; Asynchronous; Asynchronous Transfer Mode; ATM; Bandwidth; Baud Rate; Binary; Binary Digit; Bit; Bits Per Second;*

BPS; Broadband; Bus; CCITT; CCTA; Channel; Characters Per Second; Communications; Computer Power; Consultative Committee International Telegraph and Telephone; CPS; Data Bus; Data Communications; Data Transmission; Datacoms; Dial In; Dial Up; Duplex Transmission; FDDI; Fibre Distributed Data Interface; Fibre Optics; Full Duplex; Gbps; GHz; Gigahertz; Half Duplex; HD; Integrated Services Digital Network; ISDN; KHz; Kilohertz; Local Bus; Mbps; Microsecond; Million Instructions Per Second; Millisecond; MIPS; Ms; Multiplex; Multiplexer; Nanosecond; Narrowband; Ns; Open Systems Interconnect; Optical Fibre; OSI; Parallel Transmission; Pico Second; Power; Serial Interface; Serial Transmission; Simplex Transmission; Synchronous; System Bus; T-1; T-3; Telecommunication; Telecoms; Teleprocessing System; TPS; Transfer Rate; Transmission Channel; Transmit; V90;

Kbyte
Kilobyte. 1024 bytes or characters. Sometimes referred to as 1K.
See Also: *Byte; Data; Gb; Gigabyte; K; Kb; Kilobit; Kilobyte; Mb; Mbyte; Megabit; Megabyte; Terabyte; Word;*

Key
One or more fields in a record used as an index to read/store the record.
See Also: *Comma Separated Values; CSV; Data; Data Element; Data Entity; Data Flow; Data Flow Diagram; Data Item; Data Model; Data Type; Database; DB; DFD; Direct Access; Entity; Field; Index Sequential File; Indexed Sequential Access Method; Information; ISAM; Keyed Sequential Access Method; KSAM; Literal; Meta Tag; Parameter; R/W; Random Access; Read; Read/Write; Record; Search Engine; Spider; Store; Subscript; Tag; Tag File; Write;*

Keyboard
A device which allows command instructions or data to be entered into a computer.
See Also: *Carriage Return; Configuration; Device; Drop-Down Menu; Enter; Environment; Equipment; Esc; Escape; Function Key; Hardware; Hot Key; Instruction; Interactive; Kit; Menu; Mouse; Peripheral; Pop Up Menu; PS/2; Pull Down Menu; Return;*

Keyed Sequential Access Method
(KSAM). A type of access to a disk file which allows reading and writing to the file using a key.
See Also: *3.5 Inch; 5.25 Inch; Direct Access; Disk; Disk Pack; Disk Storage; Diskette; File; Five and a quarter; Floppy Disk; Index*

Sequential File; Indexed Sequential Access Method; ISAM; Key; KSAM; Magnetic Disk; Pack; R/W; Random Access; Read; Read/Write; Sequential Access; Serial Access; Three and a Half; Volume; Winchester Disk; Write;

KHz

Kilohertz. A measure of communication frequency. 1 Kilohertz is equal to one thousand cycles per second.

See Also: *Baud Rate; Bits Per Second; BPS; Characters Per Second; Chip; Chipset; Clock Speed; Communications; Computer Power; CPS; Data Communications; Data Transmission; Datacoms; Gbps; GHz; Gigahertz; Kbps; Kilohertz; Mbps; Megahertz; MHz; Power; Processor; Silicon Chip; Telecommunication; Telecoms; Transmit;*

Kilobit

A term representing 1024 bits or commonly known as 1000 bits.

See Also: *Byte; Character; Data; Gb; Gigabyte; K; Kb; Kbyte; Kilobyte; Least Significant Bit; LSB; Mb; Mbyte; Megabit; Megabyte; Most Significant Bit; MSB; Terabyte;*

Kilobyte

(Kb). 1024 bytes or characters. Sometimes referred to as 1K.

See Also: *Byte; Data; Gb; Gigabyte; K; Kb; Kbyte; Kilobit; Mb; Mbyte; Megabit; Megabyte; Terabyte; Word;*

Kilohertz

(KHz). A measure of communication frequency. 1 Kilohertz is equal to one thousand cycles per second.

See Also: *Baud Rate; Bits Per Second; BPS; Characters Per Second; Chip; Chipset; Clock Speed; Communications; Computer Power; CPS; Data Communications; Data Transmission; Datacoms; Gbps; GHz; Gigahertz; Kbps; KHz; Mbps; Megahertz; MHz; Power; Processor; Silicon Chip; Telecommunication; Telecoms; Transmit;*

Kit

The computer hardware or equipment.

See Also: *1st Generation; 2nd Generation; 3.5 Inch; 3rd Generation; 4th Generation; 5.25 Inch; Acoustic Coupler; Advanced Technology; Analogue Computer; Analogue Digital Converter; Analogue Monitor; Anti Glare Screen; Asymmetrical Modem; AT; Backing Store; Barrel Printer; Bespoke; Black Box; Bubble Jet; Cathode Ray Tube; CD-ROM Drive; CD-RW Drive; CGA; Client Server; Colour Graphics Adaptor; Computer; Configuration; Cross Platform; CRT; Cut Sheet Feeder;*

Daisywheel; DAT; Deck; Desktop; Device; Digital Analog Converter; Digital Audio Tape; Digital Computer; Digital Monitor; Digital Versatile Disk; Disk; Disk Drive; Disk Pack; Disk Storage; Diskette; Display; Distributed System/Network; Dot Matrix; Downsizing; Drive; Drum Printer; DVD; EDS; EGA; Electronic Data System; Emulate; Emulation; Enhanced Graphic Adaptor; Environment; Equipment; Extended Technology; Extended Video Array; FDD; File Server; Five and a quarter; Fixed Disk Drive; Flatbed Scanner; Floppy Disk; Floppy Disk Drive; Global; Hand Held Device; Hard Disk Drive; Hardware; HDD; Host Processor; IBM (tm) Compatible; Information System; Information Technology; Inkjet; Install; Installation; Integrated Systems; Intelligent Terminal; IS; IT; Keyboard; Laptop; Laser Jet; Laser Printer; LCD; LCD Printer; Leading Edge; Light Pen; Line Printer; Liquid Crystal Display; Liquid Crystal Display Printer; Machine; Mag Tape; Magnetic Disk; Magnetic Tape; Mailserver; Mainframe; Mass Storage; Matrix Printer; Micro; Microcomputer; Midrange System; Minicomputer; Modem; Modulator Demodulator; Monitor; Monochrome; Mouse; Multi Platform; Node; Notebook; Number Cruncher; OCR; OMR; Optical Character Reader; Optical Character Recognition; Optical Drive; Optical Mark Recognition; Optical Scanner; Pack; Page Printer; Palmtop Computer; PC; PDA; Peripheral; Personal Computer; Personal Digital Assistant; Plasma Screen; Platform; Plotter; Plug Compatible; Portable; Printer; Recording Device; Remote Device; Scanner; Screen; Server; Sheet Feeder; Standalone; State of the Art; Storage; Store; Streamer; Super Twist LCD; Super VGA; Super Video Graphics Array; SVGA; System; Tape Deck; Tape Streamer; Terminal; TFT; Thermal Printer; Thin-Film Transistor; Third Party Maintenance; Three and a Half; Touch Screen; Tower Computer; Tracker Ball; Turnkey; VDT; VDU; VGA; Video Display Terminal; Video Graphics Array; Visual Display Terminal; Visual Display Unit; Volume; Webcam; Winchester Disk; XGA; XT; Zip Drive;

KSAM
Keyed Sequential Access Method. A type of access to a disk file which allows reading and writing to the file using a key.
See Also: *3.5 Inch; 5.25 Inch; Direct Access; Disk; Disk Pack; Disk Storage; Diskette; File; Five and a quarter; Floppy Disk; Index Sequential File; Indexed Sequential Access Method; ISAM; Key; Keyed Sequential Access Method; Magnetic Disk; Pack; R/W; Random Access; Read; Read/Write; Sequential Access; Serial Access; Three and a Half; Volume; Winchester Disk; Write;*

LAN
Local Area Network. A type of network which connects multiple computers to a server in order to share data storage and peripherals. It is normally used where the equipment is close together. e.g. an office.
See Also: *AMR; Anonymous FTP; Automatic Message Routing; Backbone; Bandwidth; BBS; Broadband; Bulletin Board System; Client Server; Client Server Protocol; Distributed System/Network; Environment; Ethernet; File Server; File Sharing; Gateway; Host Processor; Intranet; LAN Port; Local Area Network; Multi User; Multitasking; Narrowband; Network; Network Information Centre; Network Operating System; NIC; Node; NOS; Open Systems Interconnect; OSI; Ring Network; Server; Star Cluster; Star Network; TCP/IP; Token Ring; Transmission Control Protocol/Internet Protocol; WAN; Wide Area Network;*

LAN Port
The connector in a computer for the Local Area Network connection.
See Also: *Backbone; Client Server; Ethernet; File Server; Gateway; LAN; Local Area Network; Network; Port; Ring Network; Server; Star Cluster; Star Network; Token Ring;*

Landscape
Printing which appears on the paper horizontally instead of vertically.
See Also: *Bi Directional; Bubble Jet; Characters Per Inch; CPI; Daisywheel; Dot Matrix; Format; Hard Copy; Inkjet; Laser Jet; Laser Printer; LCD Printer; Letter Quality; Line Printer; Liquid Crystal Display Printer; LQ; Matrix Printer; Near Letter Quality; NLQ; Output; Page Printer; Plotter; Portrait; Printer; Printout; Thermal Printer;*

Language
A set of instructions and formats in which to write programs that tell a computer what to do. e.g. BASIC, COBOL.
See Also: *A/P; ADA; ALGOL; Analyst Programmer; APL; Assembler; Assembly Code; BASIC; C or C++; CLIPPER; COBOL; CODASYL; Code; Code Generator; Conference On DAta SYstems Languages; CORAL; Extensible Hypertext Markup Language; eXtensible Markup Language; FORTH; FORTRAN; High Level Language; HTML; Hypertext Mark-Up Language; Instruction Set; JAVA; JAVASCRIPT; JCL; Job Control Language; LISP; LOGO; Low Level Language; NATURAL; Page Description Language; PASCAL; PDL; PERL; PICK; PILOT; PL/1; Practical Extraction and Reporting Language; Program; Programmer; Programming Language; PROLOG; RPG; S/P; Software; Source Code; Systems Programmer; XHTML; XML;*

Laptop
A portable computer small enough to use on your lap. The screen forms an integral part of the unit which is the lid that opens and closes the unit.
See Also: *1st Generation; 2nd Generation; 3rd Generation; 4th Generation; Advanced Technology; Analogue Computer; AT; Compatible; Computer; Computer Power; Configuration; Cross Platform; Desktop; Digital Computer; Downsizing; EDS; Electronic Data System; Environment; Equipment; Extended Technology; Hardware; IBM (tm) Compatible; Information System; Information Technology; Installation; IS; IT; Kit; Machine; Micro; Microcomputer; Multi Platform; Notebook; OEM; Original Equipment Manufacturer; Palmtop Computer; PC; Personal Computer; Platform; Portable; Power; Standalone; Tower Computer; Turnkey; Voice Activated; XT;*

Large Scale Integration
(LSI). An indication of the number of logic gates on a chip, which for LSI is above 100.
See Also: *ALU; AND gate; Application Specific Integrated Circuits; Arithmetic and Logic Unit; ASICS; Chip; Chipset; Flip Flop; IC; Integrated Circuit; I-OR gate; Logic Gate; LSI; NAND gate; NEQ gate; NOR gate; NOT gate; OR gate; Processor; Semiconductor; Silicon Chip; Solid State; Transistor; Very Large Scale Integration; VLSI; X-OR gate;*

Laser Jet
Also known as a Laser Printer. A device which prints a whole page at a time. Sometimes referred to as Page Printers. It prints very similar to a photocopier where a drum unit is electrically charged with the image to print and then passed over toner. The toner adheres to the charged area and is transferred to the paper by a heat process.
See Also: *Barrel Printer; Bubble Jet; Configuration; Daisywheel; Device; Dot Matrix; Drum Printer; Duplex Printing; Environment; Equipment; Font Cartridge; Hard Copy; Hardware; Inkjet; Installation; Kit; Landscape; Laser Printer; LCD Printer; Letter Quality; Line Printer; Lines Per Minute; Liquid Crystal Display Printer; Lpm; LPT Port; LQ; Matrix Printer; Near Letter Quality; NLQ; Page Printer; Pages Per Minute; Peripheral; Portrait; Postscript; PPM; Printer; Printer Driver; Printout; Simplex Printing; Thermal Printer; Toner;*

Laser Printer
A device which prints a whole page at a time. Sometimes referred to as Page Printers. It prints very similar to a photocopier where a drum unit is electrically charged with the image to print and then passed over toner. The toner adheres to the charged area and is transferred to the paper by a heat process.
See Also: *Barrel Printer; Bubble Jet; Configuration; Daisywheel; Device; Dot Matrix; Drum Printer; Duplex Printing; Environment; Equipment; Font Cartridge; Hard Copy; Hardware; Inkjet; Installation; Kit; Landscape; Laser Jet; LCD Printer; Letter Quality; Line Printer; Lines Per Minute; Liquid Crystal Display Printer; Lpm; LPT Port; LQ; Matrix Printer; Near Letter Quality; NLQ; Page Printer; Pages Per Minute; Peripheral; Portrait; Postscript; PPM; Printer; Printer Driver; Printout; Simplex Printing; Thermal Printer; Toner;*

LCD
Liquid Crystal Display. A screen where liquid crystal molecules form into characters when an electrical voltage is applied to them. It is used mainly on portable equipment where the screens are flat.
See Also: *Analogue Monitor; Anti Glare Screen; Cathode Ray Tube; CGA; Colour Graphics Adaptor; CRT; Device; Digital Monitor; Display; EGA; Enhanced Graphic Adaptor; Environment; Equipment; Extended Video Array; Graphics Card; Hardware; High Resolution; Installation; Intelligent Terminal; Interlaced; Kit; Liquid Crystal Display; Low Resolution; Monitor; Monochrome; Paint Screen; Peripheral; Plasma Screen; Prompt; Resolution; Screen; Screen Burn; Split Screen; Super Twist LCD; Super VGA; Super Video Graphics Array; SVGA; Terminal; TFT; Thin-Film Transistor; Touch Screen; Twip; VDT; VDU; VGA; Video Card; Video Display Terminal; Video Graphics Array; Video Random Access Memory; Visual Display Terminal; Visual Display Unit; VRAM; XGA;*

LCD Printer
A printer very similar to the laser printer. The difference being in the way the drum is charged which uses light sensitive particles that require less power.
See Also: *Barrel Printer; Bubble Jet; Configuration; Daisywheel; Device; Dot Matrix; Drum Printer; Duplex Printing; Environment; Equipment; Font Cartridge; Hard Copy; Hardware; Inkjet; Installation; Kit; Landscape; Laser Jet; Laser Printer; Letter Quality; Line Printer; Lines Per Minute; Liquid Crystal Display Printer; Lpm; LPT Port; LQ; Matrix Printer; Near Letter Quality; NLQ; Page Printer; Pages Per*

Minute; Peripheral; Portrait; Postscript; PPM; Printer; Printer Driver; Printout; Simplex Printing; Thermal Printer; Toner;

Leading Edge
The latest or newest hardware and software on the market.
See Also: *AI; Artificial Intelligence; Computer; Cross Platform; Development; Device; Digital; EDS; Electronic Data System; Equipment; Hardware; Kit; Machine; Mainframe; Midrange System; Minicomputer; Package; PC; Peripheral; Personal Computer; Platform; Plug Compatible; Recording Device; Releases; Silicon Valley; Software; Software Package; Software System; State of the Art; Tower Computer;*

Leased Line
An exclusive communication line.
See Also: *ADN; ADSL; Advanced Digital Network; AMR; Asymmetric Digital Subscriber Line; Asynchronous; Asynchronous Transfer Mode; ATM; Automatic Message Routing; Bandwidth; Broadband; CCITT; CCTA; Channel; Client Server Protocol; Communications; Consultative Committee International Telegraph and Telephone; Data Communications; Data Parity; Data Transmission; Datacoms; Digital; Direct Connection; Duplex Transmission; ECP; Enhanced Parallel Port; EPP; Extended Capabilities Port; FDDI; Fibre Distributed Data Interface; Fibre Optics; Firewire; Full Duplex; Half Duplex; Handshake; HD; Integrated Services Digital Network; ISDN; Multiplex; Multiplexer; Narrowband; Node; Open Systems Interconnect; Optical Fibre; OSI; Parallel Transmission; Parity Bit; Serial Transmission; Simplex Transmission; Synchronous; Telecommunication; Telecoms; Teleprocessing System; TPS; Transmission Channel; Transmit; V90;*

Least Significant Bit
(LSB). The bit furthest to the right in a row of binary digits.
See Also: *16 Bit; 32 Bit; 64 Bit; 8 Bit; American Standard Code for Information Interchange; ASCII; BCD; Binary; Binary Coded Decimal; Binary Digit; Bit; Bit Pattern; Digital; Eight Bit; Kilobit; LSB; Megabit; Most Significant Bit; MSB; Sixteen Bit; Sixty Four Bit; Thirty Two Bit; Word;*

LED
Light Emitting Diode. A light indicator used normally to show the status of a device.
See Also: *Device; Equipment; Light Emitting Diode; Peripheral;*

Letter Quality
(LQ). The type of print produced by some printers where the dots that make up each character are closer together, thus giving a better quality print.
See Also: *Bi Directional; Bubble Jet; Characters Per Inch; CPI; Daisywheel; DIP Switch; Dot Matrix; Dots Per Inch; DPI; Duplex Printing; Font; Font Cartridge; Format; Hard Copy; Inkjet; Landscape; Laser Jet; Laser Printer; LCD Printer; Liquid Crystal Display Printer; LQ; Matrix Printer; Near Letter Quality; NLQ; Output; Page Printer; Portrait; Postscript; Printer Driver; Printout; Scalable Fonts; Simplex Printing;*

Light Emitting Diode
(LED). A light indicator used normally to show the status of a device.
See Also: *Device; Equipment; LED; Peripheral;*

Light Pen
A handheld device which tracks or inputs data into a computer. It is achieved by positioning the light pen onto the data or by scanning the data.
See Also: *Analogue; Analogue Computer; Analogue Digital Converter; Configuration; Device; Equipment; Hand Held Device; Hardware; Input; Instruction; Kit; OCR; OMR; Optical Character Reader; Optical Character Recognition; Optical Mark Recognition; PDA; Peripheral; Personal Digital Assistant;*

Line Editor
A program which allows the user to enter and edit data in a computer one line at a time.
See Also: *Edit; Page Editor; Patch; Picture; Program; Spell Check; Split Screen; Syntax; Utility; Word Processor; Word Wrap; WP;*

Line Printer
A line printer whose mechanism includes a barrel shaped component with characters, numbers and symbols embossed on the outside. Next to the barrel is an ink ribbon and paper. Print hammers hit the paper resulting in printed characters being transferred to the paper from the barrel through the ink ribbon.
See Also: *Barrel Printer; Bubble Jet; Configuration; Daisywheel; Device; Dot Matrix; Drum Printer; Duplex Printing; Environment; Equipment; Hard Copy; Hardware; Inkjet; Installation; Kit; Landscape; Laser Jet; Laser Printer; LCD Printer; Lines Per Minute; Liquid Crystal Display Printer; Lpm; LPT Port; Matrix Printer; Output; Page Printer;*

Pages Per Minute; Peripheral; Portrait; Postscript; PPM; Printer; Printer Driver; Printout; Remote Device; Simplex Printing; Thermal Printer;

Lines Per Minute
(Lpm). The number of lines a printer can optimally print in a minute.
See Also: *Barrel Printer; Bi Directional; Bubble Jet; Daisywheel; Dot Matrix; Drum Printer; Hard Copy; Inkjet; Laser Jet; Laser Printer; LCD Printer; Line Printer; Liquid Crystal Display Printer; Lpm; Matrix Printer; Page Printer; Pages Per Minute; PPM; Printer; Printer Driver; Printout; Thermal Printer;*

Link
The web address or URL embedded in a document which takes you to the corresponding website when clicked.
See Also: *Address; Anchor; Cyberspace; Hit; Home Page; Hyperlink; Hypertext; Icon; Internet; Net; Portal; Site; The Net; The Web; Thumbnail; Universal/Uniform Resource Locator; URL; Webring; Website; World Wide Web; WWW;*

Linux
An operating system adapted from the Unix operating system.
See Also: *API; Application Program Interface; Basic Input Output System; BIOS; Boot; Boot Disk; Bootstrap; C Prompt; Cold Start; Configuration; Disk Operating System; DOS; Environment; FAT; File Allocation Table; Graphical User Interface; GUI; High Memory; Housekeeping; Installation; Network Operating System; NOS; Open System; Operating System; OS; OS/2; Re-boot; System Software; UNIX; Upper Memory; Warm Start;*

Liquid Crystal Display
(LCD). A screen where liquid crystal molecules form into characters when an electrical voltage is applied to them. Used mainly on portable equipment where the screens are flat.
See Also: *Analogue Monitor; Anti Glare Screen; Cathode Ray Tube; CGA; Colour Graphics Adaptor; CRT; Device; Digital Monitor; Display; EGA; Enhanced Graphic Adaptor; Environment; Equipment; Extended Video Array; Graphics Card; Hardware; High Resolution; Installation; Intelligent Terminal; Interlaced; Kit; LCD; Low Resolution; Monitor; Monochrome; Paint Screen; Peripheral; Plasma Screen; Prompt; Resolution; Screen; Screen Burn; Split Screen; Super Twist LCD; Super VGA; Super Video Graphics Array; SVGA; Terminal; TFT; Thin-Film Transistor; Touch Screen; Twip; VDT; VDU; VGA; Video Card; Video*

Display Terminal; Video Graphics Array; Video Random Access Memory; Visual Display Terminal; Visual Display Unit; VRAM; XGA;

Liquid Crystal Display Printer
A printer very similar to the Laser Printer. The difference being in the way the drum is charged which uses light sensitive particles that require less power.
See Also: *Barrel Printer; Bubble Jet; Configuration; Daisywheel; Device; Dot Matrix; Drum Printer; Duplex Printing; Environment; Equipment; Font Cartridge; Hard Copy; Hardware; Inkjet; Installation; Kit; Landscape; Laser Jet; Laser Printer; LCD Printer; Letter Quality; Line Printer; Lines Per Minute; Lpm; LPT Port; LQ; Matrix Printer; Near Letter Quality; NLQ; Page Printer; Pages Per Minute; Peripheral; Portrait; Postscript; PPM; Printer; Printer Driver; Printout; Simplex Printing; Thermal Printer; Toner;*

LISP
A high level computer programming language.
See Also: *3GL; 4GL; ADA; ALGOL; APL; BASIC; C or C++; CLIPPER; COBOL; Code; Code Generator; Compiler; Compiling; CORAL; FORTH; FORTRAN; Fourth Generation Language; High Level Language; Instruction Set; JAVA; JAVASCRIPT; Language; LOGO; Module; NATURAL; PASCAL; PERL; PICK; PILOT; PL/1; Practical Extraction and Reporting Language; Program; Programming Language; PROLOG; RPG; Software; Source Code; Structured Program; Syntax; Third Generation Language; Visual Basic;*

Literal
Data in a program which remains unchanged during the execution of the program.
See Also: *Character; Constant; Data; Data Element; Data Entity; Data Item; Data Type; EBCDIC; Entity; Extended Binary Coded Decimal Interchange Code; Field; Group; Information; Key; Null;*

Live
This is when hardware and software is used after being tested.
See Also: *Development; Full Project Life Cycle; Going Live; Hand Holding; Implementation; Install; Installation; Project Life Cycle; Releases; Run Time;*

Load

(1) The transfer of a program into the computer's memory. (2) The loading of a peripheral device with its storage or printing medium.

See Also: *Bubble Memory; Call; Chain; Cold Start; Command; Conventional Memory; Device; EXE; Execute; High Memory; Invoke; Memory; Mix; Peripheral; Program; Recording Device; Run; Run Time; Upper Memory;*

Local Area Network

(LAN). A type of network which connects multiple computers to a server in order to share data storage and peripherals. It is normally used where the equipment is close together. e.g. an office.

See Also: *AMR; Anonymous FTP; Automatic Message Routing; Backbone; Bandwidth; BBS; Broadband; Bulletin Board System; Client Server; Client Server Protocol; Distributed System/Network; Environment; Ethernet; File Server; File Sharing; Gateway; Host Processor; Intranet; LAN; LAN Port; Multi User; Multitasking; Narrowband; Network; Network Information Centre; Network Operating System; NIC; Node; NOS; Open Systems Interconnect; OSI; Ring Network; Server; Star Cluster; Star Network; TCP/IP; Token Ring; Transmission Control Protocol/Internet Protocol; WAN; Wide Area Network;*

Local Bus

A communication path between the central processor unit and peripheral devices.

See Also: *16 Bit; 32 Bit; 64 Bit; 8 Bit; Address Bus; Bits Per Second; BPS; Bus; Central Processing Unit; Channel; Co-processor; CPU; Data Bus; Digital; Eight Bit; Gbps; I/O; Industry Standard Architecture; Input/Output; ISA; Kbps; Maths Co-processor; Mbps; Sixteen Bit; Sixty Four Bit; System Bus; Thirty Two Bit; Transmission Channel;*

Locking

The process where a record being updated by one program is locked and thus inhibits other programs from using the record until it is released.

See Also: *Client Server; Dead Lock; Deadly Embrace; File Sharing; Hangs; Hung; Multi User; Multitasking; Record; Record Locking; Security; Server; System Hangs; Write Protect;*

Log File
A record of transactions processed or procedures performed.
See Also: *ASCII Files; Attachment; Audit Trail; Beginning of File; BOF; End of File; EOF; File; Fragmentation; Index Sequential File; Random File; Record; Sequential File; Serial File; Tag File; Temp File;*

Log In/Off
The signing on and off by a user to enable them to gain access to a computer system or Internet sites. Also referred to as "logging on or off".
See Also: *Access; End of Job; End User; EOJ; Hacker; Off Line; Online; Password;*

Logic Gate
A decision-making circuitry which operates with binary digits. Thousands of these gates are interconnected on a semiconductor chip which forms the whole circuitry on the chip.
See Also: *ALU; AMR; AND gate; Arithmetic and Logic Unit; Automatic Message Routing; Binary; Binary Digit; Bit; Boolean Algebra; Chip; Chipset; Expert System; FL; Flip Flop; Fuzzy Logic; I-OR gate; Large Scale Integration; LSI; NAND gate; NEQ gate; NOR gate; NOT gate; OR gate; Semiconductor; Silicon Chip; Solid State; Sound Chip; Transistor; Very Large Scale Integration; VLSI; X-OR gate;*

Logical Design
A hardware or software system design, normally in graphic form, which shows the logical processes of the system as opposed to the physical processes. i.e. 'what' the system does instead of 'how' it does it.
See Also: *A/P; Analyst; Analyst Programmer; Audit Trail; B/A; Bespoke; Boolean Algebra; Business Analyst; CASE; Case Tool; Computer Aided Software Engineering; Design; Development; Expert System; Flowchart; Full Project Life Cycle; Model; Modular; O & M; Object Oriented Analysis; Object Oriented Design; Object Oriented Programming; OOA; OOD; OOP; Organisation & Methods; Physical Design; Process Model; Program Specification; Programmer; Project Life Cycle; S/A; S/P; Specification; Structured Design; System Analysis; System Analyst; Systems Programmer;*

LOGO
A high level computer programming language.
See Also: *3GL; 4GL; ADA; ALGOL; APL; BASIC; C or C++; CLIPPER; COBOL; Code; Code Generator; Compiler; Compiling; CORAL; FORTH; FORTRAN; Fourth Generation Language; High Level Language; Instruction Set; JAVA; JAVASCRIPT; Language; LISP;*

Module; NATURAL; PASCAL; PERL; PICK; PILOT; PL/1; Practical Extraction and Reporting Language; Program; Programming Language; PROLOG; RPG; Software; Source Code; Structured Program; Syntax; Third Generation Language; Visual Basic;

Loop
A technique in a program to repeat a series of instructions.
See Also: *A/P; Analyst Programmer; Applet; Code; Program; Programmer; S/P; Structured Program; Systems Programmer;*

Low Level Language
A programming language in which each statement equates to one or a few machine code statements.
See Also: *Assembler; Assembly Code; Code; Code Generator; Compiler; Compiling; High Level Language; Instruction Set; Language; Machine Code; Machine Language; Object Code; Programming Language; Software;*

Low Resolution
A screen made up of 320 pixels across and 240 down where the display of data or graphics is not as good as a high resolution screen.
See Also: *Analogue Monitor; Anti Glare Screen; Cathode Ray Tube; CGA; Colour Graphics Adaptor; CRT; Digital Monitor; Display; EGA; Enhanced Graphic Adaptor; Extended Video Array; Frame Rate; Graphics; Graphics Card; Image Processing; Intelligent Terminal; Interlaced; LCD; Liquid Crystal Display; Monitor; Monochrome; Paint Screen; Pixel; Plasma Screen; Screen; Screen Burn; Split Screen; Sprite; Super Twist LCD; Super VGA; Super Video Graphics Array; SVGA; Terminal; TFT; Thin-Film Transistor; Touch Screen; Twip; VDT; VDU; VGA; Video Card; Video Display Terminal; Video Graphics Array; Visual Display Terminal; Visual Display Unit; XGA;*

Lpm
Lines Per Minute. The number of lines a printer can optimally print in a minute.
See Also: *Barrel Printer; Bi Directional; Bubble Jet; Daisywheel; Dot Matrix; Drum Printer; Hard Copy; Inkjet; Laser Jet; Laser Printer; LCD Printer; Line Printer; Lines Per Minute; Liquid Crystal Display Printer; Matrix Printer; Page Printer; Pages Per Minute; PPM; Printer; Printer Driver; Printout; Thermal Printer;*

LPT Port
The printer or parallel port on a computer.
See Also: *Barrel Printer; Bubble Jet; Daisywheel; Dot Matrix; Drum Printer; Inkjet; Laser Jet; Laser Printer; LCD Printer; Line Printer; Liquid Crystal Display Printer; Matrix Printer; Page Printer; Parallel Interface; Parallel Port; Port; Printer; Serial Port;*

LQ
Letter Quality. The type of print produced by some printers where the dots that make up each character are closer together, thus giving a better quality print.
See Also: *Bi Directional; Bubble Jet; Characters Per Inch; CPI; Daisywheel; DIP Switch; Dot Matrix; Dots Per Inch; DPI; Duplex Printing; Font; Font Cartridge; Format; Hard Copy; Inkjet; Landscape; Laser Jet; Laser Printer; LCD Printer; Letter Quality; Liquid Crystal Display Printer; Matrix Printer; Near Letter Quality; NLQ; Output; Page Printer; Portrait; Postscript; Printer Driver; Printout; Scalable Fonts; Simplex Printing;*

LSB
Least Significant Bit. The bit furthest to the right in a row of binary digits.
See Also: *16 Bit; 32 Bit; 64 Bit; 8 Bit; American Standard Code for Information Interchange; ASCII; BCD; Binary; Binary Coded Decimal; Binary Digit; Bit; Bit Pattern; Digital; Eight Bit; Kilobit; Least Significant Bit; Megabit; Most Significant Bit; MSB; Sixteen Bit; Sixty Four Bit; Thirty Two Bit; Word;*

LSI
Large Scale Integration. An indication of the number of logic gates on a chip, which for LSI is above 100.
See Also: *ALU; AND gate; Application Specific Integrated Circuits; Arithmetic and Logic Unit; ASICS; Chip; Chipset; Flip Flop; IC; Integrated Circuit; I-OR gate; Large Scale Integration; Logic Gate; NAND gate; NEQ gate; NOR gate; NOT gate; OR gate; Processor; Semiconductor; Silicon Chip; Solid State; Transistor; Very Large Scale Integration; VLSI; X-OR gate;*

Machine
A commonly used term to describe a computer of any kind.
See Also: *1st Generation; 2nd Generation; 3rd Generation; 4th Generation; Advanced Technology; Analogue Computer; AT; Compatible; Computer; Computer Power; Configuration; Cross Platform; Desktop; Digital Computer; Distributed System/Network;*

Downsizing; EDS; Electronic Data System; Emulate; Emulation; Environment; Equipment; Extended Technology; Front End Processor; Hardware; Host Processor; IBM (tm) Compatible; Information System; Information Technology; Installation; IS; IT; Kit; Laptop; Leading Edge; Mailserver; Mainframe; Micro; Microcomputer; Midrange System; Minicomputer; Multi Platform; Multimedia; Node; Notebook; Number Cruncher; OEM; Original Equipment Manufacturer; Palmtop Computer; PC; Personal Computer; Platform; Portable; Power; Standalone; State of the Art; System; Tower Computer; Turnkey; Voice Activated; XT;

Machine Code
A set of binary digits recognised by a computer to perform an instruction. Programs are converted to machine code before being used by a computer.
See Also: *Assembler; Assembly Code; BCD; Binary; Binary Coded Decimal; Binary Digit; Bit; Code Generator; Compiler; Compiling; EXE; Instruction Set; Low Level Language; Machine Language; Object Code;*

Machine Crash
(1) Mechanical failure of the read/write heads or dirt on the heads in a storage unit. (2) A state when a program stops running due to a bug in the program or the computer system.
See Also: *3.5 Inch; 5.25 Inch; Abort; Bug; Crash; Debug; Debugger; Died; Disk; Disk Drive; Disk Pack; Disk Storage; Diskette; Downtime; FDD; Five and a quarter; Fixed Disk Drive; Floppy Disk; Floppy Disk Drive; General Protection Fault; GPF; Hangs; Hard Disk Drive; HDD; Head Crash; Heads; Hung; Magnetic Disk; Pack; Program Crash; Read/Write Head; Roll Back; System Hangs; Three and a Half; Virus; Worm;*

Machine Language
A set of binary digits recognised by a computer to perform an instruction. Programs are converted to machine language before being used by a computer.
See Also: *Assembler; Assembly Code; BCD; Binary; Binary Coded Decimal; Binary Digit; Bit; Code Generator; Compiler; Compiling; EXE; Instruction Set; Low Level Language; Machine Code; Object Code;*

Macro
A set of instructions to perform a certain task on a computer.
See Also: *Applet; Audit Trail; Batch File; Batch Processing; Code; Command; Device Driver; DLL; Driver; Dynamic Link Library; Event;*

EXE; Execute; Function; Function Key; Instruction; Instruction Set; JCL; Job; Job Control Language; Module; Nesting; Process; Program; Run; Run Time; Script; Software Driver; Subroutine; Utility;

Mag Tape
Abbr. of Magnetic Tape. (1) A recording medium made of plastic tape covered with a magnetic material. (2) The device in which the magnetic tape medium is used.
See Also: *Archive; Backing Store; Backup; Bits Per Inch; Block; BPI; Configuration; DAT; Deck; Density; Device; Digital Audio Tape; Double Density; End of Tape; Environment; EOT; Equipment; Grandfather, Father, Son; Hardware; Heads; High Density; Installation; Kit; Magnetic Tape; Mass Storage; Medium; Peripheral; Read/Write Head; Recording Device; Recording Medium; Remote Device; Save; Storage; Store; Streamer; Tape Deck; Tape Streamer; Track; Write; Write Protect;*

Magnetic Core
The computer's memory before solid-state memories were invented. It consists of rows and columns of ferrite rings which can be magnetised and demagnetised to allow binary storage.
See Also: *Absolute Address; Address; Array; Block; Bubble Memory; Buffer; Cache Memory; Clipboard; Computer Power; Conventional Memory; Core; Core Dump; DDR SDRAM; DIMM; Direct Memory Access; Direct Random Access Memory; Disk Cache; DMA; Double Data Rate SDRAM; DRAM; Dual Inline Memory Module; Dump; Dynamic Memory; Dynamically; EEROM; Electrically Erasable Read Only Memory; Electronically Programmed Read Only Memory; EMS; EPROM; Erasable Programmable Read Only Memory; Expanded Memory; Expanded Memory Specification; Extended Memory; Flash Memory; High Memory; Memory; Memory Caching; Memory Resident; Mix; Overlay; Power; Programmable Read Only Memory; PROM; RAM; RAM Disk; Rambus Dynamic Random Access Memory; Random Access Memory; RDRAM; Read Only Memory; Relative Address; ROM; SDRAM; Shadow RAM Memory; SIMM; Single Inline Memory Modules; Single Inline Package; SIP; Store; Synchronous Dynamic Random Access Memory; Upper Memory; Video Random Access Memory; Volatile Memory; VRAM; Working Storage; Workspace;*

Magnetic Disk
(1) The storage medium on which information is recorded. (2) The device in which the magnetic storage medium is used.
See Also: *3.5 Inch; 5.25 Inch; Archive; ATAPI; Attachment Packet Interface; Backing Store; Backup; Bits Per Inch; Block; Boot Disk; BPI; Cluster; Computer Power; Configuration; Crash; Cylinder; Defragment; Density; Device; Directory; Disk; Disk Drive; Disk Map; Disk Operating System; Disk Pack; Disk Size; Disk Storage; Diskette; DOS; Double Density; Drive; EIDE; EISA; Enhanced Industry Standard Architecture; Enhanced Intelligent Drive Electronics; Equipment; FDD; Five and a quarter; Fixed Disk Drive; Floppy Disk; Floppy Disk Drive; Format; Fragmentation; Grandfather, Father, Son; Hard Disk Drive; Hardware; HDD; Head Crash; Heads; High Density; IDE; Indexed Sequential Access Method; Integrated Drive Electronics; ISAM; Keyed Sequential Access Method; Kit; KSAM; Machine Crash; Mass Storage; Medium; Pack; Peripheral; Power; Read/Write Head; Recording; Recording Device; Recording Medium; Remote Device; Root Directory; Save; Sector; Seek Time; Storage; Store; Sub Directory; Three and a Half; Track; Volume; Winchester Disk; Wipe; Write; Write Protect;*

Magnetic Ink Character Recognition
(MICR). The process where special ink, which contains magnetic particles, is printed onto documents and recognised by special readers that detect the shape of the characters. e.g. the base line on cheques.
See Also: *Character; EDP; Electronic Data Processing; MICR;*

Magnetic Tape
(1) A recording medium made of plastic tape covered with a magnetic material. (2) The device in which the magnetic tape medium is used.
See Also: *Archive; Backing Store; Backup; Bits Per Inch; Block; BPI; Configuration; DAT; Deck; Density; Device; Digital Audio Tape; Double Density; End of Tape; Environment; EOT; Equipment; Grandfather, Father, Son; Hardware; Heads; High Density; Installation; Kit; Mag Tape; Mass Storage; Medium; Peripheral; Read/Write Head; Recording Device; Recording Medium; Remote Device; Save; Storage; Store; Streamer; Tape Deck; Tape Streamer; Track; Write; Write Protect;*

Mail Merge
A process where information from different sources are merged together to create one document. In particular where names and addresses are merged into a standard letter.
See Also: *Application; Batch Processing; Document; Office Information System; OIS; Package; Software; Software Package; Software System; Word Processor; WP;*

Mailbox
A folder or directory within a computer to receive electronic mail.
See Also: *Body; Cybercafe; Cyberspace; Electronic Mail; E-mail; E-mail Address; Flame; Forum; Mailing List; Mailserver; POP; Post Office Protocol; Simple Mail Transfer Protocol; SMTP;*

Mailing List
A list of e-mail addresses where messages are sent.
See Also: *Address; Body; Buddy List; Cyberspace; Electronic Mail; E-mail; E-mail Address; Flame; Mailbox; Mailserver;*

Mailserver
A computer system which enables the sending and retrieval of e-mail messages.
See Also: *Client Server; Client Server Protocol; Computer; Cyberspace; Electronic Mail; E-mail; E-mail Address; Equipment; File Server; Gateway; Hardware; Host; Host Processor; IBM (tm) Compatible; Internet Relay Chat; Internet Service Provider; IRC; ISP; Kit; Machine; Mailbox; Mailing List; Midrange System; Minicomputer; Node; POP; Post Office Protocol; Provider; Proxy Server; Server; Service Provider; Simple Mail Transfer Protocol; SMTP; Webhost;*

Mainframe
A large computer built to conventional architecture.
See Also: *1st Generation; 2nd Generation; 3rd Generation; 4th Generation; Analogue Computer; Computer; Configuration; Cross Platform; Digital Computer; EDS; Electronic Data System; Environment; Equipment; Hardware; Installation; Kit; Leading Edge; Machine; Number Cruncher; Platform; State of the Art; Turnkey;*

Maintenance
The process where hardware or software is improved, fixed or serviced.
See Also: *Conversion; Defragment; Downtime; File Conversion; Hardware; Software;*

Marquee
A horizontal scrolling message displayed on the screen.
See Also: *Browser; Display; Graphics; Image Map; Image Processing; Paint Screen; Scroll; Sprite;*

Mass Storage
Many storage devices in an installation including disk and tape.
See Also: *3.5 Inch; 5.25 Inch; Archive; Backing Store; Backup; CD-RW Drive; COM; Computer Output Microfilm; Computer Power; Configuration; DAT; Deck; Density; Device; Digital Audio Tape; Digital Versatile Disk; Disk; Disk Drive; Disk Pack; Disk Size; Disk Storage; Diskette; Double Density; DVD; Equipment; FDD; Five and a quarter; Fixed Disk Drive; Floppy Disk; Floppy Disk Drive; Grandfather, Father, Son; Hard Disk Drive; Hardware; HDD; High Density; Installation; Kit; Mag Tape; Magnetic Disk; Magnetic Tape; Microfilm; Optical Drive; Pack; Paper Tape; Peripheral; Power; Recording Device; Remote Device; Save; Storage; Store; Streamer; System; Tape Deck; Tape Streamer; Three and a Half; Volume; Winchester Disk; Zip Drive;*

Maths Co-processor
A separate processor in a computer used by specialised applications to deal with separate calculations. It is also known as a co-processor.
See Also: *286; 386; 486; ALU; Application Specific Integrated Circuits; Arithmetic and Logic Unit; ASICS; Bus; Central Processing Unit; Chip; Chipset; Clock Speed; Computer Power; Co-processor; CPU; Expansion Card; Flash Memory; Floating Point; IC; Industry Standard Architecture; Integrated Circuit; Interrupt Request; IRQ; ISA; Local Bus; MCA; Megahertz; Memory; MHz; Micro Channel Architecture; Microprocessor; Mix; Parallel Processor; Power; Processor; Silicon Chip; System Bus;*

Matrix
A grid pattern made up of rows and columns as in a data table.
See Also: *Format; Subscript; Table;*

Matrix Printer
A printer in which printing is achieved by a matrix of pins on the print head that form the characters. The characters are transferred to the paper by the pins pushing against a ribbon.
See Also: *Barrel Printer; Bi Directional; Bubble Jet; Configuration; Cut Sheet Feeder; Daisywheel; Device; DIP Switch; Dot Matrix; Dots Per Inch; DPI; Drum Printer; Duplex Printing; Environment; Equipment; Font Cartridge; Hard Copy; Hardware; Inkjet; Installation; Kit;*

Landscape; Laser Jet; Laser Printer; LCD Printer; Letter Quality; Line Printer; Lines Per Minute; Liquid Crystal Display Printer; Lpm; LPT Port; LQ; Near Letter Quality; NLQ; Output; Page Printer; Pages Per Minute; Peripheral; Portrait; Postscript; PPM; Printer; Printer Driver; Printout; Sheet Feeder; Simplex Printing; Thermal Printer;

Mb
Megabyte. A size representing 1,048,576 bytes of storage, commonly known as 1 million bytes.
See Also: *Byte; Data; Gb; Gigabyte; K; Kb; Kbyte; Kilobit; Kilobyte; Mbyte; Megabit; Megabyte; Terabyte; Word;*

Mbps
Mega (million) bits per second. Represents a data transfer speed.
See Also: *16 Bit; 32 Bit; 64 Bit; 8 Bit; Access Time; Acoustic Coupler; Address Bus; ADN; ADSL; Advanced Digital Network; Asymmetric Digital Subscriber Line; Asynchronous; Asynchronous Transfer Mode; ATM; Bandwidth; Baud Rate; Binary; Binary Digit; Bit; Bits Per Second; BPS; Broadband; Bus; CCITT; CCTA; Characters Per Second; Communications; Consultative Committee International Telegraph and Telephone; CPS; Data Bus; Data Communications; Data Parity; Data Transmission; Datacoms; Dial In; Dial Up; Duplex Transmission; Eight Bit; FDDI; Fibre Distributed Data Interface; Fibre Optics; Full Duplex; Gbps; GHz; Gigahertz; Half Duplex; HD; Integrated Services Digital Network; ISDN; Kbps; KHz; Kilohertz; Local Bus; Microsecond; Million Instructions Per Second; Millisecond; MIPS; Ms; Multiplex; Multiplexer; Nanosecond; Narrowband; Ns; Open Systems Interconnect; Optical Fibre; OSI; Parallel Transmission; Parity Bit; Pico Second; Serial Transmission; Simplex Transmission; Sixteen Bit; Sixty Four Bit; Synchronous; System Bus; T-1; T-3; Telecommunication; Telecoms; Thirty Two Bit; Transfer Rate; Transmit; V90;*

Mbyte
Megabyte. A size representing 1,048,576 bytes of storage, commonly known as 1 million bytes.
See Also: *Byte; Data; Gb; Gigabyte; K; Kb; Kbyte; Kilobit; Kilobyte; Mb; Megabit; Megabyte; Terabyte; Word;*

MCA
Micro Channel Architecture. A system design which speeds up the processing between the processor and hard disk or visual display unit.
See Also: *API; Application Program Interface; Bus; Central Processing Unit; Channel; Clock Speed; Co-processor; CPU; EIDE; EISA;*

Enhanced Industry Standard Architecture; Enhanced Intelligent Drive Electronics; Firewire; Hard Disk Drive; HDD; IDE; Industry Standard Architecture; Integrated Drive Electronics; Interface; ISA; Maths Co-processor; Micro Channel Architecture; Microprocessor; Processor; SCSI; Self Monitoring Analysis and Reporting Technology; Small Computer System Interface; SMART; Transmission Channel; Universal Serial Bus; USB; Zero Wait State;

Mean Time Between Failure
(MTBF). The estimated time in which a device or computer should operate before failure occurs.
See Also: *Abort; Downtime; MTBF; Run Time; Third Party Maintenance;*

Medium
The material on which data is stored or viewed. e.g. disk, paper.
See Also: *3.5 Inch; 5.25 Inch; Backing Store; Backup; Bits Per Inch; Block; BPI; CD-ROM; COM; Computer Output Microfilm; Cylinder; DAT; Density; Digital Audio Tape; Digital Versatile Disk; Disk; Disk Pack; Disk Size; Disk Storage; Diskette; Double Density; DVD; Fiche; Five and a quarter; Floppy Disk; High Density; Mag Tape; Magnetic Disk; Magnetic Tape; Microfiche; Microfilm; Optical Disk; Pack; Paper Tape; Save; Sector; Storage; Streamer; Tape Streamer; Three and a Half; Volume; Winchester Disk;*

Megabit
A notation which represents 1,048,576 bits of storage and commonly known as 1 million bits.
See Also: *Byte; Character; Data; Gb; Gigabyte; K; Kb; Kbyte; Kilobit; Kilobyte; Least Significant Bit; LSB; Mb; Mbyte; Megabyte; Most Significant Bit; MSB; Terabyte;*

Megabyte
A size representing 1,048,576 bytes of storage, commonly known as 1 million bytes.
See Also: *Byte; Computer Power; Data; Gb; Gigabyte; K; Kb; Kbyte; Kilobit; Kilobyte; Mb; Mbyte; Megabit; Power; Terabyte; Word;*

Megahertz
(MHz). A measure of the processor's chip speed. It is the measure of speed at which the system clock operates in a computer. e.g. 450 MHz.
See Also: *286; 386; 486; Central Processing Unit; Chip; Chipset; Clock Speed; Computer Power; Co-processor; CPU; GHz; Gigahertz; KHz;*

Kilohertz; Maths Co-processor; MHz; Microprocessor; Power; Processor; Silicon Chip;

Memory
The work area within a computer where programs are executed and where data is stored, retrieved and processed.
See Also: *Absolute Address; Address; Array; Block; Bubble Memory; Buffer; Cache Memory; Central Processing Unit; Clipboard; CMOS; Complementary Metal Oxide Semiconductor Memory; Computer Power; Conventional Memory; Core; Core Dump; CPU; DDR SDRAM; DIMM; Direct Memory Access; Direct Random Access Memory; Disk Cache; DMA; Double Data Rate SDRAM; DRAM; Dual Inline Memory Module; Dump; Dynamic Memory; Dynamically; EEROM; Electrically Erasable Read Only Memory; Electronically Programmed Read Only Memory; EMS; EPROM; Erasable Programmable Read Only Memory; Expanded Memory; Expanded Memory Specification; Extended Memory; Flash Memory; High Memory; Load; Magnetic Core; Maths Co-processor; Memory Board; Memory Caching; Memory Card; Memory Resident; Mix; Operand; Overlay; Patch; Power; Programmable Read Only Memory; PROM; RAM; RAM Disk; Rambus Dynamic Random Access Memory; Random Access Memory; RDRAM; Read Only Memory; Relative Address; ROM; ROM Resident; SDRAM; Semiconductor; Shadow RAM Memory; SIMM; Single Inline Memory Modules; Single Inline Package; SIP; Solid State; Store; Synchronous Dynamic Random Access Memory; System; Upper Memory; Video Random Access Memory; Volatile Memory; VRAM; Wipe; Working Storage; Workspace;*

Memory Board
Also known as a Memory Card. A printed circuit board with a memory chip which is slotted into a computer.
See Also: *Bubble Memory; Chip; Chipset; Conventional Memory; DDR SDRAM; DIMM; Direct Random Access Memory; Double Data Rate SDRAM; DRAM; Dual Inline Memory Module; Dynamic Memory; EEROM; Electrically Erasable Read Only Memory; Electronically Programmed Read Only Memory; EMS; EPROM; Erasable Programmable Read Only Memory; Expanded Memory; Expanded Memory Specification; Expansion Slot; Extended Memory; Fax Card; Flash Memory; High Memory; IC; Integrated Circuit; Memory; Memory Caching; Memory Card; Motherboard; PCB; PCI; PCMCIA; Peripheral Component Interconnect; Personal Computer Memory Card International Association; Printed Circuit Board; Programmable Read Only Memory; PROM; RAM; RAM Disk; Rambus Dynamic Random Access Memory; Random Access Memory; RDRAM; Read Only Memory;*

ROM; SDRAM; Shadow RAM Memory; Silicon Chip; SIMM; Single Inline Memory Modules; Single Inline Package; SIP; Slot; Sound Card; Synchronous Dynamic Random Access Memory; Video Random Access Memory; VRAM;

Memory Caching

The process where a buffer of very fast memory between the central processing unit and main memory is pre-loaded with data before being transferred and thus increases the speed of processing.

See Also: *Bubble Memory; Buffer; Cache Memory; Central Processing Unit; Conventional Memory; Core; CPU; DDR SDRAM; DIMM; Direct Memory Access; Direct Random Access Memory; Disk Cache; DMA; Double Data Rate SDRAM; DRAM; Dual Inline Memory Module; Dynamic Memory; Dynamically; EEROM; Electrically Erasable Read Only Memory; Electronically Programmed Read Only Memory; EMS; EPROM; Erasable Programmable Read Only Memory; Expanded Memory; Expanded Memory Specification; Extended Memory; Flash Memory; High Memory; Magnetic Core; Memory; Memory Board; Memory Card; Mix; Programmable Read Only Memory; PROM; RAM; RAM Disk; Rambus Dynamic Random Access Memory; Random Access Memory; RDRAM; Read Only Memory; ROM; SDRAM; Shadow RAM Memory; SIMM; Single Inline Memory Modules; Single Inline Package; SIP; Store; Swapping; Synchronous Dynamic Random Access Memory; Upper Memory; Video Random Access Memory; Virtual Memory; VM; Volatile Memory; VRAM; Working Storage; Workspace;*

Memory Card

Also known as a Memory Board. A printed circuit board with a memory chip which is slotted into a computer.

See Also: *Bubble Memory; Chip; Chipset; Conventional Memory; DDR SDRAM; DIMM; Direct Random Access Memory; Double Data Rate SDRAM; DRAM; Dual Inline Memory Module; Dynamic Memory; EEROM; Electrically Erasable Read Only Memory; Electronically Programmed Read Only Memory; EMS; EPROM; Erasable Programmable Read Only Memory; Expanded Memory; Expanded Memory Specification; Expansion Slot; Extended Memory; Fax Card; Flash Memory; High Memory; IC; Integrated Circuit; Memory; Memory Board; Memory Caching; Motherboard; PCB; PCMCIA; Personal Computer Memory Card International Association; Printed Circuit Board; Programmable Read Only Memory; PROM; RAM; RAM Disk; Rambus Dynamic Random Access Memory; Random Access Memory; RDRAM; Read Only Memory; ROM; SDRAM; Shadow RAM Memory; Silicon Chip; SIMM; Single Inline Memory Modules; Single Inline*

Package; SIP; Slot; Sound Card; Synchronous Dynamic Random Access Memory; Video Random Access Memory; VRAM;

Memory Resident
Programs which are loaded into the computer's memory and remain there until activated by another process.
See Also: *Applet; Boot; Bootstrap; Bubble Memory; Conventional Memory; Core; Core Dump; DDR SDRAM; DIMM; Direct Random Access Memory; Disk Cache; Double Data Rate SDRAM; DRAM; Dual Inline Memory Module; Dynamic Memory; Dynamically; EEROM; Electrically Erasable Read Only Memory; Electronically Programmed Read Only Memory; EMS; EPROM; Erasable Programmable Read Only Memory; Expanded Memory; Expanded Memory Specification; Extended Memory; Firmware; Flash Memory; High Memory; Magnetic Core; Memory; Mix; Module; Program; Programmable Read Only Memory; PROM; RAM; RAM Disk; Rambus Dynamic Random Access Memory; Random Access Memory; RDRAM; Read Only Memory; Re-boot; ROM; Run Time; SDRAM; Shadow RAM Memory; SIMM; Single Inline Memory Modules; Single Inline Package; SIP; Stack; Store; Synchronous Dynamic Random Access Memory; Terminate and Stay Resident; TSR; Upper Memory; Utility; Virtual Memory; VM; Volatile Memory; Working Storage; Workspace;*

Menu
A list of items on the screen from which to choose. It is activated by entering specific control codes from the keyboard or with a mouse.
See Also: *Click; Display; Drop-Down Menu; Hot Key; Instruction; Keyboard; Mouse; Pop Up Menu; Pull Down Menu; Toolbar; User Friendly;*

Merge
The combining of two or more files or documents to make one file or document.
See Also: *Batch Processing; Processing;*

Message Boards
Internet sites divided into subject groups of similar topics where users can view messages or add their own opinions.
See Also: *Chatroom; Cybercafe; Cyberspace; Electronic Mail; E-mail; IM; Instant Messaging; Internet; Net; Newsgroup; Site; The Net; Thread; User Group;*

Meta Tag
A hidden tag contained in the header of an HTML page which supplies data about the page but does not affect the display. It is used to compare with search criteria when searches are made on the Internet.
See Also: *Bookmark; Browser; Cyberspace; Extensible Hypertext Markup Language; eXtensible Markup Language; Home Page; HTML; Hyperlink; Hypertext Mark-Up Language; Internet; Key; Meta-Search Engine; Net; Page; Search Engine; Spider; Surfing; The Net; Universal/Uniform Resource Locator; URL; XHTML; XML;*

Meta-Search Engine
A search engine that submits your search criteria to a program on an Internet website which retrieves the desired results from databases on that website.
See Also: *Application; Batch Processing; Bookmark; Browser; Cyberspace; Gopher; Home Page; Hyperlink; Internet; Meta Tag; Net; Search Engine; Site; Spider; Surfing; The Net; The Web; Universal/Uniform Resource Locator; URL; Utility; Webring; Website; World Wide Web; WWW;*

MHz
Megahertz. A measure of the processor's chip speed. It is the measure of speed at which the system clock operates in a computer. e.g. 450 MHz.
See Also: *286; 386; 486; Central Processing Unit; Chip; Chipset; Clock Speed; Computer Power; Co-processor; CPU; GHz; Gigahertz; KHz; Kilohertz; Maths Co-processor; Megahertz; Microprocessor; Power; Processor; Silicon Chip;*

MICR
Magnetic Ink Character Recognition. The process where special ink, which contains magnetic particles, is printed onto documents and recognised by special readers that detect the shape of the characters. e.g. the base line on cheques.
See Also: *Character; EDP; Electronic Data Processing; Magnetic Ink Character Recognition;*

Micro
Abbr. of Microcomputer. A small computer which uses a solid-state microprocessor chip. It precedes the personal computer.
See Also: *1st Generation; 2nd Generation; 3rd Generation; 4th Generation; Advanced Technology; Analogue Computer; AT; Computer; Configuration; Cross Platform; Desktop; Digital Computer; Distributed System/Network; Downsizing; EDS; Electronic Data System;*

Environment; Equipment; Extended Technology; Front End Processor; Hardware; IBM (tm) Compatible; Installation; Kit; Laptop; Machine; Microcomputer; Multi Platform; Notebook; OEM; Original Equipment Manufacturer; Palmtop Computer; PC; Personal Computer; Platform; Portable; Standalone; Tower Computer; Turnkey; XT;

Micro Channel Architecture
(MCA). A system design which speeds up the processing between the processor and hard disk or visual display unit.
See Also: *API; Application Program Interface; Bus; Central Processing Unit; Channel; Clock Speed; Co-processor; CPU; EIDE; EISA; Enhanced Industry Standard Architecture; Enhanced Intelligent Drive Electronics; Firewire; Hard Disk Drive; HDD; IDE; Industry Standard Architecture; Integrated Drive Electronics; Interface; ISA; Maths Co-processor; MCA; Microprocessor; Processor; SCSI; Self Monitoring Analysis and Reporting Technology; Small Computer System Interface; SMART; Transmission Channel; Universal Serial Bus; USB; Zero Wait State;*

Microcomputer
A small computer which uses a solid-state microprocessor chip. It precedes the personal computer.
See Also: *1st Generation; 2nd Generation; 3rd Generation; 4th Generation; Advanced Technology; Analogue Computer; AT; Computer; Configuration; Cross Platform; Desktop; Digital Computer; Distributed System/Network; Downsizing; EDS; Electronic Data System; Environment; Equipment; Extended Technology; Front End Processor; Hardware; IBM (tm) Compatible; Installation; Kit; Laptop; Machine; Micro; Multi Platform; Notebook; OEM; Original Equipment Manufacturer; Palmtop Computer; PC; Personal Computer; Platform; Portable; Standalone; Tower Computer; Turnkey; XT;*

Microfiche
A recording medium where data is reduced in size and printed onto a piece of plastic the size of a post card. A microfiche reader is needed to view the data on the fiche.
See Also: *Archive; Backing Store; Backup; Block; COM; Computer Output Microfilm; Directory; Fiche; Medium; Microfilm; Output; Recording Medium; Root Directory; Save; Sub Directory;*

Microfilm
A recording medium where data is reduced in size and printed onto a small roll of plastic film. A microfilm reader is needed to access the data.
See Also: *Archive; Backing Store; Backup; COM; Computer Output Microfilm; Fiche; Grandfather, Father, Son; Mass Storage; Medium; Microfiche; Output; Recording Medium; Save;*

Microprocessor
An electronic chip which is the central processing unit of a computer. Programs are executed, data manipulated and the computer is controlled from this processor.
See Also: *286; 386; 486; ALU; Application Specific Integrated Circuits; Arithmetic and Logic Unit; ASICS; Central Processing Unit; Chip; Chipset; Clock Speed; Computer Power; Co-processor; CPU; IC; Industry Standard Architecture; Integrated Circuit; ISA; Maths Co-processor; MCA; Megahertz; MHz; Micro Channel Architecture; Parallel Processor; Power; Processor; Reduced Instruction Set Computing; RISC; Semiconductor; Silicon Chip; Solid State; Sound Chip; Transistor;*

Microsecond
One millionth of a second.
See Also: *Access Time; Baud Rate; Bits Per Second; BPS; Characters Per Second; Clock Speed; CPS; Gbps; Kbps; Mbps; Millisecond; Ms; Nanosecond; Ns; Pico Second; Seek Time;*

MIDI
Musical Instrument Digital Interface. The connection which allows a musical instrument to be connected to a computer and which converts music to digital format.
See Also: *Analogue; Analogue Computer; Analogue Digital Converter; Digital; Handshake; Interface; Musical Instrument Digital Interface; Parallel Interface; Parallel Port; Port; SCSI; Serial Interface; Serial Port; Small Computer System Interface;*

Midrange System
A computer whose size and power is between a personal computer and a mainframe computer.
See Also: *1st Generation; 2nd Generation; 3rd Generation; 4th Generation; Analogue Computer; Compatible; Computer; Computer Power; Configuration; Cross Platform; Digital Computer; Distributed System/Network; Downsizing; EDS; Electronic Data System; Emulate; Emulation; Environment; Equipment; Front End Processor; Hardware;*

Host Processor; Information System; Information Technology; Installation; IS; IT; Kit; Leading Edge; Machine; Mailserver; Multi Platform; Platform; Power; Standalone; State of the Art; Turnkey;

Million Instructions Per Second
(MIPS). A rate of speed by which data is processed or by which a computer performs.
See Also: *Access Time; Baud Rate; Bits Per Second; BPS; Characters Per Second; Clock Speed; Computer Power; CPS; Gbps; Kbps; Mbps; MIPS; Power; Transfer Rate;*

Millisecond
(Ms). A rate of processing speed which is one thousandth of a second.
See Also: *Access Time; Baud Rate; Bits Per Second; BPS; Characters Per Second; Clock Speed; CPS; Gbps; Kbps; Mbps; Microsecond; Ms; Nanosecond; Ns; Pico Second; Seek Time;*

MIME
Multipurpose Internet Mail Extensions. A protocol which allows e-mail messages to contain a combination of text, video and audio formats.
See Also: *Attachment; BitMaP; BMP; Client Server Protocol; CODEC; COmpressor DECompressor; Electronic Mail; E-mail; GIF; Graphical Interchange Format; Handshake; Internet Protocol; IP; Joint Photographic Experts Group; JPEG; JPG; Motion Picture Experts Group; MP3; MPEG; MPG; Multimedia; Multipurpose Internet Mail Extensions; PDF; POP; Portable Document Format; Post Office Protocol; Protocol; Rich Text Format; RTF; Simple Mail Transfer Protocol; SMTP; Stream; Tag Image File Format; TIFF; WAV; Waveform Audio;*

Minicomputer
A computer whose size and power is between a personal computer and a mainframe.
See Also: *1st Generation; 2nd Generation; 3rd Generation; 4th Generation; Analogue Computer; Compatible; Computer; Computer Power; Configuration; Cross Platform; Digital Computer; Distributed System/Network; Downsizing; EDS; Electronic Data System; Emulate; Emulation; Environment; Equipment; Front End Processor; Hardware; Host Processor; Information System; Information Technology; Installation; IS; IT; Kit; Leading Edge; Machine; Mailserver; Multi Platform; Platform; Power; Standalone; State of the Art; Turnkey;*

MIPS
Million Instructions Per Second. A rate of speed by which data is processed or by which a computer performs.
See Also: *Access Time; Baud Rate; Bits Per Second; BPS; Characters Per Second; Clock Speed; Computer Power; CPS; Gbps; Kbps; Mbps; Million Instructions Per Second; Power; Transfer Rate;*

Mirror Site
An FTP site retaining the same data as the site it is mirroring and can be set up in different countries to relieve the access load on one particular site. This enables faster access and downloading of files.
See Also: *Anonymous FTP; BBS; Bulletin Board System; Cyberspace; File; File Transfer Protocol; FTP; FTP Site; FTPmail; Network Information Centre; NIC; Site; The Web; Webring; Website; World Wide Web; WWW;*

Mix
(1) The main memory of a computer. (2) The programs that are in the memory at the current time.
See Also: *Applet; Bubble Memory; Buffer; Cache Memory; Central Processing Unit; Conventional Memory; Core; Core Dump; CPU; DDR SDRAM; DIMM; Direct Random Access Memory; Disk Cache; Double Data Rate SDRAM; DRAM; Dual Inline Memory Module; Dynamic Memory; EEROM; Electrically Erasable Read Only Memory; Electronically Programmed Read Only Memory; EMS; EPROM; Erasable Programmable Read Only Memory; Expanded Memory; Expanded Memory Specification; Extended Memory; Flash Memory; High Memory; Load; Magnetic Core; Maths Co-processor; Memory; Memory Caching; Memory Resident; Multitasking; Processor; Program; Programmable Read Only Memory; PROM; RAM; RAM Disk; Rambus Dynamic Random Access Memory; Random Access Memory; RDRAM; Read Only Memory; ROM; SDRAM; Shadow RAM Memory; SIMM; Single Inline Memory Modules; Single Inline Package; SIP; Store; Synchronous Dynamic Random Access Memory; Terminate and Stay Resident; Time Share; Time Slice; Trashing; TSR; Upper Memory; Working Storage; Workspace;*

Model
(1) A process model is a graphical design of procedures for a task or application. (2) A data model is a graphical design of the relationships of the data within processes.
See Also: *B/A; Business Analyst; CASE; Case Tool; Computer Aided Software Engineering; Data Base Analyst; Data Flow; Data Flow*

Diagram; Data Model; DBA; Design; DFD; Flowchart; Full Project Life Cycle; Logical Design; Modular; O & M; Object Oriented Analysis; Object Oriented Design; Object Oriented Programming; OOA; OOD; OOP; Organisation & Methods; Physical Design; Process; Process Model; Program Specification; Project Life Cycle; Reengineering; S/A; Software Development Cycle; Specification; Structured Design; Structured Program; System Analysis; System Analyst; Top Down Technique;

Modem
MODulator/DEModulator. A device which connects to a communication line and allows data to be transferred between computers. It can be external or internal to a computer.
See Also: *Access; Acoustic Coupler; AMR; Asymmetrical Modem; Automatic Message Routing; Communications; Data Communications; Data Transmission; Datacoms; Device; Dial In; Dial Up; Duplex Transmission; Equipment; FDDI; Fibre Distributed Data Interface; Fibre Optics; Full Duplex; Half Duplex; Handshake; Hardware; HD; Information Superhighway; Integrated Services Digital Network; Interface; ISDN; Kit; Modulator Demodulator; Node; Online; Optical Fibre; Parallel Transmission; Peripheral; RS232; RS423; Serial Transmission; Simplex Transmission; Telecommunication; Telecoms; Teleprocessing System; TPS; Transmit; V90; XMODEM; YMODEM; ZMODEM;*

Modular
The design of hardware or software in which a number of modules make up an entire system.
See Also: *CASE; Case Tool; Computer Aided Software Engineering; Data Flow; Data Flow Diagram; Data Model; Design; Development; DFD; Flowchart; Full Project Life Cycle; Hardware; Integrated; Logical Design; Model; O & M; Object Oriented Analysis; Object Oriented Design; Object Oriented Programming; OOA; OOD; OOP; Organisation & Methods; Physical Design; Process; Process Model; Program Specification; Project Life Cycle; Reengineering; Software; Software Development Cycle; Specification; Structured Design; Structured Program; Top Down Technique;*

Modulator Demodulator
(Modem). A device which connects to a communication line and allows data to be transferred between computers. It can be external or internal to a computer.
See Also: *Access; Acoustic Coupler; AMR; Asymmetrical Modem; Automatic Message Routing; Communications; Data Communications; Data Transmission; Datacoms; Device; Dial In; Dial Up; Duplex Transmission; Equipment; FDDI; Fibre Distributed Data Interface; Fibre Optics; Full Duplex; Half Duplex; Handshake; Hardware; HD; Information Superhighway; Integrated Services Digital Network; Interface; ISDN; Kit; Modem; Node; Online; Optical Fibre; Parallel Transmission; Peripheral; RS232; RS423; Serial Transmission; Simplex Transmission; Telecommunication; Telecoms; Teleprocessing System; TPS; Transmit; V90; XMODEM; YMODEM; ZMODEM;*

Module
A part of a program, software or hardware system designed for a specific task and when combined with others make up the entire program or system.
See Also: *ADA; ALGOL; APL; Applet; Assembly Code; BASIC; Black Box; C or C++; CLIPPER; COBOL; Code; CORAL; Daemon; Development; Device Driver; DLL; Driver; Dynamic Link Library; EXE; Extensible Hypertext Markup Language; eXtensible Markup Language; FORTH; FORTRAN; Freeware; Function; HTML; Hypertext Mark-Up Language; Instruction Set; JAVA; JAVASCRIPT; Job; LISP; LOGO; Macro; Memory Resident; NATURAL; Nesting; Object Oriented Analysis; Object Oriented Design; Object Oriented Programming; OOA; OOD; OOP; Overlay; PASCAL; PERL; PICK; PILOT; PL/1; Practical Extraction and Reporting Language; Program; PROLOG; RPG; Script; Software Driver; Structured Design; Structured Program; XHTML; XML;*

Monitor
A device consisting of a cathode ray tube used to view data while interacting with a computer. Data entered on a keyboard is displayed on the monitor.
See Also: *Analogue Monitor; Anti Glare Screen; Cathode Ray Tube; CGA; Colour Graphics Adaptor; CRT; Device; Digital Monitor; Digital Video Interface; Display; DVI; EGA; Enhanced Graphic Adaptor; Environment; Equipment; Extended Video Array; Frame Rate; Graphics Card; Hardware; High Resolution; Installation; Intelligent Terminal; Interlaced; Kit; LCD; Liquid Crystal Display; Low Resolution; Monochrome; Output; Paint Screen; Peripheral; Plasma Screen;*

Prompt; Resolution; Screen; Screen Burn; Split Screen; Super Twist LCD; Super VGA; Super Video Graphics Array; SVGA; System; Terminal; TFT; Thin-Film Transistor; Touch Screen; Twip; VDT; VDU; VGA; Video Card; Video Display Terminal; Video Graphics Array; Video Random Access Memory; Visual Display Terminal; Visual Display Unit; VRAM; XGA;

Monochrome

A visual display unit which displays in only one colour.

See Also: *Analogue Monitor; Anti Glare Screen; Cathode Ray Tube; CGA; Colour Graphics Adaptor; CRT; Device; Digital Monitor; Display; EGA; Enhanced Graphic Adaptor; Environment; Equipment; Extended Video Array; Graphics Card; Hardware; High Resolution; Installation; Intelligent Terminal; Interlaced; Kit; LCD; Liquid Crystal Display; Low Resolution; Monitor; Paint Screen; Peripheral; Plasma Screen; Prompt; Resolution; Screen; Screen Burn; Split Screen; Super Twist LCD; Super VGA; Super Video Graphics Array; SVGA; Terminal; TFT; Thin-Film Transistor; Touch Screen; Twip; VDT; VDU; VGA; Video Card; Video Display Terminal; Video Graphics Array; Video Random Access Memory; Visual Display Terminal; Visual Display Unit; VRAM; XGA;*

Most Significant Bit

(MSB). The bit furthest to the left in a row of binary digits.

See Also: *16 Bit; 32 Bit; 64 Bit; 8 Bit; American Standard Code for Information Interchange; ASCII; BCD; Binary; Binary Coded Decimal; Binary Digit; Bit; Bit Pattern; Digital; Eight Bit; Kilobit; Least Significant Bit; LSB; Megabit; MSB; Sixteen Bit; Sixty Four Bit; Thirty Two Bit; Word;*

Motherboard

A printed circuit board which contains the chips that control the workings of a computer. Other printed circuit boards, such as the video card, are slotted into the motherboard.

See Also: *Accelerated Graphics Port; Advanced Graphics Port; AGP; AGP Slot; ALU; Application Specific Integrated Circuits; Arithmetic and Logic Unit; ASICS; Chip; Chipset; EIDE; Enhanced Intelligent Drive Electronics; Expansion Card; Expansion Slot; Fax Card; Graphics Card; IC; IDE; Integrated Circuit; Integrated Drive Electronics; Memory Board; Memory Card; PCB; PCI; PCMCIA; Peripheral Component Interconnect; Personal Computer Memory Card International Association; Printed Circuit Board; Silicon Chip; Slot; Sound Card; Video Card;*

Motion Picture Experts Group
(MPEG). Also known as MPG. A file format in which video files are stored. Filenames are given the file extension of either '.mpg' or '.mpeg'.
See Also: *Attachment; Clip Art; CODEC; COmpressor DECompressor; Extension; Filename Extension; Format; Graphics; Image Processing; MIME; MPEG; MPG; Multimedia; Multipurpose Internet Mail Extensions; Pirate Copy; Stream;*

Mouse
A hand controlled pointing device controlling the cursor movement on the screen which allows items on the screen to be selected instead of using the keyboard.
See Also: *Click; Configuration; Device; Drag; Drop-Down Menu; Environment; Equipment; Hand Held Device; Hardware; Instruction; Interactive; Keyboard; Kit; Menu; PDA; Peripheral; Personal Digital Assistant; Pop Up Menu; PS/2; Pull Down Menu; Tracker Ball;*

MP3
A standard used to compress music files so that they can be easily transferred over the Internet and stored on disk.
See Also: *Acceptable User Policy; Attachment; AUP; CODEC; COmpressor DECompressor; Download; File Transfer Protocol; FTP; MIME; Multimedia; Multipurpose Internet Mail Extensions; Pirate Copy; Stream; WAV; Waveform Audio;*

MPEG
Motion Picture Experts Group. Also known as MPG. A file format in which video files are stored. Filenames are given the file extension of either '.mpg' or '.mpeg'.
See Also: *Attachment; Clip Art; CODEC; COmpressor DECompressor; Extension; Filename Extension; Format; Graphics; Image Processing; MIME; Motion Picture Experts Group; MPG; Multimedia; Multipurpose Internet Mail Extensions; Pirate Copy; Stream;*

MPG
Motion Picture Experts Group. Also known as MPEG. A file format in which video files are stored. Filenames are given the file extension of either '.mpg' or '.mpeg'.
See Also: *Attachment; Clip Art; CODEC; COmpressor DECompressor; Extension; Filename Extension; Format; Graphics; Image Processing; MIME; Motion Picture Experts Group; MPEG; Multimedia; Multipurpose Internet Mail Extensions; Pirate Copy; Stream;*

Ms
Millisecond. A rate of processing speed which is one thousandth of a second.
See Also: *Access Time; Baud Rate; Bits Per Second; BPS; Characters Per Second; Clock Speed; CPS; Gbps; Kbps; Mbps; Microsecond; Millisecond; Nanosecond; Ns; Pico Second; Seek Time;*

MSB
Most Significant Bit. The bit furthest to the left in a row of binary digits.
See Also: *16 Bit; 32 Bit; 64 Bit; 8 Bit; American Standard Code for Information Interchange; ASCII; BCD; Binary; Binary Coded Decimal; Binary Digit; Bit; Bit Pattern; Digital; Eight Bit; Kilobit; Least Significant Bit; LSB; Megabit; Most Significant Bit; Sixteen Bit; Sixty Four Bit; Thirty Two Bit; Word;*

MTBF
Mean Time Before Failure. The estimated time in which a device or computer should operate before failure occurs.
See Also: *Abort; Downtime; Mean Time Between Failure; Run Time; Third Party Maintenance;*

Multi Platform
The design of different makes and types of computers which allows for the same software to be used on all of them.
See Also: *1st Generation; 2nd Generation; 3rd Generation; 4th Generation; Advanced Technology; Analogue Computer; Application; AT; Compatible; Computer; Configuration; Cross Platform; Desktop; Digital Computer; Distributed System/Network; EDS; Electronic Data System; Environment; Equipment; Extended Technology; Hardware; IBM (tm) Compatible; Kit; Laptop; Machine; Micro; Microcomputer; Midrange System; Minicomputer; Notebook; Open System; Open Systems Interconnect; OSI; Palmtop Computer; PC; Personal Computer; Platform; Portable; Standalone; System; Tower Computer; Turnkey; UNIX; XT;*

Multi User
A term that describes the use of a computer by more than one person at the same time and possibly for different purposes.
See Also: *Client Server; Configuration; Configuring; End User; Environment; Ethernet; File Server; File Sharing; Integrated; LAN; Local Area Network; Locking; Multitasking; Network; Record Locking; Server; Star Cluster; Star Network; Time Share; Time Slice; Token Ring; User; WAN; Wide Area Network;*

Multimedia
A term referring to computers which have a variety of facilities including text, graphics, sound and video.
See Also: *CODEC; COmpressor DECompressor; Computer; Configuration; Environment; Graphics; Image Map; Machine; MIME; Motion Picture Experts Group; MP3; MPEG; MPG; Multipurpose Internet Mail Extensions; Stream; WAV; Waveform Audio; Webcam;*

Multiplex
A term used when several pieces of information are transmitted simultaneously along the same transmission channel.
See Also: *ACK; Acoustic Coupler; ADN; ADSL; Advanced Digital Network; AMR; Asymmetric Digital Subscriber Line; Asymmetrical Modem; Asynchronous; Asynchronous Transfer Mode; ATM; Automatic Message Routing; Bandwidth; Baud Rate; Bits Per Second; BPS; Broadband; CCITT; CCTA; Characters Per Second; Communications; Consultative Committee International Telegraph and Telephone; CPS; Data Communications; Data Parity; Data Transmission; Datacoms; Dial In; Dial Up; Digital; Direct Connection; Duplex Transmission; FDDI; Fibre Distributed Data Interface; Fibre Optics; Full Duplex; Gbps; Integrated Services Digital Network; ISDN; Kbps; Leased Line; Mbps; Multiplexer; Narrowband; Open Systems Interconnect; Optical Fibre; OSI; Packet; Packet Switching; Parallel Transmission; Parity Bit; Serial Interface; Serial Transmission; Simplex Transmission; Synchronous; T-1; T-3; Telecommunication; Telecoms; Teleprocessing System; TPS; Transfer Rate; Transmit; V90;*

Multiplexer
A communications device which allows several pieces of information to transmit simultaneously along the same transmission channel.
See Also: *ACK; Acoustic Coupler; ADN; ADSL; Advanced Digital Network; AMR; Asymmetric Digital Subscriber Line; Asymmetrical Modem; Asynchronous; Asynchronous Transfer Mode; ATM; Automatic Message Routing; Bandwidth; Baud Rate; Bits Per Second; BPS; Broadband; CCITT; CCTA; Characters Per Second; Communications; Consultative Committee International Telegraph and Telephone; CPS; Data Communications; Data Parity; Data Transmission; Datacoms; Dial In; Dial Up; Digital; Direct Connection; Duplex Transmission; FDDI; Fibre Distributed Data Interface; Fibre Optics; Firewire; Full Duplex; Gbps; Integrated Services Digital Network; ISDN; Kbps; Leased Line; Mbps; Multiplex; Narrowband; Node; Open Systems Interconnect; Optical Fibre; OSI; Packet; Packet Switching; Parallel Transmission; Parity Bit; Serial Interface; Serial Transmission; Simplex Transmission;*

Synchronous; T-1; T-3; Telecommunication; Telecoms; Teleprocessing System; TPS; Transfer Rate; Transmit; V90;

Multipurpose Internet Mail Extensions
(MIME). A protocol which allows e-mail messages to contain a combination of text, video and audio formats.
See Also: *Attachment; BitMaP; BMP; Client Server Protocol; CODEC; COmpressor DECompressor; Electronic Mail; E-mail; GIF; Graphical Interchange Format; Handshake; Internet Protocol; IP; Joint Photographic Experts Group; JPEG; JPG; MIME; Motion Picture Experts Group; MP3; MPEG; MPG; Multimedia; PDF; POP; Portable Document Format; Post Office Protocol; Protocol; Rich Text Format; RTF; Simple Mail Transfer Protocol; SMTP; Stream; Tag Image File Format; TIFF; WAV; Waveform Audio;*

Multitasking
A process where more than one program or job can run on a computer at the same time.
See Also: *Batch Processing; Client Server; Computation; Compute; Data Processing; DP; Ethernet; File Server; File Sharing; Housekeeping; Integrated; Job; LAN; Local Area Network; Locking; Mix; Multi User; Network; Record Locking; Run; Run Time; Server; Star Cluster; Star Network; Time Share; Time Slice; Token Ring; WAN; Wide Area Network;*

Musical Instrument Digital Interface
(MIDI). The connection which allows a musical instrument to be connected to a computer and which converts music to digital format.
See Also: *Analogue; Analogue Computer; Analogue Digital Converter; Digital; Handshake; Interface; MIDI; Parallel Interface; Parallel Port; Port; SCSI; Serial Interface; Small Computer System Interface;*

NAND gate
A logic gate on a chip, meaning NOT AND, which operates with binary digits where an output of logic value 1 only occurs if all of the inputs do not have a logic value 1. e.g. Inp=0 and Inp=0 then Out=1, Inp=1 and Inp=0 then Out=0.
See Also: *ALU; AMR; AND gate; Arithmetic and Logic Unit; Automatic Message Routing; Binary; Binary Digit; Bit; Boolean Algebra; Chip; Chipset; Expert System; FL; Flip Flop; Fuzzy Logic; I-OR gate; Large Scale Integration; Logic Gate; LSI; NEQ gate; NOR gate; NOT gate; OR gate; Silicon Chip; Transistor; Very Large Scale Integration; VLSI; X-OR gate;*

Nanosecond
One billionth or a thousand millionth of a second.
See Also: *Access Time; Baud Rate; Bits Per Second; BPS; Characters Per Second; Clock Speed; CPS; Gbps; Kbps; Mbps; Microsecond; Millisecond; Ms; Ns; Pico Second; Seek Time;*

Narrowband
Transmission of data in a bandwidth of 64 kbits or less.
See Also: *ADN; ADSL; Advanced Digital Network; Asymmetric Digital Subscriber Line; Asymmetrical Modem; Asynchronous; Asynchronous Transfer Mode; ATM; Bandwidth; Baud Rate; Binary Digit; Bit; Bits Per Second; BPS; Broadband; CCITT; CCTA; Characters Per Second; Communications; Consultative Committee International Telegraph and Telephone; CPS; Data; Data Communications; Data Parity; Data Transmission; Data Type; Datacoms; Dial In; Dial Up; Direct Connection; Duplex Transmission; Ethernet; FDDI; Fibre Distributed Data Interface; Fibre Optics; Full Duplex; Gbps; Half Duplex; HD; Information Superhighway; Integrated Services Digital Network; Internet; ISDN; Kbps; LAN; Leased Line; Local Area Network; Mbps; Multiplex; Multiplexer; Net; Network; Open Systems Interconnect; Optical Fibre; OSI; Packet; Packet Switching; Parallel Transmission; Parity Bit; Protocol; Ring Network; Serial Interface; Serial Line Internet Protocol; Serial Transmission; Simplex Transmission; SLIP; Star Cluster; Star Network; Synchronous; T-1; T-3; TCP/IP; Telecommunication; Telecoms; Teleprocessing System; The Net; Token Ring; TPS; Transfer Rate; Transmission Control Protocol/Internet Protocol; Transmit; V90; WAN; WAP; Wide Area Network; Wireless Application Protocol;*

NATURAL
A high level computer programming language.
See Also: *3GL; 4GL; ADA; ALGOL; APL; BASIC; C or C++; CLIPPER; COBOL; CODASYL; Code; Code Generator; Compiler; Compiling; Conference On DAta SYstems Languages; CORAL; FORTH; FORTRAN; Fourth Generation Language; High Level Language; Instruction Set; JAVA; JAVASCRIPT; Language; LISP; LOGO; Module; PASCAL; PERL; PICK; PILOT; PL/1; Practical Extraction and Reporting Language; Program; Programming Language; PROLOG; RPG; Software; Source Code; Structured Program; Syntax; Third Generation Language; Visual Basic;*

NCC

The National Computing Centre. An organisation which provides standards to the computing industry.

See Also: *American National Standard Institute; ANSI; BCS; CCITT; CCTA; CERN; Conseil Europeen pour la Recherche Nucleaire; Consultative Committee International Telegraph and Telephone; IEE; International Standards Organisation; ISO;*

Near Letter Quality

(NLQ). The type of print produced by some printers where the dots that make up each character are closer together, thus giving a better quality print.

See Also: *Bi Directional; Bubble Jet; Characters Per Inch; CPI; Daisywheel; DIP Switch; Dot Matrix; Dots Per Inch; DPI; Duplex Printing; Font; Font Cartridge; Format; Hard Copy; Inkjet; Landscape; Laser Jet; Laser Printer; LCD Printer; Letter Quality; Liquid Crystal Display Printer; LQ; Matrix Printer; NLQ; Output; Page Printer; Portrait; Postscript; Printer Driver; Printout; Scalable Fonts; Simplex Printing;*

NEQ gate

NOT EQUAL gate. A logic gate on a chip which operates with binary digits where an output of logic value 1 only occurs if all the inputs are not the same logic value. e.g. Inp=0 and Inp=0 then Out=0, Inp=1 and Inp=0 then Out=1.

See Also: *ALU; AMR; AND gate; Arithmetic and Logic Unit; Automatic Message Routing; Binary; Binary Digit; Bit; Boolean Algebra; Chip; Chipset; Expert System; FL; Flip Flop; Fuzzy Logic; I-OR gate; Large Scale Integration; Logic Gate; LSI; NAND gate; NOR gate; NOT gate; OR gate; Silicon Chip; Transistor; Very Large Scale Integration; VLSI; X-OR gate;*

Nerd

A person who is fanatic about computers.

See Also: *Emoticons; Forum; IM; Instant Messaging; Netiquette; Newbie; Newsgroup; Smileys; Surfing; User; User Group;*

Nesting

A term used whereby a procedure or a program is executed within another. Nesting can occur for a number of levels.

See Also: *Applet; DLL; Dynamic Link Library; Event; Function; Instruction Set; JCL; Job; Job Control Language; Macro; Module; Program; Script; Subroutine; Utility;*

Net
The Internet. A collection of inter-connected computers and networks around the world. Often referred to as "the net".
See Also: *Acceptable User Policy; Anchor; Applet; AUP; Bandwidth; BBS; Bookmark; Broadband; Browser; Bulletin Board System; CERN; CGI; Chat; Chatroom; Client Server Protocol; Common Gateway Interface; Conseil Europeen pour la Recherche Nucleaire; Cybercafe; Cyberspace; DNS; Domain Name; Domain Name Server; Domain Name System; Dot; Gopher; Hit; Home Page; Host; Host Processor; HTML; HTTP; Hyperlink; Hypertext Mark-Up Language; Hypertext Transfer Protocol; IM; Information Superhighway; Instant Messaging; Internet; Internet Protocol; Internet Protocol Address; Internet Relay Chat; Internet Service Provider; IP; IP Address; IRC; ISP; Link; Message Boards; Meta Tag; Meta-Search Engine; Narrowband; Netiquette; Newbie; Newsgroup; PING; Point Of Presence; Point to Point Protocol; POP; PPP; Provider; Proxy Server; Search Engine; Secure Socket Layer; Serial Line Internet Protocol; Service Provider; Shareware; Simple Mail Transfer Protocol; Site; SLIP; SMTP; Spider; SSL; Surfing; T-1; T-3; TCP/IP; The Net; The Web; Transmission Control Protocol/Internet Protocol; WAP; Wap Internet Service Provider; Webhost; Webring; Website; Wireless Application Protocol; WISP; World Wide Web; Worm; WWW;*

Netiquette
Courtesy that should be used by everyone while using the Internet.
See Also: *Acceptable User Policy; AUP; Browser; Chat; Chatroom; Cybercafe; Cyberspace; Emoticons; Flame; Forum; IM; Instant Messaging; Internet; Internet Relay Chat; IRC; Nerd; Net; Newbie; Newsgroup; Smileys; Surfing; The Net; Thread; User; User Group;*

Network
Hardware and software which connects multiple computers to a server in order to share data storage and peripheral devices.
See Also: *Access; AMR; Anonymous FTP; Automatic Message Routing; Backbone; Bandwidth; BBS; Broadband; Bulletin Board System; Client Server; Client Server Protocol; Distributed System/Network; Environment; Ethernet; File Server; File Sharing; Gateway; Host Processor; Intranet; LAN; LAN Port; Local Area Network; Multi User; Multitasking; Narrowband; Network Information Centre; Network Operating System; NIC; Node; NOS; Open Systems Interconnect; OSI; Point of Sales; Polling; POS; Ring Network; Server; Star Cluster; Star Network; TCP/IP; Token Ring; Transmission Control Protocol/Internet Protocol; WAN; Wide Area Network;*

Network Information Centre
(NIC). A location where data is organised for individual networks.
See Also: *Anonymous FTP; Backbone; Client Server; Client Server Protocol; Distributed System/Network; Ethernet; File Server; Firewall; FTP Site; Gateway; Host; Intranet; LAN; Local Area Network; Mirror Site; Network; Network Operating System; NIC; Node; NOS; Open Systems Interconnect; OSI; Ring Network; Server; Star Cluster; Star Network; Token Ring; WAN; Wide Area Network;*

Network Operating System
(NOS). An operating system that runs on a server which controls shared services, such as printers or storage devices.
See Also: *API; Application Program Interface; Client Server; Client Server Protocol; Disk Operating System; Distributed System/Network; DOS; Ethernet; File Server; Gateway; Housekeeping; Intranet; LAN; Linux; Local Area Network; Network; Network Information Centre; NIC; NOS; Operating System; OS; OS/2; Ring Network; Server; Star Cluster; Star Network; System Software; Token Ring; UNIX; WAN; Wide Area Network;*

Newbie
A person new to the Internet.
See Also: *Acceptable User Policy; AUP; Chat; Chatroom; Cybercafe; Cyberspace; Emoticons; Forum; IM; Instant Messaging; Internet; Internet Relay Chat; IRC; Nerd; Net; Netiquette; Newsgroup; Smileys; Surfing; The Net; The Web; User; World Wide Web; WWW;*

Newsgroup
Discussion groups on the Internet normally categorised by subject.
See Also: *Buddy List; Chat; Chatroom; Cybercafe; Cyberspace; Emoticons; FAQ; Forum; Frequently Asked Questions; IM; Instant Messaging; Interactive; Internet; Internet Relay Chat; Internet Service Provider; IRC; ISP; Message Boards; Nerd; Net; Netiquette; Newbie; Online; Provider; Service Provider; Smileys; The Net; Thread; User; User Group;*

NIC
Network Information Centre. A location where data is organised for individual networks.
See Also: *Anonymous FTP; Backbone; Client Server; Client Server Protocol; Distributed System/Network; Ethernet; File Server; Firewall; FTP Site; Gateway; Host; Intranet; LAN; Local Area Network; Mirror Site; Network; Network Information Centre; Network Operating System;*

Node; NOS; Open Systems Interconnect; OSI; Ring Network; Server; Star Cluster; Star Network; Token Ring; WAN; Wide Area Network;

NLQ
Near Letter Quality. The type of print produced by some printers where the dots that make up each character are closer together, thus giving a better quality print.
See Also: *Bi Directional; Bubble Jet; Characters Per Inch; CPI; Daisywheel; DIP Switch; Dot Matrix; Dots Per Inch; DPI; Duplex Printing; Font; Font Cartridge; Format; Hard Copy; Inkjet; Landscape; Laser Jet; Laser Printer; LCD Printer; Letter Quality; Liquid Crystal Display Printer; LQ; Matrix Printer; Near Letter Quality; Output; Page Printer; Portrait; Postscript; Printer Driver; Printout; Scalable Fonts; Simplex Printing;*

Node
(1) A device to switch transmission from high speed channels to low speed channels and vice versa. It can also switch transmission channels or split transmission to sub channels. (2) A single computer connected to a network.
See Also: *ADN; Advanced Digital Network; AMR; Automatic Message Routing; Channel; Client Server; Communications; Computer; Cross Platform; Data Communications; Data Transmission; Datacoms; Dial In; Dial Up; Direct Connection; Distributed System/Network; Equipment; Ethernet; File Server; Gateway; Handshake; Hardware; Integrated Services Digital Network; Intranet; ISDN; Kit; LAN; Leased Line; Local Area Network; Machine; Mailserver; Modem; Modulator Demodulator; Multiplexer; Network; Network Information Centre; NIC; Open Systems Interconnect; OSI; Parallel Transmission; Platform; Proxy Server; Ring Network; Serial Transmission; Server; Star Cluster; Star Network; T-1; T-3; Telecommunication; Telecoms; Token Ring; Transmission Channel; V90; WAN; Wide Area Network;*

NOR gate
A logic gate on a chip, meaning NOT OR, which operates with binary digits where an output of logic value 1 only occurs if all inputs have a logic value 0. e.g. Inp=0 and Inp=0 then Out=1, Inp=1 and Inp=0 then Out=0.
See Also: *ALU; AMR; AND gate; Arithmetic and Logic Unit; Automatic Message Routing; Binary; Binary Digit; Bit; Boolean Algebra; Chip; Chipset; Expert System; FL; Flip Flop; Fuzzy Logic; I-OR gate; Large Scale Integration; Logic Gate; LSI; NAND gate; NEQ gate; NOT gate;*

OR gate; Silicon Chip; Transistor; Very Large Scale Integration; VLSI; X-OR gate;

NOS

Network Operating System. An operating system that runs on a server which controls shared services, such as printers or storage devices.

See Also: *API; Application Program Interface; Client Server; Client Server Protocol; Disk Operating System; Distributed System/Network; DOS; Ethernet; File Server; Gateway; Housekeeping; Intranet; LAN; Linux; Local Area Network; Network; Network Information Centre; Network Operating System; NIC; Operating System; OS; OS/2; Ring Network; Server; Star Cluster; Star Network; System Software; Token Ring; UNIX; WAN; Wide Area Network;*

NOT gate

A logic gate on a chip which operates with binary digits where the output logic value is always opposite to the input logic value. e.g. Inp=0 then Out=1.

See Also: *ALU; AMR; AND gate; Arithmetic and Logic Unit; Automatic Message Routing; Binary; Binary Digit; Bit; Boolean Algebra; Chip; Chipset; Expert System; FL; Flip Flop; Fuzzy Logic; I-OR gate; Large Scale Integration; Logic Gate; LSI; NAND gate; NEQ gate; NOR gate; OR gate; Silicon Chip; Transistor; Very Large Scale Integration; VLSI; X-OR gate;*

Notebook

A personal computer which is small enough to use on your lap. The screen forms an integral part of the unit and is the lid that opens and closes the unit.

See Also: *1st Generation; 2nd Generation; 3rd Generation; 4th Generation; Advanced Technology; Analogue Computer; AT; Compatible; Computer; Computer Power; Configuration; Cross Platform; Desktop; Digital Computer; Downsizing; EDS; Electronic Data System; Environment; Equipment; Extended Technology; Hardware; IBM (tm) Compatible; Information System; Information Technology; Installation; IS; IT; Kit; Laptop; Machine; Micro; Microcomputer; Multi Platform; OEM; Original Equipment Manufacturer; Palmtop Computer; PC; Personal Computer; Platform; Portable; Power; Standalone; Tower Computer; Turnkey; Voice Activated; XT;*

Ns
Nanosecond. One billionth or a thousand millionth of a second.
See Also: *Access Time; Baud Rate; Bits Per Second; BPS; Characters Per Second; Clock Speed; CPS; Gbps; Kbps; Mbps; Microsecond; Millisecond; Ms; Nanosecond; Pico Second; Seek Time;*

Null
A value of a data item or character, internal to a computer which contains nothing. Not even zero or space.
See Also: *Array; Constant; Data; Data Element; Data Entity; Data Item; Data Type; EBCDIC; Entity; Extended Binary Coded Decimal Interchange Code; Field; Group; Literal; String; Table; Variable; Word;*

Number Cruncher
A computer which processes large amounts of data.
See Also: *1st Generation; 2nd Generation; 3rd Generation; 4th Generation; Analogue Computer; Computer; Configuration; Cross Platform; Digital Computer; EDS; Electronic Data System; Environment; Equipment; Hardware; Installation; Kit; Machine; Mainframe; Platform; Turnkey;*

O & M
Organisation and Methods. The procedures for organising, designing and scheduling business operations.
See Also: *Analyst; B/A; Business Analyst; CASE; Case Tool; Computer Aided Software Engineering; Data Flow; Data Flow Diagram; Data Model; Development; DFD; Flowchart; Logical Design; Model; Modular; Organisation & Methods; Physical Design; Process; Process Model; S/A; Software Development Cycle; Structured Design; System Analyst;*

Object Code
The machine code produced when a computer compiles the source program code. Source code is the written program language; machine code is what computers recognise.
See Also: *Assembler; Assembly Code; BCD; Binary; Binary Coded Decimal; Binary Digit; Bit; Code Generator; Compiler; Compiling; EXE; Instruction Set; Low Level Language; Machine Code; Machine Language;*

Object Oriented Analysis

(OOA). Analysis done on new or existing function modules called Objects, which are autonomous functional modules, each containing specific processes to be performed on data.

See Also: *Analyst; B/A; Business Analyst; Development; Logical Design; Model; Modular; Module; Object Oriented Design; Object Oriented Programming; OOA; OOD; OOP; Physical Design; Process; Process Model; Program Specification; S/A; Specification; Structured Design; System Analysis; System Analyst;*

Object Oriented Design

(OOD). Designing systems where Objects are used in the system design. Objects are autonomous functional modules each containing specific processes to be performed on data.

See Also: *Analyst; B/A; Business Analyst; Development; Logical Design; Model; Modular; Module; Object Oriented Analysis; Object Oriented Programming; OOA; OOD; OOP; Physical Design; Process; Process Model; Program Specification; S/A; Specification; Structured Design; System Analysis; System Analyst;*

Object Oriented Programming

(OOP). Software development where Object modules are created or amended. Objects are autonomous functional modules each containing specific processes to be performed on data.

See Also: *Analyst; B/A; Business Analyst; Development; Logical Design; Model; Modular; Module; Object Oriented Analysis; Object Oriented Design; OOA; OOD; OOP; Physical Design; Process; Process Model; Program Specification; S/A; Specification; Structured Design; System Analysis; System Analyst;*

OCR

Optical Character Recognition OR Optical Character Reader. The process where documents are optically scanned to recognise the shapes of characters or graphics.

See Also: *CCD; Character; Charge Coupled Device; Configuration; Device; Equipment; Flatbed Scanner; Font; Hardware; Kit; Light Pen; OMR; Optical Character Reader; Optical Character Recognition; Optical Mark Recognition; Optical Scanner; Peripheral; Scanner;*

Octal
A numerical system with a base of 8 using numbers 0 - 7. Each position in the notation is times 8 starting with the right hand position as 1. e.g. 433 in octal = (4x64)+(3x8)+(3x1) = 283 in denary. Data is represented in this format.
See Also: *American Standard Code for Information Interchange; ASCII; BCD; Binary; Binary Coded Decimal; Character; Data; Data Type; Denary; Hex; Hexadecimal;*

OEM
Original Equipment Manufacturer. An organisation which assembles and sells equipment that is made up of components from other suppliers.
See Also: *Advanced Technology; Analogue Computer; AT; Compatible; Computer; Desktop; Digital Computer; Extended Technology; IBM (tm) Compatible; Laptop; Machine; Micro; Microcomputer; Notebook; Original Equipment Manufacturer; Palmtop Computer; PC; Personal Computer; Portable; Standalone; Tower Computer; Turnkey; XT;*

Off Line
The state when a peripheral device or computer is NOT ready to accept data or interface with a computer, e.g. not connected to the Internet.
See Also: *Abort; Busy; Downtime; Hangs; Hung; Interrupt; Log In/Off; Online; Peripheral; PING; Timeout;*

Office Information System
(OIS). A computer system which provides users with the facilities of office systems. i.e. word processing, spreadsheets, electronic mail, office administration.
See Also: *Application; Batch Processing; Computation; Compute; Data Processing; Desk Top Publishing; DP; DTP; EDS; Electronic Data System; Information System; Information Technology; Integrated Systems; IS; IT; Mail Merge; OIS; Package; Software; Software Package; Software System; Spreadsheet; System; Word Processor; WP;*

OIS
Office Information System. A computer system which provides users with the facilities of office systems. i.e. word processing, spreadsheets, electronic mail, office administration.
See Also: *Application; Batch Processing; Computation; Compute; Data Processing; Desk Top Publishing; DP; DTP; EDS; Electronic Data System; Information System; Information Technology; Integrated Systems; IS; IT; Mail Merge; Office Information System; Package;*

Software; Software Package; Software System; Spreadsheet; System; Word Processor; WP;

OMR
Optical Mark Recognition. The process where pre-printed characters are recognised by an optical scanner.
See Also: *CCD; Character; Charge Coupled Device; Configuration; Device; Equipment; Flatbed Scanner; Font; Hardware; Kit; Light Pen; OCR; Optical Character Reader; Optical Character Recognition; Optical Mark Recognition; Optical Scanner; Peripheral; Scanner;*

Online
The state when a peripheral device is ready to accept data or when a computer is connected to another computer, a network or the Internet.
See Also: *Access; Acoustic Coupler; Chat; Chatroom; Cyberspace; Dial In; Dial Up; Forum; Handshake; Interactive; Internet Relay Chat; IRC; Log In/Off; Modem; Modulator Demodulator; Newsgroup; Off Line; PING; Stream;*

OOA
Object Oriented Analysis. Analysis done on new or existing function modules called Objects, which are autonomous functional modules, each containing specific processes to be performed on data.
See Also: *Analyst; B/A; Business Analyst; Development; Logical Design; Model; Modular; Module; Object Oriented Analysis; Object Oriented Design; Object Oriented Programming; OOD; OOP; Physical Design; Process; Process Model; Program Specification; S/A; Specification; Structured Design; System Analysis; System Analyst;*

OOD
Object Oriented Design. Designing systems where Objects are used in the system design. Objects are autonomous functional modules each containing specific processes to be performed on data.
See Also: *Analyst; B/A; Business Analyst; Development; Logical Design; Model; Modular; Module; Object Oriented Analysis; Object Oriented Design; Object Oriented Programming; OOA; OOP; Physical Design; Process; Process Model; Program Specification; S/A; Specification; Structured Design; System Analysis; System Analyst;*

OOP

Object Oriented Programming. Software development where Object modules are created or amended. Objects are autonomous functional modules each containing specific processes to be performed on data.

See Also: *Analyst; B/A; Business Analyst; Development; Logical Design; Model; Modular; Module; Object Oriented Analysis; Object Oriented Design; Object Oriented Programming; OOA; OOD; Physical Design; Process; Process Model; Program Specification; S/A; Specification; Structured Design; System Analysis; System Analyst;*

Open System

A term where a computer uses an operating system that was designed to be used on different computers and which is not proprietary to one make of computer. This allows for the same software to be used across a range of computers.

See Also: *Configuration; Cross Platform; Disk Operating System; Distributed System/Network; DOS; Environment; Linux; Multi Platform; Operating System; OS; OS/2; Platform; UNIX;*

Open Systems Interconnect

(OSI). A standard for communications and hardware specifications for networks.

See Also: *ADN; ADSL; Advanced Digital Network; Asymmetric Digital Subscriber Line; Asymmetrical Modem; Asynchronous; Asynchronous Transfer Mode; ATM; Bandwidth; Baud Rate; Broadband; CCITT; CCTA; Characters Per Second; Client Server; Client Server Protocol; Communications; Compatible; Consultative Committee International Telegraph and Telephone; CPS; Data Communications; Data Parity; Data Transmission; Datacoms; Dial In; Dial Up; Direct Connection; Duplex Transmission; Ethernet; FDDI; Fibre Distributed Data Interface; Fibre Optics; File Server; Gateway; Half Duplex; Handshake; HD; Integrated Services Digital Network; ISDN; Kbps; LAN; Leased Line; Local Area Network; Mbps; Multi Platform; Multiplex; Multiplexer; Narrowband; Network; Network Information Centre; NIC; Node; Optical Fibre; OSI; Parallel Transmission; Parity Bit; Protocol; Ring Network; RS232; RS423; Serial Transmission; Server; Simplex Transmission; Star Cluster; Star Network; Synchronous; TCP/IP; Telecommunication; Telecoms; Token Ring; Transmission Control Protocol/Internet Protocol; Transmit; V90; WAN; Wide Area Network; XMODEM; YMODEM; ZMODEM;*

Operand
A location address in the computer's memory or an item of data within a program.
See Also: *Absolute Address; Address; Block; Data; Dump; Memory; Register; Relative Address; Stack; Working Storage; Workspace;*

Operating System
The software which controls the working of a computer. It controls the execution of programs, the input and output of data, data management and the interfaces with other devices.
See Also: *API; Application Program Interface; Basic Input Output System; BIOS; Boot; Boot Disk; Bootstrap; Cold Start; Configuration; Disk Operating System; DOS; Environment; FAT; File Allocation Table; Graphical User Interface; GUI; High Memory; Housekeeping; Installation; Linux; Network Operating System; NOS; Open System; OS; OS/2; Re-boot; Software; System Software; UNIX; Upper Memory; Warm Start;*

Operator
(1) A person who operates a computer. Normally refers to large computers. (2) A word or symbol which represents a mathematical operation.
See Also: *ALU; Arithmetic and Logic Unit; Boolean Algebra; Compute; Contractor; Hands On; User;*

Optical Character Reader
(OCR). A device which optically scans documents to recognise the shapes of characters or graphics.
See Also: *CCD; Character; Charge Coupled Device; Configuration; Device; Equipment; Flatbed Scanner; Font; Hardware; Kit; Light Pen; OCR; OMR; Optical Character Recognition; Optical Mark Recognition; Optical Scanner; Peripheral; Scanner;*

Optical Character Recognition
(OCR). The process where documents are optically scanned to recognise the shapes of characters or graphics.
See Also: *CCD; Character; Charge Coupled Device; Configuration; Device; Equipment; Flatbed Scanner; Font; Hardware; Kit; Light Pen; OCR; OMR; Optical Character Reader; Optical Mark Recognition; Optical Scanner; Peripheral; Scanner;*

Optical Disk
A disc on which information or programs are optically stored using a strong laser. A less strong laser is used to read the disc.
See Also: *Bits Per Inch; Block; Boot Disk; BPI; CD-ROM; CD-ROM Drive; CD-RW Drive; Digital Versatile Disk; Directory; DVD; Medium; Optical Drive; Recording Medium; Root Directory; Sub Directory;*

Optical Drive
A device which is integral or attached to a computer that stores and retrieves information on CD-ROMS.
See Also: *Archive; ATAPI; Attachment Packet Interface; Backing Store; Backup; CD-ROM; CD-ROM Drive; CD-RW Drive; Configuration; Device; Digital Versatile Disk; Drive; DVD; EIDE; Enhanced Intelligent Drive Electronics; Environment; Equipment; Hardware; Heads; IDE; Installation; Integrated Drive Electronics; Kit; Mass Storage; Optical Disk; Peripheral; Read/Write Head; Recording; Save; Storage; Store; Write; Write Protect;*

Optical Fibre
Very thin glass or plastic fibres which use light to transmit data along the fibres.
See Also: *Acoustic Coupler; ADN; ADSL; Advanced Digital Network; AMR; Asymmetric Digital Subscriber Line; Asymmetrical Modem; Asynchronous; Asynchronous Transfer Mode; ATM; Automatic Message Routing; Bandwidth; Baud Rate; Bits Per Second; BPS; Broadband; CCITT; CCTA; Channel; Characters Per Second; Client Server Protocol; Communications; Consultative Committee International Telegraph and Telephone; CPS; Data Communications; Data Parity; Data Transmission; Datacoms; Dial In; Dial Up; Digital; Direct Connection; Duplex Transmission; ECP; Enhanced Parallel Port; EPP; Extended Capabilities Port; FDDI; Fibre Distributed Data Interface; Fibre Optics; Full Duplex; Gbps; Half Duplex; HD; Integrated Services Digital Network; ISDN; Kbps; Leased Line; Mbps; Modem; Modulator Demodulator; Multiplex; Multiplexer; Narrowband; Open Systems Interconnect; OSI; Packet; Packet Switching; Parallel Transmission; Parity Bit; Serial Transmission; Simplex Transmission; Synchronous; Telecommunication; Telecoms; Teleprocessing System; TPS; Transfer Rate; Transmission Channel; Transmit; V90;*

Optical Mark Recognition
(OMR). The process where pre-printed characters are recognised by an optical scanner.
See Also: *CCD; Character; Charge Coupled Device; Configuration; Device; Equipment; Flatbed Scanner; Font; Hardware; Kit; Light Pen; OCR; OMR; Optical Character Reader; Optical Character Recognition; Optical Scanner; Peripheral; Scanner;*

Optical Scanner
A device which reads documents optically by recognising the shapes of characters or graphics when the document is scanned.
See Also: *Analogue Digital Converter; CCD; Charge Coupled Device; Configuration; Device; Drum; Environment; Equipment; Flatbed Scanner; Hardware; Installation; Kit; OCR; OMR; Optical Character Reader; Optical Character Recognition; Optical Mark Recognition; Peripheral; Scanner;*

OR gate
A logic gate on a chip which operates with binary digits where an output of logic value 1 occurs if any of the inputs have a logic value 1. e.g. Inp=0 and Inp=0 then Out=0, Inp=1 and Inp=0 then Out=1.
See Also: *ALU; AMR; AND gate; Arithmetic and Logic Unit; Automatic Message Routing; Binary; Binary Digit; Bit; Boolean Algebra; Chip; Chipset; Expert System; FL; Flip Flop; Fuzzy Logic; I-OR gate; Large Scale Integration; Logic Gate; LSI; NAND gate; NEQ gate; NOR gate; NOT gate; Silicon Chip; Transistor; Very Large Scale Integration; VLSI; X-OR gate;*

Organisation & Methods
(O&M). The procedures for organising, designing and scheduling business operations.
See Also: *Analyst; B/A; Business Analyst; CASE; Case Tool; Computer Aided Software Engineering; Data Flow; Data Flow Diagram; Data Model; Development; DFD; Flowchart; Logical Design; Model; Modular; O & M; Physical Design; Process; Process Model; S/A; Software Development Cycle; Structured Design; System Analyst;*

Original Equipment Manufacturer
(OEM). An organisation which assembles and sells equipment that is made up of components from other suppliers.
See Also: *Advanced Technology; Analogue Computer; AT; Compatible; Computer; Desktop; Digital Computer; Extended Technology; IBM (tm) Compatible; Laptop; Machine; Micro; Microcomputer; Notebook; OEM;*

Palmtop Computer; PC; Personal Computer; Portable; Standalone; Tower Computer; Turnkey; XT;

OS

Operating System. The software which controls the working of a computer. It controls the execution of programs, the input and output of data, data management and the interfaces with other devices.

See Also: *API; Application Program Interface; Basic Input Output System; BIOS; Boot; Boot Disk; Bootstrap; Cold Start; Configuration; Disk Operating System; DOS; Environment; FAT; File Allocation Table; Graphical User Interface; GUI; High Memory; Housekeeping; Installation; Linux; Network Operating System; NOS; Open System; Operating System; OS/2; Re-boot; Software; System Software; UNIX; Upper Memory; Warm Start;*

OS/2

An operating system for the PC.

See Also: *API; Application Program Interface; Basic Input Output System; BIOS; Boot; Boot Disk; Bootstrap; Cold Start; Configuration; Disk Operating System; DOS; Environment; FAT; File Allocation Table; Graphical User Interface; GUI; High Memory; Housekeeping; Installation; Linux; Network Operating System; NOS; Open System; Operating System; OS; Re-boot; Software; System Software; UNIX; Upper Memory; Warm Start;*

OSI

Open Systems Interconnect. A standard for communications and hardware specifications for networks.

See Also: *ADN; ADSL; Advanced Digital Network; Asymmetric Digital Subscriber Line; Asymmetrical Modem; Asynchronous; Asynchronous Transfer Mode; ATM; Bandwidth; Baud Rate; Broadband; CCITT; CCTA; Characters Per Second; Client Server; Client Server Protocol; Communications; Compatible; Consultative Committee International Telegraph and Telephone; CPS; Data Communications; Data Parity; Data Transmission; Datacoms; Dial In; Dial Up; Direct Connection; Duplex Transmission; Ethernet; FDDI; Fibre Distributed Data Interface; Fibre Optics; File Server; Gateway; Half Duplex; Handshake; HD; Integrated Services Digital Network; ISDN; Kbps; LAN; Leased Line; Local Area Network; Mbps; Multi Platform; Multiplex; Multiplexer; Narrowband; Network; Network Information Centre; NIC; Node; Open Systems Interconnect; Optical Fibre; Parallel Transmission; Parity Bit; Protocol; Ring Network; RS232; RS423; Serial Transmission; Server; Simplex Transmission; Star Cluster; Star Network; Synchronous;*

TCP/IP; Telecommunication; Telecoms; Token Ring; Transmission Control Protocol/Internet Protocol; Transmit; V90; WAN; Wide Area Network; XMODEM; YMODEM; ZMODEM;

Output
The result of manipulating data which is presented in some form or another. e.g. printed, displayed.
See Also: *Archive; Backup; Characters Per Inch; CPI; Display; Dots Per Inch; DPI; Duplex Printing; Export; Fiche; Hard Copy; Landscape; Letter Quality; Line Printer; LQ; Matrix Printer; Microfiche; Microfilm; Monitor; Near Letter Quality; NLQ; Paint Screen; Pie Chart; Plasma Screen; Plotter; Portrait; Postscript; Print Spooler; Printer; Printout; Recording; Recording Device; Recording Medium; Save; Screen; Screen Dump; Simplex Printing; Spooler; Storage; Super Twist LCD; Super VGA; Super Video Graphics Array; SVGA; Terminal; TFT; Thin-Film Transistor; Touch Screen; VDT; VDU; VGA; Video Display Terminal; Video Graphics Array; Visual Display Terminal; Visual Display Unit; Window; Write;*

Outsourcing
A term used when organisations arrange for their data to be processed by another company specifically set up to provide an outsourcing service.
See Also: *Batch Processing; Data Processing; Downsizing; DP; EDP; EDS; Electronic Data Processing; Electronic Data System; Facilities Management; FM; Information System; Information Technology; IS; IT;*

Overlay
The transfer of part of a program from a recording device into memory as and when the memory becomes available.
See Also: *API; Application Program Interface; Conventional Memory; Core; EMS; Expanded Memory; Expanded Memory Specification; Extended Memory; High Memory; Magnetic Core; Memory; Module; Program; Stack; Store; Terminate and Stay Resident; Time Share; Time Slice; TSR;*

Pack
Disk Pack. The exchangeable magnetic disk used in a disk drive.
See Also: *3.5 Inch; 5.25 Inch; Archive; ATAPI; Attachment Packet Interface; Backing Store; Backup; Bits Per Inch; Block; Boot Disk; BPI; Cluster; Computer Power; Configuration; Crash; Cylinder; Defragment; Density; Device; Directory; Disk; Disk Drive; Disk Map; Disk Operating System; Disk Pack; Disk Size; Disk Storage; Diskette; DOS; Double Density; Drive; Equipment; FDD; Five and a quarter; Fixed Disk Drive;*

Floppy Disk; Floppy Disk Drive; Format; Fragmentation; Grandfather, Father, Son; Hard Disk Drive; Hardware; HDD; Head Crash; Heads; High Density; Indexed Sequential Access Method; ISAM; Keyed Sequential Access Method; Kit; KSAM; Machine Crash; Magnetic Disk; Mass Storage; Medium; Peripheral; Power; Read/Write Head; Recording; Recording Device; Recording Medium; Root Directory; Save; Sector; Seek Time; Storage; Store; Sub Directory; Three and a Half; Track; Volume; Winchester Disk; Wipe; Write; Write Protect;

Package
A collection of programs for a specific application. e.g. accounting, word processing.
See Also: *AI; Application; Artificial Intelligence; CAD; CADCAM; CADMAT; CAE; CAI; CAM; Case Tool; CBT; Computer Aided Design; Computer Aided Design and Manufacturing; Computer Aided Design Manufacture and Test; Computer Aided Engineering; Computer Aided Instruction; Computer Aided Manufacturing; Computer Based Training; Data Base Management System; DBMS; Desk Top Publishing; DTP; EDS; Electronic Data System; Expert System; Freeware; Geographical Information System; GIS; Information System; Integrated; Integrated Systems; IS; Leading Edge; Mail Merge; Office Information System; OIS; RDBMS/RDMS; Relational Database Management System; Shareware; Software; Software Package; Software System; Spreadsheet; State of the Art; Turnkey; Vertical Market; Word Processor; WP;*

Packed Data
Data recorded in a format which takes up less storage area.
See Also: *Compressed File; Compression; Conversion; Convert; Data Compression; Decompression; Density; Double Density; High Density; PKZIP; Unzip; Zip;*

Packet
A chunk of audio, visual or data information and a destination address created for transmission purposes.
See Also: *Address; Asynchronous; Bandwidth; Broadband; Communications; Data; Data Communications; Data Parity; Data Transmission; Datacoms; Duplex Transmission; FDDI; Fibre Distributed Data Interface; Fibre Optics; Multiplex; Multiplexer; Narrowband; Optical Fibre; Packet Switching; Parallel Transmission; Parity Bit; Serial Transmission; Simplex Transmission; Synchronous; Telecommunication; Telecoms; Transmit; V90;*

Packet Switching
Audio, visual or data information divided into chunks when transmitted and reassembled at the receiving end.
See Also: *Address; Asynchronous; Bandwidth; Broadband; Communications; Data; Data Communications; Data Parity; Data Transmission; Datacoms; Duplex Transmission; FDDI; Fibre Distributed Data Interface; Fibre Optics; Multiplex; Multiplexer; Narrowband; Optical Fibre; Packet; Parallel Transmission; Parity Bit; Serial Transmission; Simplex Transmission; Synchronous; Telecommunication; Telecoms; Transmit; V90;*

Page
An HTML document or one of the pages of a website.
See Also: *Anchor; Browser; CGI; Common Gateway Interface; Extensible Hypertext Markup Language; eXtensible Markup Language; Footer; Header; Hit; Home Page; HTML; Hypertext; Hypertext Mark-Up Language; Internet; Meta Tag; Portal; Proxy Server; Site; Surfing; The Net; The Web; Thumbnail; Webring; Website; World Wide Web; WWW; XHTML; XML;*

Page Description Language
(PDL). A programming language that defines the layout and content of a page.
See Also: *APL; Code; Extensible Hypertext Markup Language; eXtensible Markup Language; High Level Language; HTML; Hypertext Mark-Up Language; Instruction Set; JAVA; JAVASCRIPT; Language; PDL; Programming Language; Software; XHTML; XML;*

Page Editor
A program which allows the user to enter and edit data in a computer one page at a time.
See Also: *Edit; Line Editor; Patch; Picture; Program; Spell Check; Split Screen; Syntax; Utility; Word Processor; Word Wrap; WP;*

Page Printer
A device which prints a whole page at a time and better known as a Laser Printer. It is very similar to a photocopier where a drum unit is charged with the image to print and then passed over toner. The toner adheres to the charged area and is transferred to the paper by a heat process.
See Also: *Barrel Printer; Bubble Jet; Configuration; Daisywheel; Device; Dot Matrix; Drum Printer; Duplex Printing; Environment; Equipment; Font Cartridge; Hard Copy; Hardware; Inkjet; Installation; Kit; Landscape; Laser Jet; Laser Printer; LCD Printer; Letter Quality;*

Line Printer; Lines Per Minute; Liquid Crystal Display Printer; Lpm; LPT Port; LQ; Matrix Printer; Near Letter Quality; NLQ; Pages Per Minute; Peripheral; Portrait; Postscript; PPM; Printer; Printer Driver; Printout; Simplex Printing; Thermal Printer; Toner;

Pages Per Minute
(PPM). The number of pages which a printer can optimally print in a minute.
See Also: *Barrel Printer; Bubble Jet; Daisywheel; Dot Matrix; Drum Printer; Duplex Printing; Hard Copy; Inkjet; Laser Jet; Laser Printer; LCD Printer; Line Printer; Lines Per Minute; Liquid Crystal Display Printer; Lpm; Matrix Printer; Page Printer; PPM; Printer; Printout; Simplex Printing; Thermal Printer;*

Paint Screen
A way in which a visual display unit screen is formatted and displayed.
See Also: *Analogue Monitor; Anti Glare Screen; Cathode Ray Tube; CGA; Colour Graphics Adaptor; CRT; Digital Monitor; Display; EGA; Enhanced Graphic Adaptor; Extended Video Array; Frame Rate; Graphics Card; Intelligent Terminal; Interlaced; LCD; Liquid Crystal Display; Low Resolution; Marquee; Monitor; Monochrome; Output; Pixel; Plasma Screen; Resolution; Screen; Screen Burn; Screen Dump; Scroll; Split Screen; Sprite; Super Twist LCD; Super VGA; Super Video Graphics Array; SVGA; Terminal; TFT; Thin-Film Transistor; Toolbar; Touch Screen; Twip; VDT; VDU; VGA; Video Card; Video Display Terminal; Video Graphics Array; Visual Display Terminal; Visual Display Unit; WIMP; Window; Windows Icons Mice and Pull-down menus; XGA;*

Palmtop Computer
A handheld computer.
See Also: *1st Generation; 2nd Generation; 3rd Generation; 4th Generation; Advanced Technology; Analogue Computer; AT; Compatible; Computer; Computer Power; Configuration; Cross Platform; Desktop; Digital Computer; Downsizing; EDS; Electronic Data System; Environment; Equipment; Extended Technology; Hardware; IBM (tm) Compatible; Information System; Information Technology; Installation; IS; IT; Kit; Laptop; Machine; Micro; Microcomputer; Multi Platform; Notebook; OEM; Original Equipment Manufacturer; PC; PDA; Personal Computer; Platform; Portable; Power; Standalone; Tower Computer; Turnkey; Voice Activated; XT;*

Paper Tape
A recording medium where a continuous paper tape has holes punched into it representing the data.
See Also: *Archive; Backing Store; Backup; Block; End of Tape; Environment; EOT; Grandfather, Father, Son; Mass Storage; Medium; Recording Medium; Save; Storage;*

Parallel Interface
A 25 pin interface in a computer which allows the transmitting and receiving of data one byte at a time using a separate transmission line for each bit of the byte being transmitted.
See Also: *Access; ECP; Enhanced Parallel Port; EPP; Extended Capabilities Port; Interface; LPT Port; MIDI; Musical Instrument Digital Interface; Parallel Port; Parallel Transmission; Port; Serial Interface; Serial Port; Serial Transmission;*

Parallel Port
A connector on a computer to which a cable is attached that allows data to be sent or received by parallel transmission, i.e. bi-directional transfer.
See Also: *Dongle; ECP; Enhanced Parallel Port; EPP; Extended Capabilities Port; Interface; LPT Port; MIDI; Musical Instrument Digital Interface; Parallel Interface; Parallel Transmission; Port; Serial Interface; Serial Port; Serial Transmission;*

Parallel Processor
A computer whose microprocessors are wired in parallel to enable different types of processing to take place simultaneously.
See Also: *286; 386; 486; ALU; Application Specific Integrated Circuits; Arithmetic and Logic Unit; ASICS; Central Processing Unit; Chip; Chipset; Computer Power; Co-processor; CPU; IC; Integrated Circuit; Maths Co-processor; Microprocessor; Power; Processor; Reduced Instruction Set Computing; RISC; Silicon Chip; Very Large Scale Integration; VLSI;*

Parallel Transmission
The communication between a computer and a device where data is transmitted and received one byte at a time using a separate transmission line for each bit of the byte being transmitted.
See Also: *ACK; Acoustic Coupler; ADN; ADSL; Advanced Digital Network; AMR; Asymmetric Digital Subscriber Line; Asymmetrical Modem; Asynchronous; Asynchronous Transfer Mode; ATM; Automatic Message Routing; Bandwidth; Baud Rate; Bits Per Second; BPS; Broadband; Bus; CCITT; CCTA; Channel; Characters Per Second;*

Communications; Consultative Committee International Telegraph and Telephone; CPS; Data Communications; Data Parity; Data Transmission; Datacoms; Dial In; Dial Up; Digital; Direct Connection; Duplex Transmission; ECP; Enhanced Parallel Port; EPP; Extended Capabilities Port; FDDI; Fibre Distributed Data Interface; Fibre Optics; Full Duplex; Gbps; Half Duplex; HD; Integrated Services Digital Network; ISDN; Kbps; Leased Line; Mbps; Modem; Modulator Demodulator; Multiplex; Multiplexer; Narrowband; Node; Open Systems Interconnect; Optical Fibre; OSI; Packet; Packet Switching; Parallel Interface; Parallel Port; Parity Bit; Serial Interface; Serial Port; Serial Transmission; Simplex Transmission; Synchronous; T-1; T-3; Telecommunication; Telecoms; Teleprocessing System; TPS; Transfer Rate; Transmission Channel; Transmit; V90;

Parameter
A variable which is set to a specific value in a program, statement or command execution.
See Also: *Data; Data Element; Data Entity; Data Item; Data Type; Entity; Information; Input; Instruction; Key; Password; String; Variable;*

Parity Bit
An extra bit attached to a set of binary digits and used to check that all the other bits were transferred from one point to another correctly.
See Also: *ACK; ADN; ADSL; Advanced Digital Network; AMR; Asymmetric Digital Subscriber Line; Asymmetrical Modem; Asynchronous; Asynchronous Transfer Mode; ATM; Automatic Message Routing; Bandwidth; Baud Rate; Binary; Binary Digit; Bit; Bits Per Second; BPS; Broadband; CCITT; CCTA; Channel; Characters Per Second; Communications; Consultative Committee International Telegraph and Telephone; CPS; Data Communications; Data Parity; Data Transmission; Datacoms; Dial In; Dial Up; Digital; Direct Connection; Duplex Transmission; FDDI; Fibre Distributed Data Interface; Fibre Optics; Full Duplex; Gbps; Half Duplex; HD; Integrated Services Digital Network; ISDN; Leased Line; Mbps; Multiplex; Multiplexer; Narrowband; Open Systems Interconnect; Optical Fibre; OSI; Packet; Packet Switching; Parallel Transmission; Serial Transmission; Simplex Transmission; Synchronous; Telecommunication; Telecoms; Transmission Channel; Transmit; V90;*

PASCAL
A high level computer programming language.
See Also: *3GL; 4GL; ADA; ALGOL; APL; BASIC; C or C++; CLIPPER; COBOL; Code; Code Generator; Compiler; Compiling;*

CORAL; FORTH; FORTRAN; Fourth Generation Language; High Level Language; Instruction Set; JAVA; JAVASCRIPT; Language; LISP; LOGO; Module; NATURAL; PERL; PICK; PILOT; PL/1; Practical Extraction and Reporting Language; Program; Programming Language; PROLOG; RPG; Software; Source Code; Structured Program; Syntax; Third Generation Language; Visual Basic;

Password
A secure code used to gain access to a computer, system or website.
See Also: *Access; Hacker; Log In/Off; Parameter; Security;*

Patch
(1) A change to a program, data or memory. (2) The process of making that change.
See Also: *Code; Data; Line Editor; Memory; Page Editor; Program;*

Path
A pointer to where files or programs are located on storage devices.
See Also: *Audit Trail; Directory; Disk; Folder; Root Directory; Storage; Sub Directory;*

PC
A Personal Computer. Another name for a microcomputer.
See Also: *1st Generation; 2nd Generation; 3rd Generation; 4th Generation; Advanced Technology; Analogue Computer; AT; Compatible; Computer; Computer Power; Configuration; Cross Platform; Desktop; Digital Computer; Downsizing; EDS; Electronic Data System; Environment; Equipment; Extended Technology; Firewire; Hardware; IBM (tm) Compatible; Information System; Information Technology; Installation; IS; IT; Kit; Laptop; Leading Edge; Machine; Micro; Microcomputer; Multi Platform; Notebook; OEM; Original Equipment Manufacturer; Palmtop Computer; Personal Computer; Platform; Portable; Power; Standalone; State of the Art; Tower Computer; Turnkey; Voice Activated; XT;*

PCB
Printed Circuit Board. A board that has electrical components soldered onto it, which are connected to each other by metal strips. The board may perform a specific task and may be connected to other boards. e.g. mother board.
See Also: *Accelerated Graphics Port; Advanced Graphics Port; AGP; AGP Slot; Application Specific Integrated Circuits; ASICS; Chip; Chipset; Expansion Card; Expansion Slot; Fax Card; Graphics Card; IC;*

Integrated Circuit; Memory Board; Memory Card; Motherboard; PCI; PCMCIA; Peripheral Component Interconnect; Personal Computer Memory Card International Association; Printed Circuit Board; Silicon Chip; SIMM; Single Inline Memory Modules; Single Inline Package; SIP; Slot; Sound Card; Video Card;

PCI
Peripheral Component Interconnect. A 32 bit expansion slot used to plug in extra expansion cards in order to upgrade the computer.
See Also: *32 Bit; Accelerated Graphics Port; Advanced Graphics Port; AGP; AGP Slot; Expansion Card; Expansion Slot; Fax Card; Graphics Card; Interface; Memory Board; Motherboard; PCB; PCMCIA; Peripheral Component Interconnect; Personal Computer Memory Card International Association; Printed Circuit Board; Slot; Sound Card; Thirty Two Bit; Video Card;*

PCMCIA
Personal Computer Memory Card International Association. An industry standard applied to the manufacture of printed circuit boards and memory cards.
See Also: *Accelerated Graphics Port; Advanced Graphics Port; AGP; AGP Slot; Application Specific Integrated Circuits; ASICS; Chipset; EIDE; Enhanced Intelligent Drive Electronics; Expansion Card; Expansion Slot; Fax Card; Graphics Card; IDE; Integrated Drive Electronics; Memory Board; Memory Card; Motherboard; PCB; PCI; Peripheral Component Interconnect; Personal Computer Memory Card International Association; Printed Circuit Board; Slot; Sound Card; Video Card;*

PDA
Personal Digital Assistant. A hand held computer that is used as a personal organiser containing address books, notes, applications, calendar etc. The later models have a stylus to navigate around the screen.
See Also: *Computer; Device; Equipment; Hand Held Device; Hardware; Kit; Light Pen; Mouse; Palmtop Computer; Personal Digital Assistant;*

PDF
Portable Document Format. A type of file containing text and graphics and has a file extension of '.pdf'.
See Also: *Attachment; BitMaP; BMP; Extension; Filename Extension; Format; GIF; Graphical Interchange Format; Graphics; Image Map; Image Processing; Joint Photographic Experts Group; JPEG; JPG;*

MIME; Multipurpose Internet Mail Extensions; Portable Document Format; Rich Text Format; RTF; Tag Image File Format; TIFF;

PDL
Page Description Language. A programming language that defines the layout and content of a page.
See Also: *APL; Code; Extensible Hypertext Markup Language; eXtensible Markup Language; High Level Language; HTML; Hypertext Mark-Up Language; Instruction Set; JAVA; JAVASCRIPT; Language; Page Description Language; Programming Language; Software; XHTML; XML;*

Peripheral
An external device connected to a computer. e.g. tape unit, printer.
See Also: *3.5 Inch; 5.25 Inch; Access; Acoustic Coupler; Analogue; Analogue Digital Converter; Analogue Monitor; Anti Glare Screen; Backing Store; Barrel Printer; Black Box; Bubble Jet; Cathode Ray Tube; CCD; CD-ROM Drive; CD-RW Drive; CGA; Charge Coupled Device; Client Server; Colour Graphics Adaptor; Compatible; Configuration; CRT; Cut Sheet Feeder; Daisywheel; DAT; Deck; Device; Device Driver; Digital Analog Converter; Digital Audio Tape; Digital Monitor; Digital Versatile Disk; DIP Switch; Disk; Disk Drive; Disk Pack; Disk Size; Disk Storage; Diskette; Display; Dongle; Dot Matrix; Drive; Drum Printer; DVD; EGA; Emulate; Emulation; Enhanced Graphic Adaptor; Environment; Equipment; Extended Video Array; FDD; Five and a quarter; Fixed Disk Drive; Flatbed Scanner; Floppy Disk; Floppy Disk Drive; Front End Processor; Hand Held Device; Hard Disk Drive; Hardware; HDD; Inkjet; Intelligent Terminal; Interface; Keyboard; Kit; Laser Jet; Laser Printer; LCD; LCD Printer; Leading Edge; LED; Light Emitting Diode; Light Pen; Line Printer; Liquid Crystal Display; Liquid Crystal Display Printer; Load; Mag Tape; Magnetic Disk; Magnetic Tape; Mass Storage; Matrix Printer; Modem; Modulator Demodulator; Monitor; Monochrome; Mouse; OCR; Off Line; OMR; Optical Character Reader; Optical Character Recognition; Optical Drive; Optical Mark Recognition; Optical Scanner; Pack; Page Printer; Plasma Screen; Plotter; Plug and Play; Plug Compatible; Printer; Recording Device; Remote Device; Scanner; Screen; Server; Sheet Feeder; State of the Art; Storage; Store; Streamer; Super Twist LCD; Super VGA; Super Video Graphics Array; SVGA; System; Tape Deck; Tape Streamer; Terminal; TFT; Thermal Printer; Thin-Film Transistor; Three and a Half; Touch Screen; Tracker Ball; VDT; VDU; VGA; Video Display Terminal; Video Graphics Array; Visual Display*

Terminal; Visual Display Unit; Webcam; Winchester Disk; XGA; Zip Drive;

Peripheral Component Interconnect
(PCI). A 32 bit expansion slot used to plug in extra expansion cards in order to upgrade the computer.
See Also: *32 Bit; Accelerated Graphics Port; Advanced Graphics Port; AGP; AGP Slot; Expansion Card; Expansion Slot; Fax Card; Graphics Card; Interface; Memory Board; Motherboard; PCB; PCI; PCMCIA; Personal Computer Memory Card International Association; Printed Circuit Board; Slot; Sound Card; Thirty Two Bit; Video Card;*

PERL
Practical Extraction and Reporting Language. A high level programming language used mainly to create Common Gateway Interfaces.
See Also: *3GL; 4GL; ADA; ALGOL; APL; BASIC; C or C++; CGI; CLIPPER; COBOL; Code; Code Generator; Common Gateway Interface; Compiler; Compiling; CORAL; FORTH; FORTRAN; Fourth Generation Language; High Level Language; Instruction Set; JAVA; JAVASCRIPT; Language; LISP; LOGO; Module; NATURAL; PASCAL; PICK; PILOT; PL/1; Practical Extraction and Reporting Language; Program; Programming Language; PROLOG; RPG; Software; Source Code; Structured Program; Syntax; Third Generation Language; Visual Basic;*

Personal Computer
(PC). Another name for a microcomputer.
See Also: *1st Generation; 2nd Generation; 3rd Generation; 4th Generation; Advanced Technology; Analogue Computer; AT; Compatible; Computer; Computer Power; Configuration; Cross Platform; Desktop; Digital Computer; Downsizing; EDS; Electronic Data System; Environment; Equipment; Extended Technology; Firewire; Hardware; IBM (tm) Compatible; Information System; Information Technology; Installation; IS; IT; Kit; Laptop; Leading Edge; Machine; Micro; Microcomputer; Multi Platform; Notebook; OEM; Original Equipment Manufacturer; Palmtop Computer; PC; Platform; Portable; Power; Standalone; State of the Art; Tower Computer; Turnkey; Voice Activated; XT;*

Personal Computer Memory Card International Association
(PCMCIA). An industry standard applied to the manufacture of printed circuit boards and memory cards.
See Also: *Accelerated Graphics Port; Advanced Graphics Port; AGP; AGP Slot; Application Specific Integrated Circuits; ASICS; Chipset; EIDE; Enhanced Intelligent Drive Electronics; Expansion Card; Expansion Slot; Fax Card; Graphics Card; IDE; Integrated Drive Electronics; Memory Board; Memory Card; Motherboard; PCB; PCI; PCMCIA; Peripheral Component Interconnect; Printed Circuit Board; Slot; Sound Card; Video Card;*

Personal Digital Assistant
(PDA). A hand held computer that is used as a personal organiser containing address books, notes, applications, calendar etc. The later models have a stylus to navigate around the screen.
See Also: *Computer; Device; Equipment; Hand Held Device; Hardware; Kit; Light Pen; Mouse; PDA;*

Physical Design
A hardware or software system design, normally in graphic form, which shows the physical processes of the system as opposed to the logical processes. i.e. 'how' the system does it instead of 'what' it does.
See Also: *A/P; Analyst; Analyst Programmer; Audit Trail; B/A; Bespoke; Business Analyst; CASE; Case Tool; Computer Aided Software Engineering; Design; Development; Flowchart; Full Project Life Cycle; Logical Design; Model; Modular; O & M; Object Oriented Analysis; Object Oriented Design; Object Oriented Programming; OOA; OOD; OOP; Organisation & Methods; Process Model; Program Specification; Programmer; Project Life Cycle; S/A; S/P; Specification; Structured Design; System Analysis; System Analyst; Systems Programmer;*

PICK
A high level computer programming language.
See Also: *3GL; 4GL; ADA; ALGOL; APL; BASIC; C or C++; CLIPPER; COBOL; Code; Code Generator; Compiler; Compiling; CORAL; FORTH; FORTRAN; Fourth Generation Language; High Level Language; Instruction Set; JAVA; JAVASCRIPT; Language; LISP; LOGO; Module; NATURAL; PASCAL; PERL; PILOT; PL/1; Practical Extraction and Reporting Language; Program; Programming Language; PROLOG; RPG; Software; Source Code; Structured Program; Syntax; Third Generation Language; Visual Basic;*

Pico Second
One million millionth of a second.
See Also: *Access Time; Baud Rate; Bits Per Second; BPS; Characters Per Second; Clock Speed; CPS; Gbps; Kbps; Mbps; Microsecond; Millisecond; Ms; Nanosecond; Ns; Seek Time;*

Picture
An edit mask used when data is printed or displayed which formats the data into a required format. e.g. an internal number in the computer of 001234 with a mask of ZZZZ.ZZ will print or display the number as 12.34.
See Also: *Code; Line Editor; Page Editor; Printout; Syntax; Wildcard;*

Pie Chart
A graphical representation in the form of a pie showing the breakdown of percentages or amounts where each breakdown is represented by a sector of the pie.
See Also: *Graphics; Image Map; Image Processing; Output;*

PILOT
A high level computer programming language.
See Also: *3GL; 4GL; ADA; ALGOL; APL; BASIC; C or C++; CLIPPER; COBOL; Code; Code Generator; Compiler; Compiling; CORAL; FORTH; FORTRAN; Fourth Generation Language; High Level Language; Instruction Set; JAVA; JAVASCRIPT; Language; LISP; LOGO; Module; NATURAL; PASCAL; PERL; PICK; PL/1; Practical Extraction and Reporting Language; Program; Programming Language; PROLOG; RPG; Software; Source Code; Structured Program; Syntax; Third Generation Language; Visual Basic;*

PING
A method of checking if a computer is connected to the Internet.
See Also: *Access; ACK; Busy; Cyberspace; Handshake; Internet; Internet Protocol; Internet Service Provider; IP; ISP; Net; Off Line; Online; Point Of Presence; Point to Point Protocol; Polling; POP; PPP; Provider; Serial Line Internet Protocol; Service Provider; SLIP; Surfing; The Net;*

Pirate Copy
An illegal copy of software, music or video pictures.
See Also: *Hacker; Motion Picture Experts Group; MP3; MPEG; MPG; Public Domain; Software;*

Pixel
A single dot on a screen which is the smallest unit of resolution and which formats the characters or graphics seen on the screen. It is an abbreviation of 'picture element' and pronounced "picksil".
See Also: *BitMaP; BMP; Clip Art; Cursor; Display; GIF; Graphical Interchange Format; Graphics; High Resolution; Image Map; Image Processing; Joint Photographic Experts Group; JPEG; JPG; Low Resolution; Paint Screen; Resolution; Screen Burn; Sprite; Twip; Video Card; Window;*

PKZIP
A program which compresses and decompresses data files to reduce storage space and data transmission times.
See Also: *Compressed File; Compression; Data Compression; Decompression; Packed Data; Program; Self Extracting File; Zip;*

PL/1
A high-level computer programming language used for both scientific and commercial applications.
See Also: *3GL; 4GL; ADA; ALGOL; APL; BASIC; C or C++; CLIPPER; COBOL; Code; Code Generator; Compiler; Compiling; CORAL; FORTH; FORTRAN; Fourth Generation Language; High Level Language; Instruction Set; JAVA; JAVASCRIPT; Language; LISP; LOGO; Module; NATURAL; PASCAL; PERL; PICK; PILOT; Practical Extraction and Reporting Language; Program; Programming Language; PROLOG; RPG; Software; Source Code; Structured Program; Syntax; Third Generation Language; Visual Basic;*

Plasma Screen
A screen which displays characters made up from gas being ionised to form each character.
See Also: *Analogue Monitor; Anti Glare Screen; Cathode Ray Tube; CGA; Colour Graphics Adaptor; CRT; Device; Digital Monitor; Display; EGA; Enhanced Graphic Adaptor; Environment; Equipment; Extended Video Array; Graphics Card; Hardware; High Resolution; Installation; Intelligent Terminal; Interlaced; Kit; LCD; Liquid Crystal Display; Low Resolution; Monitor; Monochrome; Output; Paint Screen; Peripheral; Prompt; Resolution; Screen; Screen Burn; Split Screen; Super Twist LCD; Super VGA; Super Video Graphics Array; SVGA; Terminal; TFT; Thin-Film Transistor; Touch Screen; Twip; VDT; VDU; VGA; Video Card; Video Display Terminal; Video Graphics Array; Video Random Access Memory; Visual Display Terminal; Visual Display Unit; VRAM; XGA;*

Platform
A computer or range of computers designed with the same standard to allow the same operating system or applications to run on them.
See Also: *Advanced Technology; Analogue Computer; AT; Compatible; Computer; Computer Power; Configuration; Cross Platform; Desktop; Digital Computer; Downsizing; EDS; Electronic Data System; Emulate; Emulation; Environment; Equipment; Extended Technology; Hardware; IBM (tm) Compatible; Information System; Information Technology; Installation; IS; IT; Kit; Laptop; Leading Edge; Machine; Mainframe; Micro; Microcomputer; Midrange System; Minicomputer; Multi Platform; Node; Notebook; Number Cruncher; Open System; Palmtop Computer; PC; Personal Computer; Portable; Power; Standalone; State of the Art; System; Tower Computer; Turnkey; Voice Activated; XT;*

Plotter
A peripheral device attached to a computer which is used for printing graphical designs.
See Also: *Bi Directional; Configuration; Device; Environment; Equipment; Hard Copy; Hardware; Installation; Kit; Landscape; Output; Peripheral; Portrait; Printer; Printout;*

Plug and Play
A term used to describe the upgrading of computers with devices or printed circuit boards where the computer reconfigures itself to recognise the new additions and does not rely on manual configuration. The computer is automatically readied for use after plugging in the additions.
See Also: *Compatible; Configuration; Configuring; Convert; Device; Peripheral; Plug Compatible; Upgrade;*

Plug Compatible
Hardware which can be connected as a replacement to existing equipment without any changes.
See Also: *Compatible; Configuration; Configuring; Device; Equipment; Hardware; Kit; Leading Edge; Peripheral; Plug and Play; State of the Art; Upgrade;*

Point Of Presence
(POP). An access point location to the Internet.
See Also: *Acceptable User Policy; Access; AUP; CGI; Common Gateway Interface; Cyberspace; Host; HTTP; Hypertext Transfer Protocol; Internet; Internet Protocol Address; Internet Service Provider; IP Address; ISP; Net; PING; Point to Point Protocol; POP; PPP; Provider; Proxy Server; Service Provider; The Net;*

Point of Sales
(POS). A device in a retail outlet which records items purchased, and may be connected to a computer to update stock totals.
See Also: *Distributed System/Network; Download; EDI; EFT; EFTPOS; Electronic Data Interchange; Electronic Fund Transfer; Electronic Fund Transfer Point of Sales; Front End Processor; Intelligent Terminal; Network; POS; Upload;*

Point to Point Protocol
(PPP). An Internet connection which allows the use of a computer to become part of the Internet.
See Also: *Acceptable User Policy; Access; AUP; Chat; Chatroom; Client Server Protocol; Cybercafe; Cyberspace; Handshake; Host; Host Processor; HTTP; Hypertext Transfer Protocol; Internet; Internet Protocol; Internet Protocol Address; Internet Relay Chat; Internet Service Provider; IP; IP Address; IRC; ISP; Net; PING; Point Of Presence; POP; PPP; Provider; Proxy Server; Secure Socket Layer; Serial Line Internet Protocol; Service Provider; Simple Mail Transfer Protocol; SLIP; SMTP; SSL; The Net; WAP; Wap Internet Service Provider; Webhost; Wireless Application Protocol; WISP;*

Polling
The automatic checking of ports and circuits in a computer to detect if any data is to be processed. Each port or circuit is allocated a time slice to work in and polling takes place many times a second.
See Also: *Busy; Client Server; Intranet; Network; PING; Ring Network; Server;*

POP
Point Of Presence. An access point to locate an Internet Service Provider on the Internet.
See Also: *Acceptable User Policy; Access; AUP; CGI; Common Gateway Interface; Cyberspace; Host; HTTP; Hypertext Transfer Protocol; Internet; Internet Protocol Address; Internet Service Provider; IP Address; ISP; Net; PING; Point Of Presence; Point to Point Protocol; PPP; Provider; Proxy Server; Service Provider; The Net;*

POP
Post Office Protocol. A method of e-mail storage.
See Also: *Body; Electronic Mail; E-mail; Internet Service Provider; ISP; Mailbox; Mailserver; MIME; Multipurpose Internet Mail Extensions; Post Office Protocol; Protocol; Provider; Service Provider;*

Pop Up Menu
A list of items on the screen from which to choose. It is activated by entering specific control codes from the keyboard or with a mouse.
See Also: *Click; Display; Drop-Down Menu; Hot Key; Instruction; Keyboard; Menu; Mouse; Pull Down Menu; Toolbar; User Friendly;*

Port
An interface connection socket on a computer or peripheral device.
See Also: *Accelerated Graphics Port; Access; Advanced Graphics Port; AGP; AGP Slot; Dongle; ECP; Enhanced Parallel Port; EPP; Expansion Slot; Extended Capabilities Port; Interface; LAN Port; LPT Port; MIDI; Musical Instrument Digital Interface; Parallel Interface; Parallel Port; RS232; RS423; Serial Interface; Serial Port; Slot; UART; Universal Asynchronous Receiver/Transmitter;*

Portable
A portable computer small enough to use on your lap. The screen, which is in the lid that opens and closes the unit, forms an integral part of the unit.
See Also: *1st Generation; 2nd Generation; 3rd Generation; 4th Generation; Advanced Technology; Analogue Computer; AT; Compatible; Computer; Computer Power; Configuration; Cross Platform; Desktop; Digital Computer; Downsizing; EDS; Electronic Data System; Environment; Equipment; Extended Technology; Hardware; IBM (tm) Compatible; Information System; Information Technology; Installation; IS; IT; Kit; Laptop; Machine; Micro; Microcomputer; Multi Platform; Notebook; OEM; Original Equipment Manufacturer; Palmtop Computer; PC; Personal Computer; Platform; Power; Standalone; Tower Computer; Turnkey; Voice Activated; XT;*

Portable Document Format
(PDF). A type of file containing text and graphics and has a file extension of '.pdf'.
See Also: *Attachment; BitMaP; BMP; Extension; Filename Extension; Format; GIF; Graphical Interchange Format; Graphics; Image Map; Image Processing; Joint Photographic Experts Group; JPEG; JPG; MIME; Multipurpose Internet Mail Extensions; PDF; Rich Text Format; RTF; Tag Image File Format; TIFF;*

Portal
The first website a surfer sees when browsing the web from where they can select a range of services, a search engine or another website.
See Also: *Anchor; Browser; CGI; Common Gateway Interface; Cyberspace; Home Page; Host; Internet Service Provider; ISP; Link; Page; Provider; Search Engine; Service Provider; Site; Spider; Surfing; The Web; Universal/Uniform Resource Locator; URL; Webhost; Webring; Website; World Wide Web; WWW;*

Portrait
Printing which appears on the paper vertically instead of horizontally.
See Also: *Bi Directional; Bubble Jet; Characters Per Inch; CPI; Daisywheel; Dot Matrix; Format; Hard Copy; Inkjet; Landscape; Laser Jet; Laser Printer; LCD Printer; Letter Quality; Line Printer; Liquid Crystal Display Printer; LQ; Matrix Printer; Near Letter Quality; NLQ; Output; Page Printer; Plotter; Printer; Printout; Thermal Printer;*

POS
Point of Sales. A device in a retail outlet which records items purchased, and may be connected to a computer to update stock totals.
See Also: *Distributed System/Network; Download; EDI; EFT; EFTPOS; Electronic Data Interchange; Electronic Fund Transfer; Electronic Fund Transfer Point of Sales; Front End Processor; Intelligent Terminal; Network; Point of Sales; Upload;*

Post Office Protocol
(POP). A method of e-mail storage.
See Also: *Body; Electronic Mail; E-mail; Internet Service Provider; ISP; Mailbox; Mailserver; MIME; Multipurpose Internet Mail Extensions; POP; Protocol; Provider; Service Provider;*

Postscript
A standard format for page printing with its own fonts.
See Also: *Bi Directional; Bubble Jet; Dot Matrix; Font; Font Cartridge; Format; Hard Copy; Inkjet; Laser Jet; Laser Printer; LCD Printer; Letter Quality; Line Printer; Liquid Crystal Display Printer; LQ; Matrix Printer; Near Letter Quality; NLQ; Output; Page Printer; Printer; Printer Driver; Printout; Scalable Fonts;*

Power

The speed and size of a computer, in particular the chip processing speed, the disks access speed and the size of memory and storage capacities.

See Also: *286; 3.5 Inch; 32 Bit; 386; 486; 5.25 Inch; Backing Store; Central Processing Unit; Chip; Chipset; Clock Speed; Computer; Computer Power; Conventional Memory; Co-processor; Core; Core Dump; CPU; Cross Platform; DDR SDRAM; Desktop; Digital Computer; Digital Versatile Disk; DIMM; Direct Random Access Memory; Disk; Disk Cache; Disk Drive; Disk Pack; Disk Size; Disk Storage; Diskette; Double Data Rate SDRAM; DRAM; Drive; Dual Inline Memory Module; DVD; Dynamic Memory; EEROM; Electrically Erasable Read Only Memory; Electronically Programmed Read Only Memory; EMS; EPROM; Erasable Programmable Read Only Memory; Expanded Memory; Expanded Memory Specification; Extended Memory; FDD; Five and a quarter; Fixed Disk Drive; Flash Memory; Floppy Disk; Floppy Disk Drive; GHz; Gigahertz; Hard Disk Drive; HDD; High Memory; IBM (tm) Compatible; Kbps; KHz; Kilohertz; Laptop; Machine; Magnetic Core; Magnetic Disk; Mass Storage; Maths Co-processor; Megabyte; Megahertz; Memory; MHz; Microprocessor; Midrange System; Million Instructions Per Second; Minicomputer; MIPS; Notebook; Pack; Palmtop Computer; Parallel Processor; PC; Personal Computer; Platform; Portable; Processor; Programmable Read Only Memory; PROM; RAM; RAM Disk; Rambus Dynamic Random Access Memory; Random Access Memory; RDRAM; Read Only Memory; ROM; SDRAM; Shadow RAM Memory; Silicon Chip; SIMM; Single Inline Memory Modules; Single Inline Package; SIP; Storage; Store; Synchronous Dynamic Random Access Memory; System; Thirty Two Bit; Three and a Half; Tower Computer;*

PPM

Pages Per Minute. The number of pages which a printer can optimally print in a minute.

See Also: *Barrel Printer; Bubble Jet; Daisywheel; Dot Matrix; Drum Printer; Duplex Printing; Hard Copy; Inkjet; Laser Jet; Laser Printer; LCD Printer; Line Printer; Lines Per Minute; Liquid Crystal Display Printer; Lpm; Matrix Printer; Page Printer; Pages Per Minute; Printer; Printout; Simplex Printing; Thermal Printer;*

PPP

Point to Point Protocol. An Internet connection which allows the use of a computer to become part of the Internet.

See Also: *Acceptable User Policy; Access; AUP; Chat; Chatroom; Client Server Protocol; Cybercafe; Cyberspace; Handshake; Host; Host*

Processor; HTTP; Hypertext Transfer Protocol; Internet; Internet Protocol; Internet Protocol Address; Internet Relay Chat; Internet Service Provider; IP; IP Address; IRC; ISP; Net; PING; Point Of Presence; Point to Point Protocol; POP; Provider; Proxy Server; Secure Socket Layer; Serial Line Internet Protocol; Service Provider; Simple Mail Transfer Protocol; SLIP; SMTP; SSL; The Net; WAP; Wap Internet Service Provider; Webhost; Wireless Application Protocol; WISP;

Practical Extraction and Reporting Language
(PERL). A high level programming language used mainly to create Common Gateway Interfaces.
See Also: *3GL; 4GL; ADA; ALGOL; APL; BASIC; C or C++; CGI; CLIPPER; COBOL; Code; Code Generator; Common Gateway Interface; Compiler; Compiling; CORAL; FORTH; FORTRAN; Fourth Generation Language; High Level Language; Instruction Set; JAVA; JAVASCRIPT; Language; LISP; LOGO; Module; NATURAL; PASCAL; PERL; PICK; PILOT; PL/1; Program; Programming Language; PROLOG; RPG; Software; Source Code; Structured Program; Syntax; Third Generation Language; Visual Basic;*

Print Spooler
Software which remains in memory and is activated when output is sent to the printer. It captures the output and stores it temporarily until the printer becomes available. The word SPOOL is an acronym of Simultaneous Peripheral Operation On-Line.
See Also: *Batch Processing; Output; Printer Driver; Printout; Program; System Software;*

Printed Circuit Board
(PCB). A board that has electrical components soldered onto it, which are connected to each other by metal strips. The board may perform a specific task and may be connected to other boards. e.g. mother board.
See Also: *Accelerated Graphics Port; Advanced Graphics Port; AGP; AGP Slot; Application Specific Integrated Circuits; ASICS; Chip; Chipset; Expansion Card; Expansion Slot; Fax Card; Graphics Card; IC; Integrated Circuit; Memory Board; Memory Card; Motherboard; PCB; PCI; PCMCIA; Peripheral Component Interconnect; Personal Computer Memory Card International Association; Silicon Chip; SIMM; Single Inline Memory Modules; Single Inline Package; SIP; Slot; Sound Card; Video Card;*

Printer
A device which produces paper output from a computer. e.g. dot matrix, laser.
See Also: *Barrel Printer; Bi Directional; Bubble Jet; Characters Per Inch; Configuration; CPI; Cut Sheet Feeder; Daisywheel; Device; Digital Analog Converter; Dot Matrix; Drum Printer; Duplex Printing; Environment; Equipment; Font Cartridge; Hard Copy; Hardware; Inkjet; Installation; Kit; Landscape; Laser Jet; Laser Printer; LCD Printer; Line Printer; Lines Per Minute; Liquid Crystal Display Printer; Lpm; LPT Port; Matrix Printer; Output; Page Printer; Pages Per Minute; Peripheral; Plotter; Portrait; Postscript; PPM; Printer Driver; Printout; Remote Device; Sheet Feeder; Simplex Printing; Spooler; System; Thermal Printer; Toner;*

Printer Driver
A program which allows application software to control the printer.
See Also: *Barrel Printer; Bi Directional; Bubble Jet; Configuring; Daisywheel; Device Driver; Dot Matrix; Driver; Drum Printer; Duplex Printing; Inkjet; Laser Jet; Laser Printer; LCD Printer; Letter Quality; Line Printer; Lines Per Minute; Liquid Crystal Display Printer; Lpm; LQ; Matrix Printer; Near Letter Quality; NLQ; Page Printer; Postscript; Print Spooler; Printer; Printout; Simplex Printing; Software Driver; Thermal Printer;*

Printout
The result of formatted information produced on paper.
See Also: *Barrel Printer; Bi Directional; Bubble Jet; Characters Per Inch; Core Dump; CPI; Daisywheel; Dot Matrix; Drum Printer; Dump; Duplex Printing; Hard Copy; Inkjet; Landscape; Laser Jet; Laser Printer; LCD Printer; Letter Quality; Line Printer; Lines Per Minute; Liquid Crystal Display Printer; Lpm; LQ; Matrix Printer; Near Letter Quality; NLQ; Output; Page Printer; Pages Per Minute; Picture; Plotter; Portrait; Postscript; PPM; Print Spooler; Printer; Printer Driver; Simplex Printing; Thermal Printer; Toner;*

Process
(1) A set of tasks to achieve a specific job. (2) The processing of those tasks.
See Also: *Audit Trail; AUTOEXEC.BAT; Batch Processing; Computation; Compute; End of Job; EOJ; Instruction Set; JCL; Job Control Language; Macro; Model; Modular; O & M; Object Oriented Analysis; Object Oriented Design; Object Oriented Programming; OOA; OOD; OOP; Organisation & Methods; Process Model; Processing;*

Program; Reengineering; Run; Run Time; Script; Software System; Subroutine;

Process Model
A graphical design of procedures for a task or application showing what data is used and what happens to that data.
See Also: *B/A; Business Analyst; CASE; Case Tool; Computer Aided Software Engineering; Data Base Analyst; Data Flow; Data Flow Diagram; Data Model; DBA; Design; DFD; Flowchart; Full Project Life Cycle; Logical Design; Model; Modular; O & M; Object Oriented Analysis; Object Oriented Design; Object Oriented Programming; OOA; OOD; OOP; Organisation & Methods; Physical Design; Process; Program Specification; Project Life Cycle; Reengineering; S/A; Software Development Cycle; Specification; Structured Design; Structured Program; System Analysis; System Analyst; Top Down Technique;*

Processing
The manipulation, analysis and storage of data on a computer.
See Also: *Audit Trail; Batch Processing; Bespoke; CAD; CADCAM; CADMAT; CAE; CAI; CAM; CBT; Computation; Compute; Computer Aided Design; Computer Aided Design and Manufacturing; Computer Aided Design Manufacture and Test; Computer Aided Engineering; Computer Aided Instruction; Computer Aided Manufacturing; Computer Based Training; Data Base Management System; Data Processing; DBMS; DP; Dynamically; EDS; Electronic Data System; Facilities Management; FM; Geographical Information System; GIS; Information Technology; Intelligent Terminal; IT; Merge; Process; RDBMS/RDMS; Reengineering; Relational Database Management System; Run; Run Time; Software System; Spreadsheet; Teleprocessing System; TPS; Transaction Processing; Word Processor; WP;*

Processor
The Central Processing Unit or CPU. The central area of a computer which controls the entire operation of a computer. It contains the memory and executes program instructions.
See Also: *286; 386; 486; ALU; Application Specific Integrated Circuits; Arithmetic and Logic Unit; ASICS; Central Processing Unit; Chip; Chipset; Clock Speed; Computer Power; Co-processor; CPU; Flip Flop; GHz; Gigahertz; IC; Industry Standard Architecture; Integrated Circuit; ISA; KHz; Kilohertz; Large Scale Integration; LSI; Maths Co-processor; MCA; Megahertz; MHz; Micro Channel Architecture; Microprocessor; Mix; Parallel Processor; Power; Reduced Instruction Set Computing;*

RISC; Semiconductor; Silicon Chip; Solid State; Sound Chip; System; Transistor; Zero Wait State;

Program
A collection of statements, instructions and commands instructing a computer to perform specific tasks.
See Also: *3GL; 4GL; A/P; Abort; ADA; ALGOL; Analyst Programmer; API; APL; Applet; Application; Application Program Interface; Assembler; Assembly Code; BASIC; Bloatware; Bubble Sort; Bug; C or C++; Call; Chain; CLIPPER; COBOL; Code; Code Generator; CODEC; Command; COmpressor DECompressor; Configuration; CORAL; Daemon; Debugger; Desk Top Publishing; Development; Device Driver; DLL; Driver; DTP; Dynamic Link Library; Edit; EXE; Execute; Firmware; FORTH; FORTRAN; Fourth Generation Language; Freeware; Function; Gopher; Graphical User Interface; GUI; Information Technology; Instruction; Instruction Set; Internet Relay Chat; Invoke; IRC; IT; JAVA; JAVASCRIPT; Language; Line Editor; LISP; Load; LOGO; Loop; Macro; Memory Resident; Mix; Module; NATURAL; Nesting; Overlay; Page Editor; PASCAL; Patch; PERL; PICK; PILOT; PKZIP; PL/1; Practical Extraction and Reporting Language; Print Spooler; Process; Program Crash; Program Specification; Programmer; Programming Language; PROLOG; Query Language; RPG; Run; Run Time; S/P; Script; Self Extracting File; Software; Software Driver; Software System; Source Code; Spooler; SQL; Structured Program; Structured Query Language; Subroutine; Swapping; Syntax; System Software; Systems Programmer; Terminate and Stay Resident; Third Generation Language; TSR; Virus; Visual Basic;*

Program Crash
A state when a program stops running due to a bug in the program.
See Also: *Abort; Bug; Crash; Debug; Debugger; Died; Downtime; General Protection Fault; GPF; Hangs; Head Crash; Hung; Machine Crash; Program; Roll Back; System Hangs; Virus; Worm;*

Program Specification
A document defining what a program is required to do.
See Also: *A/P; Analyst Programmer; Design; Development; Flowchart; Full Project Life Cycle; Logical Design; Model; Modular; Object Oriented Analysis; Object Oriented Design; Object Oriented Programming; OOA; OOD; OOP; Physical Design; Process Model; Program; Programmer; Project Life Cycle; Reengineering; S/P; Software*

Development Cycle; Structured Design; System Analyst; Systems Programmer;

Programmable Read Only Memory
(PROM). A ROM chip whose contents cannot be changed unless programmed using a special device.
See Also: *Basic Input Output System; BIOS; Bubble Memory; Buffer; Cache Memory; CMOS; Complementary Metal Oxide Semiconductor Memory; Computer Power; Conventional Memory; Core; Core Dump; DDR SDRAM; DIMM; Direct Memory Access; Direct Random Access Memory; Disk Cache; DMA; Double Data Rate SDRAM; DRAM; Dual Inline Memory Module; Dynamic Memory; Dynamically; EEROM; Electrically Erasable Read Only Memory; Electronically Programmed Read Only Memory; EMS; EPROM; Erasable Programmable Read Only Memory; Expanded Memory; Expanded Memory Specification; Extended Memory; Flash Memory; High Memory; Magnetic Core; Memory; Memory Board; Memory Caching; Memory Card; Memory Resident; Mix; Power; PROM; RAM; RAM Disk; Rambus Dynamic Random Access Memory; Random Access Memory; RDRAM; Read Only Memory; ROM; ROM Resident; SDRAM; Shadow RAM Memory; SIMM; Single Inline Memory Modules; Single Inline Package; SIP; Stack; Store; Swapping; Synchronous Dynamic Random Access Memory; Upper Memory; Video Random Access Memory; VRAM; Working Storage; Workspace;*

Programmer
A person who writes or codes a program for a computer.
See Also: *A/P; Analyst; Analyst Programmer; B/A; Business Analyst; Code; Contractor; Data Base Analyst; Data Processing Manager; DBA; Design; Development; DPM; Full Project Life Cycle; Language; Logical Design; Loop; Physical Design; Program; Program Specification; Programming Language; Project Life Cycle; S/A; S/P; Software; Software Development Cycle; Software House; Specification; Structured Design; Structured Program; System Analyst; Systems Programmer; Technical Author;*

Programming Language
A set of instructions and formats in which to write programs that tell a computer what to do. e.g. BASIC, COBOL.
See Also: *A/P; ADA; ALGOL; Analyst Programmer; APL; Assembler; Assembly Code; BASIC; C or C++; CLIPPER; COBOL; CODASYL; Code; Code Generator; Conference On DAta SYstems Languages; CORAL; Extensible Hypertext Markup Language; eXtensible Markup Language; FORTH; FORTRAN; High Level Language; HTML;*

Hypertext Mark-Up Language; Instruction Set; JAVA; JAVASCRIPT; JCL; Job Control Language; Language; LISP; LOGO; Low Level Language; NATURAL; Page Description Language; PASCAL; PDL; PERL; PICK; PILOT; PL/1; Practical Extraction and Reporting Language; Program; Programmer; PROLOG; RPG; S/P; Software; Source Code; Systems Programmer; XHTML; XML;

Project Life Cycle
All aspects in the development of a project for both hardware and software systems.
See Also: *A/P; Analyst; Analyst Programmer; B/A; Business Analyst; Design; Development; Full Project Life Cycle; Going Live; Hand Holding; Live; Logical Design; Model; Modular; Physical Design; Process Model; Program Specification; Programmer; Reengineering; S/A; S/P; Software Development Cycle; Software House; Specification; Structured Design; System Analysis; System Analyst; Systems Programmer; Technical Author; Upgrade; Walkthrough;*

PROLOG
PROgramming LOGic. A high level computer programming language.
See Also: *3GL; 4GL; ADA; ALGOL; APL; BASIC; C or C++; CLIPPER; COBOL; Code; Code Generator; Compiler; Compiling; CORAL; FORTH; FORTRAN; Fourth Generation Language; High Level Language; Instruction Set; JAVA; JAVASCRIPT; Language; LISP; LOGO; Module; NATURAL; PASCAL; PERL; PICK; PILOT; PL/1; Practical Extraction and Reporting Language; Program; Programming Language; RPG; Software; Source Code; Structured Program; Syntax; Third Generation Language; Visual Basic;*

PROM
Programmable Read Only Memory. A ROM chip whose contents cannot be changed unless programmed using a special device.
See Also: *Basic Input Output System; BIOS; Bubble Memory; Buffer; Cache Memory; CMOS; Complementary Metal Oxide Semiconductor Memory; Computer Power; Conventional Memory; Core; Core Dump; DDR SDRAM; DIMM; Direct Memory Access; Direct Random Access Memory; Disk Cache; DMA; Double Data Rate SDRAM; DRAM; Dual Inline Memory Module; Dynamic Memory; Dynamically; EEROM; Electrically Erasable Read Only Memory; Electronically Programmed Read Only Memory; EMS; EPROM; Erasable Programmable Read Only Memory; Expanded Memory; Expanded Memory Specification; Extended Memory; Flash Memory; High Memory; Magnetic Core; Memory; Memory Board; Memory Caching; Memory Card; Memory Resident;*

Mix; Power; Programmable Read Only Memory; RAM; RAM Disk; Rambus Dynamic Random Access Memory; Random Access Memory; RDRAM; Read Only Memory; ROM; ROM Resident; SDRAM; Shadow RAM Memory; SIMM; Single Inline Memory Modules; Single Inline Package; SIP; Stack; Store; Swapping; Synchronous Dynamic Random Access Memory; Upper Memory; Video Random Access Memory; VRAM; Working Storage; Workspace;

Prompt
A symbol or description on a screen indicating where data is to be entered into the computer.
See Also: *Analogue Monitor; Anti Glare Screen; C Prompt; Cathode Ray Tube; CGA; Colour Graphics Adaptor; CRT; Cursor; Digital Monitor; Display; EGA; Enhanced Graphic Adaptor; Extended Video Array; LCD; Liquid Crystal Display; Monitor; Monochrome; Plasma Screen; Screen; Super Twist LCD; Super VGA; Super Video Graphics Array; SVGA; Terminal; TFT; Thin-Film Transistor; Touch Screen; VDT; VDU; VGA; Video Display Terminal; Video Graphics Array; Visual Display Terminal; Visual Display Unit; XGA;*

Protocol
A standard set of rules applied in the design of equipment and software which allows communication between different equipment and different software.
See Also: *Acceptable User Policy; Access; Acoustic Coupler; AMR; Anonymous FTP; AUP; Automatic Message Routing; Bandwidth; Bluetooth (tm); Broadband; Client Server Protocol; Communications; Compatible; Data Communications; File Transfer Protocol; FTP; Gateway; Handshake; HTTP; Hypertext Transfer Protocol; International Standards Organisation; Internet Protocol; Internet Protocol Address; IP; IP Address; ISO; MIME; Multipurpose Internet Mail Extensions; Narrowband; Open Systems Interconnect; OSI; POP; Post Office Protocol; Secure Socket Layer; Serial Line Internet Protocol; Simple Mail Transfer Protocol; SLIP; SMTP; SSL; TCP/IP; Transmission Control Protocol/Internet Protocol; V90; WAP; Wi-Fi; Wireless Application Protocol; Wireless Fidelity; XMODEM; YMODEM; ZMODEM;*

Provider
Internet Service Provider or ISP. A company which provide users with access to the Internet.
See Also: *Acceptable User Policy; AUP; Browser; CGI; Common Gateway Interface; Cookie; Cyberspace; DNS; Domain Name; Domain*

Name Server; Domain Name System; E-commerce; EDI; Electronic Data Interchange; Handshake; Hit; Home Page; Host; Host Processor; HTTP; Hypertext Transfer Protocol; Information Superhighway; Internet; Internet Relay Chat; Internet Service Provider; IRC; ISP; Mailserver; Net; Newsgroup; PING; Point Of Presence; Point to Point Protocol; POP; POP; Portal; Post Office Protocol; PPP; Proxy Server; Search Engine; Serial Line Internet Protocol; Service Provider; SLIP; Spider; Surfing; The Net; Wap Internet Service Provider; Webhost; WISP;

Proxy Server
A system which protects your computer from the Internet and stores web pages to give faster access to the Internet.
See Also: *Access; CGI; Client Server; Client Server Protocol; Common Gateway Interface; Cookie; Cyberspace; Domain Name Server; Host Processor; Information Superhighway; Interface; Internet; Internet Service Provider; ISP; Mailserver; Net; Node; Page; Point Of Presence; Point to Point Protocol; POP; PPP; Provider; Server; Service Provider; Site; The Net; The Web; Webhost; Webring; Website; World Wide Web; WWW;*

PS/2
A connection on most personal computers used to plug in the mouse and keyboard.
See Also: *Interface; Keyboard; Mouse;*

Public Domain
Programs and files which can be used and modified without permission.
See Also: *BBS; Bulletin Board System; Cybercafe; Cyberspace; Freeware; Gopher; Pirate Copy; Shareware;*

Pull Down Menu
A menu which is displayed on the screen and activated by entering certain control codes from the keyboard or using a mouse.
See Also: *Click; Display; Drop-Down Menu; Hot Key; Instruction; Keyboard; Menu; Mouse; Pop Up Menu; Toolbar; User Friendly;*

Query Language
A language designed to access databases and to manipulate the data in order to format and produce reports easily.
See Also: *Code; Code Generator; Gopher; High Level Language; Instruction Set; Program; Software; Source Code; SQL; Structured Program; Structured Query Language; Syntax;*

R/W

Abbr. of Read/Write. The reading and writing of data to a peripheral device.

See Also: *Access; Archive; Backup; Dead Lock; Deadly Embrace; Direct Access; Heads; I/O; Indexed Sequential Access Method; Input/Output; ISAM; Key; Keyed Sequential Access Method; KSAM; Random Access; Read; Read/Write; Read/Write Head; Recording; Recording Device; Recording Medium; Save; Seek Time; Sequential Access; Serial Access; Store; Write;*

Radio Button

A field on a screen that the user may select by clicking. There is normally more than one Radio Button on a form and when another is selected, the previously selected one is deselected.

See Also: *Click; Data; Data Element; Data Entity; Data Item; Data Type; Field; Graphics; Image Map; Image Processing; Information; Input; Toggle; Variable;*

RAM

Random Access Memory. The memory in a computer from which data can be read as well as written. It is used by programs to process data and the contents are lost when the machine is switched off or reset.

See Also: *Basic Input Output System; BIOS; Bubble Memory; Buffer; Cache Memory; CMOS; Complementary Metal Oxide Semiconductor Memory; Computer Power; Conventional Memory; Core; Core Dump; DDR SDRAM; DIMM; Direct Memory Access; Direct Random Access Memory; Disk Cache; DMA; Double Data Rate SDRAM; DRAM; Dual Inline Memory Module; Dynamic Memory; Dynamically; EEROM; Electrically Erasable Read Only Memory; Electronically Programmed Read Only Memory; EMS; EPROM; Erasable Programmable Read Only Memory; Expanded Memory; Expanded Memory Specification; Extended Memory; Flash Memory; High Memory; Magnetic Core; Memory; Memory Board; Memory Caching; Memory Card; Memory Resident; Mix; Power; Programmable Read Only Memory; PROM; RAM Disk; Rambus Dynamic Random Access Memory; Random Access Memory; RDRAM; Read Only Memory; ROM; SDRAM; Shadow RAM Memory; SIMM; Single Inline Memory Modules; Single Inline Package; SIP; Stack; Store; Swapping; Synchronous Dynamic Random Access Memory; Upper Memory; Video Random Access Memory; VRAM; Working Storage; Workspace;*

RAM Disk
The part of a computers memory set aside for storing files to allow faster access than a disk drive.
See Also: *Absolute Address; Basic Input Output System; BIOS; Bubble Memory; Buffer; Cache Memory; CMOS; Complementary Metal Oxide Semiconductor Memory; Computer Power; Conventional Memory; Core; Core Dump; DDR SDRAM; DIMM; Direct Memory Access; Direct Random Access Memory; Disk Cache; DMA; Double Data Rate SDRAM; DRAM; Dual Inline Memory Module; Dynamic Memory; Dynamically; EEROM; Electrically Erasable Read Only Memory; Electronically Programmed Read Only Memory; EMS; EPROM; Erasable Programmable Read Only Memory; Expanded Memory; Expanded Memory Specification; Extended Memory; Flash Memory; High Memory; Magnetic Core; Memory; Memory Board; Memory Caching; Memory Card; Memory Resident; Mix; Power; Programmable Read Only Memory; PROM; RAM; Rambus Dynamic Random Access Memory; Random Access Memory; RDRAM; Read Only Memory; Relative Address; ROM; SDRAM; Shadow RAM Memory; SIMM; Single Inline Memory Modules; Single Inline Package; SIP; Stack; Store; Swapping; Synchronous Dynamic Random Access Memory; Upper Memory; Video Random Access Memory; VRAM; Working Storage; Workspace;*

Rambus Dynamic Random Access Memory
(RDRAM). A very fast memory with speeds of up to 1,066Mbytes/sec.
See Also: *Basic Input Output System; BIOS; Bubble Memory; Buffer; Cache Memory; CMOS; Complementary Metal Oxide Semiconductor Memory; Computer Power; Conventional Memory; Core; Core Dump; DDR SDRAM; DIMM; Direct Memory Access; Direct Random Access Memory; Disk Cache; DMA; Double Data Rate SDRAM; DRAM; Dual Inline Memory Module; Dynamic Memory; Dynamically; EEROM; Electrically Erasable Read Only Memory; Electronically Programmed Read Only Memory; EMS; EPROM; Erasable Programmable Read Only Memory; Expanded Memory; Expanded Memory Specification; Extended Memory; Flash Memory; High Memory; Magnetic Core; Memory; Memory Board; Memory Caching; Memory Card; Memory Resident; Mix; Power; Programmable Read Only Memory; PROM; RAM; RAM Disk; Random Access Memory; RDRAM; Read Only Memory; ROM; SDRAM; Shadow RAM Memory; SIMM; Single Inline Memory Modules; Single Inline Package; SIP; Stack; Store; Swapping; Synchronous Dynamic Random Access Memory; Upper Memory; Video Random Access Memory; VRAM; Working Storage; Workspace;*

Random Access

The process by which records are read or written to a random file. Records in a random file are physically stored anywhere within the file but are accessed using a key.

See Also: *Access; Access Time; Beginning of File; BOF; Database; DB; Direct Access; End of File; EOF; File; Index Sequential File; Indexed Sequential Access Method; ISAM; Key; Keyed Sequential Access Method; KSAM; R/W; Random File; Read; Read/Write; Sequential Access; Serial Access; Tag; Tag File; Write;*

Random Access Memory

(RAM). The memory in a computer from which data can be read as well as written. It is used by programs to process data and the contents are lost when the machine is switched off or reset.

See Also: *Basic Input Output System; BIOS; Bubble Memory; Buffer; Cache Memory; CMOS; Complementary Metal Oxide Semiconductor Memory; Computer Power; Conventional Memory; Core; Core Dump; DDR SDRAM; DIMM; Direct Memory Access; Direct Random Access Memory; Disk Cache; DMA; Double Data Rate SDRAM; DRAM; Dual Inline Memory Module; Dynamic Memory; Dynamically; EEROM; Electrically Erasable Read Only Memory; Electronically Programmed Read Only Memory; EMS; EPROM; Erasable Programmable Read Only Memory; Expanded Memory; Expanded Memory Specification; Extended Memory; Flash Memory; High Memory; Magnetic Core; Memory; Memory Board; Memory Caching; Memory Card; Memory Resident; Mix; Power; Programmable Read Only Memory; PROM; RAM; RAM Disk; Rambus Dynamic Random Access Memory; RDRAM; Read Only Memory; ROM; SDRAM; Shadow RAM Memory; SIMM; Single Inline Memory Modules; Single Inline Package; SIP; Stack; Store; Swapping; Synchronous Dynamic Random Access Memory; Upper Memory; Video Random Access Memory; VRAM; Working Storage; Workspace;*

Random File

A file in which records are randomly stored. An algorithm is used to decide where the records are stored.

See Also: *ASCII Files; Attachment; Beginning of File; BOF; Compressed File; Database; DB; Direct Access; File; Fragmentation; Index Sequential File; Log File; Random Access; Sequential File; Serial File; Tag File; Temp File;*

RDB
Relational Database. A collection of files whose records are linked to each other if there is some relationship between them.
See Also: *Beginning of File; BOF; Comma Separated Values; CSV; Data Base Analyst; Data Base Management System; Data Dictionary; Data Entity; Database; DB; DBA; DBMS; End of File; Entity; EOF; File; Index Sequential File; Integrated; RDBMS/RDMS; Record; Relational Database; Relational Database Management System; Sequential File; Serial File;*

RDBMS/RDMS
Relational Database Management System. (1) A collection of files whose records are linked to each other if there is some relationship between them. (2) The software system which enables a database to be set up and maintained.
See Also: *Bespoke; Data Base Analyst; Data Base Management System; Data Dictionary; Data Processing; Database; DB; DBA; DBMS; DP; File; Information System; Information Technology; IS; IT; Package; Processing; RDB; Relational Database; Relational Database Management System; Roll Back; Software; Software Package; Software System; System;*

RDRAM
Rambus Dynamic Random Access Memory. A very fast memory with speeds of up to 1,066Mbytes/sec.
See Also: *Basic Input Output System; BIOS; Bubble Memory; Buffer; Cache Memory; CMOS; Complementary Metal Oxide Semiconductor Memory; Computer Power; Conventional Memory; Core; Core Dump; DDR SDRAM; DIMM; Direct Memory Access; Direct Random Access Memory; Disk Cache; DMA; Double Data Rate SDRAM; DRAM; Dual Inline Memory Module; Dynamic Memory; Dynamically; EEROM; Electrically Erasable Read Only Memory; Electronically Programmed Read Only Memory; EMS; EPROM; Erasable Programmable Read Only Memory; Expanded Memory; Expanded Memory Specification; Extended Memory; Flash Memory; High Memory; Magnetic Core; Memory; Memory Board; Memory Caching; Memory Card; Memory Resident; Mix; Power; Programmable Read Only Memory; PROM; RAM; RAM Disk; Rambus Dynamic Random Access Memory; Random Access Memory; Read Only Memory; ROM; SDRAM; Shadow RAM Memory; SIMM; Single Inline Memory Modules; Single Inline Package; SIP; Stack; Store; Swapping; Synchronous Dynamic Random Access Memory; Upper Memory; Video Random Access Memory; VRAM; Working Storage; Workspace;*

Read
The process where a program or recording peripheral such as a disk or tape unit access information from the recording medium. i.e. the reading of a record.
See Also: *Access; Dead Lock; Deadly Embrace; Direct Access; Heads; I/O; Indexed Sequential Access Method; Input/Output; ISAM; Key; Keyed Sequential Access Method; KSAM; R/W; Random Access; Read/Write; Read/Write Head; Recording Medium; Seek Time; Sequential Access; Serial Access;*

Read Only Memory
(ROM). Memory in a computer which contains data or instructions that cannot be changed. e.g. BIOS instructions.
See Also: *Basic Input Output System; BIOS; Bubble Memory; Buffer; Cache Memory; CMOS; Complementary Metal Oxide Semiconductor Memory; Computer Power; Conventional Memory; Core; Core Dump; DDR SDRAM; DIMM; Direct Memory Access; Direct Random Access Memory; Disk Cache; DMA; Double Data Rate SDRAM; DRAM; Dual Inline Memory Module; Dynamic Memory; Dynamically; EEROM; Electrically Erasable Read Only Memory; Electronically Programmed Read Only Memory; EMS; EPROM; Erasable Programmable Read Only Memory; Expanded Memory; Expanded Memory Specification; Extended Memory; Flash Memory; High Memory; Magnetic Core; Memory; Memory Board; Memory Caching; Memory Card; Memory Resident; Mix; Power; Programmable Read Only Memory; PROM; RAM; RAM Disk; Rambus Dynamic Random Access Memory; Random Access Memory; RDRAM; ROM; ROM Resident; SDRAM; Shadow RAM Memory; SIMM; Single Inline Memory Modules; Single Inline Package; SIP; Stack; Store; Swapping; Synchronous Dynamic Random Access Memory; Upper Memory; Video Random Access Memory; VRAM; Working Storage; Workspace;*

Read/Write
(R/W). The reading and writing of data to a peripheral device.
See Also: *Access; Archive; Backup; Dead Lock; Deadly Embrace; Direct Access; Heads; I/O; Indexed Sequential Access Method; Input/Output; ISAM; Key; Keyed Sequential Access Method; KSAM; R/W; Random Access; Read; Read/Write Head; Recording; Recording Device; Recording Medium; Save; Seek Time; Sequential Access; Serial Access; Store; Write;*

Read/Write Head
A part of a recording device which enables data to be read from or written to the recording medium.
See Also: *3.5 Inch; 5.25 Inch; CD-RW Drive; Crash; Digital Versatile Disk; Disk; Disk Drive; Disk Pack; Disk Storage; Diskette; DVD; FDD; Five and a quarter; Fixed Disk Drive; Floppy Disk; Floppy Disk Drive; Hard Disk Drive; HDD; Head Crash; Heads; Machine Crash; Mag Tape; Magnetic Disk; Magnetic Tape; Optical Drive; Pack; R/W; Read; Read/Write; Recording Device; Storage; Store; Streamer; Tape Deck; Tape Streamer; Three and a Half; Winchester Disk; Write; Zip Drive;*

Real Time
The processing of data immediately it is entered into a computer.
See Also: *Audit Trail; EDI; EFT; EFTPOS; Electronic Data Interchange; Electronic Fund Transfer; Electronic Fund Transfer Point of Sales; Forum; IM; Instant Messaging; Interactive; Stream; Virtual Reality; VR; WAP; Wireless Application Protocol;*

Re-boot
A procedure using a set of instructions to initialise a computer when switched on or reset.
See Also: *AUTOEXEC.BAT; Basic Input Output System; BIOS; Boot; Boot Disk; Bootstrap; CMOS; Cold Start; Complementary Metal Oxide Semiconductor Memory; CONFIG.SYS; Disk Operating System; DOS; Instruction; Linux; Memory Resident; Operating System; OS; OS/2; Recovery; Registry; ROM Resident; UNIX; Warm Start;*

Record
A data structure containing one or more data items or fields.
See Also: *Archive; Backup; Comma Separated Values; CSV; Data; Data Element; Data Entity; Data Item; Data Type; Database; DB; Field; Format; Index Sequential File; Information; Key; Locking; Log File; RDB; Record Locking; Recording; Relational Database; Save; Sequential File; Serial File; String; Table; Tag; Trailer; Transaction; Variable;*

Record Locking
The process where a record being updated by one program is locked and thus inhibits other programs from using the record until the lock is released.
See Also: *Client Server; Dead Lock; Deadly Embrace; File Sharing; Hangs; Hung; Locking; Multi User; Multitasking; Record; Security; Server; System Hangs; Write Protect;*

Recording
The process where data is recorded onto a storage device. e.g. disk.
See Also: *3.5 Inch; 5.25 Inch; Access Time; Archive; Backing Store; Backup; Bits Per Inch; BPI; CD-RW Drive; DAT; Data; Data Element; Data Entity; Data Item; Digital Audio Tape; Disk; Disk Drive; Disk Pack; Disk Storage; Diskette; FDD; Five and a quarter; Fixed Disk Drive; Floppy Disk; Floppy Disk Drive; Grandfather, Father, Son; Hard Disk Drive; HDD; Magnetic Disk; Optical Drive; Output; Pack; R/W; Read/Write; Record; Recording Device; Recording Medium; Save; Storage; Store; Streamer; Tag; Tape Deck; Tape Streamer; Three and a Half; Winchester Disk; Write; Zip; Zip Drive;*

Recording Device
A peripheral in which data is stored using a recording medium like floppy disk or magnetic tape.
See Also: *3.5 Inch; 5.25 Inch; Access; Access Time; Archive; Backing Store; Backup; CD-RW Drive; Configuration; DAT; Deck; Device; Device Driver; Digital Audio Tape; Digital Versatile Disk; Disk; Disk Drive; Disk Pack; Disk Storage; Diskette; Drive; DVD; Environment; Equipment; FDD; Five and a quarter; Fixed Disk Drive; Floppy Disk; Floppy Disk Drive; Grandfather, Father, Son; Hand Held Device; Hard Disk Drive; Hardware; HDD; Heads; I/O; Input/Output; Kit; Leading Edge; Load; Mag Tape; Magnetic Disk; Magnetic Tape; Mass Storage; Output; Pack; Peripheral; R/W; Read/Write; Read/Write Head; Recording; Recording Medium; Remote Device; Save; State of the Art; Storage; Store; Streamer; System; Tape Deck; Tape Streamer; Three and a Half; Winchester Disk; Wipe; Write; Zip Drive;*

Recording Medium
The material on which data is stored. It can be floppy disk, hard disk, magnetic tape, CD-ROM etc.
See Also: *3.5 Inch; 5.25 Inch; Archive; Backing Store; Backup; Bits Per Inch; Block; Boot Disk; BPI; CD-ROM; COM; Computer Output Microfilm; Cylinder; DAT; Density; Digital Audio Tape; Digital Versatile Disk; Directory; Disk; Disk Pack; Disk Size; Disk Storage; Diskette; Double Density; DVD; Fiche; Five and a quarter; Floppy Disk; Grandfather, Father, Son; High Density; Mag Tape; Magnetic Disk; Magnetic Tape; Microfiche; Microfilm; Optical Disk; Output; Pack; Paper Tape; R/W; Read; Read/Write; Recording; Recording Device; Root Directory; Save; Sector; Storage; Streamer; Sub Directory; Tape Streamer; Three and a Half; Volume; Winchester Disk;*

Recovery
The process of recovering a computer system to a correct state after there has been a failure. Some computers keep a log of processing and transactions to enable the database to be 'rolled back' to a point in time when the data is known to be correct.
See Also: *Abort; Batch Processing; Boot; Bootstrap; General Protection Fault; GPF; Grandfather, Father, Son; Re-boot; Reengineering; Registry; Restore; Roll Back; Temp File; Warm Start;*

Reduced Instruction Set Computing
(RISC). A computer architecture whose microprocessor has a reduced number of instructions which are the ones most frequently used. This enables the processor to operate at faster speeds.
See Also: *286; 386; 486; Advanced Technology; AT; Extended Technology; Instruction Set; Microprocessor; Parallel Processor; Processor; RISC; XT;*

Reengineering
The process of recreating source designs or programs and redeveloping or redesigning software.
See Also: *Audit Trail; Bloatware; CASE; Case Tool; Computer Aided Software Engineering; Development; Full Project Life Cycle; Model; Modular; Process; Process Model; Processing; Program Specification; Project Life Cycle; Recovery; Software Development Cycle; Specification; Top Down Technique; Walkthrough;*

Register
A storage area in the central processing unit which holds data that is currently being processed.
See Also: *16 Bit; 32 Bit; 64 Bit; 8 Bit; Absolute Address; Address; Eight Bit; Operand; Relative Address; Sixteen Bit; Sixty Four Bit; Store; Thirty Two Bit; Working Storage; Workspace;*

Registry
A data file on a personal computer which contains the configuration settings for the PC.
See Also: *AUTOEXEC.BAT; Batch File; Boot; Bootstrap; CMOS; Cold Start; Command; Complementary Metal Oxide Semiconductor Memory; CONFIG.SYS; Configuration; Configuring; Re-boot; Recovery; Tuning; Tweaking; Warm Start;*

Relational Database
(RDB). A collection of files whose records are linked to each other if there is some relationship between them.
See Also: *Beginning of File; BOF; Comma Separated Values; CSV; Data Base Analyst; Data Base Management System; Data Dictionary; Data Entity; Database; DB; DBA; DBMS; End of File; Entity; EOF; File; Index Sequential File; Integrated; RDB; RDBMS/RDMS; Record; Relational Database Management System; Sequential File; Serial File;*

Relational Database Management System
(RDBMS/RDMS). (1) A collection of files whose records are linked to each other if there is some relationship between them. (2) The software system which enables a database to be set up and maintained.
See Also: *Bespoke; Data Base Analyst; Data Base Management System; Data Dictionary; Data Processing; Database; DB; DBA; DBMS; DP; File; Information System; Information Technology; IS; IT; Package; Processing; RDB; RDBMS/RDMS; Relational Database; Roll Back; Software; Software Package; Software System; System;*

Relative Address
(1) A location in the computers memory referenced by a number in relation to another number. e.g. the 4th item in a list is relative to the 1st + 3. (2) The reference numbers of that location.
See Also: *Absolute Address; Address; Block; Bubble Memory; Buffer; Cache Memory; Conventional Memory; Core; Core Dump; Disk Cache; Flash Memory; Magnetic Core; Memory; Operand; RAM Disk; Register; Store; Upper Memory; Virtual Memory; VM; Volatile Memory; Working Storage; Workspace;*

Releases
New and updated versions of software or hardware.
See Also: *Application; Bespoke; Going Live; Hardware; Install; Installation; Leading Edge; Live; Software; State of the Art; Upgrade;*

Remote Device
A peripheral device connected to a computer and situated at a different location to the computer.
See Also: *Analogue; Anonymous FTP; Client Server; Configuration; Device; Device Driver; Disk Storage; Distributed System/Network; Drive; Environment; Equipment; File Server; Front End Processor; Hand Held Device; Hardware; Interface; Intranet; Kit; Line Printer; Mag Tape; Magnetic Disk; Magnetic Tape; Mass Storage; Peripheral; Printer; Recording Device; Server; Storage; Store;*

Resolution
The density in which graphics are displayed on a monitor. i.e. the number of dots or pixels.
See Also: *Analogue Monitor; Anti Glare Screen; BitMaP; BMP; Cathode Ray Tube; CGA; Colour Graphics Adaptor; CRT; Digital Monitor; Display; EGA; Enhanced Graphic Adaptor; Extended Video Array; Frame Rate; GIF; Graphical Interchange Format; Graphics; Graphics Card; High Resolution; Image Processing; Interlaced; Joint Photographic Experts Group; JPEG; JPG; LCD; Liquid Crystal Display; Monitor; Monochrome; Paint Screen; Pixel; Plasma Screen; Screen; Screen Burn; Super Twist LCD; Super VGA; Super Video Graphics Array; SVGA; Tag Image File Format; Terminal; TFT; Thin-Film Transistor; TIFF; Touch Screen; Twip; VDT; VDU; VGA; Video Card; Video Display Terminal; Video Graphics Array; Visual Display Terminal; Visual Display Unit; XGA;*

Restore
The procedure where the data in a database or file is reset to a previous point in time. This is done by referencing a log file to reprocess the previous transactions or by copying the previous files.
See Also: *Abort; Archive; Audit Trail; Batch Processing; Grandfather, Father, Son; Recovery; Roll Back;*

Return
A key on the keyboard used to input typed information into a computer when depressed. Also known as the ENTER key.
See Also: *Carriage Return; Command; Enter; Instruction; Keyboard;*

Rich Text Format
(RTF). A type of file format.
See Also: *ASCII Files; Attachment; BitMaP; BMP; Extension; Filename Extension; Format; GIF; Graphical Interchange Format; Joint Photographic Experts Group; JPEG; JPG; MIME; Multipurpose Internet Mail Extensions; PDF; Portable Document Format; RTF; Tag Image File Format; TIFF;*

Ring Network
A type of network that connects multiple computers to a server to share data storage and peripherals. It is known as a 'Ring' as cables from each computer are connected to a main ring cable which in turn is connected to a server.
See Also: *AMR; Anonymous FTP; Automatic Message Routing; Backbone; Bandwidth; BBS; Broadband; Bulletin Board System; Client*

Server; Client Server Protocol; Distributed System/Network; Environment; Ethernet; File Server; File Sharing; Gateway; Intranet; LAN; LAN Port; Local Area Network; Narrowband; Network; Network Information Centre; Network Operating System; NIC; Node; NOS; Open Systems Interconnect; OSI; Polling; Server; Star Cluster; Star Network; TCP/IP; Token Ring; Transmission Control Protocol/Internet Protocol; WAN; Wide Area Network;

RISC

Reduced Instruction Set Computer. A computer architecture whose microprocessor has a reduced number of instructions which are the ones most frequently used. This enables the processor to operate at a faster speed.

See Also: *286; 386; 486; Advanced Technology; AT; Extended Technology; Instruction Set; Microprocessor; Parallel Processor; Processor; Reduced Instruction Set Computing; XT;*

Roll Back

The procedure where the data in a database is reset to a previous point in time by reference to a log file in order to reprocess the transactions.

See Also: *Abort; Audit Trail; Backup; Batch Processing; Data Base Management System; DBMS; Grandfather, Father, Son; Machine Crash; Program Crash; RDBMS/RDMS; Recovery; Relational Database Management System; Restore; Save;*

ROM

Read Only Memory. Memory in a computer which contains data or instructions that cannot be changed. e.g. BIOS instructions.

See Also: *Basic Input Output System; BIOS; Bubble Memory; Buffer; Cache Memory; CMOS; Complementary Metal Oxide Semiconductor Memory; Computer Power; Conventional Memory; Core; Core Dump; DDR SDRAM; DIMM; Direct Memory Access; Direct Random Access Memory; Disk Cache; DMA; Double Data Rate SDRAM; DRAM; Dual Inline Memory Module; Dynamic Memory; Dynamically; EEROM; Electrically Erasable Read Only Memory; Electronically Programmed Read Only Memory; EMS; EPROM; Erasable Programmable Read Only Memory; Expanded Memory; Expanded Memory Specification; Extended Memory; Flash Memory; High Memory; Magnetic Core; Memory; Memory Board; Memory Caching; Memory Card; Memory Resident; Mix; Power; Programmable Read Only Memory; PROM; RAM; RAM Disk; Rambus Dynamic Random Access Memory; Random Access Memory; RDRAM; Read Only Memory; ROM Resident; SDRAM; Shadow RAM Memory; SIMM; Single Inline Memory Modules; Single Inline*

Package; SIP; Stack; Store; Swapping; Synchronous Dynamic Random Access Memory; Upper Memory; Video Random Access Memory; VRAM; Working Storage; Workspace;

ROM Resident
Programs or instructions for a computer which are recorded in Read Only Memory.
See Also: *Basic Input Output System; BIOS; Boot; Bootstrap; CMOS; Complementary Metal Oxide Semiconductor Memory; Daemon; EEROM; Electrically Erasable Read Only Memory; Electronically Programmed Read Only Memory; EPROM; Erasable Programmable Read Only Memory; Firmware; Instruction Set; Memory; Programmable Read Only Memory; PROM; Read Only Memory; Re-boot; ROM; Shadow RAM Memory;*

Root Directory
The highest level of directory on a storage device which can contain other directories and also its own files.
See Also: *3.5 Inch; 5.25 Inch; C Prompt; CD-ROM; Directory; Disk; Disk Pack; Disk Storage; Diskette; FAT; Fiche; File; File Allocation Table; Five and a quarter; Floppy Disk; Folder; Magnetic Disk; Microfiche; Optical Disk; Pack; Path; Recording Medium; Storage; Streamer; Sub Directory; Tape Streamer; Three and a Half; Volume;*

RPG
Report Program Generator. A high level computer programming language.
See Also: *3GL; 4GL; ADA; ALGOL; APL; BASIC; C or C++; CLIPPER; COBOL; Code; Code Generator; Compiler; Compiling; CORAL; FORTH; FORTRAN; Fourth Generation Language; High Level Language; Instruction Set; JAVA; JAVASCRIPT; Language; LISP; LOGO; Module; NATURAL; PASCAL; PERL; PICK; PILOT; PL/1; Practical Extraction and Reporting Language; Program; Programming Language; PROLOG; Software; Source Code; Structured Program; Syntax; Third Generation Language; Visual Basic;*

RS232
A standard code for serial transmission to a computer or peripheral device.
See Also: *Access; Acoustic Coupler; Interface; Modem; Modulator Demodulator; Open Systems Interconnect; OSI; Port; RS423; Serial Interface; Serial Port; Serial Transmission; UART; Universal Asynchronous Receiver/Transmitter;*

RS423
A standard code for a serial interface to a computer or peripheral device.
See Also: *Access; Acoustic Coupler; Interface; Modem; Modulator Demodulator; Open Systems Interconnect; OSI; Port; RS232; Serial Interface; Serial Port; Serial Transmission; UART; Universal Asynchronous Receiver/Transmitter;*

RTF
Rich Text Format. A type of file format.
See Also: *ASCII Files; Attachment; BitMaP; BMP; Extension; Filename Extension; Format; GIF; Graphical Interchange Format; Joint Photographic Experts Group; JPEG; JPG; MIME; Multipurpose Internet Mail Extensions; PDF; Portable Document Format; Rich Text Format; Tag Image File Format; TIFF;*

Run
(1) A program or a series of programs which perform specific tasks on a computer. e.g. invoicing. (2) The procedure or command to execute those tasks.
See Also: *Batch Processing; Call; Chain; Data Processing; DP; EXE; Execute; Function; Instruction Set; Invoke; Job; Load; Macro; Multitasking; Process; Processing; Program; Run Time; Script; Time Share; Time Slice;*

Run Time
The period of time when an application or program has started running.
See Also: *Batch Processing; Call; Chain; Data Processing; DP; EXE; Execute; Function; Going Live; Hand Holding; Instruction Set; Invoke; Job; Live; Load; Macro; Mean Time Between Failure; Memory Resident; MTBF; Multitasking; Process; Processing; Program; Run; Script; Time Share; Time Slice;*

S/A
Systems Analyst. A person who analyses, designs and documents a computer software system.
See Also: *A/P; Analyst; Analyst Programmer; B/A; Business Analyst; Contractor; Data Base Analyst; Data Flow Diagram; Data Model; Data Processing Manager; DBA; Design; Development; DFD; DPM; Flowchart; Full Project Life Cycle; Hand Holding; Logical Design; Model; O & M; Object Oriented Analysis; Object Oriented Design; Object Oriented Programming; OOA; OOD; OOP; Organisation & Methods; Physical Design; Process Model; Programmer; Project Life Cycle; S/P; Software Development Cycle; Software House; Specification;*

Structured Design; System Analysis; System Analyst; Systems Programmer; Technical Author; Walkthrough;

S/P

Systems Programmer. A person who is responsible for implementing and maintaining the system software in a computer system.

See Also: *A/P; Analyst; Analyst Programmer; B/A; Business Analyst; Code; Contractor; Data Base Analyst; Data Processing Manager; DBA; Design; Development; DPM; Full Project Life Cycle; Language; Logical Design; Loop; Physical Design; Program; Program Specification; Programmer; Programming Language; Project Life Cycle; S/A; Software; Software Development Cycle; Software House; Specification; Structured Design; Structured Program; System Analyst; Systems Programmer; Technical Author;*

Save

The copying of data, graphics or sound from the computer to a permanent storage device.

See Also: *3.5 Inch; 5.25 Inch; Archive; Backing Store; Backup; CD-RW Drive; COM; Computer Output Microfilm; DAT; Deck; Digital Audio Tape; Disk; Disk Drive; Disk Pack; Disk Storage; Diskette; Drive; Event; FDD; Fiche; File; Five and a quarter; Fixed Disk Drive; Floppy Disk; Floppy Disk Drive; Grandfather, Father, Son; Hard Disk Drive; HDD; Mag Tape; Magnetic Disk; Magnetic Tape; Mass Storage; Medium; Microfiche; Microfilm; Optical Drive; Output; Pack; Paper Tape; R/W; Read/Write; Record; Recording; Recording Device; Recording Medium; Roll Back; Storage; Store; Streamer; Tape Deck; Tape Streamer; Three and a Half; Unzip; Volume; Winchester Disk; Write; Zip; Zip Drive;*

Scalable Fonts

A font defined to be used on any size of character.

See Also: *Character; Characters Per Inch; CPI; Font; Font Cartridge; Format; Letter Quality; LQ; Near Letter Quality; NLQ; Postscript; WYSIWYG;*

Scanner

A flat device like a photocopier which optically reads a document into the computer by recognising the shapes of characters or graphics when the document is scanned.

See Also: *Analogue Digital Converter; CCD; Charge Coupled Device; Configuration; Device; Drum; Environment; Equipment; Flatbed Scanner; Hardware; Installation; Kit; OCR; OMR; Optical Character*

Reader; Optical Character Recognition; Optical Mark Recognition; Optical Scanner; Peripheral;

Screen
A device consisting of a cathode ray tube and used for displaying data and graphics.
See Also: *Analogue Monitor; Anti Glare Screen; Cathode Ray Tube; CGA; Colour Graphics Adaptor; CRT; Device; Digital Monitor; Digital Video Interface; Display; DVI; EGA; Enhanced Graphic Adaptor; Environment; Equipment; Extended Video Array; Frame Rate; Graphics Card; Hardware; High Resolution; Installation; Intelligent Terminal; Interlaced; Kit; LCD; Liquid Crystal Display; Low Resolution; Monitor; Monochrome; Output; Paint Screen; Peripheral; Plasma Screen; Prompt; Resolution; Screen Burn; Screen Dump; Scroll; Split Screen; Sprite; Super Twist LCD; Super VGA; Super Video Graphics Array; SVGA; System; Terminal; TFT; Thin-Film Transistor; Toolbar; Touch Screen; Twip; VDT; VDU; VGA; Video Card; Video Display Terminal; Video Graphics Array; Video Random Access Memory; Visual Display Terminal; Visual Display Unit; VRAM; XGA;*

Screen Burn
A term used when the phosphorus in the screen etches the display characters onto the cathode ray tube glass. This occurs to a visual display unit screen when it is on for a long period of time.
See Also: *Analogue Monitor; Anti Glare Screen; Cathode Ray Tube; CGA; Colour Graphics Adaptor; CRT; Digital Monitor; Display; EGA; Enhanced Graphic Adaptor; Extended Video Array; High Resolution; Intelligent Terminal; LCD; Liquid Crystal Display; Low Resolution; Monitor; Monochrome; Paint Screen; Pixel; Plasma Screen; Resolution; Screen; Super Twist LCD; Super VGA; Super Video Graphics Array; SVGA; Terminal; TFT; Thin-Film Transistor; Touch Screen; Twip; VDT; VDU; VGA; Video Card; Video Display Terminal; Video Graphics Array; Visual Display Terminal; Visual Display Unit; XGA;*

Screen Dump
Also known as Screen Grab or Screen Shot. An image of a screen display captured for printing or saving.
See Also: *Display; Dump; Graphics; Output; Paint Screen; Screen; Window; WYSIWYG;*

Script
A set of programmed commands used to communicate between computers.
See Also: *Applet; Audit Trail; Batch File; Batch Processing; Code; Command; Device Driver; DLL; Dynamic Link Library; Event; EXE; Execute; Function; Function Key; Instruction; Instruction Set; JCL; Job; Job Control Language; Macro; Module; Nesting; Process; Program; Run; Run Time; Subroutine; Utility;*

Scroll
The upward, downward or side to side movement of the display on a screen.
See Also: *Cursor; Display; Drag; Marquee; Paint Screen; Screen; Sprite;*

SCSI
Small Computer System Interface. An interface between a computer and its peripherals. Pronounced "scuzzy".
See Also: *Channel; EIDE; EISA; Enhanced Industry Standard Architecture; Enhanced Intelligent Drive Electronics; Firewire; Industry Standard Architecture; Interface; ISA; MCA; Micro Channel Architecture; MIDI; Musical Instrument Digital Interface; Self Monitoring Analysis and Reporting Technology; Serial Interface; Small Computer System Interface; SMART; Transmission Channel; Ultra DMA; Universal Serial Bus; USB;*

SDRAM
Synchronous Dynamic Random Access Memory. A fast type of computer memory.
See Also: *Basic Input Output System; BIOS; Bubble Memory; Buffer; Cache Memory; CMOS; Complementary Metal Oxide Semiconductor Memory; Computer Power; Conventional Memory; Core; Core Dump; DDR SDRAM; DIMM; Direct Memory Access; Direct Random Access Memory; Disk Cache; DMA; Double Data Rate SDRAM; DRAM; Dual Inline Memory Module; Dynamic Memory; Dynamically; EEROM; Electrically Erasable Read Only Memory; Electronically Programmed Read Only Memory; EMS; EPROM; Erasable Programmable Read Only Memory; Expanded Memory; Expanded Memory Specification; Extended Memory; Flash Memory; High Memory; Magnetic Core; Memory; Memory Board; Memory Caching; Memory Card; Memory Resident; Mix; Power; Programmable Read Only Memory; PROM; RAM; RAM Disk; Rambus Dynamic Random Access Memory; Random Access Memory; RDRAM; Read Only Memory; ROM; Shadow RAM Memory;*

SIMM; Single Inline Memory Modules; Single Inline Package; SIP; Stack; Store; Swapping; Synchronous Dynamic Random Access Memory; Upper Memory; Video Random Access Memory; VRAM; Working Storage; Workspace;

Search Engine
A system used on the Internet which scans Internet sites in search of key words and phrases.
See Also: *Anchor; Application; Batch Processing; BBS; Bookmark; Browser; Bulletin Board System; Cyberspace; Gopher; Hit; Host; Internet; Internet Service Provider; ISP; Key; Meta Tag; Meta-Search Engine; Net; Portal; Provider; Service Provider; Site; Software System; Spider; Surfing; The Net; The Web; Utility; Webhost; Webring; Website; World Wide Web; WWW;*

Sector
A section of a track on a disk storage medium where data is stored.
See Also: *3.5 Inch; 5.25 Inch; Bits Per Inch; Block; BPI; Cluster; Cylinder; Data; Disk; Disk Pack; Disk Storage; Diskette; Five and a quarter; Floppy Disk; Magnetic Disk; Medium; Pack; Recording Medium; Storage; Three and a Half; Track; Volume; Winchester Disk;*

Secure Socket Layer
(SSL). A protocol to enable secure or private transmissions across the Internet.
See Also: *CGI; Common Gateway Interface; Cyberspace; EFT; EFTPOS; Electronic Fund Transfer; Electronic Fund Transfer Point of Sales; Encryption; Firewall; Gateway; Handshake; Internet; Internet Protocol; IP; Net; Point to Point Protocol; PPP; Protocol; Serial Line Internet Protocol; Simple Mail Transfer Protocol; SLIP; SMTP; SSL; TCP/IP; The Net; Transmission Control Protocol/Internet Protocol; WAP; Wireless Application Protocol; XMODEM; YMODEM; ZMODEM;*

Security
(1) The inhibiting of access into a computer system by the use of passwords and user codes. (2) The backing up of data onto a storage device.
See Also: *Archive; Audit Trail; Backing Store; Backup; Disk Storage; Dongle; Encryption; Firewall; Grandfather, Father, Son; Locking; Password; Record Locking; Storage; Write Protect;*

Seek Time
The time it takes for the read/write head on a storage device to position itself to read or write data.
See Also: *3.5 Inch; 5.25 Inch; Access; Access Time; Disk; Disk Drive; Disk Pack; Disk Storage; Diskette; FDD; Five and a quarter; Fixed Disk Drive; Floppy Disk; Floppy Disk Drive; Hard Disk Drive; HDD; Magnetic Disk; Microsecond; Millisecond; Ms; Nanosecond; Ns; Pack; Pico Second; R/W; Read; Read/Write; Storage; Three and a Half; Volume; Winchester Disk; Write;*

Self Extracting File
A program compressed to save space that will decompress into one or more component files when activated.
See Also: *Compressed File; Compression; Decompression; File; PKZIP; Program; Unzip; Zip;*

Self Monitoring Analysis and Reporting Technology
(SMART). A method where the EIDE disk interface communicates with the BIOS about hard disk performance and can inform the user of problems with the hard disk.
See Also: *ATAPI; Attachment Packet Interface; Basic Input Output System; BIOS; EIDE; EISA; Enhanced Industry Standard Architecture; Enhanced Intelligent Drive Electronics; IDE; Integrated Drive Electronics; Interface; MCA; Micro Channel Architecture; SCSI; Small Computer System Interface; SMART; Ultra DMA;*

Semiconductor
A solid-state electronic component made from a material which is neither a good or bad conductor of electricity. e.g. silicon.
See Also: *Application Specific Integrated Circuits; ASICS; Chip; Chipset; IC; Integrated Circuit; Large Scale Integration; Logic Gate; LSI; Memory; Microprocessor; Processor; Silicon Chip; Solid State; Sound Chip; Transistor; Very Large Scale Integration; VLSI;*

Sequential Access
A method of reading and writing records in a file by searching the records in a logical sequence from the beginning of the file until the desired record is found or where the next record is to be written.
See Also: *Access; Access Time; Index Sequential File; Indexed Sequential Access Method; ISAM; Keyed Sequential Access Method; KSAM; R/W; Random Access; Read; Read/Write; Sequential File; Serial Access; Write;*

Sequential File
A file in which records are stored sequentially but in a logical manner.
See Also: *ASCII Files; Attachment; Batch File; Beginning of File; BOF; Comma Separated Values; CSV; Database; DB; End of File; EOF; File; Index Sequential File; Log File; Random File; RDB; Record; Relational Database; Sequential Access; Serial File; Tag File; Temp File;*

Serial Access
A method of reading or writing records in a file by searching the records in a physical sequence from the beginning of the file.
See Also: *Access; Access Time; Index Sequential File; Indexed Sequential Access Method; ISAM; Keyed Sequential Access Method; KSAM; R/W; Random Access; Read; Read/Write; Sequential Access; Serial File; Write;*

Serial File
A file in which records are stored physically in a serial manner. i.e. one after the other.
See Also: *ASCII Files; Attachment; Batch File; Beginning of File; BOF; Comma Separated Values; CSV; Database; DB; End of File; EOF; File; Fragmentation; Index Sequential File; Log File; Random File; RDB; Record; Relational Database; Sequential File; Serial Access; Tag File; Temp File;*

Serial Interface
A connection between a computer and devices where data is transmitted and received one bit at a time using separate transmission lines.
See Also: *Access; Acoustic Coupler; ADN; ADSL; Advanced Digital Network; Asymmetric Digital Subscriber Line; Asymmetrical Modem; Asynchronous; Bandwidth; Broadband; CCITT; CCTA; Consultative Committee International Telegraph and Telephone; Duplex Transmission; Firewire; Full Duplex; Integrated Services Digital Network; Interface; ISDN; Kbps; MIDI; Multiplex; Multiplexer; Musical Instrument Digital Interface; Narrowband; Parallel Interface; Parallel Port; Parallel Transmission; Port; RS232; RS423; SCSI; Serial Port; Serial Transmission; Simplex Transmission; Small Computer System Interface; Synchronous; Telecommunication; Telecoms; Teleprocessing System; TPS; UART; Universal Asynchronous Receiver/Transmitter; Universal Serial Bus; USB;*

Serial Line Internet Protocol
(SLIP). A way in which a user can connect to the Internet without using a host computer.
See Also: *Bandwidth; Broadband; CGI; Client Server Protocol; Common Gateway Interface; Cyberspace; Gateway; Handshake; Interface; Internet; Internet Protocol; Internet Protocol Address; Internet Relay Chat; Internet Service Provider; IP; IP Address; IRC; ISP; Narrowband; Net; PING; Point to Point Protocol; PPP; Protocol; Provider; Secure Socket Layer; Service Provider; Simple Mail Transfer Protocol; SLIP; SMTP; SSL; TCP/IP; The Net; Transmission Control Protocol/Internet Protocol; WAP; Wap Internet Service Provider; Wireless Application Protocol; WISP;*

Serial Port
A connector on a computer to which a cable is attached that allows data to be sent or received by serial transmission, i.e. one bit at a time using separate transmission lines. Also known as a Com port.
See Also: *Dongle; ECP; Enhanced Parallel Port; EPP; Extended Capabilities Port; Interface; LPT Port; MIDI; Parallel Interface; Parallel Port; Parallel Transmission; Port; RS232; RS423; Serial Interface; Serial Transmission; UART; Universal Asynchronous Receiver/Transmitter;*

Serial Transmission
The transmission between a computer and a device where data is transmitted and received one bit at a time using separate transmission lines.
See Also: *ACK; Acoustic Coupler; ADN; ADSL; Advanced Digital Network; AMR; Asymmetric Digital Subscriber Line; Asymmetrical Modem; Asynchronous; Asynchronous Transfer Mode; ATM; Automatic Message Routing; Bandwidth; Baud Rate; Bits Per Second; BPS; Broadband; Bus; CCITT; CCTA; Channel; Characters Per Second; Communications; Consultative Committee International Telegraph and Telephone; CPS; Data Communications; Data Parity; Data Transmission; Datacoms; Dial In; Dial Up; Digital; Direct Connection; Duplex Transmission; FDDI; Fibre Distributed Data Interface; Fibre Optics; Full Duplex; Gbps; Half Duplex; HD; Integrated Services Digital Network; ISDN; Kbps; Leased Line; Mbps; Modem; Modulator Demodulator; Multiplex; Multiplexer; Narrowband; Node; Open Systems Interconnect; Optical Fibre; OSI; Packet; Packet Switching; Parallel Interface; Parallel Port; Parallel Transmission; Parity Bit; RS232; RS423; Serial Interface; Serial Port; Simplex Transmission; Synchronous; T-1; T-3; Telecommunication; Telecoms; Teleprocessing*

System; TPS; Transfer Rate; Transmission Channel; Transmit; UART; Universal Asynchronous Receiver/Transmitter; V90;

Server

Hardware and software, which control the sharing of peripherals and data files for computers, connected together in a network.

See Also: *Access; AMR; Anonymous FTP; Automatic Message Routing; CGI; Client Server; Client Server Protocol; Common Gateway Interface; Configuration; Database; DB; Device; Distributed System/Network; Domain Name Server; Environment; Equipment; Ethernet; File Server; File Sharing; Firewall; Front End Processor; Gateway; Handshake; Hardware; Host Processor; Installation; Intranet; Kit; LAN; LAN Port; Local Area Network; Locking; Mailserver; Multi User; Multitasking; Network; Network Information Centre; Network Operating System; NIC; Node; NOS; Open Systems Interconnect; OSI; Peripheral; Polling; Proxy Server; Record Locking; Remote Device; Ring Network; Software; Star Cluster; Star Network; System; Time Share; Time Slice; Token Ring; WAN; Wide Area Network;*

Service Provider

Internet Service Provider or ISP. A company which provide users with access to the Internet.

See Also: *Acceptable User Policy; AUP; Browser; CGI; Common Gateway Interface; Cookie; Cyberspace; DNS; Domain Name; Domain Name Server; Domain Name System; E-commerce; EDI; Electronic Data Interchange; Handshake; Hit; Home Page; Host; Host Processor; HTTP; Hypertext Transfer Protocol; Information Superhighway; Internet; Internet Relay Chat; Internet Service Provider; IRC; ISP; Mailserver; Net; Newsgroup; PING; Point Of Presence; Point to Point Protocol; POP; POP; Portal; Post Office Protocol; PPP; Provider; Proxy Server; Search Engine; Serial Line Internet Protocol; SLIP; Spider; Surfing; The Net; Wap Internet Service Provider; Webhost; WISP;*

Shadow RAM Memory

Memory used to speed up access to Read Only Memory.

See Also: *Basic Input Output System; BIOS; Bubble Memory; Buffer; Cache Memory; CMOS; Complementary Metal Oxide Semiconductor Memory; Computer Power; Conventional Memory; Core; Core Dump; DDR SDRAM; DIMM; Direct Memory Access; Direct Random Access Memory; Disk Cache; DMA; Double Data Rate SDRAM; DRAM; Dual Inline Memory Module; Dynamic Memory; Dynamically; EEROM; Electrically Erasable Read Only Memory; Electronically Programmed Read Only Memory; EMS; EPROM; Erasable Programmable Read Only*

Memory; Expanded Memory; Expanded Memory Specification; Extended Memory; Flash Memory; High Memory; Magnetic Core; Memory; Memory Board; Memory Caching; Memory Card; Memory Resident; Mix; Power; Programmable Read Only Memory; PROM; RAM; RAM Disk; Rambus Dynamic Random Access Memory; Random Access Memory; RDRAM; Read Only Memory; ROM; ROM Resident; SDRAM; SIMM; Single Inline Memory Modules; Single Inline Package; SIP; Stack; Store; Swapping; Synchronous Dynamic Random Access Memory; Upper Memory; Video Random Access Memory; VRAM; Working Storage; Workspace;

Shareware
Free software distributed on a trial basis with no product support unless paid for or registered.
See Also: *Application; BBS; Bulletin Board System; CAD; CADCAM; CADMAT; CAE; CAI; CAM; CBT; Code; Computer Aided Design; Computer Aided Design and Manufacturing; Computer Aided Design Manufacture and Test; Computer Aided Engineering; Computer Aided Instruction; Computer Aided Manufacturing; Computer Based Training; Desk Top Publishing; DTP; EXE; Geographical Information System; GIS; Net; Package; Public Domain; Software; Software Package; Software System; Utility;*

Sheet Feeder
A device attached to a printer which allows for single sheets of paper to be fed to the printer.
See Also: *Bubble Jet; Cut Sheet Feeder; Daisywheel; Device; Dot Matrix; Equipment; Hard Copy; Inkjet; Kit; Matrix Printer; Peripheral; Printer; Thermal Printer;*

Signature
Information appended at the end of an e-mail, normally consists of the sender's personal details.
See Also: *Attachment; Body; Electronic Mail; E-mail; Emoticons; Flame; Smileys; Spam;*

Silicon Chip
A printed circuit etched on a number of layers of silicon which form either a memory chip or a chip to perform a specific task.
See Also: *286; 386; 486; Advanced Technology; ALU; AND gate; Application Specific Integrated Circuits; Arithmetic and Logic Unit; ASICS; AT; Central Processing Unit; Chip; Chipset; Clock Speed; Computer Power; Co-processor; CPU; Extended Technology; Flip Flop;*

GHz; Gigahertz; IC; Integrated Circuit; I-OR gate; KHz; Kilohertz; Large Scale Integration; Logic Gate; LSI; Maths Co-processor; Megahertz; Memory Board; Memory Card; MHz; Microprocessor; Motherboard; NAND gate; NEQ gate; NOR gate; NOT gate; OR gate; Parallel Processor; PCB; Power; Printed Circuit Board; Processor; Semiconductor; Solid State; Sound Chip; Transistor; UART; Universal Asynchronous Receiver/Transmitter; Very Large Scale Integration; VLSI; X-OR gate; XT;

Silicon Valley
An area in San Francisco where computer hardware and software organisations are concentrated.
See Also: *Leading Edge; State of the Art;*

SIMM
Single Inline Memory Modules. A number of RAM chips on a printed circuit board which has edge connectors that allow easy memory upgrades to a computer.
See Also: *Basic Input Output System; BIOS; Bubble Memory; Buffer; Cache Memory; CMOS; Complementary Metal Oxide Semiconductor Memory; Computer Power; Conventional Memory; Core; Core Dump; DDR SDRAM; DIMM; Direct Memory Access; Direct Random Access Memory; Disk Cache; DMA; Double Data Rate SDRAM; DRAM; Dual Inline Memory Module; Dynamic Memory; Dynamically; EEROM; Electrically Erasable Read Only Memory; Electronically Programmed Read Only Memory; EMS; EPROM; Erasable Programmable Read Only Memory; Expanded Memory; Expanded Memory Specification; Extended Memory; Flash Memory; High Memory; Magnetic Core; Memory; Memory Board; Memory Caching; Memory Card; Memory Resident; Mix; PCB; Power; Printed Circuit Board; Programmable Read Only Memory; PROM; RAM; RAM Disk; Rambus Dynamic Random Access Memory; Random Access Memory; RDRAM; Read Only Memory; ROM; SDRAM; Shadow RAM Memory; Single Inline Memory Modules; Single Inline Package; SIP; Stack; Store; Swapping; Synchronous Dynamic Random Access Memory; Upper Memory; Video Random Access Memory; VRAM; Working Storage; Workspace;*

Simple Mail Transfer Protocol
(SMTP). A way in which e-mails are exchanged over the Internet.
See Also: *Acceptable User Policy; AUP; Body; Client Server Protocol; Cyberspace; Electronic Mail; E-mail; Internet; Internet Protocol; Internet Protocol Address; Internet Relay Chat; IP; IP Address; IRC; Mailbox; Mailserver; MIME; Multipurpose Internet Mail Extensions;*

Net; Point to Point Protocol; PPP; Protocol; Secure Socket Layer; Serial Line Internet Protocol; SLIP; SMTP; SSL; TCP/IP; The Net; Transmission Control Protocol/Internet Protocol;

Simplex Printing
Printing on one side of the paper.
See Also: *Barrel Printer; Bi Directional; Bubble Jet; Daisywheel; Dot Matrix; Drum Printer; Duplex Printing; Hard Copy; Inkjet; Laser Jet; Laser Printer; LCD Printer; Letter Quality; Line Printer; Liquid Crystal Display Printer; LQ; Matrix Printer; Near Letter Quality; NLQ; Output; Page Printer; Pages Per Minute; PPM; Printer; Printer Driver; Printout; Thermal Printer;*

Simplex Transmission
Transmission in only one direction along a communication line.
See Also: *ACK; Acoustic Coupler; ADN; ADSL; Advanced Digital Network; AMR; Asymmetric Digital Subscriber Line; Asymmetrical Modem; Asynchronous; Asynchronous Transfer Mode; ATM; Automatic Message Routing; Bandwidth; Baud Rate; Bits Per Second; BPS; Broadband; Bus; CCITT; CCTA; Channel; Characters Per Second; Communications; Consultative Committee International Telegraph and Telephone; CPS; Data Communications; Data Parity; Data Transmission; Datacoms; Dial In; Dial Up; Digital; Direct Connection; Duplex Transmission; FDDI; Fibre Distributed Data Interface; Fibre Optics; Firewire; Full Duplex; Gbps; Half Duplex; HD; Integrated Services Digital Network; ISDN; Kbps; Leased Line; Mbps; Modem; Modulator Demodulator; Multiplex; Multiplexer; Narrowband; Open Systems Interconnect; Optical Fibre; OSI; Packet; Packet Switching; Parallel Transmission; Parity Bit; Serial Interface; Serial Transmission; Synchronous; Telecommunication; Telecoms; Transfer Rate; Transmission Channel; Transmit; V90;*

Single Inline Memory Modules
(SIMM). A number of RAM chips on a printed circuit board which has edge connectors that allow easy memory upgrades to a computer.
See Also: *Basic Input Output System; BIOS; Bubble Memory; Buffer; Cache Memory; CMOS; Complementary Metal Oxide Semiconductor Memory; Computer Power; Conventional Memory; Core; Core Dump; DDR SDRAM; DIMM; Direct Memory Access; Direct Random Access Memory; Disk Cache; DMA; Double Data Rate SDRAM; DRAM; Dual Inline Memory Module; Dynamic Memory; Dynamically; EEROM; Electrically Erasable Read Only Memory; Electronically Programmed Read Only Memory; EMS; EPROM; Erasable Programmable Read Only*

Memory; Expanded Memory; Expanded Memory Specification; Extended Memory; Flash Memory; High Memory; Magnetic Core; Memory; Memory Board; Memory Caching; Memory Card; Memory Resident; Mix; PCB; Power; Printed Circuit Board; Programmable Read Only Memory; PROM; RAM; RAM Disk; Rambus Dynamic Random Access Memory; Random Access Memory; RDRAM; Read Only Memory; ROM; SDRAM; Shadow RAM Memory; SIMM; Single Inline Package; SIP; Stack; Store; Swapping; Synchronous Dynamic Random Access Memory; Upper Memory; Video Random Access Memory; VRAM; Working Storage; Workspace;

Single Inline Package
(SIP). A number of RAM chips on a printed circuit board which has pin connectors that allow easy memory upgrades to a computer.
See Also: *Basic Input Output System; BIOS; Bubble Memory; Buffer; Cache Memory; CMOS; Complementary Metal Oxide Semiconductor Memory; Computer Power; Conventional Memory; Core; Core Dump; DDR SDRAM; DIMM; Direct Memory Access; Direct Random Access Memory; Disk Cache; DMA; Double Data Rate SDRAM; DRAM; Dual Inline Memory Module; Dynamic Memory; Dynamically; EEROM; Electrically Erasable Read Only Memory; Electronically Programmed Read Only Memory; EMS; EPROM; Erasable Programmable Read Only Memory; Expanded Memory; Expanded Memory Specification; Extended Memory; Flash Memory; High Memory; Magnetic Core; Memory; Memory Board; Memory Caching; Memory Card; Memory Resident; Mix; PCB; Power; Printed Circuit Board; Programmable Read Only Memory; PROM; RAM; RAM Disk; Rambus Dynamic Random Access Memory; Random Access Memory; RDRAM; Read Only Memory; ROM; SDRAM; Shadow RAM Memory; SIMM; Single Inline Memory Modules; SIP; Stack; Store; Swapping; Synchronous Dynamic Random Access Memory; Upper Memory; Video Random Access Memory; VRAM; Working Storage; Workspace;*

SIP
Single Inline Package. A number of RAM chips on a printed circuit board which has pin connectors that allow easy memory upgrades to a computer.
See Also: *Basic Input Output System; BIOS; Bubble Memory; Buffer; Cache Memory; CMOS; Complementary Metal Oxide Semiconductor Memory; Computer Power; Conventional Memory; Core; Core Dump; DDR SDRAM; DIMM; Direct Memory Access; Direct Random Access Memory; Disk Cache; DMA; Double Data Rate SDRAM; DRAM; Dual Inline Memory Module; Dynamic Memory; Dynamically; EEROM;*

Electrically Erasable Read Only Memory; Electronically Programmed Read Only Memory; EMS; EPROM; Erasable Programmable Read Only Memory; Expanded Memory; Expanded Memory Specification; Extended Memory; Flash Memory; High Memory; Magnetic Core; Memory; Memory Board; Memory Caching; Memory Card; Memory Resident; Mix; PCB; Power; Printed Circuit Board; Programmable Read Only Memory; PROM; RAM; RAM Disk; Rambus Dynamic Random Access Memory; Random Access Memory; RDRAM; Read Only Memory; ROM; SDRAM; Shadow RAM Memory; SIMM; Single Inline Memory Modules; Single Inline Package; Stack; Store; Swapping; Synchronous Dynamic Random Access Memory; Upper Memory; Video Random Access Memory; VRAM; Working Storage; Workspace;

Site
A World Wide Web Internet site which provides information to anyone accessing it and is identified by a Domain Name.
See Also: *Acceptable User Policy; Address; Anchor; AUP; Bookmark; Browser; CERN; CGI; Common Gateway Interface; Conseil Europeen pour la Recherche Nucleaire; Cyberspace; DNS; Domain Name; Domain Name Server; Domain Name System; Forum; FTP Site; FTPmail; Hit; Home Page; Host; HTML; HTTP; Hyperlink; Hypertext Mark-Up Language; Hypertext Transfer Protocol; Internet; Link; Message Boards; Meta-Search Engine; Mirror Site; Net; Page; Portal; Proxy Server; Search Engine; Spider; Surfing; The Net; The Web; Thumbnail; Universal/Uniform Resource Locator; URL; Webcam; Webhost; Webring; Website; World Wide Web; WWW;*

Sixteen Bit
(16 bit). A term describing the architecture of a computer in which data is stored in 16 bit registers, or transferred from one part of a computer to another in a 16 bit wide data bus.
See Also: *16 Bit; 286; 32 Bit; 386; 64 Bit; 8 Bit; Address; Address Bus; Advanced Technology; Analogue Computer; AT; Binary; Binary Digit; Bit; Bits Per Second; BPS; Bus; Channel; Data Bus; Digital; Eight Bit; Extended Technology; Gbps; Least Significant Bit; Local Bus; LSB; Mbps; Most Significant Bit; MSB; Register; Sixty Four Bit; System Bus; Thirty Two Bit; Transmission Channel; XT;*

Sixty Four Bit
A term describing the architecture of a computer in which data is stored in 64 bit registers, or transferred from one part of a computer to another in a 64 bit wide data bus.
See Also: *16 Bit; 32 Bit; 64 Bit; 8 Bit; Address; Address Bus; Analogue Computer; Binary; Binary Digit; Bit; Bits Per Second; BPS; Bus; Channel; Data Bus; Digital; Eight Bit; Gbps; Least Significant Bit; Local Bus; LSB; Mbps; Most Significant Bit; MSB; Register; Sixteen Bit; System Bus; Thirty Two Bit; Transmission Channel;*

SLIP
Serial Line Internet Protocol. A way in which a user can connect to the Internet without using a host computer.
See Also: *Bandwidth; Broadband; CGI; Client Server Protocol; Common Gateway Interface; Cyberspace; Gateway; Handshake; Interface; Internet; Internet Protocol; Internet Protocol Address; Internet Relay Chat; Internet Service Provider; IP; IP Address; IRC; ISP; Narrowband; Net; PING; Point to Point Protocol; PPP; Protocol; Provider; Secure Socket Layer; Serial Line Internet Protocol; Service Provider; Simple Mail Transfer Protocol; SMTP; SSL; TCP/IP; The Net; Transmission Control Protocol/Internet Protocol; WAP; Wap Internet Service Provider; Wireless Application Protocol; WISP;*

Slot
A location within a computer which allows printed circuit boards or cards to be slotted in for upgrades to the system.
See Also: *Accelerated Graphics Port; Advanced Graphics Port; AGP; AGP Slot; Expansion Card; Expansion Slot; Fax Card; Memory Board; Memory Card; Motherboard; PCB; PCI; PCMCIA; Peripheral Component Interconnect; Personal Computer Memory Card International Association; Port; Printed Circuit Board; Sound Card;*

Small Computer System Interface
(SCSI). An interface between a computer and its peripherals. Pronounced "scuzzy".
See Also: *Channel; EIDE; EISA; Enhanced Industry Standard Architecture; Enhanced Intelligent Drive Electronics; Firewire; Industry Standard Architecture; Interface; ISA; MCA; Micro Channel Architecture; MIDI; Musical Instrument Digital Interface; SCSI; Self Monitoring Analysis and Reporting Technology; Serial Interface; SMART; Transmission Channel; Ultra DMA; Universal Serial Bus; USB;*

SMART

Self Monitoring Analysis and Reporting Technology. A method where the EIDE disk interface communicates with the BIOS about hard disk performance and can inform the user of problems with the hard disk.

See Also: *ATAPI; Attachment Packet Interface; Basic Input Output System; BIOS; EIDE; EISA; Enhanced Industry Standard Architecture; Enhanced Intelligent Drive Electronics; IDE; Integrated Drive Electronics; Interface; MCA; Micro Channel Architecture; SCSI; Self Monitoring Analysis and Reporting Technology; Small Computer System Interface; Ultra DMA;*

Smileys

Character symbols that shows facial emotions, e.g. happy :-) and sad :-(

See Also: *Character; Chat; Chatroom; Emoticons; Forum; Graphics; IM; Instant Messaging; Nerd; Netiquette; Newbie; Newsgroup; Signature;*

SMTP

Simple Mail Transfer Protocol. A way in which e-mails are exchanged over the Internet.

See Also: *Acceptable User Policy; AUP; Body; Client Server Protocol; Cyberspace; Electronic Mail; E-mail; Internet; Internet Protocol; Internet Protocol Address; Internet Relay Chat; IP; IP Address; IRC; Mailbox; Mailserver; MIME; Multipurpose Internet Mail Extensions; Net; Point to Point Protocol; PPP; Protocol; Secure Socket Layer; Serial Line Internet Protocol; Simple Mail Transfer Protocol; SLIP; SSL; TCP/IP; The Net; Transmission Control Protocol/Internet Protocol;*

Snail Mail

Ordinary letter post as opposed to e-mail.

See Also: *Electronic Mail; E-mail;*

Software

A collective term to describe programs, operating systems and applications.

See Also: *3GL; 4GL; A/P; ADA; ALGOL; Analyst Programmer; API; APL; Application; Application Program Interface; Assembler; Assembly Code; BASIC; BBS; Bespoke; Bloatware; Browser; Bulletin Board System; C or C++; CAD; CADCAM; CADMAT; CAE; CAI; CAM; CBT; Client Server; CLIPPER; COBOL; Code; Code Generator; CODEC; COmpressor DECompressor; Computer Aided Design; Computer Aided Design and Manufacturing; Computer Aided Design Manufacture and Test; Computer Aided Engineering; Computer Aided Instruction;*

Computer Aided Manufacturing; Computer Based Training; Configuration; Cookie; CORAL; Data Base Management System; DBMS; Desk Top Publishing; Development; Device Driver; Disk Operating System; DOS; Driver; DTP; EDS; Electronic Data System; EXE; FORTH; FORTRAN; Fourth Generation Language; Freeware; Gateway; Geographical Information System; GIS; Global; High Level Language; Information System; Information Technology; Install; Installation; Instruction Set; Integrated; Interpreter; IS; IT; JAVA; JAVASCRIPT; Language; Leading Edge; LISP; LOGO; Low Level Language; Mail Merge; Maintenance; Modular; NATURAL; Office Information System; OIS; Operating System; OS; OS/2; Package; Page Description Language; PASCAL; PDL; PERL; PICK; PILOT; Pirate Copy; PL/1; Practical Extraction and Reporting Language; Program; Programmer; Programming Language; PROLOG; Query Language; RDBMS/RDMS; Relational Database Management System; Releases; RPG; S/P; Server; Shareware; Software Driver; Software Package; Software System; Spooler; SQL; State of the Art; Structured Query Language; Subroutine; System; System Software; Systems Programmer; Terminate and Stay Resident; Third Generation Language; Trojan; TSR; Turnkey; UNIX; Utility; Vertical Market; Virus; Virus Checker; Visual Basic; Worm;

Software Development Cycle
A term used to cover stages of development during a software development project.
See Also: *A/P; Analyst; Analyst Programmer; B/A; Bespoke; Business Analyst; Code; Development; Full Project Life Cycle; In-house; Model; Modular; O & M; Organisation & Methods; Process Model; Program Specification; Programmer; Project Life Cycle; Reengineering; S/A; S/P; Software House; Specification; System Analysis; System Analyst; Systems Programmer; Upgrade; Walkthrough; Wizard;*

Software Driver
A program used by the operating system which converts another program's commands into those used by a hardware device. e.g. printer.
See Also: *API; Application Program Interface; ATAPI; Attachment Packet Interface; Code; CODEC; COmpressor DECompressor; Configuring; Device Driver; DLL; Driver; Dynamic Link Library; EXE; Freeware; Function; Instruction Set; Macro; Module; Printer Driver; Program; Software; System Software; Utility;*

Software House
An organisation that develops software for other companies.
See Also: *A/P; Analyst; Analyst Programmer; Application; B/A; Business Analyst; Code; Data Centre; Development; Facilities Management; FM; Full Project Life Cycle; In-house; Programmer; Project Life Cycle; S/A; S/P; Software Development Cycle; System Analyst; Systems Programmer; Technical Author;*

Software Package
A collection of programs for a specific application. e.g. accounting, word processing.
See Also: *AI; Application; Artificial Intelligence; CAD; CADCAM; CADMAT; CAE; CAI; CAM; Case Tool; CBT; Computer Aided Design; Computer Aided Design and Manufacturing; Computer Aided Design Manufacture and Test; Computer Aided Engineering; Computer Aided Instruction; Computer Aided Manufacturing; Computer Based Training; Data Base Management System; DBMS; Desk Top Publishing; DTP; EDS; Electronic Data System; Expert System; Freeware; Geographical Information System; GIS; Information System; Integrated; Integrated Systems; IS; Leading Edge; Mail Merge; Office Information System; OIS; Package; RDBMS/RDMS; Relational Database Management System; Shareware; Software; Software System; Spreadsheet; State of the Art; System; Turnkey; Vertical Market; Word Processor; WP;*

Software System
A collection of programs for a specific application. e.g. accounting, word processing.
See Also: *3GL; 4GL; AI; Application; Artificial Intelligence; Bespoke; CAD; CADCAM; CADMAT; CAE; CAI; CAM; CBT; Code; Computation; Compute; Computer Aided Design; Computer Aided Design and Manufacturing; Computer Aided Design Manufacture and Test; Computer Aided Engineering; Computer Aided Instruction; Computer Aided Manufacturing; Computer Based Training; Configuration; Data Base Management System; Data Processing; DBMS; Debugger; Desk Top Publishing; Development; DP; DTP; EDP; EDS; Electronic Data Processing; Electronic Data System; Facilities Management; Firewall; FM; Fourth Generation Language; Freeware; Geographical Information System; GIS; Graphical User Interface; GUI; Information System; Information Technology; In-house; Integrated; Integrated Systems; IS; IT; Leading Edge; Mail Merge; Office Information System; OIS; Package; Process; Processing; Program; RDBMS/RDMS; Relational Database Management System; Search Engine; Shareware; Software; Software Package; Spider; Spreadsheet;*

State of the Art; System; System Software; Third Generation Language; Turnkey; Vertical Market; Virtual Reality; VR; Word Processor; WP;

Solid State
An electronic component made of solid material with no moving parts. e.g. silicon chip.
See Also: *Application Specific Integrated Circuits; ASICS; Chip; Chipset; IC; Integrated Circuit; Large Scale Integration; Logic Gate; LSI; Memory; Microprocessor; Processor; Semiconductor; Silicon Chip; Sound Chip; Transistor; Very Large Scale Integration; VLSI;*

Sound Card
A printed circuit board in the computer, which controls all the complexities of music and noises, we hear from the computer.
See Also: *Accelerated Graphics Port; Advanced Graphics Port; AGP; AGP Slot; Chipset; Expansion Card; Expansion Slot; Fax Card; Graphics Card; Memory Board; Memory Card; Motherboard; PCB; PCI; PCMCIA; Peripheral Component Interconnect; Personal Computer Memory Card International Association; Printed Circuit Board; Slot; Sound Chip; Stream; Video Card;*

Sound Chip
A chip which allows sound channels to be used on a computer.
See Also: *Application Specific Integrated Circuits; ASICS; Chip; Chipset; Flip Flop; IC; Integrated Circuit; Logic Gate; Microprocessor; Processor; Semiconductor; Silicon Chip; Solid State; Sound Card; Stream; Transistor;*

Source Code
Program instructions written in a high level language which are converted into machine code by a compiler or interpreter.
See Also: *3GL; 4GL; ADA; ALGOL; APL; Assembler; BASIC; C or C++; CLIPPER; COBOL; Code Generator; Compiler; Compiling; CORAL; Extensible Hypertext Markup Language; eXtensible Markup Language; FORTH; FORTRAN; Fourth Generation Language; Instruction Set; Interpreter; JAVA; JAVASCRIPT; Language; LISP; LOGO; NATURAL; PASCAL; PERL; PICK; PILOT; PL/1; Practical Extraction and Reporting Language; Program; Programming Language; PROLOG; Query Language; RPG; SQL; Structured Program; Structured Query Language; Subroutine; Syntax; Third Generation Language; Visual Basic; XHTML; XML;*

Spam
Unsolicited e-mail.
See Also: *Attachment; Body; Chat; Chatroom; Cyberspace; Electronic Mail; E-mail; Hacker; Signature; Trojan; Virus; Virus Checker;*

Specification
A document that defines system requirements. e.g. program specification, hardware specification.
See Also: *A/P; Analyst; Analyst Programmer; B/A; Business Analyst; CASE; Case Tool; Computer Aided Software Engineering; Design; Development; Flowchart; Full Project Life Cycle; Logical Design; Model; Modular; Object Oriented Analysis; Object Oriented Design; Object Oriented Programming; OOA; OOD; OOP; Physical Design; Process Model; Programmer; Project Life Cycle; Reengineering; S/A; S/P; Software Development Cycle; Structured Design; Structured Program; System Analysis; System Analyst; Systems Programmer; Table; Technical Author; Top Down Technique; Tutorial; User Guide; User Manual; Walkthrough;*

Spell Check
A procedure where a document is checked for spelling mistakes by using a pre-recorded dictionary.
See Also: *Batch Processing; Document; Edit; Line Editor; Page Editor; Utility; Word Processor; WP;*

Spider
A tool used by Internet search programs to scan Meta tags on websites which then stores information about those websites for future use.
See Also: *Anchor; Application; Batch Processing; BBS; Bookmark; Browser; Bulletin Board System; Cyberspace; Gopher; Hit; Host; Internet; Internet Service Provider; ISP; Key; Meta Tag; Meta-Search Engine; Net; Portal; Provider; Search Engine; Service Provider; Site; Software System; Surfing; The Net; The Web; Utility; Webhost; Webring; Website; World Wide Web; Worm; WWW;*

Split Screen
A state when the display on a screen is split in two to enable the user to view two separate parts of the same document. This is a standard facility in a word processor.
See Also: *Analogue Monitor; Anti Glare Screen; Cathode Ray Tube; CGA; Colour Graphics Adaptor; CRT; Digital Monitor; Display; EGA; Enhanced Graphic Adaptor; Extended Video Array; Graphics Card; Intelligent Terminal; LCD; Line Editor; Liquid Crystal Display; Low*

Resolution; Monitor; Monochrome; Page Editor; Paint Screen; Plasma Screen; Screen; Super Twist LCD; Super VGA; Super Video Graphics Array; SVGA; Terminal; TFT; Thin-Film Transistor; Touch Screen; VDT; VDU; VGA; Video Display Terminal; Video Graphics Array; Visual Display Terminal; Visual Display Unit; Window; Word Processor; WP; XGA;

Spooler
Software which remains in memory and is activated when output is sent to the printer. It captures the output and stores it temporarily until the printer becomes available. The word SPOOL is an acronym of Simultaneous Peripheral Operation On Line.
See Also: *Batch Processing; Housekeeping; Output; Printer; Program; Software; System Software; Utility;*

Spreadsheet
An application which allows data to be entered in rows and columns that can be totalled or manipulated. Data is entered into cells in the row or column and is manipulated using formulas applied to cells.
See Also: *Application; Computation; Compute; Data Processing; DP; Office Information System; OIS; Package; Processing; Software Package; Software System; Table;*

Sprite
A graphical shape designed to be displayed and moved on the screen.
See Also: *BitMaP; BMP; Clip Art; Cursor; Display; Drag; Floating Toolbar; Frame Rate; GIF; Graphical Interchange Format; Graphics; High Resolution; Icon; Image Map; Image Processing; Joint Photographic Experts Group; JPEG; JPG; Low Resolution; Marquee; Paint Screen; Pixel; Screen; Scroll; Toolbar; Twip;*

SQL
Structured Query Language. A language designed to access databases and to manipulate the data in order to format and produce reports easily.
See Also: *Code; Code Generator; Gopher; High Level Language; Instruction Set; Program; Query Language; Software; Source Code; Structured Program; Structured Query Language; Syntax;*

SSL
Secure Socket Layer. A protocol to enable secure or private transmissions across the Internet.
See Also: *CGI; Common Gateway Interface; Cyberspace; EFT; EFTPOS; Electronic Fund Transfer; Electronic Fund Transfer Point of*

Sales; Encryption; Firewall; Gateway; Handshake; Internet; Internet Protocol; IP; Net; Point to Point Protocol; PPP; Protocol; Secure Socket Layer; Serial Line Internet Protocol; Simple Mail Transfer Protocol; SLIP; SMTP; TCP/IP; The Net; Transmission Control Protocol/Internet Protocol; WAP; Wireless Application Protocol; XMODEM; YMODEM; ZMODEM;

Stack

Memory area allocated to hold temporary data. Data is stored in stack format and each item added to the stack moves the next one down one place.

See Also: *Address; Array; Bubble Memory; Bubble Sort; Buffer; Cache Memory; Clipboard; DDR SDRAM; DIMM; Direct Random Access Memory; Double Data Rate SDRAM; DRAM; Dual Inline Memory Module; Dynamic Memory; EEROM; Electrically Erasable Read Only Memory; Electronically Programmed Read Only Memory; EMS; EPROM; Erasable Programmable Read Only Memory; Expanded Memory; Expanded Memory Specification; Extended Memory; High Memory; Memory Resident; Operand; Overlay; Programmable Read Only Memory; PROM; RAM; RAM Disk; Rambus Dynamic Random Access Memory; Random Access Memory; RDRAM; Read Only Memory; ROM; SDRAM; Shadow RAM Memory; SIMM; Single Inline Memory Modules; Single Inline Package; SIP; Store; Synchronous Dynamic Random Access Memory; Table; Upper Memory; Video Random Access Memory; Virtual Memory; VM; Volatile Memory; VRAM; Working Storage; Workspace;*

Standalone

A computer not connected to any other computer or network.

See Also: *1st Generation; 2nd Generation; 3rd Generation; 4th Generation; Advanced Technology; Analogue Computer; AT; Computer; Cross Platform; Desktop; Digital Computer; Downsizing; EDS; Electronic Data System; Environment; Equipment; Extended Technology; Hardware; IBM (tm) Compatible; Installation; Kit; Laptop; Machine; Micro; Microcomputer; Midrange System; Minicomputer; Multi Platform; Notebook; OEM; Original Equipment Manufacturer; Palmtop Computer; PC; Personal Computer; Platform; Portable; Tower Computer; Turnkey; XT;*

Star Cluster
A type of network that connects multiple computers to a server to share data storage and peripherals. It is known as a 'Star' as the transmission cables are connected directly to the server from each computer.
See Also: *AMR; Anonymous FTP; Automatic Message Routing; Backbone; Bandwidth; BBS; Broadband; Bulletin Board System; Client Server; Client Server Protocol; Distributed System/Network; Environment; Ethernet; File Server; File Sharing; Gateway; Host Processor; Intranet; LAN; LAN Port; Local Area Network; Multi User; Multitasking; Narrowband; Network; Network Information Centre; Network Operating System; NIC; Node; NOS; Open Systems Interconnect; OSI; Ring Network; Server; Star Network; TCP/IP; Token Ring; Transmission Control Protocol/Internet Protocol; WAN; Wide Area Network;*

Star Network
A type of network that connects multiple computers to a server to share data storage and peripherals. It is known as a 'Star' as the transmission cables are connected directly to the server from each computer.
See Also: *AMR; Anonymous FTP; Automatic Message Routing; Backbone; Bandwidth; BBS; Broadband; Bulletin Board System; Client Server; Client Server Protocol; Distributed System/Network; Environment; Ethernet; File Server; File Sharing; Gateway; Host Processor; Intranet; LAN; LAN Port; Local Area Network; Multi User; Multitasking; Narrowband; Network; Network Information Centre; Network Operating System; NIC; Node; NOS; Open Systems Interconnect; OSI; Ring Network; Server; Star Cluster; TCP/IP; Token Ring; Transmission Control Protocol/Internet Protocol; WAN; Wide Area Network;*

State of the Art
The latest or newest hardware and software on the market.
See Also: *AI; Artificial Intelligence; Computer; Cross Platform; Development; Device; Digital; EDS; Electronic Data System; Equipment; Hardware; Kit; Leading Edge; Machine; Mainframe; Midrange System; Minicomputer; Package; PC; Peripheral; Personal Computer; Platform; Plug Compatible; Recording Device; Releases; Silicon Valley; Software; Software Package; Software System; Tower Computer;*

Storage

(1) The recording medium on which data is stored. e.g. hard disk or magnetic tape. (2) The storage device which uses the medium.

See Also: *3.5 Inch; 5.25 Inch; Archive; ATAPI; Attachment Packet Interface; Backing Store; Backup; Bits Per Inch; Block; Boot Disk; BPI; CD-RW Drive; Cluster; Compressed File; Computer Power; Configuration; Cylinder; DAT; Deck; Density; Device; Digital Audio Tape; Digital Versatile Disk; Direct Memory Access; Directory; Disk; Disk Drive; Disk Pack; Disk Size; Disk Storage; Diskette; DMA; Double Density; Drive; DVD; Equipment; FDD; Five and a quarter; Fixed Disk Drive; Floppy Disk; Floppy Disk Drive; Fragmentation; Grandfather, Father, Son; Hard Disk Drive; Hardware; HDD; Heads; High Density; Installation; Kit; Mag Tape; Magnetic Disk; Magnetic Tape; Mass Storage; Medium; Optical Drive; Output; Pack; Paper Tape; Path; Peripheral; Power; Read/Write Head; Recording; Recording Device; Recording Medium; Remote Device; Root Directory; Save; Sector; Security; Seek Time; Store; Streamer; Sub Directory; Tape Deck; Tape Streamer; Three and a Half; Track; Volume; Winchester Disk; Wipe; Write; Write Protect; Zip; Zip Drive;*

Store

(1) The computers memory. (2) Storage devices. (3) The process of storing information on those devices.

See Also: *3.5 Inch; 5.25 Inch; Absolute Address; Address; Archive; Array; Backing Store; Backup; Bits Per Inch; Block; BPI; Bubble Memory; Buffer; Cache Memory; CD-RW Drive; CMOS; Complementary Metal Oxide Semiconductor Memory; Computer Power; Configuration; Conventional Memory; Core; Core Dump; DAT; DDR SDRAM; Deck; Device; Digital Audio Tape; Digital Versatile Disk; DIMM; Direct Memory Access; Direct Random Access Memory; Disk; Disk Cache; Disk Drive; Disk Pack; Disk Size; Disk Storage; Diskette; DMA; Double Data Rate SDRAM; DRAM; Drive; Dual Inline Memory Module; Dump; DVD; Dynamic Memory; Dynamically; EEROM; EIDE; EISA; Electrically Erasable Read Only Memory; Electronically Programmed Read Only Memory; EMS; Enhanced Industry Standard Architecture; Enhanced Intelligent Drive Electronics; EPROM; Equipment; Erasable Programmable Read Only Memory; Expanded Memory; Expanded Memory Specification; Extended Memory; FDD; Five and a quarter; Fixed Disk Drive; Flash Memory; Floppy Disk; Floppy Disk Drive; Grandfather, Father, Son; Hard Disk Drive; Hardware; HDD; Heads; High Memory; Installation; Key; Kit; Mag Tape; Magnetic Core; Magnetic Disk; Magnetic Tape; Mass Storage; Memory; Memory Caching; Memory Resident; Mix; Optical Drive; Overlay; Pack;*

Peripheral; Power; Programmable Read Only Memory; PROM; R/W; RAM; RAM Disk; Rambus Dynamic Random Access Memory; Random Access Memory; RDRAM; Read Only Memory; Read/Write; Read/Write Head; Recording; Recording Device; Register; Relative Address; Remote Device; ROM; Save; SDRAM; Shadow RAM Memory; SIMM; Single Inline Memory Modules; Single Inline Package; SIP; Stack; Storage; Streamer; Synchronous Dynamic Random Access Memory; System; Tape Deck; Tape Streamer; Three and a Half; Upper Memory; Video Random Access Memory; Volatile Memory; Volume; VRAM; Winchester Disk; Wipe; Working Storage; Workspace; Write; Write Protect; Zip; Zip Drive;

Stream
A term used when music or video clips are downloaded from the Internet to be listened to or viewed without the data being saved on the computer.
See Also: *CODEC; COmpressor DECompressor; Download; Internet; MIME; Motion Picture Experts Group; MP3; MPEG; MPG; Multimedia; Multipurpose Internet Mail Extensions; Online; Real Time; Sound Card; Sound Chip; Video Card; WAV; Waveform Audio; Webcam;*

Streamer
(1) A magnetic tape medium. (2) The device which uses the tape medium.
See Also: *Archive; Backing Store; Backup; Bits Per Inch; Block; BPI; Configuration; Deck; Density; Device; Double Density; Drive; Equipment; Grandfather, Father, Son; Hardware; Heads; High Density; Installation; Kit; Mag Tape; Magnetic Tape; Mass Storage; Medium; Peripheral; Read/Write Head; Recording; Recording Device; Recording Medium; Root Directory; Save; Storage; Store; Tape Deck; Tape Streamer; Track; Write; Write Protect; Zip Drive;*

String
A data item made up of alphanumeric characters.
See Also: *Character; Comma Separated Values; Concatenate; CSV; Data; Data Element; Data Entity; Data Item; Data Type; EBCDIC; Extended Binary Coded Decimal Interchange Code; Information; Input; Null; Parameter; Record; Variable; Word;*

Structured Design
A design which is constructed in a logical and modular format.
See Also: *A/P; Analyst; Analyst Programmer; B/A; Business Analyst; Data Flow; Data Flow Diagram; Data Model; Development; DFD; Full Project Life Cycle; Logical Design; Model; Modular; Module; O & M; Object Oriented Analysis; Object Oriented Design; Object Oriented*

Programming; OOA; OOD; OOP; Organisation & Methods; Physical Design; Process Model; Program Specification; Programmer; Project Life Cycle; S/A; S/P; Specification; Structured Program; System Analysis; System Analyst; Systems Programmer; Top Down Technique; Walkthrough;

Structured Program
A program which is divided into modules where each module performs a specific task.
See Also: *A/P; ADA; ALGOL; Analyst Programmer; API; APL; Application Program Interface; BASIC; C or C++; CLIPPER; COBOL; Code; CORAL; Development; FORTH; FORTRAN; LISP; LOGO; Loop; Model; Modular; Module; NATURAL; PASCAL; PERL; PICK; PILOT; PL/1; Practical Extraction and Reporting Language; Process Model; Program; Programmer; PROLOG; Query Language; RPG; S/P; Source Code; Specification; SQL; Structured Design; Structured Query Language; Systems Programmer; Top Down Technique;*

Structured Query Language
(SQL). A language designed to access databases and to manipulate the data in order to format and produce reports easily.
See Also: *Code; Code Generator; Gopher; High Level Language; Instruction Set; Program; Query Language; Software; Source Code; SQL; Structured Program; Syntax;*

Sub Directory
A directory within another directory of an index of files on a storage device.
See Also: *3.5 Inch; 5.25 Inch; CD-ROM; Directory; Disk; Disk Pack; Disk Storage; Diskette; FAT; Fiche; File; File Allocation Table; Five and a quarter; Floppy Disk; Folder; Magnetic Disk; Microfiche; Optical Disk; Pack; Path; Recording Medium; Root Directory; Storage; Three and a Half; Volume;*

Subroutine
A set of instructions within a program which can be executed many times from different parts of the program to perform a specific task.
See Also: *Call; Chain; Code; Command; DLL; Dynamic Link Library; Function; Instruction Set; Invoke; JCL; Job Control Language; Macro; Nesting; Process; Program; Script; Software; Source Code;*

Subscript
(1) A number which refers to the position of an item in a table or array.
(2) Characters printed lower than the normal characters. e.g. H_2O.
See Also: *Array; Character; Data Element; Data Item; Entity; Field; Key; Matrix; Table; Tag; Variable;*

Super Twist LCD
A visual display unit design technology that switches a shutter on and off in the display which allows for a faster display.
See Also: *Analogue Monitor; Anti Glare Screen; Cathode Ray Tube; CGA; Colour Graphics Adaptor; CRT; Device; Digital Monitor; Display; EGA; Enhanced Graphic Adaptor; Environment; Equipment; Extended Video Array; Graphics Card; Hardware; High Resolution; Installation; Intelligent Terminal; Interlaced; Kit; LCD; Liquid Crystal Display; Low Resolution; Monitor; Monochrome; Output; Paint Screen; Peripheral; Plasma Screen; Prompt; Resolution; Screen; Screen Burn; Split Screen; Super VGA; Super Video Graphics Array; SVGA; Terminal; TFT; Thin-Film Transistor; Touch Screen; Twip; VDT; VDU; VGA; Video Card; Video Display Terminal; Video Graphics Array; Video Random Access Memory; Visual Display Terminal; Visual Display Unit; VRAM; XGA;*

Super VGA
Super Video Graphics Array. A visual display unit design which has a resolution of 800x600 dots with 256 colours or 1024x768 dots with 16 colours.
See Also: *Analogue Monitor; Anti Glare Screen; Cathode Ray Tube; CGA; Colour Graphics Adaptor; CRT; Device; Digital Monitor; Display; EGA; Enhanced Graphic Adaptor; Environment; Equipment; Extended Video Array; Graphics Card; Hardware; High Resolution; Installation; Intelligent Terminal; Interlaced; Kit; LCD; Liquid Crystal Display; Low Resolution; Monitor; Monochrome; Output; Paint Screen; Peripheral; Plasma Screen; Prompt; Resolution; Screen; Screen Burn; Split Screen; Super Twist LCD; Super Video Graphics Array; SVGA; Terminal; TFT; Thin-Film Transistor; Touch Screen; Twip; VDT; VDU; VGA; Video Card; Video Display Terminal; Video Graphics Array; Video Random Access Memory; Visual Display Terminal; Visual Display Unit; VRAM; XGA;*

Super Video Graphics Array
(SVGA). A visual display unit design which has a resolution of 800x600 dots with 256 colours or 1024x768 dots with 16 colours.
See Also: *Analogue Monitor; Anti Glare Screen; Cathode Ray Tube; CGA; Colour Graphics Adaptor; CRT; Device; Digital Monitor; Display;*

EGA; Enhanced Graphic Adaptor; Environment; Equipment; Extended Video Array; Graphics Card; Hardware; High Resolution; Installation; Intelligent Terminal; Interlaced; Kit; LCD; Liquid Crystal Display; Low Resolution; Monitor; Monochrome; Output; Paint Screen; Peripheral; Plasma Screen; Prompt; Resolution; Screen; Screen Burn; Split Screen; Super Twist LCD; Super VGA; SVGA; Terminal; TFT; Thin-Film Transistor; Touch Screen; Twip; VDT; VDU; VGA; Video Card; Video Display Terminal; Video Graphics Array; Video Random Access Memory; Visual Display Terminal; Visual Display Unit; VRAM; XGA;

Surfing

Surf or surfing the net. Searching for websites on the Internet using Search Engines and search criteria.

See Also: *Bookmark; Browser; Cyberspace; Forum; Hacker; Hit; Home Page; Host; Hyperlink; Information Superhighway; Internet; Internet Service Provider; ISP; Meta Tag; Meta-Search Engine; Nerd; Net; Netiquette; Newbie; Page; PING; Portal; Provider; Search Engine; Service Provider; Site; Spider; The Net; The Web; Universal/Uniform Resource Locator; URL; Webcam; Webhost; Webring; Website; World Wide Web; WWW;*

SVGA

Super Video Graphics Array. A visual display unit design which has a resolution of 800x600 dots with 256 colours or 1024x768 dots with 16 colours.

See Also: *Analogue Monitor; Anti Glare Screen; Cathode Ray Tube; CGA; Colour Graphics Adaptor; CRT; Device; Digital Monitor; Display; EGA; Enhanced Graphic Adaptor; Environment; Equipment; Extended Video Array; Graphics Card; Hardware; High Resolution; Installation; Intelligent Terminal; Interlaced; Kit; LCD; Liquid Crystal Display; Low Resolution; Monitor; Monochrome; Output; Paint Screen; Peripheral; Plasma Screen; Prompt; Resolution; Screen; Screen Burn; Split Screen; Super Twist LCD; Super VGA; Super Video Graphics Array; Terminal; TFT; Thin-Film Transistor; Touch Screen; Twip; VDT; VDU; VGA; Video Card; Video Display Terminal; Video Graphics Array; Video Random Access Memory; Visual Display Terminal; Visual Display Unit; VRAM; XGA;*

Swapping
The transfer of data, part of a program or a program in and out of memory to disk, which allows the memory to become available for other processing.
See Also: *Bloatware; Bubble Memory; Buffer; Cache Memory; Data; DDR SDRAM; DIMM; Direct Random Access Memory; Double Data Rate SDRAM; DRAM; Dual Inline Memory Module; Dynamic Memory; EEROM; Electrically Erasable Read Only Memory; Electronically Programmed Read Only Memory; EMS; EPROM; Erasable Programmable Read Only Memory; Expanded Memory; Expanded Memory Specification; Extended Memory; High Memory; Housekeeping; Memory Caching; Program; Programmable Read Only Memory; PROM; RAM; RAM Disk; Rambus Dynamic Random Access Memory; Random Access Memory; RDRAM; Read Only Memory; ROM; SDRAM; Shadow RAM Memory; SIMM; Single Inline Memory Modules; Single Inline Package; SIP; Synchronous Dynamic Random Access Memory; Terminate and Stay Resident; Time Share; Time Slice; Trashing; TSR; Upper Memory; Virtual Memory; VM; Volatile Memory;*

Synchronous
Communication where prepared sets of data are transmitted in blocks at fixed rates of time.
See Also: *ACK; Acoustic Coupler; ADN; ADSL; Advanced Digital Network; Asymmetric Digital Subscriber Line; Asymmetrical Modem; Asynchronous; Asynchronous Transfer Mode; ATM; Bandwidth; Baud Rate; Bits Per Second; BPS; Broadband; Bus; CCITT; CCTA; Characters Per Second; Communications; Consultative Committee International Telegraph and Telephone; CPS; Data Communications; Data Parity; Data Transmission; Datacoms; Dial In; Dial Up; Digital; Direct Connection; Duplex Transmission; FDDI; Fibre Distributed Data Interface; Fibre Optics; Full Duplex; Gbps; Half Duplex; HD; Information Superhighway; Integrated Services Digital Network; ISDN; Kbps; Leased Line; Mbps; Multiplex; Multiplexer; Narrowband; Open Systems Interconnect; Optical Fibre; OSI; Packet; Packet Switching; Parallel Transmission; Parity Bit; Serial Interface; Serial Transmission; Simplex Transmission; T-1; T-3; Telecommunication; Telecoms; Teleprocessing System; TPS; Transmit; V90;*

Synchronous Dynamic Random Access Memory
(SDRAM). A type of computer memory.
See Also: *Basic Input Output System; BIOS; Bubble Memory; Buffer; Cache Memory; CMOS; Complementary Metal Oxide Semiconductor Memory; Computer Power; Conventional Memory; Core; Core Dump;*

DDR SDRAM; DIMM; Direct Memory Access; Direct Random Access Memory; Disk Cache; DMA; Double Data Rate SDRAM; DRAM; Dual Inline Memory Module; Dynamic Memory; Dynamically; EEROM; Electrically Erasable Read Only Memory; Electronically Programmed Read Only Memory; EMS; EPROM; Erasable Programmable Read Only Memory; Expanded Memory; Expanded Memory Specification; Extended Memory; Flash Memory; High Memory; Magnetic Core; Memory; Memory Board; Memory Caching; Memory Card; Memory Resident; Mix; Power; Programmable Read Only Memory; PROM; RAM; RAM Disk; Rambus Dynamic Random Access Memory; Random Access Memory; RDRAM; Read Only Memory; ROM; SDRAM; Shadow RAM Memory; SIMM; Single Inline Memory Modules; Single Inline Package; SIP; Stack; Store; Swapping; Upper Memory; Video Random Access Memory; VRAM; Working Storage; Workspace;

Syntax
The rules for coding program instructions, entering commands or writing statements.
See Also: *3GL; 4GL; ADA; ALGOL; APL; BASIC; C or C++; CLIPPER; COBOL; CODASYL; Code; Command; Compiler; Conference On DAta SYstems Languages; CORAL; Development; FORTH; FORTRAN; Fourth Generation Language; Instruction; Instruction Set; Interpreter; JAVA; JAVASCRIPT; JCL; Job Control Language; Line Editor; LISP; LOGO; NATURAL; Page Editor; PASCAL; PERL; PICK; Picture; PILOT; PL/1; Practical Extraction and Reporting Language; Program; PROLOG; Query Language; RPG; Source Code; SQL; Structured Query Language; Third Generation Language; Visual Basic;*

System
A collective term for hardware or software.
See Also: *1st Generation; 2nd Generation; 3GL; 3rd Generation; 4GL; 4th Generation; Access; Application; Backing Store; Bespoke; Central Processing Unit; Client Server; Computer; Computer Power; Configuration; Configuring; Core; CPU; Cross Platform; Data Base Management System; DBMS; Deck; Desktop; Device; Disk Storage; Distributed System/Network; EDS; Electronic Data System; Environment; Equipment; Fourth Generation Language; Hardware; Information System; Installation; Integrated Systems; IS; Kit; Machine; Mass Storage; Memory; Monitor; Multi Platform; Office Information System; OIS; Peripheral; Platform; Power; Printer; Processor; RDBMS/RDMS; Recording Device; Relational Database Management System; Screen; Server; Software; Software Package; Software System; Store; Terminal; TFT; Thin-Film Transistor; Third Generation*

Language; Third Party Maintenance; Touch Screen; Turnkey; VDT; VDU; VGA; Video Display Terminal; Video Graphics Array; Visual Display Terminal; Visual Display Unit;

System Analysis
The procedure for capturing user requirements, analysing those requirements and designing a computer system.
See Also: *Analyst; B/A; Business Analyst; Design; Development; Full Project Life Cycle; Logical Design; Model; Object Oriented Analysis; Object Oriented Design; Object Oriented Programming; OOA; OOD; OOP; Physical Design; Process Model; Project Life Cycle; S/A; Software Development Cycle; Specification; Structured Design; System Analyst; Walkthrough;*

System Analyst
(S/A). A person who analyses, designs and documents a computer software system.
See Also: *A/P; Analyst; Analyst Programmer; B/A; Business Analyst; Contractor; Data Base Analyst; Data Processing Manager; DBA; Design; Development; DPM; Full Project Life Cycle; Hand Holding; Logical Design; Model; O & M; Object Oriented Analysis; Object Oriented Design; Object Oriented Programming; OOA; OOD; OOP; Organisation & Methods; Physical Design; Process Model; Program Specification; Programmer; Project Life Cycle; S/A; S/P; Software Development Cycle; Software House; Specification; Structured Design; System Analysis; Systems Programmer; Technical Author; Walkthrough;*

System Bus
A transmission channel within the computer which transfers data between the memory and the processor.
See Also: *16 Bit; 32 Bit; 64 Bit; 8 Bit; Address Bus; Bits Per Second; BPS; Bus; Central Processing Unit; Channel; Characters Per Second; Co-processor; CPS; CPU; Data Bus; Digital; Eight Bit; Gbps; I/O; Industry Standard Architecture; Input/Output; ISA; Kbps; Local Bus; Maths Co-processor; Mbps; Sixteen Bit; Sixty Four Bit; Thirty Two Bit; Transfer Rate; Transmission Channel;*

System Hangs
A term used when a computer hardware or software system stops in the middle of processing with no indication of the cause.
See Also: *Abort; Bug; Busy; Crash; Dead Lock; Deadly Embrace; Debug; Debugger; Died; Downtime; General Protection Fault; GPF;*

Hangs; Head Crash; Hung; Locking; Machine Crash; Program Crash; Record Locking;

System Software
Programs used in a computer which are not application programs.
See Also: *3GL; 4GL; API; Application Program Interface; Basic Input Output System; BIOS; Boot; Bootstrap; Command; Configuration; Development; Device Driver; Disk Operating System; DLL; DOS; Driver; Dynamic Link Library; Firmware; Fourth Generation Language; Function; Graphical User Interface; GUI; Housekeeping; Instruction; Linux; Network Operating System; NOS; Operating System; OS; OS/2; Print Spooler; Program; Software; Software Driver; Software System; Spooler; Third Generation Language; UNIX;*

Systems Programmer
(S/P). A person who is responsible for implementing and maintaining the system software in a computer system.
See Also: *A/P; Analyst; Analyst Programmer; B/A; Business Analyst; Code; Contractor; Data Base Analyst; Data Processing Manager; DBA; Design; Development; DPM; Full Project Life Cycle; Language; Logical Design; Loop; Physical Design; Program; Program Specification; Programmer; Programming Language; Project Life Cycle; S/A; S/P; Software; Software Development Cycle; Software House; Specification; Structured Design; Structured Program; System Analyst; Technical Author;*

T-1
A network link on the Internet allowing transmission speeds of up to 1.54 megabits per second.
See Also: *Access; ADN; ADSL; Advanced Digital Network; Asymmetric Digital Subscriber Line; Asymmetrical Modem; Asynchronous; Asynchronous Transfer Mode; ATM; Bandwidth; Baud Rate; BBS; Bits Per Second; BPS; Broadband; Bulletin Board System; Characters Per Second; CPS; Gbps; Integrated Services Digital Network; Internet; ISDN; Kbps; Mbps; Multiplex; Multiplexer; Narrowband; Net; Node; Parallel Transmission; Serial Transmission; Synchronous; T-3; Telecommunication; Telecoms; The Net; Transmit;*

T-3
A network link on the Internet allowing transmission speeds of up to 45 megabits per second.
See Also: *Access; ADN; ADSL; Advanced Digital Network; Asymmetric Digital Subscriber Line; Asymmetrical Modem; Asynchronous;*

Asynchronous Transfer Mode; ATM; Bandwidth; Baud Rate; BBS; Bits Per Second; BPS; Broadband; Bulletin Board System; Characters Per Second; CPS; Gbps; Integrated Services Digital Network; Internet; ISDN; Kbps; Mbps; Multiplex; Multiplexer; Narrowband; Net; Node; Parallel Transmission; Serial Transmission; Synchronous; T-1; Telecommunication; Telecoms; The Net; Transmit;

Table
A list of items in a database or in the computers memory set up by a program. It can be a single list (one dimensional), double list (two dimensional) etc. Each item in the table is referenced by a subscript.
See Also: *Array; Comma Separated Values; CSV; Data; Data Element; Data Entity; Data Item; Data Type; Database; DB; File; Information; Matrix; Null; Record; Specification; Spreadsheet; Stack; Subscript; Tag; Tag File; Variable; Word;*

Tag
(1) To mark an item for later processing. (2) An index record in a file which serves as a pointer to a record in another file and allows for faster processing.
See Also: *Bookmark; Comma Separated Values; CSV; Direct Access; Key; Random Access; Record; Recording; Subscript; Table; Tag File; Temp File;*

Tag File
A file of index records which points to records in another file and used for faster processing.
See Also: *ASCII Files; Attachment; Beginning of File; BOF; Database; DB; Direct Access; End of File; EOF; File; Fragmentation; Index Sequential File; Key; Log File; Random Access; Random File; Sequential File; Serial File; Table; Tag; Temp File;*

Tag Image File Format
(TIFF). A file format in which graphic images are stored.
See Also: *Attachment; BitMaP; BMP; Clip Art; Extension; Filename Extension; Format; GIF; Graphical Interchange Format; Graphics; Image Processing; Joint Photographic Experts Group; JPEG; JPG; MIME; Multipurpose Internet Mail Extensions; PDF; Portable Document Format; Resolution; Rich Text Format; RTF; Thumbnail; TIFF;*

Tape Deck
A peripheral device which uses magnetic tape to store information.
See Also: *Archive; Backing Store; Backup; Configuration; DAT; Deck; Device; Digital Audio Tape; Drive; End of Tape; Environment; EOT; Equipment; Grandfather, Father, Son; Hardware; Heads; Installation; Kit; Mag Tape; Magnetic Tape; Mass Storage; Peripheral; Read/Write Head; Recording; Recording Device; Save; Storage; Store; Streamer; Tape Streamer;*

Tape Streamer
(1) A magnetic tape medium. (2) The device which uses the tape medium.
See Also: *Archive; Backing Store; Backup; Bits Per Inch; Block; BPI; Configuration; DAT; Deck; Density; Device; Digital Audio Tape; Double Density; Drive; End of Tape; Environment; EOT; Equipment; Grandfather, Father, Son; Hardware; Heads; High Density; Installation; Kit; Mag Tape; Magnetic Tape; Mass Storage; Medium; Peripheral; Read/Write Head; Recording; Recording Device; Recording Medium; Root Directory; Save; Storage; Store; Streamer; Tape Deck;*

TCP/IP
Transmission Control Protocol/Internet Protocol. A set of rules that determine the exchange of information from one computer or network to another.
See Also: *Acceptable User Policy; Anonymous FTP; AUP; Bandwidth; Broadband; Client Server Protocol; Compatible; Download; Ethernet; File Server; File Transfer Protocol; FTP; Gateway; Handshake; HTTP; Hypertext Transfer Protocol; Interface; Internet; Internet Protocol; IP; LAN; Local Area Network; Narrowband; Net; Network; Open Systems Interconnect; OSI; Protocol; Ring Network; Secure Socket Layer; Serial Line Internet Protocol; Simple Mail Transfer Protocol; SLIP; SMTP; SSL; Star Cluster; Star Network; The Net; Token Ring; Transmission Control Protocol/Internet Protocol; WAN; Wide Area Network; XMODEM; YMODEM; ZMODEM;*

Technical Author
A person who prepares manuals, user guides or any supporting documentation for a system.
See Also: *A/P; Analyst; Analyst Programmer; B/A; Business Analyst; Contractor; Data Base Analyst; Data Processing Manager; DBA; DPM; Full Project Life Cycle; Programmer; Project Life Cycle; S/A; S/P; Software House; Specification; System Analyst; Systems Programmer; User; User Guide; User Manual; Walkthrough;*

Telecommunication
The transmission of data along telecommunication lines or through the air.
See Also: *ACK; Acoustic Coupler; ADN; ADSL; Advanced Digital Network; AMR; Asymmetric Digital Subscriber Line; Asymmetrical Modem; Asynchronous; Asynchronous Transfer Mode; ATM; Automatic Message Routing; Bandwidth; Baud Rate; Bits Per Second; Bluetooth (tm); BPS; Broadband; CCITT; CCTA; Characters Per Second; Client Server Protocol; Communications; Consultative Committee International Telegraph and Telephone; CPS; Data Communications; Data Parity; Data Transmission; Datacoms; Dial In; Dial Up; Direct Connection; Download; Duplex Transmission; FDDI; Fibre Distributed Data Interface; Fibre Optics; Full Duplex; Gbps; GHz; Gigahertz; Half Duplex; HD; Integrated Services Digital Network; ISDN; Kbps; KHz; Kilohertz; Leased Line; Mbps; Modem; Modulator Demodulator; Multiplex; Multiplexer; Narrowband; Node; Open Systems Interconnect; Optical Fibre; OSI; Packet; Packet Switching; Parallel Transmission; Parity Bit; Serial Interface; Serial Transmission; Simplex Transmission; Synchronous; T-1; T-3; Telecoms; Teleprocessing System; TPS; Transfer Rate; Transmit; V90; WAP; Wi-Fi; Wireless Application Protocol; Wireless Fidelity;*

Telecoms
Telecommunication. The transmission of data along telecommunication lines or through the air.
See Also: *ACK; Acoustic Coupler; ADN; ADSL; Advanced Digital Network; AMR; Asymmetric Digital Subscriber Line; Asymmetrical Modem; Asynchronous; Asynchronous Transfer Mode; ATM; Automatic Message Routing; Bandwidth; Baud Rate; Bits Per Second; Bluetooth (tm); BPS; Broadband; CCITT; CCTA; Characters Per Second; Client Server Protocol; Communications; Consultative Committee International Telegraph and Telephone; CPS; Data Communications; Data Parity; Data Transmission; Datacoms; Dial In; Dial Up; Direct Connection; Download; Duplex Transmission; FDDI; Fibre Distributed Data Interface; Fibre Optics; Full Duplex; Gbps; GHz; Gigahertz; Half Duplex; HD; Integrated Services Digital Network; ISDN; Kbps; KHz; Kilohertz; Leased Line; Mbps; Modem; Modulator Demodulator; Multiplex; Multiplexer; Narrowband; Node; Open Systems Interconnect; Optical Fibre; OSI; Packet; Packet Switching; Parallel Transmission; Parity Bit; Serial Interface; Serial Transmission; Simplex Transmission; Synchronous; T-1; T-3; Telecommunication; Teleprocessing System; TPS; Transfer Rate; Transmit; V90; WAP; Wi-Fi; Wireless Application Protocol; Wireless Fidelity;*

Teleprocessing System
(TPS). A system where data processing is performed on a remote computer which is linked to a main computer elsewhere.
See Also: *Acoustic Coupler; ADN; ADSL; Advanced Digital Network; AMR; Asymmetric Digital Subscriber Line; Asymmetrical Modem; Asynchronous; Asynchronous Transfer Mode; ATM; Automatic Message Routing; Bandwidth; Baud Rate; Broadband; CCITT; CCTA; Communications; Computation; Compute; Consultative Committee International Telegraph and Telephone; Data Communications; Data Processing; Data Transmission; Datacoms; Dial In; Dial Up; Direct Connection; Distributed System/Network; DP; EFT; EFTPOS; Electronic Fund Transfer; Electronic Fund Transfer Point of Sales; FDDI; Fibre Distributed Data Interface; Fibre Optics; File Server; Full Duplex; Integrated Services Digital Network; ISDN; Kbps; Leased Line; Modem; Modulator Demodulator; Multiplex; Multiplexer; Narrowband; Optical Fibre; Parallel Transmission; Processing; Serial Interface; Serial Transmission; Synchronous; Telecommunication; Telecoms; TPS; Transmit; V90;*

Temp File
A data file created within a program for temporary use and deleted when the program terminates.
See Also: *ASCII Files; Attachment; Batch File; Beginning of File; BOF; End of File; EOF; File; Fragmentation; Index Sequential File; Log File; Random File; Recovery; Sequential File; Serial File; Tag; Tag File;*

Terabyte
1000 gigabytes of information.
See Also: *Byte; Character; Data; Gb; Gigabyte; K; Kb; Kbyte; Kilobit; Kilobyte; Mb; Mbyte; Megabit; Megabyte;*

Terminal
A device consisting of a cathode ray tube and used to view data or used with a keyboard to input data and interact with a computer.
See Also: *Analogue Monitor; Anti Glare Screen; Cathode Ray Tube; CGA; Colour Graphics Adaptor; Configuration; CRT; Device; Digital Monitor; Display; EGA; Enhanced Graphic Adaptor; Environment; Equipment; Extended Video Array; Graphics Card; Hardware; High Resolution; Installation; Intelligent Terminal; Interlaced; Kit; LCD; Liquid Crystal Display; Low Resolution; Monitor; Monochrome; Output; Paint Screen; Peripheral; Plasma Screen; Prompt; Resolution; Screen; Screen Burn; Split Screen; Super Twist LCD; Super VGA; Super Video Graphics Array; SVGA; System; TFT; Thin-Film Transistor; Touch*

Screen; VDT; VDU; VGA; Video Card; Video Display Terminal; Video Graphics Array; Video Random Access Memory; Visual Display Terminal; Visual Display Unit; VRAM; XGA;

Terminate and Stay Resident
(TSR). Programs that are loaded into the computer's memory and remain dormant until activated by another process.
See Also: *Code; DLL; Dynamic Link Library; Dynamically; High Memory; Interrupt; Interrupt Request; IRQ; Memory Resident; Mix; Overlay; Program; Software; Swapping; Trojan; TSR; Upper Memory;*

TFT
Thin-Film Transistor. Technology used to create thin, flat colour screens for VDU monitors.
See Also: *Analogue Monitor; Anti Glare Screen; Cathode Ray Tube; CGA; Colour Graphics Adaptor; Configuration; CRT; Device; Digital Monitor; Display; EGA; Enhanced Graphic Adaptor; Environment; Equipment; Extended Video Array; Frame Rate; Graphics Card; Hardware; High Resolution; Installation; Intelligent Terminal; Interlaced; Kit; LCD; Liquid Crystal Display; Low Resolution; Monitor; Monochrome; Output; Paint Screen; Peripheral; Plasma Screen; Prompt; Resolution; Screen; Screen Burn; Split Screen; Super Twist LCD; Super VGA; Super Video Graphics Array; SVGA; System; Terminal; Thin-Film Transistor; Touch Screen; VDT; VDU; VGA; Video Card; Video Display Terminal; Video Graphics Array; Video Random Access Memory; Visual Display Terminal; Visual Display Unit; VRAM; XGA;*

The Net
The Internet. A collection of inter-connected computers and networks around the world.
See Also: *Acceptable User Policy; Anchor; Applet; AUP; Bandwidth; BBS; Bookmark; Broadband; Browser; Bulletin Board System; CERN; CGI; Chat; Chatroom; Client Server Protocol; Common Gateway Interface; Conseil Europeen pour la Recherche Nucleaire; Cybercafe; Cyberspace; DNS; Domain Name; Domain Name Server; Domain Name System; Dot; Gopher; Hit; Home Page; Host; Host Processor; HTML; HTTP; Hyperlink; Hypertext Mark-Up Language; Hypertext Transfer Protocol; IM; Information Superhighway; Instant Messaging; Internet; Internet Protocol; Internet Protocol Address; Internet Relay Chat; Internet Service Provider; IP; IP Address; IRC; ISP; Link; Message Boards; Meta Tag; Meta-Search Engine; Narrowband; Net; Netiquette; Newbie; Newsgroup; Page; PING; Point Of Presence; Point to Point*

Protocol; POP; PPP; Provider; Proxy Server; Search Engine; Secure Socket Layer; Serial Line Internet Protocol; Service Provider; Simple Mail Transfer Protocol; Site; SLIP; SMTP; Spider; SSL; Surfing; T-1; T-3; TCP/IP; The Web; Transmission Control Protocol/Internet Protocol; WAP; Wap Internet Service Provider; Webhost; Webring; Website; Wireless Application Protocol; WISP; World Wide Web; Worm; WWW;

The Web
The World Wide Web or WWW. All the websites available on the Internet.
See Also: *Acceptable User Policy; Anchor; AUP; Bookmark; Browser; CERN; CGI; Common Gateway Interface; Conseil Europeen pour la Recherche Nucleaire; Cybercafe; Cyberspace; DNS; Domain Name; Domain Name Server; Domain Name System; Extensible Hypertext Markup Language; eXtensible Markup Language; Forum; FTP Site; Global; Hit; Home Page; Host; HTML; HTTP; Hyperlink; Hypertext; Hypertext Mark-Up Language; Hypertext Transfer Protocol; Information Superhighway; Internet; Link; Meta-Search Engine; Mirror Site; Net; Newbie; Page; Portal; Proxy Server; Search Engine; Site; Spider; Surfing; The Net; Universal/Uniform Resource Locator; URL; Webcam; Webhost; Webring; Website; World Wide Web; Worm; WWW; XHTML; XML;*

Thermal Printer
A printer where characters formed on the print head are transferred to thermal paper using a heat process.
See Also: *Barrel Printer; Bi Directional; Bubble Jet; Configuration; Cut Sheet Feeder; Daisywheel; Device; Dot Matrix; Drum Printer; Duplex Printing; Environment; Equipment; Font Cartridge; Hard Copy; Hardware; Inkjet; Installation; Kit; Landscape; Laser Jet; Laser Printer; LCD Printer; Line Printer; Lines Per Minute; Liquid Crystal Display Printer; Lpm; Matrix Printer; Page Printer; Pages Per Minute; Peripheral; Portrait; PPM; Printer; Printer Driver; Printout; Sheet Feeder; Simplex Printing;*

Thin-Film Transistor
(TFT). Technology used to create thin, flat colour screens for VDU monitors
See Also: *Analogue Monitor; Anti Glare Screen; Cathode Ray Tube; CGA; Colour Graphics Adaptor; Configuration; CRT; Device; Digital Monitor; Display; EGA; Enhanced Graphic Adaptor; Environment; Equipment; Extended Video Array; Frame Rate; Graphics Card; Hardware; High Resolution; Installation; Intelligent Terminal;*

Interlaced; Kit; LCD; Liquid Crystal Display; Low Resolution; Monitor; Monochrome; Output; Paint Screen; Peripheral; Plasma Screen; Prompt; Resolution; Screen; Screen Burn; Split Screen; Super Twist LCD; Super VGA; Super Video Graphics Array; SVGA; System; Terminal; TFT; Touch Screen; VDT; VDU; VGA; Video Card; Video Display Terminal; Video Graphics Array; Video Random Access Memory; Visual Display Terminal; Visual Display Unit; VRAM; XGA;

Third Generation Language
A high level computer programming language which is used to write source code on different processors. The source code is converted to machine code by compiling or using an interpreter. e.g. COBOL, BASIC.
See Also: *3GL; 3rd Generation; 4GL; ADA; ALGOL; APL; BASIC; C or C++; CLIPPER; COBOL; CODASYL; Code; Code Generator; Compiler; Compiling; Conference On DAta SYstems Languages; CORAL; FORTH; FORTRAN; Fourth Generation Language; High Level Language; Instruction Set; Interpreter; LISP; LOGO; NATURAL; PASCAL; PERL; PICK; PILOT; PL/1; Practical Extraction and Reporting Language; Program; PROLOG; RPG; Software; Software System; Source Code; Syntax; System; System Software; Visual Basic;*

Third Party Maintenance
Maintenance performed on hardware by an organisation other than the supplier of the equipment.
See Also: *Downtime; EDS; Electronic Data System; Equipment; Facilities Management; FM; Hardware; Kit; Mean Time Between Failure; MTBF; System;*

Thirty Two Bit
(32 bit). A term describing the architecture of a computer in which data is stored in 32 bit registers, or transferred from one part of a computer to another in a 32 bit wide data bus.
See Also: *16 Bit; 32 Bit; 486; 64 Bit; 8 Bit; Address; Address Bus; Analogue Computer; Binary; Binary Digit; Bit; Bits Per Second; BPS; Bus; Channel; Computer Power; Data Bus; Digital; Eight Bit; Gbps; Least Significant Bit; Local Bus; LSB; Mbps; Most Significant Bit; MSB; PCI; Peripheral Component Interconnect; Power; Register; Sixteen Bit; Sixty Four Bit; System Bus; Transmission Channel;*

Thread
All the communicated replies to a discussion in a newsgroup, e.g. Instant Messaging, Internet chat.
See Also: *Attachment; Body; Chat; Chatroom; Cybercafe; Cyberspace; Electronic Mail; E-mail; Forum; IM; Instant Messaging; Internet Relay Chat; IRC; Message Boards; Netiquette; Newsgroup; User Group;*

Three and a Half
(1) A floppy disk which is 3.5 inches in diameter with a storage capacity of up to 1.44 Mb. (2) The disk drive to take a 3.5 inch disk.
See Also: *3.5 Inch; 5.25 Inch; Archive; ATAPI; Attachment Packet Interface; Backing Store; Backup; Bits Per Inch; Block; Boot Disk; BPI; Cluster; Computer Power; Configuration; Crash; Cylinder; Defragment; Density; Device; Directory; Disk; Disk Drive; Disk Map; Disk Pack; Disk Size; Disk Storage; Diskette; Double Density; Drive; EIDE; Enhanced Intelligent Drive Electronics; Equipment; FDD; Five and a quarter; Fixed Disk Drive; Floppy Disk; Floppy Disk Drive; Format; Fragmentation; Grandfather, Father, Son; Hard Disk Drive; Hardware; HDD; Head Crash; Heads; High Density; IDE; Indexed Sequential Access Method; Integrated Drive Electronics; ISAM; Keyed Sequential Access Method; Kit; KSAM; Machine Crash; Magnetic Disk; Mass Storage; Medium; Pack; Peripheral; Power; Read/Write Head; Recording; Recording Device; Recording Medium; Root Directory; Save; Sector; Seek Time; Storage; Store; Sub Directory; Track; Volume; Winchester Disk; Wipe; Write; Write Protect;*

Thumbnail
An image on a web page reduced in size to save space, which contains a hyperlink to the full size image.
See Also: *Anchor; Bookmark; Browser; GIF; Graphical Interchange Format; Hyperlink; Hypertext; Joint Photographic Experts Group; JPEG; JPG; Link; Page; Site; Tag Image File Format; TIFF; Webring; Website;*

TIFF
Tag Image File Format. A file format in which graphic images are stored.
See Also: *Attachment; BitMaP; BMP; Clip Art; Extension; Filename Extension; Format; GIF; Graphical Interchange Format; Graphics; Image Processing; Joint Photographic Experts Group; JPEG; JPG; MIME; Multipurpose Internet Mail Extensions; PDF; Portable Document Format; Resolution; Rich Text Format; RTF; Tag Image File Format; Thumbnail;*

Time Share
Also known as Time Slice. A mode of operation in which two or more programs make use of the same resources at allocated intervals of time.
See Also: *Client Server; Interrupt; Mix; Multi User; Multitasking; Overlay; Run; Run Time; Server; Swapping; Time Slice; Trashing; Working Storage; Workspace; Zero Wait State;*

Time Slice
Also known as Time Share. A mode of operation in which two or more programs make use of the same resources at allocated intervals of time.
See Also: *Client Server; Interrupt; Mix; Multi User; Multitasking; Overlay; Run; Run Time; Server; Swapping; Time Share; Trashing; Working Storage; Workspace; Zero Wait State;*

Timeout
The state when a connection is deactivated after a period of inactivity.
See Also: *Abort; Busy; Died; Hangs; Hung; Off Line;*

Toggle
(1) A switch. (2) The setting 'on' or 'off' of a switch or function.
See Also: *Binary; Binary Digit; Bit; Check Box; DIP Switch; Flip Flop; Function; Radio Button;*

Token Ring
A type of network that connects multiple computers to a server to share data storage and peripherals. It is known as a 'Token Ring' as cables from each computer are connected to a main ring cable which in turn is connected to the server.
See Also: *AMR; Anonymous FTP; Automatic Message Routing; Backbone; Bandwidth; BBS; Broadband; Bulletin Board System; Client Server; Client Server Protocol; Distributed System/Network; Environment; Ethernet; File Server; File Sharing; Gateway; Host Processor; Intranet; LAN; LAN Port; Local Area Network; Multi User; Multitasking; Narrowband; Network; Network Information Centre; Network Operating System; NIC; Node; NOS; Open Systems Interconnect; OSI; Ring Network; Server; Star Cluster; Star Network; TCP/IP; Transmission Control Protocol/Internet Protocol; WAN; Wide Area Network;*

Toner
A carbon powder which is attracted to the electronically charged drum in a laser printer and then transferred to print on paper using a heat process.
See Also: *Laser Jet; Laser Printer; LCD Printer; Liquid Crystal Display Printer; Page Printer; Printer; Printout;*

Toolbar
A set of buttons arranged in a strip on the screen each having an icon denoting different programs or commands.
See Also: *Click; Command; Display; Drag; Drop-Down Menu; Floating Toolbar; Graphics; Icon; Menu; Paint Screen; Pop Up Menu; Pull Down Menu; Screen; Sprite;*

Top Down Technique
Modular design or programming where an entire task is broken down into a hierarchical structure of small modules relating to each other.
See Also: *CASE; Case Tool; Computer Aided Software Engineering; Data Flow; Data Flow Diagram; Data Model; Design; Development; DFD; Model; Modular; Process Model; Reengineering; Specification; Structured Design; Structured Program;*

Touch Screen
A visual display unit which allows input to a computer by touching sensitive areas on the screen that relate to commands or data.
See Also: *Analogue Monitor; Anti Glare Screen; Cathode Ray Tube; CGA; Colour Graphics Adaptor; CRT; Device; Digital Monitor; Display; EGA; Enhanced Graphic Adaptor; Environment; Equipment; Extended Video Array; Graphics Card; Hardware; High Resolution; Installation; Intelligent Terminal; Interlaced; Kit; LCD; Liquid Crystal Display; Low Resolution; Monitor; Monochrome; Output; Paint Screen; Peripheral; Plasma Screen; Prompt; Resolution; Screen; Screen Burn; Split Screen; Super Twist LCD; Super VGA; Super Video Graphics Array; SVGA; System; Terminal; TFT; Thin-Film Transistor; Twip; VDT; VDU; VGA; Video Card; Video Display Terminal; Video Graphics Array; Video Random Access Memory; Visual Display Terminal; Visual Display Unit; VRAM; XGA;*

Tower Computer
A personal computer supplied in an upright casing.
See Also: *1st Generation; 2nd Generation; 3rd Generation; 4th Generation; Advanced Technology; Analogue Computer; AT; Compatible; Computer; Computer Power; Configuration; Cross Platform; Desktop; Digital Computer; Downsizing; EDS; Electronic*

Data System; Environment; Equipment; Extended Technology; Hardware; IBM (tm) Compatible; Information System; Information Technology; Installation; IS; IT; Kit; Laptop; Leading Edge; Machine; Micro; Microcomputer; Multi Platform; Notebook; OEM; Original Equipment Manufacturer; Palmtop Computer; PC; Personal Computer; Platform; Portable; Power; Standalone; State of the Art; Turnkey; Voice Activated; XT;

TPS
Teleprocessing System. A system where data processing is performed on a remote computer which is linked to a main computer elsewhere.
See Also: *Acoustic Coupler; ADN; ADSL; Advanced Digital Network; AMR; Asymmetric Digital Subscriber Line; Asymmetrical Modem; Asynchronous; Asynchronous Transfer Mode; ATM; Automatic Message Routing; Bandwidth; Baud Rate; Broadband; CCITT; CCTA; Communications; Computation; Compute; Consultative Committee International Telegraph and Telephone; Data Communications; Data Processing; Data Transmission; Datacoms; Dial In; Dial Up; Direct Connection; Distributed System/Network; DP; EFT; EFTPOS; Electronic Fund Transfer; Electronic Fund Transfer Point of Sales; FDDI; Fibre Distributed Data Interface; Fibre Optics; File Server; Full Duplex; Integrated Services Digital Network; ISDN; Kbps; Leased Line; Modem; Modulator Demodulator; Multiplex; Multiplexer; Narrowband; Optical Fibre; Parallel Transmission; Processing; Serial Interface; Serial Transmission; Synchronous; Telecommunication; Telecoms; Teleprocessing System; Transmit; V90;*

Trace
The procedure of stepping through a program one instruction at a time.
See Also: *Audit Trail; Debug; Walkthrough;*

Track
A section on disk or tape medium in which data is stored.
See Also: *3.5 Inch; 5.25 Inch; Bits Per Inch; Block; BPI; Cluster; Cylinder; Data; Disk; Disk Pack; Disk Storage; Diskette; Five and a quarter; Floppy Disk; Mag Tape; Magnetic Disk; Magnetic Tape; Pack; Sector; Storage; Streamer; Three and a Half; Volume;*

Tracker Ball
A tracking device that has a ball component which is rotated by the hand to position or track the cursor on the screen.
See Also: *Device; Equipment; Hardware; Kit; Mouse; Peripheral;*

Trailer
A record at the end of a file which contains information relating to the file, such as totals, and may indicate end of file.
See Also: *Batch File; Beginning of File; BOF; Comma Separated Values; CSV; End of File; EOF; Record;*

Transaction
(1) A record. (2) The processing of a record through a set of procedures.
See Also: *Comma Separated Values; CSV; Data; Data Element; Data Entity; Data Item; Data Type; Database; DB; Field; Record; Transaction Processing;*

Transaction Processing
The processing of transactions as and when they are input into the computer.
See Also: *Audit Trail; Batch Processing; Processing; Transaction;*

Transfer Rate
The rate at which data is transferred from one computer or device to another, usually in characters per second.
See Also: *Acoustic Coupler; ADN; ADSL; Advanced Digital Network; Asymmetric Digital Subscriber Line; Asymmetrical Modem; Asynchronous Transfer Mode; ATM; Bandwidth; Baud Rate; Bits Per Second; BPS; Broadband; Bus; CCITT; CCTA; Channel; Characters Per Second; Communications; Consultative Committee International Telegraph and Telephone; CPS; Data Communications; Data Transmission; Datacoms; Dial In; Dial Up; Duplex Transmission; ECP; Enhanced Parallel Port; EPP; Extended Capabilities Port; FDDI; Fibre Distributed Data Interface; Fibre Optics; Full Duplex; Gbps; Half Duplex; HD; Integrated Services Digital Network; ISDN; Kbps; Mbps; Million Instructions Per Second; MIPS; Multiplex; Multiplexer; Narrowband; Optical Fibre; Parallel Transmission; Serial Transmission; Simplex Transmission; System Bus; Telecommunication; Telecoms; Transmission Channel; Transmit; V90; XMODEM; YMODEM; ZMODEM;*

Transistor
A solid-state device made from a semiconductor material. It is capable of performing simple operations such as amplification or a switching decision as in the case of a logic gate.
See Also: *ALU; AND gate; Application Specific Integrated Circuits; Arithmetic and Logic Unit; ASICS; Chip; Chipset; Flip Flop; IC; Integrated Circuit; I-OR gate; Large Scale Integration; Logic Gate; LSI;*

Microprocessor; NAND gate; NEQ gate; NOR gate; NOT gate; OR gate; Processor; Semiconductor; Silicon Chip; Solid State; Sound Chip; Very Large Scale Integration; VLSI; X-OR gate;

Transmission Channel
A path between a computer and its peripherals along which data is transferred.
See Also: *16 Bit; 32 Bit; 64 Bit; 8 Bit; Access; Address Bus; Asymmetrical Modem; Backbone; Bus; Channel; Characters Per Second; Communications; CPS; Data Bus; Data Communications; Data Parity; Data Transmission; Datacoms; Digital; Direct Connection; Duplex Transmission; Eight Bit; FDDI; Fibre Distributed Data Interface; Fibre Optics; Firewire; Full Duplex; Half Duplex; HD; I/O; Industry Standard Architecture; Input/Output; ISA; Kbps; Leased Line; Local Bus; MCA; Micro Channel Architecture; Node; Optical Fibre; Parallel Transmission; Parity Bit; SCSI; Serial Transmission; Simplex Transmission; Sixteen Bit; Sixty Four Bit; Small Computer System Interface; System Bus; Thirty Two Bit; Transfer Rate; Transmit; Universal Serial Bus; USB;*

Transmission Control Protocol/Internet Protocol
(TCP/IP). A set of rules that determine the exchange of information from one computer or network to another.
See Also: *Acceptable User Policy; Anonymous FTP; AUP; Bandwidth; Broadband; Client Server Protocol; Compatible; Download; Ethernet; File Server; File Transfer Protocol; FTP; Gateway; Handshake; HTTP; Hypertext Transfer Protocol; Interface; Internet; Internet Protocol; IP; LAN; Local Area Network; Narrowband; Net; Network; Open Systems Interconnect; OSI; Protocol; Ring Network; Secure Socket Layer; Serial Line Internet Protocol; Simple Mail Transfer Protocol; SLIP; SMTP; SSL; Star Cluster; Star Network; TCP/IP; The Net; Token Ring; WAN; Wide Area Network; XMODEM; YMODEM; ZMODEM;*

Transmit
The transfer of data along communication lines or through the air from one computer or device to another.
See Also: *ACK; Acoustic Coupler; ADN; ADSL; Advanced Digital Network; Asymmetric Digital Subscriber Line; Asymmetrical Modem; Asynchronous; Asynchronous Transfer Mode; ATM; Backbone; Bandwidth; Baud Rate; Bits Per Second; Bluetooth (tm); BPS; Broadband; CCITT; CCTA; Channel; Characters Per Second; Communications; Consultative Committee International Telegraph and Telephone; CPS; Data Communications; Data Parity; Data*

Transmission; Datacoms; Dial In; Dial Up; Digital; Direct Connection; Download; Duplex Transmission; ECP; Enhanced Parallel Port; EPP; Extended Capabilities Port; FDDI; Fibre Distributed Data Interface; Fibre Optics; Full Duplex; Gbps; GHz; Gigahertz; Half Duplex; HD; Integrated Services Digital Network; ISDN; Kbps; KHz; Kilohertz; Leased Line; Mbps; Modem; Modulator Demodulator; Multiplex; Multiplexer; Narrowband; Open Systems Interconnect; Optical Fibre; OSI; Packet; Packet Switching; Parallel Transmission; Parity Bit; Serial Transmission; Simplex Transmission; Synchronous; T-1; T-3; Telecommunication; Telecoms; Teleprocessing System; TPS; Transfer Rate; Transmission Channel; V90; Wi-Fi; Wireless Fidelity;

Trashing
The working of programs or jobs within a computer's memory.
See Also: *Mix; Swapping; Time Share; Time Slice; Working Storage; Workspace;*

Trojan
A virus program that remains dormant in the computer and when activated will sabotage the computer.
See Also: *Bug; Daemon; Hacker; Software; Spam; Terminate and Stay Resident; TSR; Utility; Virus; Virus Checker; Worm;*

TSR
Terminate and Stay Resident. Programs that are loaded into the computer's memory and remain dormant until activated by another process.
See Also: *Code; DLL; Dynamic Link Library; Dynamically; High Memory; Interrupt; Interrupt Request; IRQ; Memory Resident; Mix; Overlay; Program; Software; Swapping; Terminate and Stay Resident; Trojan; Upper Memory;*

Tuning
The process where a computer is made to run faster and/or more efficient.
See Also: *CMOS; Complementary Metal Oxide Semiconductor Memory; CONFIG.SYS; Configuring; Registry; Tweaking; Upgrade;*

Turnkey
A computer system which includes both hardware and software. The system is loaded with all the required application programs when switched on.
See Also: *1st Generation; 2nd Generation; 3rd Generation; 4th Generation; Advanced Technology; Analogue Computer; Application;*

AT; Bespoke; CAD; CADCAM; CADMAT; CAE; CAI; CAM; CBT; Computer; Computer Aided Design; Computer Aided Design and Manufacturing; Computer Aided Design Manufacture and Test; Computer Aided Engineering; Computer Aided Instruction; Computer Aided Manufacturing; Computer Based Training; Configuration; Cross Platform; Desk Top Publishing; Desktop; Digital Computer; Distributed System/Network; Downsizing; DTP; EDS; Electronic Data System; Environment; Equipment; Extended Technology; Front End Processor; Hardware; IBM (tm) Compatible; Information System; Installation; Integrated; Integrated Systems; IS; Kit; Laptop; Machine; Mainframe; Micro; Microcomputer; Midrange System; Minicomputer; Multi Platform; Notebook; Number Cruncher; OEM; Original Equipment Manufacturer; Package; Palmtop Computer; PC; Personal Computer; Platform; Portable; Software; Software Package; Software System; Standalone; System; Tower Computer; Word Processor; WP; XT;

Tutorial
Documentation held on a file in the computer that enables the user to learn and understand how hardware or software systems work.
See Also: *Specification; User Guide; User Manual;*

Tweaking
The process where a computer is made to run faster and/or more efficient.
See Also: *CMOS; Complementary Metal Oxide Semiconductor Memory; CONFIG.SYS; Configuring; Registry; Tuning; Upgrade;*

Twip
A screen measurement that is resolution dependent. It is normally referred to as a dot on the screen but it is not a pixel.
See Also: *Analogue Monitor; Anti Glare Screen; Cathode Ray Tube; CGA; Clip Art; Colour Graphics Adaptor; CRT; Cursor; Digital Monitor; Display; EGA; Enhanced Graphic Adaptor; Extended Video Array; Frame Rate; Graphics; Image Map; Image Processing; Intelligent Terminal; LCD; Liquid Crystal Display; Low Resolution; Monitor; Monochrome; Paint Screen; Pixel; Plasma Screen; Resolution; Screen; Screen Burn; Sprite; Super Twist LCD; Super VGA; Super Video Graphics Array; SVGA; Touch Screen; Video Card; XGA;*

UART
Universal Asynchronous Receiver/Transmitter. A chip controlling the serial input/output port in a personal computer.
See Also: *Application Specific Integrated Circuits; ASICS; Chip; Chipset; I/O; IC; Input/Output; Integrated Circuit; Port; RS232; RS423;*

Serial Interface; Serial Port; Serial Transmission; Silicon Chip; Universal Asynchronous Receiver/Transmitter; Universal Serial Bus; USB;

Ultra DMA
A standard used when linking the hard disk drive with the computer. Currently DMA 66 and DMA 100.
See Also: *EIDE; EISA; Enhanced Industry Standard Architecture; Enhanced Intelligent Drive Electronics; IDE; Industry Standard Architecture; Integrated Drive Electronics; ISA; SCSI; Self Monitoring Analysis and Reporting Technology; Small Computer System Interface; SMART;*

Universal Asynchronous Receiver/Transmitter
(UART). A chip controlling the serial input/output port in a personal computer.
See Also: *Application Specific Integrated Circuits; ASICS; Chip; Chipset; I/O; IC; Input/Output; Integrated Circuit; Port; RS232; RS423; Serial Interface; Serial Port; Serial Transmission; Silicon Chip; UART; Universal Serial Bus; USB;*

Universal Serial Bus
(USB). A standard used when connecting external devices to the computer with transfer speeds of 12Mbits/sec to 480Mbits/sec
See Also: *Access; Bus; Channel; Interface; MCA; Micro Channel Architecture; SCSI; Serial Interface; Small Computer System Interface; Transmission Channel; UART; Universal Asynchronous Receiver/Transmitter; USB;*

Universal/Uniform Resource Locator
(URL). The electronic address or domain name of a website.
See Also: *Address; Anchor; Bookmark; Browser; CERN; CGI; Common Gateway Interface; Conseil Europeen pour la Recherche Nucleaire; DNS; Domain Name; Domain Name Server; Domain Name System; Dot; E-mail Address; Hit; Home Page; Host; Hyperlink; Hypertext; Link; Meta Tag; Meta-Search Engine; Portal; Site; Surfing; The Web; URL; Webring; Website; World Wide Web; WWW;*

UNIX
An operating system which can be run on many platforms.
See Also: *Boot; Bootstrap; Configuration; Disk Operating System; DOS; Environment; High Memory; Housekeeping; Linux; Multi Platform;*

Network Operating System; NOS; Open System; Operating System; OS; OS/2; Re-boot; Software; System Software; Upper Memory;

Unzip
The decompression of stored information held on a recording medium. i.e. programs, data files.
See Also: *Archive; Backup; Compressed File; Compression; Data Compression; Decompression; Packed Data; Save; Self Extracting File; Zip;*

Upgrade
The improvement of hardware or software with a later release of the product or with a new system.
See Also: *Configuring; Convert; Development; Full Project Life Cycle; Going Live; Implementation; Install; Installation; Plug and Play; Plug Compatible; Project Life Cycle; Releases; Software Development Cycle; Tuning; Tweaking;*

Upload
The transfer of data and files from a local computer to a remote computer.
See Also: *Attachment; BBS; Bulletin Board System; Download; EFT; EFTPOS; Electronic Fund Transfer; Electronic Fund Transfer Point of Sales; File Server; Point of Sales; POS;*

Upper Memory
A partition of the computer's main memory where the operating system and any programs that remain resident are stored.
See Also: *Absolute Address; Address; Block; Bubble Memory; CMOS; Complementary Metal Oxide Semiconductor Memory; Conventional Memory; Core; Core Dump; DDR SDRAM; DIMM; Direct Random Access Memory; Disk Cache; Disk Operating System; DOS; Double Data Rate SDRAM; DRAM; Dual Inline Memory Module; Dynamic Memory; Dynamically; EEROM; Electrically Erasable Read Only Memory; Electronically Programmed Read Only Memory; EMS; EPROM; Erasable Programmable Read Only Memory; Expanded Memory; Expanded Memory Specification; Extended Memory; Flash Memory; General Protection Fault; GPF; High Memory; Linux; Load; Magnetic Core; Memory; Memory Caching; Memory Resident; Mix; Operating System; OS; OS/2; Programmable Read Only Memory; PROM; RAM; RAM Disk; Rambus Dynamic Random Access Memory; Random Access Memory; RDRAM; Read Only Memory; Relative Address; ROM; SDRAM; Shadow RAM Memory; SIMM; Single Inline Memory Modules; Single Inline Package; SIP; Stack; Store; Swapping; Synchronous*

Dynamic Random Access Memory; Terminate and Stay Resident; TSR; UNIX; Virtual Memory; VM; Volatile Memory; Working Storage; Workspace;

URL

Universal/Uniform Resource Locator. The electronic address or domain name of a website.

See Also: *Address; Anchor; Bookmark; Browser; CERN; CGI; Common Gateway Interface; Conseil Europeen pour la Recherche Nucleaire; DNS; Domain Name; Domain Name Server; Domain Name System; Dot; E-mail Address; Hit; Home Page; Host; Hyperlink; Hypertext; Link; Meta Tag; Meta-Search Engine; Portal; Site; Surfing; The Web; Universal/Uniform Resource Locator; Webring; Website; World Wide Web; WWW;*

USB

Universal Serial Bus. A standard used when connecting external devices to the computer with transfer speeds of 12Mbits/sec to 480Mbits/sec.

See Also: *Access; Bus; Channel; Interface; MCA; Micro Channel Architecture; SCSI; Serial Interface; Small Computer System Interface; Transmission Channel; UART; Universal Asynchronous Receiver/Transmitter; Universal Serial Bus;*

User

A person who uses a computer. Normally refers to people in large organisations.

See Also: *Cybercafe; Dead Lock; Deadly Embrace; End User; Hand Holding; Hands On; Help Desk; IM; In-house; Instant Messaging; Multi User; Nerd; Netiquette; Newbie; Newsgroup; Operator; Technical Author; User Friendly; User Group; User Guide; User Manual; Walkthrough;*

User Friendly

A term used when a computer system has been designed to allow a user to use the system with ease. Visual aids are used to prompt and notify the user what to do and what is happening. e.g. menu selection, message display.

See Also: *Drop-Down Menu; End User; Graphical User Interface; GUI; Menu; Pop Up Menu; Pull Down Menu; User; WIMP; Windows Icons Mice and Pull-down menus;*

User Group
A group of people who have a common interest in data processing requirements or computer systems.
See Also: *BCS; Buddy List; Chat; Chatroom; Cybercafe; End User; Forum; Help Desk; Message Boards; Nerd; Netiquette; Newsgroup; Thread; User;*

User Guide
Also known as User Manual. A manual instructing users in the use of software or hardware.
See Also: *End User; Hand Holding; Help Desk; Specification; Technical Author; Tutorial; User; User Manual;*

User Manual
Also known as User Guide. A manual instructing users in the use of software or hardware.
See Also: *End User; Hand Holding; Help Desk; Specification; Technical Author; Tutorial; User; User Guide;*

Utility
A program that works independently from others to perform a specific task.
See Also: *Code; CODEC; COmpressor DECompressor; Configuration; Daemon; Device Driver; DLL; Driver; Dynamic Link Library; EXE; Format; Function; Gopher; Instruction Set; Job; Line Editor; Macro; Memory Resident; Meta-Search Engine; Nesting; Page Editor; Script; Search Engine; Shareware; Software; Software Driver; Spell Check; Spider; Spooler; Trojan;*

V90
A standard for the speed of data transfer using modems over a telephone line.
See Also: *Acoustic Coupler; ADN; ADSL; Advanced Digital Network; AMR; Asymmetric Digital Subscriber Line; Asymmetrical Modem; Asynchronous; Asynchronous Transfer Mode; ATM; Automatic Message Routing; Bandwidth; Baud Rate; Bits Per Second; BPS; Broadband; CCITT; CCTA; Characters Per Second; Communications; Consultative Committee International Telegraph and Telephone; CPS; Data Communications; Data Parity; Data Transmission; Datacoms; Dial In; Dial Up; Digital; Direct Connection; Duplex Transmission; FDDI; Fibre Distributed Data Interface; Fibre Optics; Firewire; Full Duplex; Gbps; Half Duplex; HD; Integrated Services Digital Network; ISDN; Kbps; Leased Line; Mbps; Modem; Modulator Demodulator; Multiplex;*

Multiplexer; Narrowband; Node; Open Systems Interconnect; Optical Fibre; OSI; Packet; Packet Switching; Parallel Transmission; Parity Bit; Protocol; Serial Transmission; Simplex Transmission; Synchronous; Telecommunication; Telecoms; Teleprocessing System; TPS; Transfer Rate; Transmit;

Variable
A data item whose value may be changed during the execution of a program.
See Also: *Character; Comma Separated Values; CSV; Data; Data Element; Data Entity; Data Item; Data Type; Entity; Field; Group; Information; Input; Null; Parameter; Radio Button; Record; String; Subscript; Table; Word;*

VDT
Video/Visual Display Terminal. Also known as Visual Display Unit (VDU). A device consisting of a cathode ray tube and used to view data or used with a keyboard to input data and interact with a computer.
See Also: *Analogue Monitor; Anti Glare Screen; Cathode Ray Tube; CGA; Colour Graphics Adaptor; Configuration; CRT; Device; Digital Monitor; Display; EGA; Enhanced Graphic Adaptor; Environment; Equipment; Extended Video Array; Graphics Card; Hardware; High Resolution; Installation; Intelligent Terminal; Interlaced; Kit; LCD; Liquid Crystal Display; Low Resolution; Monitor; Monochrome; Output; Paint Screen; Peripheral; Plasma Screen; Prompt; Resolution; Screen; Screen Burn; Split Screen; Super Twist LCD; Super VGA; Super Video Graphics Array; SVGA; System; Terminal; TFT; Thin-Film Transistor; Touch Screen; VDU; VGA; Video Card; Video Display Terminal; Video Graphics Array; Video Random Access Memory; Visual Display Terminal; Visual Display Unit; VRAM; XGA;*

VDU
Visual Display Unit. Also known as Video/Visual Display Terminal (VDT). A device consisting of a cathode ray tube and used to view data or used with a keyboard to input data and interact with a computer.
See Also: *Analogue Monitor; Anti Glare Screen; Cathode Ray Tube; CGA; Colour Graphics Adaptor; Configuration; CRT; Device; Digital Monitor; Display; EGA; Enhanced Graphic Adaptor; Environment; Equipment; Extended Video Array; Frame Rate; Graphics Card; Hardware; High Resolution; Installation; Intelligent Terminal; Interlaced; Kit; LCD; Liquid Crystal Display; Low Resolution; Monitor; Monochrome; Output; Paint Screen; Peripheral; Plasma Screen; Prompt; Resolution; Screen; Screen Burn; Split Screen; Super Twist*

LCD; Super VGA; Super Video Graphics Array; SVGA; System; Terminal; TFT; Thin-Film Transistor; Touch Screen; VDT; VGA; Video Card; Video Display Terminal; Video Graphics Array; Video Random Access Memory; Visual Display Terminal; Visual Display Unit; VRAM; XGA;

Vertical Market

An industry for which software is specifically written. e.g. software for doctors surgeries.

See Also: *Application; CAD; CADCAM; CADMAT; CAE; CAI; CAM; CBT; Computation; Compute; Computer Aided Design; Computer Aided Design and Manufacturing; Computer Aided Design Manufacture and Test; Computer Aided Engineering; Computer Aided Instruction; Computer Aided Manufacturing; Computer Based Training; Data Processing; Desk Top Publishing; DP; DTP; EDS; Electronic Data System; Geographical Information System; GIS; Information System; Integrated Systems; IS; Package; Software; Software Package; Software System;*

Very Large Scale Integration

(VLSI). An indication of the number of logic gates on a chip which for VLSI is above 5000.

See Also: *ALU; AMR; AND gate; Application Specific Integrated Circuits; Arithmetic and Logic Unit; ASICS; Automatic Message Routing; Chip; Chipset; Flip Flop; IC; Integrated Circuit; I-OR gate; Large Scale Integration; Logic Gate; LSI; NAND gate; NEQ gate; NOR gate; NOT gate; OR gate; Parallel Processor; Semiconductor; Silicon Chip; Solid State; Transistor; VLSI; X-OR gate;*

VGA

Video Graphics Array. A visual display unit design which has a resolution of 320x200 dots with 256 colours or 640x480 dots with 16 colours.

See Also: *Analogue Monitor; Anti Glare Screen; Cathode Ray Tube; CGA; Colour Graphics Adaptor; Configuration; CRT; Device; Digital Monitor; Display; EGA; Enhanced Graphic Adaptor; Environment; Equipment; Extended Video Array; Graphics Card; Hardware; High Resolution; Installation; Intelligent Terminal; Interlaced; Kit; LCD; Liquid Crystal Display; Low Resolution; Monitor; Monochrome; Output; Paint Screen; Peripheral; Plasma Screen; Prompt; Resolution; Screen; Screen Burn; Split Screen; Super Twist LCD; Super VGA; Super Video Graphics Array; SVGA; System; Terminal; TFT; Thin-Film Transistor; Touch Screen; VDT; VDU; Video Card; Video Display Terminal; Video*

Graphics Array; Video Random Access Memory; Visual Display Terminal; Visual Display Unit; VRAM; XGA;

Video Card

A printed circuit board which determines the resolution of the visual display unit screen. e.g. 800 x 600 pixels.

See Also: *Accelerated Graphics Port; Advanced Graphics Port; AGP; AGP Slot; Analogue Monitor; Anti Glare Screen; Application Specific Integrated Circuits; ASICS; Cathode Ray Tube; CGA; Colour Graphics Adaptor; CRT; Digital Monitor; Digital Video Interface; Display; DVI; EGA; Enhanced Graphic Adaptor; Extended Video Array; Fax Card; Frame Rate; Graphics; Graphics Card; High Resolution; IC; Image Processing; Integrated Circuit; LCD; Liquid Crystal Display; Low Resolution; Monitor; Monochrome; Motherboard; Paint Screen; PCB; PCI; PCMCIA; Peripheral Component Interconnect; Personal Computer Memory Card International Association; Pixel; Plasma Screen; Printed Circuit Board; Resolution; Screen; Screen Burn; Sound Card; Stream; Super Twist LCD; Super VGA; Super Video Graphics Array; SVGA; Terminal; TFT; Thin-Film Transistor; Touch Screen; Twip; VDT; VDU; VGA; Video Display Terminal; Video Graphics Array; Video Random Access Memory; Visual Display Terminal; Visual Display Unit; VRAM; XGA;*

Video Display Terminal

(VDT). Also known as Visual Display Unit (VDU). A device consisting of a cathode ray tube and used to view data or used with a keyboard to input data and interact with a computer.

See Also: *Analogue Monitor; Anti Glare Screen; Cathode Ray Tube; CGA; Colour Graphics Adaptor; Configuration; CRT; Device; Digital Monitor; Display; EGA; Enhanced Graphic Adaptor; Environment; Equipment; Extended Video Array; Graphics Card; Hardware; High Resolution; Installation; Intelligent Terminal; Interlaced; Kit; LCD; Liquid Crystal Display; Low Resolution; Monitor; Monochrome; Output; Paint Screen; Peripheral; Plasma Screen; Prompt; Resolution; Screen; Screen Burn; Split Screen; Super Twist LCD; Super VGA; Super Video Graphics Array; SVGA; System; Terminal; TFT; Thin-Film Transistor; Touch Screen; VDT; VDU; VGA; Video Card; Video Graphics Array; Video Random Access Memory; Visual Display Terminal; Visual Display Unit; VRAM; XGA;*

Video Graphics Array
(VGA). A visual display unit design which has a resolution of 320x200 dots with 256 colours or 640x480 dots with 16 colours.
See Also: *Analogue Monitor; Anti Glare Screen; Cathode Ray Tube; CGA; Colour Graphics Adaptor; Configuration; CRT; Device; Digital Monitor; Display; EGA; Enhanced Graphic Adaptor; Environment; Equipment; Extended Video Array; Graphics Card; Hardware; High Resolution; Installation; Intelligent Terminal; Interlaced; Kit; LCD; Liquid Crystal Display; Low Resolution; Monitor; Monochrome; Output; Paint Screen; Peripheral; Plasma Screen; Prompt; Resolution; Screen; Screen Burn; Split Screen; Super Twist LCD; Super VGA; Super Video Graphics Array; SVGA; System; Terminal; TFT; Thin-Film Transistor; Touch Screen; VDT; VDU; VGA; Video Card; Video Display Terminal; Video Random Access Memory; Visual Display Terminal; Visual Display Unit; VRAM; XGA;*

Video Random Access Memory
(VRAM). Memory used in a monitor.
See Also: *Analogue Monitor; Anti Glare Screen; Block; Bubble Memory; Cathode Ray Tube; CGA; Colour Graphics Adaptor; Conventional Memory; Core; Core Dump; CRT; DDR SDRAM; Digital Monitor; DIMM; Direct Random Access Memory; Disk Cache; Display; Double Data Rate SDRAM; DRAM; Dual Inline Memory Module; Dynamic Memory; EEROM; EGA; Electrically Erasable Read Only Memory; Electronically Programmed Read Only Memory; EMS; Enhanced Graphic Adaptor; EPROM; Erasable Programmable Read Only Memory; Expanded Memory; Expanded Memory Specification; Extended Memory; Extended Video Array; Flash Memory; Graphics Card; High Memory; LCD; Liquid Crystal Display; Magnetic Core; Memory; Memory Board; Memory Caching; Memory Card; Monitor; Monochrome; Plasma Screen; Programmable Read Only Memory; PROM; RAM; RAM Disk; Rambus Dynamic Random Access Memory; Random Access Memory; RDRAM; Read Only Memory; ROM; Screen; SDRAM; Shadow RAM Memory; SIMM; Single Inline Memory Modules; Single Inline Package; SIP; Stack; Store; Super Twist LCD; Super VGA; Super Video Graphics Array; SVGA; Synchronous Dynamic Random Access Memory; Terminal; TFT; Thin-Film Transistor; Touch Screen; VDT; VDU; VGA; Video Card; Video Display Terminal; Video Graphics Array; Visual Display Terminal; Visual Display Unit; Volatile Memory; VRAM; XGA;*

Virtual Memory
(VM). A procedure where data and programs are transferred to disk from the main memory and back again as required by the priority of the program running. This allows the main memory to be available for use by other programs and the disk to be used for storage as an extension to the main memory.
See Also: *Absolute Address; Block; Bubble Memory; Buffer; Cache Memory; Dynamically; Memory Caching; Memory Resident; Relative Address; Stack; Swapping; Upper Memory; VM; Volatile Memory;*

Virtual Reality
(VR). A technology which allows a person to be immersed inside a three dimensional artificial world and to interact with other people or objects within that world.
See Also: *AI; Artificial Intelligence; Expert System; Real Time; Software System; VR;*

Virus
A program which is designed to disrupt the workings of a computer.
See Also: *Abort; Bug; Daemon; Firewall; Hacker; Machine Crash; Program; Program Crash; Software; Spam; Trojan; Virus Checker; Worm;*

Virus Checker
A suite of programs which checks a computer's memory and disks for viruses that may have invaded the computer system.
See Also: *Bug; Daemon; Firewall; Hacker; Housekeeping; Software; Spam; Trojan; Virus; Worm;*

Visual Basic
A high level computer programming language.
See Also: *3GL; 4GL; ADA; ALGOL; APL; BASIC; C or C++; CLIPPER; COBOL; Code; Code Generator; CORAL; FORTH; FORTRAN; Fourth Generation Language; High Level Language; Instruction Set; JAVA; JAVASCRIPT; LISP; LOGO; NATURAL; PASCAL; PERL; PICK; PILOT; PL/1; Practical Extraction and Reporting Language; Program; PROLOG; RPG; Software; Source Code; Syntax; Third Generation Language;*

Visual Display Terminal
(VDT). Also known as Visual Display Unit (VDU). A device consisting of a cathode ray tube and used to view data or used with a keyboard to input data and interact with a computer.
See Also: *Analogue Monitor; Anti Glare Screen; Cathode Ray Tube; CGA; Colour Graphics Adaptor; Configuration; CRT; Device; Digital Monitor; Display; EGA; Enhanced Graphic Adaptor; Environment; Equipment; Extended Video Array; Graphics Card; Hardware; High Resolution; Installation; Intelligent Terminal; Interlaced; Kit; LCD; Liquid Crystal Display; Low Resolution; Monitor; Monochrome; Output; Paint Screen; Peripheral; Plasma Screen; Prompt; Resolution; Screen; Screen Burn; Split Screen; Super Twist LCD; Super VGA; Super Video Graphics Array; SVGA; System; Terminal; TFT; Thin-Film Transistor; Touch Screen; VDT; VDU; VGA; Video Card; Video Display Terminal; Video Graphics Array; Video Random Access Memory; Visual Display Unit; VRAM; XGA;*

Visual Display Unit
(VDU). Also known as Visual Display Terminal (VDT). A device consisting of a cathode ray tube and used to view data or used with a keyboard to input data and interact with a computer.
See Also: *Analogue Monitor; Anti Glare Screen; Cathode Ray Tube; CGA; Colour Graphics Adaptor; Configuration; CRT; Device; Digital Monitor; Display; EGA; Enhanced Graphic Adaptor; Environment; Equipment; Extended Video Array; Frame Rate; Graphics Card; Hardware; High Resolution; Installation; Intelligent Terminal; Interlaced; Kit; LCD; Liquid Crystal Display; Low Resolution; Monitor; Monochrome; Output; Paint Screen; Peripheral; Plasma Screen; Prompt; Resolution; Screen; Screen Burn; Split Screen; Super Twist LCD; Super VGA; Super Video Graphics Array; SVGA; System; Terminal; TFT; Thin-Film Transistor; Touch Screen; VDT; VDU; VGA; Video Card; Video Display Terminal; Video Graphics Array; Video Random Access Memory; Visual Display Terminal; VRAM; XGA;*

VLSI
Very Large Scale Integration. An indication of the number of logic gates on a chip which for VLSI is above 5000.
See Also: *ALU; AMR; AND gate; Application Specific Integrated Circuits; Arithmetic and Logic Unit; ASICS; Automatic Message Routing; Chip; Chipset; Flip Flop; IC; Integrated Circuit; I-OR gate; Large Scale Integration; Logic Gate; LSI; NAND gate; NEQ gate; NOR gate; NOT gate; OR gate; Parallel Processor; Semiconductor; Silicon Chip; Solid State; Transistor; Very Large Scale Integration; X-OR gate;*

VM

Virtual Memory. A procedure where data and programs are transferred to disk from the main memory and back again as required by the priority of the program running. This allows the main memory to be available for use by other programs and the disk to be used for storage as an extension to the main memory.

See Also: *Absolute Address; Block; Bubble Memory; Buffer; Cache Memory; Dynamically; Memory Caching; Memory Resident; Relative Address; Stack; Swapping; Upper Memory; Virtual Memory; Volatile Memory;*

Voice Activated

A computer system which uses a human's voice to enter data or to issue commands.

See Also: *Analogue; Analogue Computer; Analogue Digital Converter; Computer; Cross Platform; Desktop; Digital Computer; Execute; IBM (tm) Compatible; Instruction; Interactive; Laptop; Machine; Notebook; Palmtop Computer; PC; Personal Computer; Platform; Portable; Tower Computer;*

Volatile Memory

Any memory which loses its contents when the computer is switched off or reset. e.g. Random Access Memory.

See Also: *Absolute Address; Address; Block; Bubble Memory; Buffer; Cache Memory; Clipboard; CMOS; Complementary Metal Oxide Semiconductor Memory; Conventional Memory; Core; Core Dump; Direct Memory Access; Disk Cache; DMA; Dynamically; Flash Memory; Magnetic Core; Memory; Memory Caching; Memory Resident; Relative Address; Stack; Store; Swapping; Upper Memory; Video Random Access Memory; Virtual Memory; VM; VRAM; Working Storage; Workspace;*

Volume

A name given to a disk storage medium.

See Also: *3.5 Inch; 5.25 Inch; Backing Store; Backup; Bits Per Inch; Block; BPI; Cluster; Defragment; Density; Directory; Disk; Disk Map; Disk Pack; Disk Size; Disk Storage; Diskette; Double Density; Equipment; Five and a quarter; Floppy Disk; Fragmentation; Grandfather, Father, Son; Hardware; High Density; Indexed Sequential Access Method; ISAM; Keyed Sequential Access Method; Kit; KSAM; Magnetic Disk; Mass Storage; Medium; Pack; Recording Medium; Root Directory; Save; Sector; Seek Time; Storage; Store; Sub Directory; Three and a Half; Track; Winchester Disk;*

VR
Virtual Reality. A technology which allows a person to be immersed inside a three dimensional artificial world and to interact with other people or objects within that world.
See Also: *AI; Artificial Intelligence; Expert System; Real Time; Software System; Virtual Reality;*

VRAM
Video Random Access Memory. Memory used in a monitor.
See Also: *Analogue Monitor; Anti Glare Screen; Block; Bubble Memory; Cathode Ray Tube; CGA; Colour Graphics Adaptor; Conventional Memory; Core; Core Dump; CRT; DDR SDRAM; Digital Monitor; DIMM; Direct Random Access Memory; Disk Cache; Display; Double Data Rate SDRAM; DRAM; Dual Inline Memory Module; Dynamic Memory; EEROM; EGA; Electrically Erasable Read Only Memory; Electronically Programmed Read Only Memory; EMS; Enhanced Graphic Adaptor; EPROM; Erasable Programmable Read Only Memory; Expanded Memory; Expanded Memory Specification; Extended Memory; Extended Video Array; Flash Memory; Graphics Card; High Memory; LCD; Liquid Crystal Display; Magnetic Core; Memory; Memory Board; Memory Caching; Memory Card; Monitor; Monochrome; Plasma Screen; Programmable Read Only Memory; PROM; RAM; RAM Disk; Rambus Dynamic Random Access Memory; Random Access Memory; RDRAM; Read Only Memory; ROM; Screen; SDRAM; Shadow RAM Memory; SIMM; Single Inline Memory Modules; Single Inline Package; SIP; Stack; Store; Super Twist LCD; Super VGA; Super Video Graphics Array; SVGA; Synchronous Dynamic Random Access Memory; Terminal; TFT; Thin-Film Transistor; Touch Screen; VDT; VDU; VGA; Video Card; Video Display Terminal; Video Graphics Array; Video Random Access Memory; Visual Display Terminal; Visual Display Unit; Volatile Memory; XGA;*

Walkthrough
A procedure where work is evaluated manually by others.
See Also: *Analyst; Audit Trail; B/A; Business Analyst; Development; Full Project Life Cycle; Hand Holding; Help Desk; Project Life Cycle; Reengineering; S/A; Software Development Cycle; Specification; Structured Design; System Analysis; System Analyst; Technical Author; Trace; User;*

WAN

Wide Area Network. A type of network which connects multiple computers to a server to share data storage and peripherals. It is normally used where the equipment is some distance away form the server nationally and internationally.

See Also: *AMR; Anonymous FTP; Automatic Message Routing; Backbone; Bandwidth; BBS; Broadband; Bulletin Board System; Client Server; Client Server Protocol; Distributed System/Network; Environment; Ethernet; File Server; File Sharing; Gateway; Intranet; LAN; Local Area Network; Multi User; Multitasking; Narrowband; Network; Network Information Centre; Network Operating System; NIC; Node; NOS; Open Systems Interconnect; OSI; Ring Network; Server; Star Cluster; Star Network; TCP/IP; Token Ring; Transmission Control Protocol/Internet Protocol; Wide Area Network;*

WAP

Wireless Application Protocol. The method of connecting mobile telephones to the Internet.

See Also: *Acceptable User Policy; Access; Asynchronous Transfer Mode; ATM; AUP; Bandwidth; Bluetooth (tm); Broadband; Client Server Protocol; Cyberspace; HTTP; Hypertext Transfer Protocol; Interface; Internet; Internet Protocol; Internet Protocol Address; IP; IP Address; Narrowband; Net; Point to Point Protocol; PPP; Protocol; Real Time; Secure Socket Layer; Serial Line Internet Protocol; SLIP; SSL; Telecommunication; Telecoms; The Net; Wap Internet Service Provider; Wi-Fi; Wireless Application Protocol; Wireless Fidelity; WISP;*

Wap Internet Service Provider

(WISP). A company which provides access to WAP services on the Internet.

See Also: *Acceptable User Policy; AUP; Cyberspace; Handshake; Host; HTTP; Hypertext Transfer Protocol; Information Superhighway; Internet; Internet Service Provider; ISP; Net; Point to Point Protocol; PPP; Provider; Serial Line Internet Protocol; Service Provider; SLIP; The Net; WAP; Webhost; Wireless Application Protocol; WISP;*

Warm Start

The re-initialising of a computer system after it has been on for some time.

See Also: *AUTOEXEC.BAT; Boot; Boot Disk; Bootstrap; CMOS; Cold Start; Complementary Metal Oxide Semiconductor Memory; CONFIG.SYS; Disk Operating System; DOS; Linux; Operating System; OS; OS/2; Re-boot; Recovery; Registry;*

WAV
Waveform Audio. A file format in which audio data is stored digitally. The audio file has a file extension of '.wav'.
See Also: *Extension; Filename Extension; MIME; MP3; Multimedia; Multipurpose Internet Mail Extensions; Stream; Waveform Audio;*

Waveform Audio
(WAV). A file format in which audio data is stored digitally. The audio file has a file extension of '.wav'.
See Also: *Extension; Filename Extension; MIME; MP3; Multimedia; Multipurpose Internet Mail Extensions; Stream; WAV;*

Webcam
A camera connected to a PC that shows live pictures of locations, people etc. to anyone who connects to the website that provides the pictures.
See Also: *Chat; Chatroom; Cyberspace; Device; Equipment; Hardware; Kit; Multimedia; Peripheral; Site; Stream; Surfing; The Web; Website; World Wide Web; WWW;*

Webhost
The Internet Service Provider or computer that administers websites.
See Also: *Browser; CGI; Common Gateway Interface; Cyberspace; DNS; Domain Name; Domain Name Server; Domain Name System; Host; Host Processor; HTTP; Hypertext Transfer Protocol; Information Superhighway; Internet; Internet Relay Chat; Internet Service Provider; IRC; ISP; Mailserver; Net; Point to Point Protocol; Portal; PPP; Provider; Proxy Server; Search Engine; Service Provider; Site; Spider; Surfing; The Net; The Web; Wap Internet Service Provider; Website; WISP; World Wide Web; WWW;*

Webring
A group of linked websites that allow you to navigate from one to the other at the press of a button.
See Also: *Address; Anchor; Bookmark; Browser; Cyberspace; DNS; Domain Name; Domain Name Server; Domain Name System; Forum; FTP Site; Home Page; Host; HTML; HTTP; Hyperlink; Hypertext Mark-Up Language; Hypertext Transfer Protocol; Internet; Link; Meta-Search Engine; Mirror Site; Net; Page; Portal; Proxy Server; Search Engine; Site; Spider; Surfing; The Net; The Web; Thumbnail; Universal/Uniform Resource Locator; URL; Website; World Wide Web; WWW;*

Website
A World Wide Web Internet site which provides information to anyone accessing it and is identified by a Domain Name.
See Also: *Acceptable User Policy; Address; Anchor; AUP; Bookmark; Browser; CERN; CGI; Common Gateway Interface; Conseil Europeen pour la Recherche Nucleaire; Cyberspace; DNS; Domain Name; Domain Name Server; Domain Name System; Forum; FTP Site; FTPmail; Hit; Home Page; Host; HTML; HTTP; Hyperlink; Hypertext Mark-Up Language; Hypertext Transfer Protocol; Internet; Link; Meta-Search Engine; Mirror Site; Net; Page; Portal; Proxy Server; Search Engine; Site; Spider; Surfing; The Net; The Web; Thumbnail; Universal/Uniform Resource Locator; URL; Webcam; Webhost; Webring; World Wide Web; WWW;*

Wide Area Network
(WAN). A type of network which connects multiple computers to a server to share data storage and peripherals. It is normally used where the equipment is some distance away from the server nationally and internationally.
See Also: *AMR; Anonymous FTP; Automatic Message Routing; Backbone; Bandwidth; BBS; Broadband; Bulletin Board System; Client Server; Client Server Protocol; Distributed System/Network; Environment; Ethernet; File Server; File Sharing; Gateway; Intranet; LAN; Local Area Network; Multi User; Multitasking; Narrowband; Network; Network Information Centre; Network Operating System; NIC; Node; NOS; Open Systems Interconnect; OSI; Ring Network; Server; Star Cluster; Star Network; TCP/IP; Token Ring; Transmission Control Protocol/Internet Protocol; WAN;*

Wi-Fi
Wireless Fidelity. Compliance standards used for wireless communications.
See Also: *Access; Bluetooth (tm); Communications; Data Communications; Data Transmission; Interface; Internet Protocol; IP; Protocol; Telecommunication; Telecoms; Transmit; WAP; Wireless Application Protocol; Wireless Fidelity;*

Wildcard
A wildcard is a character used when entering search criteria. The standard is an asterisk (*). Instead of typing the whole name, the '*' is entered after any number of characters typed and the search will result in all items that contain the characters before the asterisk regardless of the following characters. e.g. filename.* will retrieve all files whose name is represented by 'filename', regardless of the file extension.
See Also: *Character; Picture;*

WIMP
Windows Icons Mice and Pull-down menus. A graphical user interface (GUI) that has images displayed in a window on the screen which has icons or pull down menus for selection.
See Also: *Clip Art; Display; Environment; Graphical User Interface; Graphics; GUI; Image Map; Image Processing; Paint Screen; User Friendly; Window; Windows Icons Mice and Pull-down menus;*

Winchester Disk
A peripheral device in which information is stored on a sealed magnetic disk.
See Also: *3.5 Inch; 5.25 Inch; Archive; ATAPI; Attachment Packet Interface; Backing Store; Backup; Boot Disk; Cluster; Configuration; Defragment; Density; Device; Disk; Disk Drive; Disk Pack; Disk Size; Disk Storage; Diskette; Double Density; Drive; EIDE; EISA; Enhanced Industry Standard Architecture; Enhanced Intelligent Drive Electronics; Environment; Equipment; FDD; Five and a quarter; Fixed Disk Drive; Floppy Disk; Floppy Disk Drive; Fragmentation; Grandfather, Father, Son; Hard Disk Drive; Hardware; HDD; Heads; High Density; IDE; Indexed Sequential Access Method; Installation; Integrated Drive Electronics; ISAM; Keyed Sequential Access Method; Kit; KSAM; Magnetic Disk; Mass Storage; Medium; Pack; Peripheral; Read/Write Head; Recording; Recording Device; Recording Medium; Save; Sector; Seek Time; Storage; Store; Three and a Half; Volume; Wipe; Write; Write Protect;*

Window
A part of a display screen sectioned off with specific information for a program. More than one window can appear on a screen.
See Also: *Graphics; Image Map; Image Processing; Output; Paint Screen; Pixel; Screen Dump; Split Screen; WIMP; Windows Icons Mice and Pull-down menus;*

Windows Icons Mice and Pull-down menus
(WIMP). A graphical user interface (GUI) that has images displayed in a window on the screen which has icons or pull down menus for selection.
See Also: *Clip Art; Display; Environment; Graphical User Interface; Graphics; GUI; Image Map; Image Processing; Paint Screen; User Friendly; WIMP; Window;*

Wipe
To delete data from memory or from a recording device.
See Also: *3.5 Inch; 5.25 Inch; Disk; Disk Pack; Disk Storage; Diskette; Five and a quarter; Floppy Disk; Magnetic Disk; Memory; Pack; Recording Device; Storage; Store; Three and a Half; Winchester Disk;*

Wireless Application Protocol
(WAP). The method of connecting mobile telephones to the Internet.
See Also: *Acceptable User Policy; Access; Asynchronous Transfer Mode; ATM; AUP; Bandwidth; Bluetooth (tm); Broadband; Client Server Protocol; Cyberspace; HTTP; Hypertext Transfer Protocol; Interface; Internet; Internet Protocol; Internet Protocol Address; IP; IP Address; Narrowband; Net; Point to Point Protocol; PPP; Protocol; Real Time; Secure Socket Layer; Serial Line Internet Protocol; SLIP; SSL; Telecommunication; Telecoms; The Net; WAP; Wap Internet Service Provider; Wi-Fi; Wireless Fidelity; WISP;*

Wireless Fidelity
(Wi-Fi). Compliance standards used for wireless communications.
See Also: *Access; Bluetooth (tm); Communications; Data Communications; Data Transmission; Interface; Internet Protocol; IP; Protocol; Telecommunication; Telecoms; Transmit; WAP; Wi-Fi; Wireless Application Protocol;*

WISP
Wap Internet Service Provider. A company which provides access to WAP services on the Internet.
See Also: *Acceptable User Policy; AUP; Cyberspace; Handshake; Host; HTTP; Hypertext Transfer Protocol; Information Superhighway; Internet; Internet Service Provider; ISP; Net; Point to Point Protocol; PPP; Provider; Serial Line Internet Protocol; Service Provider; SLIP; The Net; WAP; Wap Internet Service Provider; Webhost; Wireless Application Protocol;*

Wizard
A wizard is a program which helps the user create a design by offering a choice of selections. The wizard then creates the required design by performing all the work for the user.
See Also: *CASE; Case Tool; Computer Aided Software Engineering; Design; Development; Software Development Cycle;*

Word
(1) A group of characters. (2) A set of bits which constitute a location of memory or storage.
See Also: *Binary; Binary Digit; Bit; Bit Pattern; Byte; Character; Data; Data Element; Data Entity; Data Item; Data Type; Field; K; Kb; Kbyte; Kilobyte; Least Significant Bit; LSB; Mb; Mbyte; Megabyte; Most Significant Bit; MSB; Null; String; Table; Variable;*

Word Processor
(WP). A collection of programs which allow documents to be created, amended and printed in different formats.
See Also: *Application; Computation; Compute; Data Processing; Desk Top Publishing; DP; DTP; Edit; EDS; Electronic Data System; Integrated Systems; Line Editor; Mail Merge; Office Information System; OIS; Package; Page Editor; Processing; Software Package; Software System; Spell Check; Split Screen; Turnkey; Word Wrap; WP;*

Word Wrap
A facility in a word processor or text editor that transfers a whole word being typed to the next line if the end of line is reached in the middle of the word.
See Also: *Edit; Line Editor; Page Editor; Word Processor; WP;*

Working Storage
An area in a program or in the computer's memory set aside for processing.
See Also: *Absolute Address; Address; Array; Bloatware; Block; Bubble Sort; Conventional Memory; Core; Core Dump; DDR SDRAM; Development; DIMM; Direct Memory Access; Direct Random Access Memory; Disk Cache; DMA; Double Data Rate SDRAM; DRAM; Dual Inline Memory Module; Dynamic Memory; EEROM; Electrically Erasable Read Only Memory; Electronically Programmed Read Only Memory; EMS; EPROM; Erasable Programmable Read Only Memory; Expanded Memory; Expanded Memory Specification; Extended Memory; Flash Memory; High Memory; Magnetic Core; Memory; Memory Caching; Memory Resident; Mix; Operand; Programmable Read Only*

Memory; PROM; RAM; RAM Disk; Rambus Dynamic Random Access Memory; Random Access Memory; RDRAM; Read Only Memory; Register; Relative Address; ROM; SDRAM; Shadow RAM Memory; SIMM; Single Inline Memory Modules; Single Inline Package; SIP; Stack; Store; Synchronous Dynamic Random Access Memory; Time Share; Time Slice; Trashing; Upper Memory; Volatile Memory; Workspace;

Workspace
An area in a program or in the computer's memory set aside for processing.
See Also: *Absolute Address; Address; Array; Bloatware; Block; Bubble Sort; Conventional Memory; Core; Core Dump; DDR SDRAM; Development; DIMM; Direct Memory Access; Direct Random Access Memory; Disk Cache; DMA; Double Data Rate SDRAM; DRAM; Dual Inline Memory Module; Dynamic Memory; EEROM; Electrically Erasable Read Only Memory; Electronically Programmed Read Only Memory; EMS; EPROM; Erasable Programmable Read Only Memory; Expanded Memory; Expanded Memory Specification; Extended Memory; Flash Memory; High Memory; Magnetic Core; Memory; Memory Caching; Memory Resident; Mix; Operand; Programmable Read Only Memory; PROM; RAM; RAM Disk; Rambus Dynamic Random Access Memory; Random Access Memory; RDRAM; Read Only Memory; Register; Relative Address; ROM; SDRAM; Shadow RAM Memory; SIMM; Single Inline Memory Modules; Single Inline Package; SIP; Stack; Store; Synchronous Dynamic Random Access Memory; Time Share; Time Slice; Trashing; Upper Memory; Volatile Memory; Working Storage;*

World Wide Web
(WWW). All the websites available on the Internet.
See Also: *Acceptable User Policy; Anchor; AUP; Bookmark; Browser; CERN; CGI; Common Gateway Interface; Conseil Europeen pour la Recherche Nucleaire; Cybercafe; Cyberspace; DNS; Domain Name; Domain Name Server; Domain Name System; Extensible Hypertext Markup Language; eXtensible Markup Language; Forum; FTP Site; Global; Hit; Home Page; Host; HTML; HTTP; Hyperlink; Hypertext; Hypertext Mark-Up Language; Hypertext Transfer Protocol; Information Superhighway; Internet; Link; Meta-Search Engine; Mirror Site; Net; Newbie; Page; Portal; Proxy Server; Search Engine; Site; Spider; Surfing; The Net; The Web; Universal/Uniform Resource Locator; URL; Webcam; Webhost; Webring; Website; Worm; WWW; XHTML; XML;*

Worm

(1) A type of computer virus. (2) A search program which locates data on the Internet/WWW depending on user requests.

See Also: *Bug; Daemon; Gopher; Internet; Machine Crash; Net; Program Crash; Software; Spider; The Net; The Web; Trojan; Virus; Virus Checker; World Wide Web; WWW;*

WP

Word Processing/Word Processor. A collection of programs which allow documents to be created, amended and printed in different formats.

See Also: *Application; Computation; Compute; Data Processing; Desk Top Publishing; DP; DTP; Edit; EDS; Electronic Data System; Integrated Systems; Line Editor; Mail Merge; Office Information System; OIS; Package; Page Editor; Processing; Software Package; Software System; Spell Check; Split Screen; Turnkey; Word Processor; Word Wrap;*

Write

The process where a program or recording peripheral such as a disk or tape unit transfers information to the recording medium. e.g. the writing of a record.

See Also: *3.5 Inch; 5.25 Inch; Access; Archive; Backup; CD-RW Drive; Data; Dead Lock; Deadly Embrace; Direct Access; Disk; Disk Drive; Disk Pack; Disk Storage; Diskette; FDD; Five and a quarter; Fixed Disk Drive; Floppy Disk; Floppy Disk Drive; Hard Disk Drive; HDD; Heads; I/O; Indexed Sequential Access Method; Input/Output; ISAM; Key; Keyed Sequential Access Method; KSAM; Mag Tape; Magnetic Disk; Magnetic Tape; Optical Drive; Output; Pack; R/W; Random Access; Read/Write; Read/Write Head; Recording; Recording Device; Save; Seek Time; Sequential Access; Serial Access; Storage; Store; Streamer; Three and a Half; Winchester Disk; Write Protect; Zip; Zip Drive;*

Write Protect

The setting on a disk or tape medium so that information cannot be written to it.

See Also: *3.5 Inch; 5.25 Inch; Access; CD-RW Drive; Disk; Disk Drive; Disk Pack; Disk Storage; Diskette; FDD; Five and a quarter; Fixed Disk Drive; Floppy Disk; Floppy Disk Drive; Hard Disk Drive; HDD; Locking; Mag Tape; Magnetic Disk; Magnetic Tape; Optical Drive; Pack; Record Locking; Security; Storage; Store; Streamer; Three and a Half; Winchester Disk; Write; Zip Drive;*

WWW
World Wide Web or the Web. All the websites available on the Internet.
See Also: *Acceptable User Policy; Anchor; AUP; Bookmark; Browser; CERN; CGI; Common Gateway Interface; Conseil Europeen pour la Recherche Nucleaire; Cybercafe; Cyberspace; DNS; Domain Name; Domain Name Server; Domain Name System; Extensible Hypertext Markup Language; eXtensible Markup Language; Forum; FTP Site; Global; Hit; Home Page; Host; HTML; HTTP; Hyperlink; Hypertext; Hypertext Mark-Up Language; Hypertext Transfer Protocol; Information Superhighway; Internet; Link; Meta-Search Engine; Mirror Site; Net; Newbie; Page; Portal; Proxy Server; Search Engine; Site; Spider; Surfing; The Net; The Web; Universal/Uniform Resource Locator; URL; Webcam; Webhost; Webring; Website; World Wide Web; Worm; XHTML; XML;*

WYSIWYG
What You See Is What You Get. A term indicating that the result you are looking at is the formatted design in the fonts and styles selected.
See Also: *Bespoke; Display; Font; Format; Graphics; Scalable Fonts; Screen Dump;*

XGA
Extended Video Array. A standard of visual display unit design which allows faster speeds, a better resolution and more colours.
See Also: *Analogue Monitor; Anti Glare Screen; Cathode Ray Tube; CGA; Colour Graphics Adaptor; CRT; Device; Digital Monitor; Display; EGA; Enhanced Graphic Adaptor; Environment; Equipment; Extended Video Array; Graphics Card; Hardware; High Resolution; Installation; Intelligent Terminal; Interlaced; Kit; LCD; Liquid Crystal Display; Low Resolution; Monitor; Monochrome; Paint Screen; Peripheral; Plasma Screen; Prompt; Resolution; Screen; Screen Burn; Split Screen; Super Twist LCD; Super VGA; Super Video Graphics Array; SVGA; Terminal; TFT; Thin-Film Transistor; Touch Screen; Twip; VDT; VDU; VGA; Video Card; Video Display Terminal; Video Graphics Array; Video Random Access Memory; Visual Display Terminal; Visual Display Unit; VRAM;*

XHTML
Extensible Hypertext Markup Language. A web page programming language that is a hybrid between HTML and XML.
See Also: *Anchor; Applet; Browser; Code; Extensible Hypertext Markup Language; eXtensible Markup Language; High Level Language; HTML; Hyperlink; Hypertext; Hypertext Mark-Up Language; Instruction Set;*

JAVA; JAVASCRIPT; Language; Meta Tag; Module; Page; Page Description Language; PDL; Programming Language; Source Code; The Web; World Wide Web; WWW; XML;

XML
eXtensible Markup Language. A programming language used to create a website or web pages.
See Also: *Anchor; Applet; Browser; Code; Extensible Hypertext Markup Language; eXtensible Markup Language; High Level Language; HTML; Hyperlink; Hypertext; Hypertext Mark-Up Language; Instruction Set; JAVA; JAVASCRIPT; Language; Meta Tag; Module; Page; Page Description Language; PDL; Programming Language; Source Code; The Web; World Wide Web; WWW; XHTML;*

XMODEM
A slow file transfer protocol.
See Also: *Access; Acoustic Coupler; Anonymous FTP; Client Server Protocol; File Server; Gateway; Handshake; Interface; Modem; Modulator Demodulator; Open Systems Interconnect; OSI; Protocol; Secure Socket Layer; SSL; TCP/IP; Transfer Rate; Transmission Control Protocol/Internet Protocol; YMODEM; ZMODEM;*

X-OR gate
Exclusive OR gate. A logic gate on a chip which operates with binary digits where an output of logic value 1 occurs if any of the inputs have a logic value 1 but not if all are logic value 1. e.g. Inp=1 and Inp=1 then Out=0, Inp=1 and Inp=0 then Out= 1, Inp=0 and Inp=0 then Out=0.
See Also: *ALU; AMR; AND gate; Arithmetic and Logic Unit; Automatic Message Routing; Binary; Binary Digit; Bit; Boolean Algebra; Chip; Chipset; Expert System; FL; Flip Flop; Fuzzy Logic; I-OR gate; Large Scale Integration; Logic Gate; LSI; NAND gate; NEQ gate; NOR gate; NOT gate; OR gate; Silicon Chip; Transistor; Very Large Scale Integration; VLSI;*

XT
Extended Technology. The basis in which some personal computers were designed before the 286 chip was developed. Internally the processor can handle 16 bit data transfer but only communicated with external devices using 8 bit data transfer.
See Also: *16 Bit; 1st Generation; 286; 2nd Generation; 386; 3rd Generation; 486; 4th Generation; Advanced Technology; Analogue Computer; AT; Chip; Chipset; Computer; Cross Platform; Desktop; Digital Computer; EDS; Electronic Data System; Environment;*

Equipment; Extended Technology; Front End Processor; Hardware; IBM (tm) Compatible; Installation; Kit; Laptop; Machine; Micro; Microcomputer; Multi Platform; Notebook; OEM; Original Equipment Manufacturer; Palmtop Computer; PC; Personal Computer; Platform; Portable; Reduced Instruction Set Computing; RISC; Silicon Chip; Sixteen Bit; Standalone; Tower Computer; Turnkey;

YMODEM
A file transfer protocol, slightly faster than the XMODEM protocol.
See Also: *Access; Anonymous FTP; Client Server Protocol; File Server; Gateway; Handshake; Interface; Modem; Modulator Demodulator; Open Systems Interconnect; OSI; Protocol; Secure Socket Layer; SSL; TCP/IP; Transfer Rate; Transmission Control Protocol/Internet Protocol; XMODEM; ZMODEM;*

Zero Wait State
A term meaning that the central processor does not wait to process while information is being stored or retrieved.
See Also: *Central Processing Unit; CPU; Direct Memory Access; DMA; MCA; Micro Channel Architecture; Processor; Time Share; Time Slice;*

Zip
(1) To compress the storage of information. (2) The compressed file format with a file extension of '.zip'.
See Also: *Archive; Attachment; Backing Store; Backup; Bloatware; Compressed File; Compression; Data Compression; Decompression; Grandfather, Father, Son; Packed Data; PKZIP; Recording; Save; Self Extracting File; Storage; Store; Unzip; Write; Zip Drive;*

Zip Drive
An external drive capable of reading and writing special disks or cartridges of a large capacity.
See Also: *Archive; Backing Store; Backup; Configuration; DAT; Device; Digital Audio Tape; Drive; End of Tape; EOT; Equipment; Grandfather, Father, Son; Hardware; Heads; Installation; Kit; Mass Storage; Peripheral; Read/Write Head; Recording; Recording Device; Save; Storage; Store; Streamer; Write; Write Protect; Zip;*

ZMODEM
A very fast file transfer protocol.
See Also: *Access; Anonymous FTP; Client Server Protocol; File Server; Gateway; Handshake; Interface; Modem; Modulator Demodulator; Open Systems Interconnect; OSI; Protocol; Secure Socket Layer; SSL; TCP/IP;*

Transfer Rate; Transmission Control Protocol/Internet Protocol; XMODEM; YMODEM;

Notes

Notes

Notes

Notes

Notes

Notes

Notes

Notes

Notes

Notes

Notes

Notes

Notes

ADDENDUM/CORRECTIONS

Hex should read 'Abbr. of Hexadecimal. A numerical system with a base of 16 using numbers 0 - 9 and the letters A - F representing eleven to sixteen. Data can be represented in this format.'

Hexadecimal should read 'A numerical system with a base of 16 using numbers 0 - 9 and the letters A - F representing eleven to sixteen. Data can be represented in this format.'

Book Ordering

Please order using one of the following methods:-

1) Our secure website at: www.specialist-uk.com

2) By email to: sales@specialist-uk.com

3) By telephone to: +44 (0) 1892 723717

4) By fax to: +44 (0) 1892 723717

5) By writing to: Specialist Computing Ltd,
PO Box 128,
Tonbridge,
Kent.
TN12 7WD
United Kingdom